D0198628

THE OFFICIAL GUIDE TO

THE X FILES™

created by Chris Carter

VOLUME 6

all things

Marc Shapiro

HarperEntertainment
An Imprint of HarperCollins*Publishers*

The X-Files is a trademark of Twentieth Century Fox Film Corporation. All rights reserved.

ALL THINGS. Copyright © 2001 by Twentieth Century Fox Film Corporation. All rights reserved. Printed in the United States of America. No part of this book may be used or reproduced in any manner whatsoever without written permission except in the case of brief quotations embodied in critical articles and reviews. For information address HarperCollins Publishers Inc., 10 East 53rd Street, New York, NY 10022.

HarperCollins books may be purchased for educational, business, or sales promotional use. For information please write: Special Markets Department, HarperCollins Publishers Inc., 10 East 53rd Street, New York, NY 10022.

FIRST EDITION

Cover and interior designed by Hotfoot Studio

Front cover photographs courtesy of Fox Broadcasting Company
Video grabs provided by Omni Graphic Solutions

Library of Congress Cataloging-in-Publication Data
Shapiro, Marc, 1949–
All things / Marc Shapiro.– 1st ed.
p. cm.– (The official guide to the X-Files; v. 6)
ISBN 0-06-107611-2 (trade pbk.)
1. X-files (Television program) I. Title. II. Series.

PN1992.77.X22 S513 2001
791.45'72–dc21 2001016671

Other *The X-Files* titles published by HarperCollins

Fiction

The X-Files *Goblins*
The X-Files *Whirlwind*
The X-Files *Ground Zero*
The X-Files *Ruins*
The X-Files *Antibodies*
The X-Files *Skin*

Nonfiction

The Truth Is Out There: The Official Guide to The X-Files
Trust No One: The Official Third Season Guide to The X-Files
I Want to Believe: The Official Guide to The X-Files, *volume 3*
Resist or Serve: The Official Guide to The X-Files, *volume 4*
The End and the Beginning: The Official Guide to The X-Files, *volume 5*
The X-Files *Book of the Unexplained Volume One*
The X-Files *Book of the Unexplained Volume Two*
The X-Files *2001 Wall Calendar*
The Official Map of The X-Files
The X-Files *Postcard Book*
The X-Files *Postcard Book: Monsters and Mutants*
The X-Files *Postcard Book: Unexplained Phenomena*
The Art of The X-Files
The Making of The X-Files: Fight the Future *Film*
The X-Files: Fight the Future *Film Novel*

10 9 8 7 6 5 4 3 2 1

For Nancy and Rachael with love

Acknowledgments

Many thanks to Chris Carter, Frank Spotnitz, Paul Rabwin, David Amann, Corey Kaplan, Kim Manners, Gillian Anderson, William Davis, Mitch Pileggi, Vince Gilligan, Rick Millikan, John Shiban, Harry Bring, Bruce Harwood, Michelle Maclaren, Jeffrey Bell, Greg Walker, Steve Maeda, John Vulich, Danny Weselis, Mary Astadourian, Juli Wilburn and the many cast and crew members for their kindness and patience in opening up the world of *The X-Files* to me. Thanks to the good folks at HarperCollins, and especially Caitlin Blasdell and April Benavides for their skills, guidance, and constant encouragement. Thanks to agent extraordinaire, Lori Perkins, for the constant hustle on my behalf. And finally thanks for a wide variety of reasons to Mike Kirby, Bennie, Freda, Kerri, Bad Baby, Chaos, Charles Bukowski, Howard Stern, Black Sabbath, Kiss, Cirith Ungol, Bentley Little, John Shirley, Patti Smith, Allen Ginsberg, Jack Kerouac, David McDonnell, Tony Timpone, Salvador Dali, Picasso, Selma Howe, Jim Rhome, Jefferson Airplane, The Doors, Mountain, The Ramones, Michael Slade, Kathi Koja, and all the subversive forces that populate my own personal X-Files.

CONTENTS

INTRODUCTION

How does one top six seasons of double-crossing federal agents, aliens, and things that go bump in the night? Easy. Go forward and produce a seventh one. Undaunted by a tally of 163 previous episodes praised by critics and fans alike, *The X-Files* faced the challenge of creating fresh stories that still provoked fear and wonder, and took Mulder, Scully, and

the audience deeper into the unknown. The show's creator, cast, and crew saw one way to meet this challenge: Take creative risks. Throughout the season, fans watched the series close the door on many of its long-running story arcs and well-known characters while opening new ones to entirely different possibilities. It's no mistake that the seventh season began with the exploration of something called "The Sixth Extinction" and ended with the promise of Scully's surprising pregnancy. In many ways, what was happening before viewers' eyes was the death of numerous familiar elements of the show and the birth of intriguing new ones—in short, the reinvention of *The X-Files*.

Closure, something *The X-Files* had generally avoided in its open-ended storytelling, became a watchword for the season. The episode "Closure" marked one of the most significant resolutions in *The X-Files* mythology: the end of Mulder's search for his abducted sister, Samantha. This quest had led Mulder to the X-Files and had remained the driving force behind his examination of the fantastic and bizarre world of the paranormal. Bringing one of the seminal mysteries of the series to a close was quite a chance to take, but the result breathed new life into Mulder's pursuit of the truth.

"Orison" also served to tie up loose ends from the past, in this case Scully's. Bringing back death fetishist Donnie Pfaster from the second season was a daring move that made for powerful drama as Scully faced down her own personal demon. Like Mulder, she found some resolution to a past that had haunted her, while raising new questions in its disturbing wake.

This season even offered closure for another series, *Millennium*. "Millennium" marked a trek into new territory, as Scully and Mulder ventured into Frank Black's apocalyptic world as the dawning of the year 2000 loomed before them. It also succeeded in concluding Frank's journey and bidding him a touching farewell.

Finally, the seventh season said good-bye to two characters who had been with the series from the beginning. The shocking death of Mulder's mother was followed by the possible demise of the Cigarette-Smoking Man, the menacing figure who had been at the heart of the far-reaching shadow conspiracy from the start of the first season. Again, these were risky moves, eliminating Mulder's only remaining family and the series' primary villain. But as loyal viewers know, nothing can be taken for granted on *The X-Files*, and whether these characters are gone for good remains to be seen.

All of these resolutions were balanced with the exploration of new paths on which the characters found themselves. Scully's emotional life and romantic past were reexamined in such episodes as "all things," revealing the soul-searching complexity of a character we thought we knew. Her complicated relationship with Mulder also developed and took new turns, as confirmed by the unexpected kiss in "Millennium." Even the long-running conceit of Mulder the believer always challenged by Scully the skeptic was altered by fresh questions Scully faced in the opening two-parter as she gazed at an alien spacecraft on an exotic beach.

One need only survey a few of Season 7's episodes to see that the series was pushing the creative envelope. "X-Cops" was notable for being a crossover with the reality series *Cops* and a unique way of filming the show; it blurred the lines between fantasy and reality by bringing *The X-Files* into our world and having Mulder and Scully hunt a monster with film crew in tow. Similarly, "Hollywood A.D." considered what would happen if Tinseltown threw its garish lights on Mulder and Scully's dark exploits. "What would happen if...?" seemed to be the question that inspired many of the radically varied episodes. By doing this, *The X-Files* challenged many of its viewers' preconceived notions of what to expect.

Something must have been in the air with all of these risk-taking adventures onscreen; behind the scenes, cast and crew began stretching their creative wings and entering untested waters as well. While David Duchovny followed up the previous season's "The Unnatural" with an even more ambitious writing/directing sophomore effort, "Hollywood A.D.," Gillian Anderson gave her character a revelatory experience in her writing and directing debut, "all things." William B. Davis also tried his hand at writing, adding subtle shadings to the Cigarette-Smoking Man's adversarial relationship with Scully in "En Ami." Longtime writer/executive producer Vince Gilligan tried on the director's cap for the first time for the hilarious *X-Files* take on *I Dream of Jeannie*, "Je Souhaite." The payoff from such creative risks? Incredibly effective episodes that ran the gamut, from lighthearted humor to touching emotion to nefarious scheming.

As the season wound down, the theme of closure and rebirth was brought into sharp relief by the uncertainty of whether the series would return for Season 8. Even as "Requiem" was being filmed, there was no definitive answer. The episode could be seen as a brilliant cliffhanger to take the show in a fresh direction or the shocking finale of its television run. This tension seemed to be reflected by the events of the episode. Mulder's boarding of the spacecraft was the fulfillment of his longtime search for true alien contact, in many ways the culmination of the central quest of *The X-Files*. Yet even as questions were being answered and mysteries resolved with Mulder aboard the ship, his disappearance became a new puzzle. And, in one of the most stunning twists in *X-Files* history, Scully's final words of the episode revealed how, remarkably, the possibilities of the show were truly limitless. The promise (or threat?) of her unborn baby raised more questions and promised more startling new directions for a series that was, rather than drawing to a close, only announcing the beginning of yet another journey.

According to executive producer Frank Spotnitz, those working on *The X-Files* had gone into Season 7 knowing it would be "a fairly risky season. . . . We knew it was all going to be very tricky but we knew that we could rise to the occasion." With the airing of the powerful final episode, Chris Carter, cast, and crew had proven that they could indeed meet these challenges—that they were true masters of reinvention.

Which was good news, since word had come at last that there would be a Season 8. And if Season 7 was any indication, this reborn *X-Files* was not to be missed.

episode 7X03

THE SIXTH EXTINCTION

EPISODE: 7X03
FIRST AIRED: November 7, 1999
EDITOR: Louise A. Innes
WRITTEN BY: Chris Carter
DIRECTED BY: Kim Manners

Scully continues to probe the spaceship off the Ivory Coast of Africa. Skinner enlists the help of Kritschgau in an attempt to get to the bottom of Mulder's madness while avoiding the suspicions of Diana Fowley.

GUEST STARS:

Mitch Pileggi (A.D. Skinner)
Mimi Rogers (Agent Diana Fowley)
Jo Nell Kennedy (Amina Ngebe)
Warren Sweeney (Dr. Geoff Harriman)
Michael Ensign (Dr. Barnes)
John Finn (Michael Kritschgau)
Conrad Roberts (Primitive African Man)
Mari Weiss (ICU Nurse)
Anthony Okungbowa (Barnes's Driver)

PRINCIPAL SETTINGS:

Ivory Coast, West Africa; Washington, D.C.

The episode opens with a recap of the storyline of "Biogenesis" (6X22), which concluded with Mulder in the grip of insanity in a padded room and Scully standing in shallow water on an African shore, staring at what is undoubtedly a spacecraft.

Surf crashes on a long crescent shore. Moonlight bounces off a great expanse of water, defining a vague meeting of sea and sky on the shores of the Ivory Coast, West Africa.

Scully's voice breaks with the crashing of waves.

"I came in search of something I did not believe existed."

A white tent glows on the beach, lit from within by lantern light.

"I've stayed on now in spite of myself. In spite of everything I've ever held to be true."

Inside the tent, Scully sits at a table, studying a photo with a magnifying glass by flickering lamplight.

"I will continue here as long as I can. As long as you're beset by the haunting illness which I saw consume your beautiful mind."

Scully looks deeper into the photo of what appears to be a spaceship in the shallow water.

"What is this discovery I've made? How can I reconcile what I see with what I know? I feel this was meant not for me to find, but for you. To make sense of, make the connections which can't be ignored."

Scully reaches for a mysterious paper rubbing. As she brings it close to the photo for comparison, the lantern flame begins to flicker and dance.

"Connections which for me deny all logic and reason," she solemnly intones as she compares the photo and the rubbing, and finds that their mysterious symbols match. "What is this source of power I hold in my hand? This rubbing. A simple impression taken from the surface of the craft."

Scully lays the rubbing down. A moth lands on it.

"I watched this rubbing take its undeniable hold on you, saw you succumb to its spiraling effect. Now I must work to uncover what your illness prevents you from finding. In the source of every illness lies its cure."

More and more bugs land on the lantern. As Scully rises and reaches to turn it off, the figure of an old, primitively dressed African man materializes behind Scully. She sees the figure in reflection a second before she turns off the light. She quickly whips around.

"Who's there?" she asks. "Who's there?"

She relights the lantern and sees that there is no one else in the tent. Scully grabs a machete and cautiously steps toward the tent opening, unaware that the table she is working on is now crawling with bugs. She throws back the tent flap and steps out into the moonlight. She scans the darkness, sees nothing, and turns back into the tent.

The tent is now swarming with bugs. She tries to turn off the lantern, but as she reaches for the switch the bugs turn their attention to Scully and swarm around her. The bugs are in her eyes, her face, all over her body. She flails wildly with her arms. Scully screams in terror.

•

Mulder is huddled in his padded cell.

"He's been quiet for the last thirty-six hours," says the voice of Dr. Harriman. "But he doesn't sleep."

Mulder is being held in a neuropsych ward. Each door has a video monitor situated next to it. Watching Mulder through one of these monitors with deep concern are Dr. Harriman and FBI Assistant Director Skinner.

Harriman says, "There's activity in the temporal lobe we've just never seen. It won't allow his brain to rest or shut down. Manifesting in episodes of aggression, sometimes against himself."

"You can't sedate him?" asks Skinner.

"Yes," says Harriman. "We slow him down for short periods and put him in the neuro ward. It's the only way we're able to run tests. But over time his brain is going to just die."

Mulder's face is drawn, his eyes sunken, his gown ripped and coated with blood. He does not look up as the door to his room opens.

"Agent Mulder," says Skinner as he and Dr. Harriman enter the room.

"Agent Mulder," repeats Skinner. "Can you hear me?" He gets no reaction.

Mulder makes eye contact with Skinner. He doesn't appear to recognize him.

"Do you know who I am? It's Skinner. Walter Skinner."

Skinner is upset by what he sees. He turns to Dr. Harriman.

"Can we get him out of here, give him some fresh air at least?" asks Skinner.

Mulder suddenly jumps to his feet and attacks Skinner, shoving him against the wall and wrapping his hands around his neck, choking him.

"Let him go, he can't breathe!" says Harriman as he tries to separate the two men. Mulder is not letting go. The two men fall to the floor as Dr. Harriman races from the room and presses a PANIC button. Skinner is bleeding from the nose, his eyes bulging as he tries to fight off Mulder with a straight arm.

"Let go, Mulder," says Skinner. "I don't want to hurt you."

Two male orderlies race into the room and rip Mulder off Skinner, pinning him against the wall. Harriman moves to Skinner.

"It's all right. Just let me get up," says Skinner.

Mulder raves like a madman as Skinner, wiping blood from his face, leaves the room. Dr. Harriman orders up mega-restraints and sedatives.

Outside the padded cell, Skinner notices something in his shirt pocket. He pulls out a small piece of ripped cloth the color of Mulder's hospital gown.

Written in dried blood are the words HELP ME.

•

The tent sits silently in the early-morning sun. There is no sign of Scully. Two old rusted-out Jeeps round into view, carrying loads of African men who jump out near the water's edge and head straight for the shallows and the submerged craft, where they begin to sweep away the sand. One of the drivers is speaking to a woman passenger. Questions, answers, and furtive gestures in the direction of the water and the tent pass between them.

The woman gets out of the truck and walks over to the tent. She pulls open the flap.

"My God," the woman says. "What happened here?"

Scully's hair is wet. Inside the tent is the residue of thousands of dead bugs. She does not respond to the question. The woman steps into the tent. "They say you speak English."

"What do you want?" asks Scully.

"I'm sorry!" the woman says. "You must wonder who I am. I am Amina Ngebe. I have come to see your discovery."

"I asked that no one be told about it. Nor that I'm here."

"Yes, well, it's still a secret," says Amina. "But a well-known one, I'm afraid. Dr. Merkmallen called it the African Internet. God rest him."

"You knew Dr. Merkmallen?" asks Scully.

Amina introduces herself as a professor of biology. "But hardly one qualified to say what must have gone on here."

"I was working late last night by lamplight," says Scully. "And I saw a man who vanished. And then they just swarmed."

"You must not let the men know what happened to you last night," says Amina. "The vanishing man. None of it."

"Why?"

"They are animists, believing nature is vengeful. They'll take this as a sign to leave what you've found alone. A bad omen."

"Caused by the ship out there?"

Amina shakes her head no. "Caused by God," she says. "Who will be much less helpful than those men if we are to continue this work."

•

The workers continue to expose the alien craft with scoops and shovels. Some are taking photos, others are diving underneath the waves. Suddenly a cry comes from deep water. The sea is boiling up, steam escaping into the atmosphere. A man rises from the center of

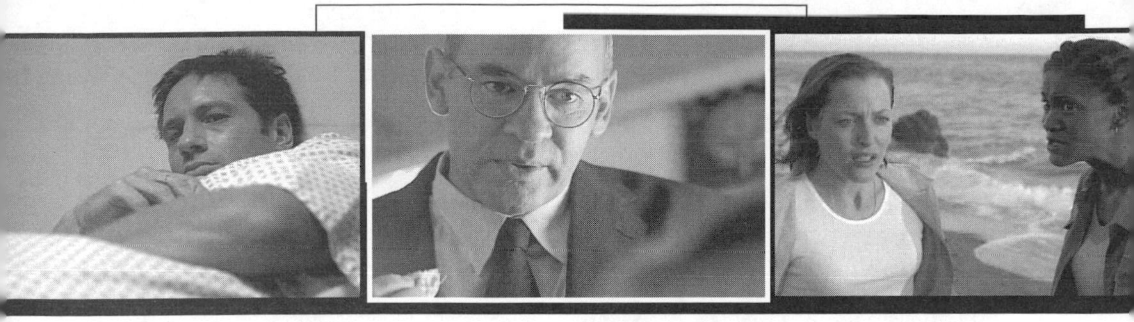

the boiling water, screaming as he rips his diving mask off.

Scully and Amina run to the shoreline, where the screaming diver has been brought to shore. His skin is a series of open bleeding blisters. Scully wades into the shallows to help the man.

"Let's get him to the truck!" says Scully. "He's got to get to a hospital."

Amina says, "You see—another warning."

•

Skinner returns to the psych ward later that night and enters Mulder's room, where he sees him strapped to his bed.

"Agent Mulder?" says Skinner, holding up the note Mulder had put in his pocket. "I want to help you."

Mulder continues to stare. His only movement is a difficulty in swallowing.

"I don't know what to do," says Skinner. "I don't have much time."

Mulder's fingers begin to tap on his blanket. Skinner takes Mulder's hand in his own. Skinner asks, "Can you write?" Mulder makes a faint nod yes. Skinner takes a pen from his pocket and transfers it to Mulder's hand.

Mulder begins to scrawl the crude letter *K* in Skinner's palm. He labors and finally manages the letter *R*. As Skinner watches Mulder struggle, we hear Scully's voice.

•

"I feel you slipping away from me with every minute I fail here," she says.

The photos of the spaceship lie on the table in Scully's tent.

"What are the elusive meanings I cannot see? That are hidden here?"

While Amina sleeps in a nearby cot, Scully lies awake, troubled.

"If I could understand it, know how it affected you. Learn how to use its power to save you."

There are bright lights in her face. She rises. Outside a truck sits with its lights shining on the wall of the tent. Scully emerges from the tent, machete in hand. She moves toward the truck and spots a young African driver at the wheel. He gestures, trying to tell her something in a language she does not understand. He shines a flashlight toward the beach.

"Look, I'm sorry. I don't speak your language," says Scully.

The driver gestures toward the beach and heads in that direction. Scully turns away, and comes face-to-face with Dr. Barnes.

"Perhaps you need an interpreter," says Dr. Barnes.

"Stay away from me," she says.

"Are you going to hack me up in front of my driver?" he says. "Word is you're under suspicion already."

"You're the murderer here!" she says.

Amina, hearing the yelling, has come out of the tent. She asks who Barnes murdered. Scully tells her Dr. Merkmallen.

Barnes says, "I murdered no one. But I won't be sent away from here. I know what we've got. This craft that's come ashore . . . its extraterrestrial origins."

"You don't even believe in that," says Scully.

"Nor do you," says Barnes. "But here we are."

Scully lets her weapon down.

"I'm here only to help my partner," she says.

Barnes says, "Then let me help you. To read it."

He pulls a journal out of his back pocket.

"I've spent my life looking for what's out there," says Barnes. "The answer to what theologians have pondered for millennia. The key to everything, to life itself. I've already been threatened by men in Washington about what I know. How long would your secret keep if you were to send me away?"

They are distracted by yells from Barnes's driver coming from the beach. They race to the water's edge, where Barnes asks his driver what he found.

The driver looks to his feet.

"It's a sea of blood," says Amina.

Scully looks around and sees the figure of the old African man, standing on some rocks out beyond the surf line. Scully continues to look.

The old African man is gone.

•

On Skinner's palm, Mulder has scrawled the name Kritschgau. Skinner tracks the man to a low-rent apartment building. He knocks on the apartment door and a man peers out.

"Michael Kritschgau?" asks Skinner.

"All I know is that he asked for you," says Skinner.

•

Skinner has convinced Kritschgau to accompany him to the neuropsych unit, where Mulder continues to stare, dull-eyed, into space.

"Can he even recognize me?" asks Kritschgau.

Skinner says, "To be honest, I don't know."

Kritschgau's eyes dart to the monitors. The lines on the monitors jump. Skinner looks from Mulder to Kritschgau. "Agent Mulder?" he asks. Kritschgau notes that again the monitor lines jumped at Skinner's voice.

"His brain's on constant redline," says

Kritschgau says, "It's six o'clock in the morning."

"I don't know if you remember me. My name is Skinner. I'm here to talk to you about Fox Mulder."

"Yeah. I'm listening."

"He's in serious condition, Mr. Kritschgau. He asked to talk to you."

"I got nothing to say to the man," says Kritschgau as he starts to close the door.

Skinner puts his hand on the door, stopping him from shutting it.

Kritschgau says, "I had a job, with a government pension coming. And two years ago Fox Mulder asks me to do him a favor. Blow the whistle on Uncle Sam's UFO propaganda mill. And all it got me was this swanky address."

Skinner says that Mulder does not have a lot of time.

"I'm not a doctor. What is it you think I can do for him?"

Skinner. "They've got him on haldoperidol just to keep him on the monitors."

"Haldoperidol?"

"He becomes violently agitated. He just won't speak. Or sleep. Even when he's medicated. There's activity in a part of his brain they've never seen before."

"Was his . . ."

Kritschgau is cut off in midsentence as the monitor lines once again jump.

"'Was his' what?" Skinner prompts.

"I started to ask you a question about his prior mental state," says Kritschgau. "But he anticipated it. Second time. Agent Mulder." The monitor lines jump yet again.

Skinner says, "He claimed to be hearing voices."

"I might know why Agent Mulder asked for me. But it doesn't mean that I can do anything for him."

"What just happened?" asks Skinner.

"I think he responded to a question I didn't ask," says Kritschgau.

•

Kritschgau finishes picking the lock to the hospital pharmacy dispensary. The door is pushed open and Skinner, pushing Mulder in a wheelchair with an IV bag attached, eases into the darkened room. Kritschgau turns on the lights and begins scanning the shelves of medicine.

"I don't know how long we can keep him out of that unit," says Skinner. "We could be held responsible."

Kritschgau shoots back, "You asked me to come down here. You better be prepared to accept the responsibility, Mr. Skinner."

Kritschgau reaches up and grabs a syringe.

"You're going to inject him?" asks Skinner.

"No, you are," he says. "With 1,000 milligrams of phenytoin."

"I'm not injecting him with anything," says Skinner. "Not now and not until after I talk to his doctor."

"He's being given the wrong treatment."

"You're not a doctor!" says Skinner.

Kritschgau completes the works for injection.

"No, but I've seen his condition. Who do you want to trust?" asks Kritschgau.

Skinner considers this. "Seen it where?" asks Skinner.

"In a study," Kritschgau says. "Of something like ESP, called remote viewing."

Skinner wants to know whose study.

"The Company. The CIA, Mr. Skinner. Extreme subjects would go into arrest, their minds working harder than their bodies could sustain. They became, in effect, all brain. Phenytoin was the only thing that could slow the electrical impulses to a normal rate." He holds out the syringe for Skinner.

"Agent Mulder knew about this," says Skinner. "That's why he asked for you." He takes the loaded syringe.

Skinner kneels before the catatonic Mulder and plunges the syringe into his IV bag. Mulder has an immediate reaction to the drug. His eyes begin to blink, then close, and his breathing becomes heavy and labored.

"They're coming," whispers Mulder.

•

Agent Diana Fowley bursts through the hospital hallway doors. She is agitated, angry, and taking it out on a nurse, who is matching her stride through the hospital.

"Who last saw him?" asks Fowley.

The nurse checks her files and charts.

"I come here and find a patient missing and nobody knew?" asks Fowley.

The nurse says, "I just came on . . . sorry. Fox Mulder, right? He's restrained, it says. And he's not in his bed?"

"No," says Fowley. "How many times can I say it?" she asks as she pushes open the doors to Mulder's room.

They find Skinner standing over Mulder, who appears exactly as he was before Kritschgau entered the picture. "He's right here," observes the nurse.

Fowley says, "He wasn't here when I came in."

"No," says Skinner. "I just found him down the hall. I got him back into bed."

The nurse notices that Mulder's restraints are off and the contacts to his monitors have been removed.

"Who are you?" she asks.

Skinner says, "I'm his boss. And hers."

"Well, I don't know how he could have gotten up by himself," the nurse comments, "or pulled all this stuff out."

"I hope someone's calling his doctor, making a report of this," Skinner says.

"He's got to remain in his bed." The nurse turns and leaves.

"I'll stay with him," says Skinner. "Agent Fowley, why don't you see if you can help her."

Fowley is suspicious of Skinner's intentions.

"That's an order, Agent Fowley," says Skinner. With a look at Mulder, Fowley exits.

"She knows," says Mulder.

"You can read her mind?" asks Skinner.

"Yeah, we gotta act fast," says Mulder.

"The doctor's on his way."

"No doctors," says Mulder. "Get Scully."

Skinner indicates that he does not know where she is.

"HIS BRAIN'S ON CONSTANT REDLINE. THEY'VE GOT HIM ON HALDOPERIDOL JUST TO KEEP HIM ON THE MONITORS."—Skinner

Mulder says, "Look, I know you've been compromised. I know Krycek is threatening your life. Blackmailing you. You don't think I can trust you. But it's not you that I need."

"Then who?" asks Skinner.

"Him," says Mulder, looking in the direction of Kritschgau, who has been lingering near the door.

"Kritschgau. Ask him to prove it," says Mulder.

"Prove what?" asks Kritschgau.

"What's causing this?" asks Mulder.

"A brain abnormality. It's how you're able to read minds."

"What's causing this is alien," says Mulder. "It's why my doctors can't help me."

"I don't believe in aliens, Agent Mulder," says Kritschgau. "I think you know that."

"I do," says Mulder. "That's why I need you."

•

Scully is hard at work alone and has not had much sleep.

"The work here is painstaking. A slow and tedious piecing together."

On the floor she has begun to reconstruct the shape of the craft from black-and-white photos laid out like a mosaic.

"It appears to be a craft, its skin covered in the intricate symbols you and I both saw. But which I now understand are part of a complex communication."

Scully continues her research amid a jumble of drawn boxes and lines connecting symbols. She picks up one of the photos and lays it down next to a piece of paper. The paper is covered in Dr. Barnes's handwriting.

"Dr. Barnes has broken some of the symbols into letters using an ancient Navajo alphabet. And though it has helped to uncover some of what's here, it has also made for greater confusion."

Strange words—adenine, thymine, cytosine—are beginning to take shape.

"On the top surface of the craft I'm finding words describing human genetics."

Men continue to work at the ship, exposing more of its symbols.

"Efforts to read the bottom of the craft have been harder. Our workers were scared away by phenomena I admit I can't explain. A sea of blood, a swarm of insects. But what little we've found has been staggering. Passages from the Christian Bible, from pagan religions. From ancient Sumeria."

Amina and Dr. Barnes are also hard at work. They barely speak. There is a sense of tension and suspicion between them.

"Science and mysticism conjoined. But more than words, they are somehow imbued with power.

"I've ignored warnings to quit this work, remaining committed to finding answers. Afraid only that our secret here won't last . . ."

"And that I might be too late."

Scully picks up the original carbon rubbing and looks at it intently. Her thoughts are interrupted by Amina.

"I have something to show you. More pieces of the puzzle," says Amina.

Amina moves around the spaceship pictures and lays new photos on the mosaic.

"I couldn't believe it," says Amina. "I thought I was making it up in my head. That it could not be true."

"What?" asks Scully.

Amina looks at one particular section of the symbols. "What this is, what the symbols spell out, is a passage from the Koran. Qiyaamah. The Day of Final Judgment. On a spacecraft? Teachings of the ancient Prophet Muhammad!"

"I've found more, too," says Scully.

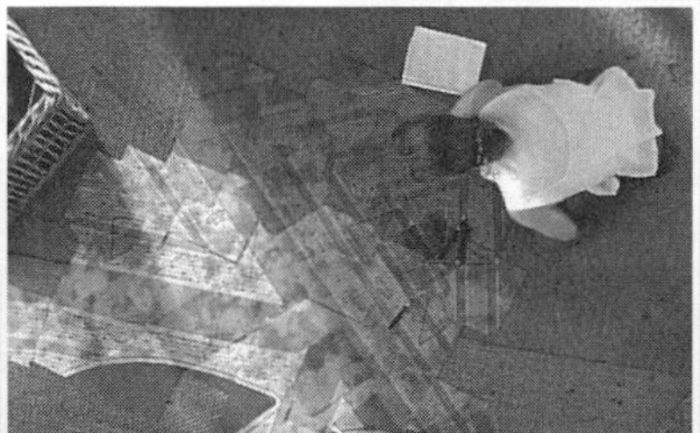

She runs her hand over a section of the grid.

"Twenty-four panels, one for each human chromosome," she says. "A map of their makeup. Maybe a map of our entire genetic makeup. A complete human genome. It's like the most beautiful, intricate work of art."

"It's the word of God," says Amina.

"You're wrong," says Dr. Barnes. "There is no God."

Barnes enters the tent, carrying a burlap sack. He sets the sack down.

"What's out there in the water is only what we call God," says Barnes. "What we call creation. The spark that ignited the fire, that cooked the ol' primordial soup. Made animate from inanimate. Made us."

"I believe he's mad from the sun," says Amina.

Barnes walks slowly toward the two women. "Mad? I am perfectly sane. Because today I understand everything. Beginning and end. Alpha and omega. Everything in between. It's all been written. But the word is extraterrestrial."

"You're sick, Dr. Barnes," says Scully. "You need to get off your feet. Lie down."

Barnes picks up a machete and brandishes it menacingly.

"You think you're going to take the credit?" he says. "This is my discovery!"

"I'm only here to help my friend," says Scully.

"You can't help him," Barnes says. "You're wasting your time reading it!"

Scully insists the symbols have power.

Barnes says, "It is power! The ultimate power. Your friend just got too close."

He crosses the room and sits down by the door, guarding it with the machete. "No one leaves here before me."

•

Kritschgau and Skinner are flanking Mulder's bed, showing him a series of mundane objects on three monitors, punctuated occasionally by the photo of a spaceship.

Kritschgau says, "We've developed this to test remote-viewing capabilities. It works much like a card trick. You tap the monitor where the saucer image appears, when it appears. Or when you think it does."

"Who you gonna call?" says Mulder. Kritschgau acknowledges this joke with a small smile.

The test continues. Mulder taps the monitors, occasionally corresponding to when the saucer images come up.

Kritschgau says, "All right. Agent Mulder, fine. You're at about five percent accuracy."

"I'm assuming that's low," says Skinner.

"At the CIA, a high degree of ability was twenty percent," says Kritschgau. "Twenty-five percent was extraordinary."

Mulder leans his head back on his pillow and closes his eyes.

"But I see them in my head," says Mulder.

Skinner says, "You saw his ability earlier. It was you who pointed it out."

"Our tests showed that some people have psychic ability. Sure. ESP, clairvoyance, remote viewing. But it was never attributed to aliens," says Kritschgau.

"You don't wanna believe," says Mulder. "You're not looking hard enough."

Kritschgau is about to stop the test when Skinner insists he repeat the test, only faster. The monitors are put on fast-scan mode. Mulder touches the monitors in perfect synch with the spaceship image. The cynical Kritschgau is now convinced.

"He's ahead of the images," says Kritschgau. "He's anticipating."

•

Scully and Amina are wide awake in their cots, eyeing Barnes, who is dozing at the tent entrance, machete still in hand. An earthquake-like sound rattles through the tent. It awakens Dr. Barnes, who makes for the burlap sack he had brought into the tent earlier. His hand reaches into the sack and comes out with live wiggling bait fish.

Barnes says, "They're back! They were dead! They've come back to life! The ship, it brought them back to life!"

He turns to show the wiggling fish to Scully, who brings a wooden chair hard on him, knocking him out. Scully and Amina run out of the tent to Barnes's truck. With Amina at the wheel, they drive from the beach onto the blacktop.

"We have to get to the police," says Scully.

"That's where I'm going," says Amina. "This is the road to Abidjan."

Suddenly Scully's attention is drawn to a figure standing in the middle of the road.

"Stop!" says Scully.

Amina slams on the brakes. The truck fishtails out of control, before coming to a stop.

"That was him," says Scully. "That was the man I saw in the tent. In the road."

Scully orders Amina to turn the car around.

"I'm going home," she says.

•

Skinner is trying to revive Mulder from his latest bout of madness.

"Agent Mulder, I don't know if you can hear me, but we're going to try to get you out of here," he says. He begins untying the restraints.

Kritschgau enters the room. "A.M. nurse is on in five minutes. We've got to move."

Skinner says, "I don't think he's in any shape."

Kritschgau produces a bottle and a syringe. "I'm going to hit him pretty hard. Maybe we can get him on his feet."

Kritschgau loads the needle and prepares to give Mulder the injection. Skinner stops him. He asks what he's doing.

"I'm trying to help him," says Kritschgau.

"This isn't about him. It's about you. It's about revenge against the government. For trying to destroy your life."

"I WAS DESTROYED TO PROTECT WHAT MULDER KNEW ALL ALONG. AND NOW HE'S THE PROOF. HE'S THE X-FILE!"—Kritschgau

The headlights fall on an empty road.

She turns to Amina, who is no longer in the driver's seat. In her place sits the old African man. He stares at Scully.

"Some truths are not for you," says the African man.

The specter reaches out to Scully and touches her on the forehead as Scully opens her eyes to find Amina over her, touching her forehead.

"Are you all right?" asks Amina.

Scully is still jittery and jumps at Amina's touch.

"What are you doing?" asks Scully.

"You were cold. I was feeling to see if you were still alive."

"What happened to you?" asks Scully.

"To me?" asks Amina.

"You slammed on the brakes," she says. "There was a man."

Amina says, "That's right. In the road."

"No," says Scully. "He was right there. Sitting right where you are, in your seat."

"The men were right. This is a bad sign. A sign to give up."

"I was destroyed to protect what Mulder knew all along," says the angry Kritschgau. "And now he's the proof. He's the X-File!"

"We can't just keep shooting him full of drugs," says Skinner. "It's gone too far."

"How far should it go? How far would Mulder go?"

Skinner backs off as Kritschgau sticks the needle into Mulder's IV bag, just as Agent Fowley, Dr. Harriman, and the nurse enter the room. Harriman demands to know what's going on. Fowley rushes at Kritschgau.

"Let me see your hands," she says. "Hands!"

He brings them up without the syringe. "Step away," she orders.

"Agent Fowley," says Skinner. "What the hell do you think you're doing?"

"What am I doing? What are you doing, sir? With this?" she asks, holding up the syringe and turning her rage on Kritschgau. "I want you to face the wall. Do you hear me? Face the wall!"

"Let me explain," says Skinner.

"What was this man given?" asks Dr.

Harriman. "What was in this syringe?"

"Phenytoin," says Fowley, reading the bottle.

"Let me tell you what it does," says Skinner.

"How much did you give him?" Dr. Harriman asks. "What dosage was this?"

"Let me tell you why we did it," Skinner continues.

Mulder suddenly starts to violently convulse as Fowley, Harriman, and Skinner attempt to hold him down.

•

It's daytime when Dr. Barnes's driver appears inside the tent to tell him that Scully and Amina have taken the truck. The driver turns to see Barnes standing behind him with the machete poised to strike.

"I'm so sorry," says Barnes.

He plunges the blade into the driver.

•

Mulder's eyes are open. They fall on Diana Fowley. They are alone.

"I know what's happened to you," she says. "I know what you're suffering from. I've been sitting back and watching."

Mulder does not seem to recognize her.

"I know you know. I know you know about me, that my loyalties aren't just to you, but to a man you've grown to despise. You have your reasons, but as you look inside me now, you know that I have mine. Fox, I love you. I've loved you for so long. You know that, too. And I won't let you die. To prove what you are, to prove what's inside you. There's no need to prove it. It's been known for so long. Now we can be together."

She kisses Mulder softly on the forehead, then turns and walks out of the room.

•

An elevator opens at the FBI Building. Scully, still dressed in her jungle outfit, steps out and heads down the hallway. Scully strides past Skinner's secretary and into his office.

"Where is he? Is he still in the hospital?" she asks.

"Where have you been?" Skinner questions.

Scully asks if Mulder is still in Georgetown Memorial. Skinner hesitates and then tells her that she can't get to him.

"Do you know where he is or don't you?" she asks.

"He's in the neuropsych ward," he says. "But it's no good, Agent Scully."

Scully turns to leave. Skinner tries to stop her.

"I've been on a plane for twenty-two hours," she says. "I have to see him."

Skinner says, "Then I think you should know what you're going to see, if you can even get on the ward. There's been some trouble."

"What kind of trouble?"

"I got this man Kritschgau involved."

"Kritschgau?" she asks.

"It's a long story, but it ended badly. They've got Mulder under security now, 'round the clock. I take full responsibility."

"Responsibility for what?" asks Scully.

"He can't even communicate, Agent Scully. They won't treat him because they don't know what's wrong with him. They said he was dying. I had to do something."

Scully insists that Mulder is not dying.

"I'm afraid it's true," says Skinner.

"He is not dying. He is more alive than he's ever been. He's more alive than his body can withstand. And what's causing it may be extraterrestrial in origin."

Skinner is not shocked by Scully's very Mulder-like statement.

"I know. But there's nothing to be done about it," he says. "They're going to deny you access."

"Maybe as his partner. But not as his doctor," Scully declares as she exits.

Dr. Barnes is gathering up the photos and paperwork in the tent when he is startled by a clatter behind him. A pitcher has tipped over and is pouring a stream of liquid onto the ground. He follows the stream to the point where we last saw the dead driver's body, which is now gone.

"He's alive," says Barnes. "He's come back to life. Holy Mother of God."

Taking a lantern, he heads out of the tent. Looking around in the darkness, he finds fresh footprints in the sand, heading toward the beach. The footprints lead into the water. He turns with a start to discover the driver he killed standing behind him, zombie-eyed and holding the still-bloody machete. He raises it and brings it down on Barnes, whose death fall lands right at the tip of the alien ship.

•

In the neuropsych ward, Mulder turns his head toward the sound of Scully arguing with Dr. Harriman. Scully soon enters the room.

She says, "Mulder, it's me. I know that you can hear me. If you could just give me some sign."

There is no visible response from Mulder, but Scully is determined. Overwhelming emotion is beginning to well up inside her. "I want you to know where I've been, what I've found. I think that if you know, that you can find a way to hold on. I need you to hold on. I've found a key. The key. To every question that has ever been asked. It's a puzzle. The pieces are there for us to put together. And I know that it can save you, if you can just hold on.

"Mulder, please hold on." She fights to hold back tears and takes his hand.

•

Amina is moving up the beach with some uniformed police. They move to the water's edge, where they discover Dr. Barnes's body lying face down in the surf.

The spacecraft has disappeared.

TO BE CONTINUED

BACK STORY:

There was much more to "The Sixth Extinction" than merely continuing the compelling storyline of last season's cliffhanger, "Biogenesis." The die had been cast midway through the sixth season when one mythology had ended. Now it was time to turn the page and begin another.

"Since the episodes 'Two Fathers' and 'One Son,' the mythology of the show had really been reinvented," says executive producer Frank Spotnitz. "We've destroyed all the stuff about Mulder's father, the project, and the Syndicate. All the things that had sustained us for six years were suddenly gone. We had no crutches. From that point on, every time we sat down to write a mythology show, we knew it was going to be a completely different challenge."

Although "The Sixth Extinction," written by Chris Carter, did touch on the mysterious correlation between aliens and religion, Chris Carter saw "The Sixth Extinction" as a transitional episode to something more important in the evolution of the show.

"I felt that, with 'The Sixth Extinction,' I was just playing a supporting role and that the episode, essentially the middle episode of a three-episode arc, was just a transitional episode to get us to 'Amor Fati,' which was really less about the mythology and more about Mulder's choices in life."

Given the very busy schedules of everyone involved in *The X-Files*, it did not come as a surprise that this all important two-part season opener was played out amid chaos. David Duchovny's and Gillian Anderson's off-season film work had already forced *The X-Files*'s production team to juggle the filming order, filming the third episode, "Hungry," first. Now, with the emphasis of "Amor Fati" being on Mulder's psychological and emotional turmoil, it was hard to refuse when Duchovny offered his assistance in writing that all-important script. It was finally agreed that Duchovny would cowrite "Amor Fati" with Carter at the same time Carter was writing "The Sixth Extinction."

Kim Manners remembers watching the preparations for "The Sixth Extinction" with some confusion about exactly how the storyline would unfold. "I was looking at the episode in the context of the three-story arc that had begun with 'Biogenesis' and thinking, 'What the hell is that about?' Looking back in hindsight, now it makes a little more sense. But at the time it was very confusing to us."

But despite the ambitious mythology elements, "The Sixth Extinction," in hindsight, was really a simple story. Frank Spotnitz argues that "For me, it was a lot like a fifties monster movie with Scully out on the beach with this guy going nuts with a machete, the bug attacks, and the sea of blood. Yeah, it was supposed to be serious business but, overall, I thought it was shaping up as a pretty entertaining hour."

Logistically, "The Sixth Extinction" ran into an immediate continuity problem in regard to its beach location. "Biogenesis" had been filmed on the sands of Malibu Beach, California. However, "The Sixth Extinction" was being filmed at a different time of the year (midsummer 1999). Consequently the tides had changed, making the location basically unusable. The problem was solved when the production moved some miles to the south and the shooting-friendly confines of Leo Carrillo State Beach.

For the African sequences to appear authentic, Rick Millikan was faced with a double challenge in casting the natives. "We needed people who not only looked African but who could speak both African and English. Believe me, finding actors who fit all those requirements was not easy."

The episode was quick out of the box with a prominent action sequence in which a number of natives swimming in the "cursed" water get boiled by a sudden heat surge. The elaborate scene was accomplished with the aid of an underwater camera filming stuntmen in varying degrees of burn makeup.

Shooting on the beach in the middle of summer was a lot of fun for director Kim Manners. But things got a little dicey and pungent once the production moved back to the familiar confines of Stage 8 on the Fox lot for interiors.

"We had millions of dead insects on Stage 8 that stunk the place to high hell." Manners chuckled at the memory, but it was not a laughing matter when the script called for Scully to fight off a swarm of insects that stubbornly refused to swarm for the camera.

"What we ended up doing," says Manners, "was to blow popcorn and packing foam at her with big fans and added the insects in postproduction."

This episode was essentially Duchovny and Anderson's first full episode of the season (having only shot a total of two days on "Hungry"), and there was a sense of renewal in their performances that would set the tone for the season to come. Duchovny, although limited to moments of anguish and turmoil, was moving and believable in his vulnerability. And Anderson, in the role of seeker with a growing belief in the truly strange world around her, would ultimately turn in an emotionally balanced and quietly showstopping performance.

"The Sixth Extinction" provided an intriguing opening to Season 7. For Frank Spotnitz, the episode hearkened back to another time and another challenge. "What happened with 'The Sixth Extinction' and 'Amor Fati' was a lot like what happened at the end of season one, beginning of season two, when Gillian got pregnant. That really was the birth of the mythology proper. Now it's kind of happened again."

FACTS:

A friendly neighborhood entomologist rented out the 50,000 dead crickets that littered the floor during the sequences of Scully's bug attack.

The spaceship in the water was computer-generated.

Mimi Rogers, formerly married to Tom Cruise, appeared with David Duchovny in the pre–*X-Files* film *The Rapture*.

episode 7X04

THE SIXTH EXTINCTION II
AMOR FATI

EPISODE: 7X04
FIRST AIRED: November 14, 1999
EDITOR: Heather MacDougall
WRITTEN BY: David Duchovny & Chris Carter
DIRECTED BY: Michael Watkins

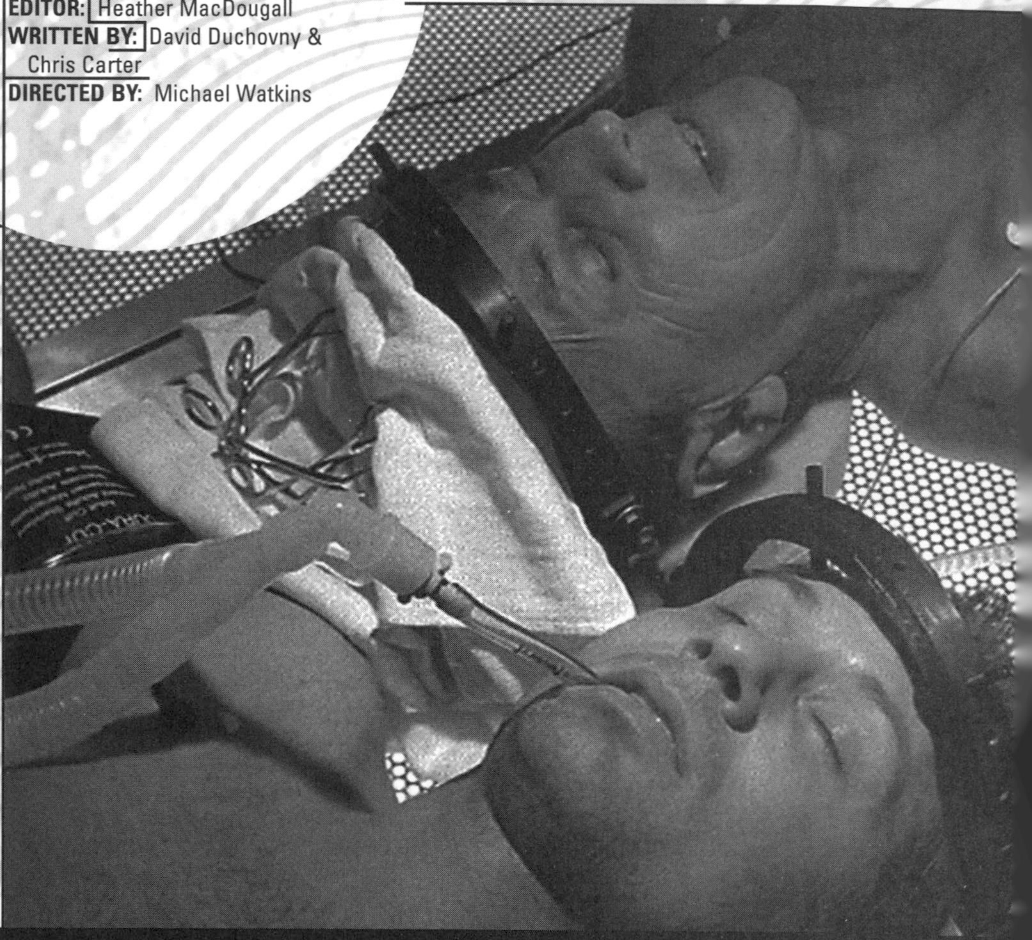

Scully continues to try to find a cure for Mulder's illness as the Cigarette-Smoking Man ups the emotional ante with surprising revelations, dire promises, and a genetic transplant procedure that will make the promise of world domination a reality.

GUEST STARS:

Mitch Pileggi (A.D. Skinner)
William B. Davis (The Cigarette-Smoking Man)
Nicholas Lea (Krycek)
Mimi Rogers (Agent Diana Fowley)
Jerry Hardin (Deep Throat)
Martin Grey (Special Agent Flagler)
Rebecca Toolan (Mrs. Mulder)
Floyd Red Crow Westerman (Albert Hosteen)
John Finn (Michael Kritschgau)
Brian George (Project Doctor)
Warren Sweeney (Dr. Geoff Harriman)
Fritz Greve (Bearded Man)
Anthony Anselmi (Paramedic)
Arlene Pileggi (Skinner's Secretary)
Megan Leitch (Samantha Mulder)
Henry Schwartz (Toddler)
Andrew and Steven Cavarno (Dream Boy)

PRINCIPAL SETTING:

Washington, D.C.

The episode begins with a recap of the previous episode, in which Mulder's sickness has been revealed as psychic activity, possibly of alien origin. Scully has returned from Africa and ultimately comes to Mulder to beg him to hang on while she finds help.

Mulder sits in the middle of a pristine, surreal beach. He watches as a couple coaxes their young child to take his first steps. A doctor's detached, clinical voice rustles in the background.

"We've exhausted all medical and scientific avenues."

Mulder is at peace.

"By that I mean nothing we can find . . . no disease, no hint of disease, only symptoms. The brute fact is he's experiencing so much activity in his temporal lobe that it is effectively destroying his brain."

We switch to Georgetown Memorial Hospital, where Mulder's mother is speaking with Dr. Harriman.

"Enough!" she insists. "There's only so much bluntness a mother can take."

Dr. Harriman tries to apologize but is waved off by Mrs. Mulder.

"All you do is sedate him," she says. "You're turning him into a zombie."

His mother's voice intensifies in Mulder's head. He opens his eyes, but there remains no expression in them. Mrs. Mulder leans close to gently turn his head to face her.

"I know you can hear me, Fox," she says. "Can you give me a sign?"

His lips don't move. But we hear him trying to speak to her.

Mulder's mind cries out, "I can hear you, Mom . . . No, Mom, I'm here! Come back, Mom! Mommmm!" As Mrs. Mulder walks away, Mulder hears her thoughts for him. He desperately screams louder, but no one can hear.

His mother and Dr. Harriman are gone.

Later, a man is standing in Mulder's room, his back to us.

It is the Cigarette-Smoking Man. He is speaking telepathically and cryptically.

"When in disgrace with fortune and men's eyes . . . Ah, but your mommy will still love you."

CSM continues his assault on Mulder's senses.

"All a mother wants is to shield her boy from pain and danger; safe in the world as he was once in the womb. But maybe we think a father demands more than mere survival. Maybe we're afraid a father demands worldly adulation, success, heroism."

The Cigarette-Smoking Man is at Mulder's bedside. He puts his face right next to Mulder's ear, yet still speaks only in his mind. "I know you can hear me."

Mulder's mind says, "I could always hear you. Even when my mind is jammed with a thousand voices I can hear you like a snake hissing underneath. How did you get in here?"

CSM removes a small ampoule and begins loading a syringe. Mulder's mind fights.

"How does anything I do surprise you now?" asks CSM. "Aren't you expecting me to sprout vampire fangs?"

"You've come to kill me," says Mulder.

The CSM says, "Be better than living like a zombie, wouldn't it?"

The CSM sticks the needle in Mulder's head and injects the mystery liquid. Mulder goes through excruciating pain. When the two men speak, their lips now move.

"I'm giving you a choice," says CSM.

"What choice?" asks Mulder.

"Life or death," says CSM. "Your account is squared with me, with God, with the IRS, with the FBI. Rise out of your bed and come with me."

Mulder says, "I'm dying, you idiot. If I could get up, I'd kick your ass."

"Don't be so dramatic," says CSM. "Only part of you is dying, the part that played the hero. You've suffered enough for the X-Files, for your partner, for the world. You're not Christ, you're not Prince Hamlet, you're not even Ralph Nader. You can walk out of this hospital and the world will forget you. Arise."

Mulder sits upright in his bed. He wants to know what CSM has done to him.

CSM says, "I'm showing you how to take the road not taken. Take my hand." He holds out a hand.

"Why should I take your hand?" asks Mulder.

CSM asks, "You can't read my mind?"

"No. I can't. All the voices are gone."

"Take my hand, Fox. You have to take the first step."

Mulder's eyes roll back and he is back on the serene beach, watching the toddler taking his first steps toward the outstretched hands of his parents. "Take my hand." The scene melts back to the real world and the Cigarette-Smoking Man.

"I'm your father."

•

After spending the night in Mulder's office poring over the mysterious symbols that she has transferred to her computer, Scully has fallen asleep amid a jumble of medical textbooks and notepads.

"Sleep is a luxury, Agent Scully," says Kritschgau. "A self-indulgence we have no time for. Nor does Agent Mulder."

Scully jumps up and sees Kritschgau standing behind her.

"How did you get in here?"

"Getting in's easy," says Kritschgau. "It's what you do once you're inside that's key."

"What's that supposed to mean?" she asks.

"You are the only one with access to Mulder. I need you to use it wisely."

"Like you?" says Scully. "Almost killing him by shooting him full of phenytoin for a few moments of lucidity."

"It's what Agent Mulder wanted," he says. "He knows what's wrong. What he wants now is to prove it. It's why he asked for me, not you."

"I don't believe that."

Kritschgau reveals the reason for Mulder's illness.

"Two years ago your partner was infected with a virus he claimed was alien. A virus reactivated in him by exposure to a source of energy, also alien. Agent Mulder is living proof of what he tried so long to substantiate. The existence of alien life."

Scully says, "Well, whatever it is, it's killing him. And we have to get it out of him."

Kritschgau speaks threateningly. "You destroy this and I'll destroy you."

Their standoff is broken by the sound of a telephone ring, and Kritschgau exits. Scully answers the phone and hears the voice of A.D. Skinner.

"Agent Scully, you need to go to the hospital," he says.

"What? Why? What's happened?"

Skinner says, "Mulder's gone. He's disappeared."

Scully races to the hospital, where she finds Skinner standing next to an empty bed.

Scully says, "There were guards posted here. A man who's gravely ill doesn't just get up and disappear."

"I know, I know."

"How did this happen?"

"His mother checked him out," says Skinner.

"His mother?"

"That's what they're saying."

"Has anybody spoken with her?" she asks.

"I'm leaving that up to you," he says. "It's better I not be involved any further in this case."

"Sir, this isn't just a case," Scully says. "This is Agent Mulder we're speaking about."

Skinner says, "And I'm trying to help him. By staying out of this from now on."

"Sir?"

"I'm in a compromised position. The less I know about Agent Mulder's whereabouts, and yours, the better."

•

Mulder is once again inside his head and on the sandy beach. A small boy walks toward him and starts to speak . . . in the voice of the Cigarette-Smoking Man.

"The child is father to the man."

Mulder awakens in the passenger seat of a car, still dressed in hospital garb, his hands manacled by handcuffs. He looks over and sees the Cigarette-Smoking Man in the driver's seat.

"You've been asleep quite a while," CSM says. "I suspect it'll be some time before your sleep patterns return to normal. Would you like an explanation?"

Mulder is not sure. CSM tells Mulder that his doctors worked on him while he was unconscious at the hospital.

"At some point I realized that if the Syndicate didn't kill you, the FBI would, and if the FBI didn't kill you, your own misguided heroism would. There's really no way out for you. There's no way to cheat death except by disappearing."

"Maybe now you do."

•

A weary and distraught Scully enters her apartment. A noise startles her. Someone else is in the apartment. Scully draws her weapon and moves warily through the apartment. She turns around and . . .

"Don't move! Who's there?" she yells at the sight of a man standing in the darkness by her front door.

"I don't mean to frighten you. Albert Hosteen," says the Navajo elder as he steps forward into the light.

"What are you doing here? How did you get here?"

"I'm sorry to surprise you," says Hosteen.

"Surprise? That you're standing here. Last time I saw you was in New Mexico. They'd taken you from the hospital. Your doctors feared the worst."

Hosteen says, "I was hoping to see your partner."

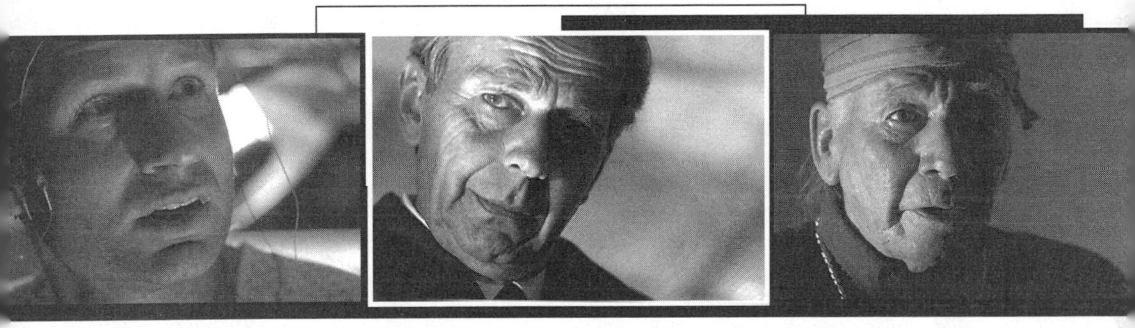

"A man can't just disappear," says Mulder.

CSM says, "We've made entire cultures disappear. Like me now, you'll become a man without a name. But even while you miss your former identity, you'll learn to love life's simpler pleasures."

"That'll be kind of tough with these on," says Mulder, indicating the handcuffs on his wrists.

CSM says, "When you no longer want to run, those will come off. How do you feel?"

"I feel better than I did," says Mulder. "I've got to tell Scully. I've got to tell her."

"If you do have contact with her, you'll put her in danger. You're entering a kind of witness protection program for want of a better term."

CSM lights up two smokes. "Can I offer you a cigarette?"

"I don't smoke," Mulder reminds him.

Scully tells Hosteen that Mulder is missing.

"You must save him," says Hosteen.

"He's very ill," says Scully.

"You must find him before something happens. Not only for his sake. For the sake of us all."

•

After driving all night, the car containing Mulder and CSM pulls up to the curb in a suburb.

"Where are we?" asks Mulder.

"Home," says CSM. "This is your new life." He holds out a key to Mulder.

Mulder looks out the car window at an idyllic suburban paradise. "I don't understand," he says, taking the key.

CSM gets out of the car, leaving the keys In the ignition.

"You can drive away right now. Drive back to Scully and your X-Files and imminent death . . . wouldn't be surprised if you did. But I think you should take a look around. Why leave something behind until you know what it is you're leaving?"

CSM turns and walks away. Mulder looks out the car window at the house.

•

Scully is in Mulder's office, talking with FBI surveillance specialist Agent Flagler. Flagler looks at a series of monitors as he fills Scully in on what the agency knows.

"Mulder was taken out of the hospital just before two A.M. His mother's signature is on the hospital documents. It's her handwriting. She checked him out AMA—against medical advice. It's all legitimate until you go to surveillance. This is the camera in the hall outside Mulder's room."

On the monitor a hand appears and darkens the frame. Then, on the monitor in Mulder's room, a hand comes up and slaps something over the lens, obscuring its view.

"We're guesstimating there were at least three others involved. Check this out. Where's Waldo," says Flagler as he hits the FAST FORWARD button on the deck of the first monitor. He pauses the deck and points to a sliver of visible picture. Scully leans in and looks at the reflection in one of Mulder's hospital room windows. In it we can see Mulder's mother talking to someone who is not visible. But we can see a cigarette.

"She's talking to someone," says Flagler.

"Yeah, I know who that is," says Scully.

•

Mulder gets out of a car and goes up the walk to the house. He puts the key in the lock, pushes the door open, and sticks his head in, calling hello. He sees a nice but modest and comfortable house. He wanders through the cozy home and into the kitchen, where he pulls open a refrigerator. It is well stocked with bags of sunflower seeds. Mulder smiles at the sight of his favorite snack food, opens a bag, and puts some in his mouth.

He is startled by a familiar voice.

"They can change your name."

He turns and sees Deep Throat smiling back at him.

"But they can't change the things you love."

Mulder says, "It can't be. You're dead."

"No," says Deep Throat. "Just really relaxed."

Mulder is overcome by joy as he realizes that Deep Throat is alive.

"Scully saw you get shot," says Mulder. "On the bridge. Six years ago. I was sure you were dead."

He reaches out to touch his face and hugs the man.

Deep Throat lifts his shirt to reveal a nasty bullet scar. "One well-placed bullet, like a punctuation mark in a man's life, and you get to start a whole new chapter. I'm fine, son. Aside from a little tennis elbow."

Mulder, still in shock, sits down. "I felt responsible for your death."

"You can let that go," says Deep Throat. "Clearly, I'm alive."

"I thought that you died for my quest," says Mulder.

"Yes, along with Scully's sister, and the man you thought was your father, and Duane Barry, and even Scully's mysterious illness, and on and on. You can let go of all that guilt. I'm here to tell you that you're not the hub of the universe, the cause of life and death. We—you and I—are merely puppets in a master plan, no more, no less. You've suffered enough, now you should enjoy your life. Let me show you something."

Deep Throat pulls out his wallet and shows Mulder a picture.

"That's my wife and daughters. We live just down the street. I hope you visit us for dinner."

•

Mulder is asleep in an easy chair, a pile of sunflower seeds in a nearby ashtray. As he dozes, he dreams . . .

Mulder is back on the beach, watching as the young boy builds a sand castle. A wave washes over the sand castle and floods it out. The boy looks upset. Mulder is now by his side.

"Hey, buddy, it's okay," says Mulder. "You can build it again. Just start again, okay?"

Mulder awakens from his dream in a darkened room, now wearing jeans and still handcuffed. Unsure of where he is, he looks around the room. His eyes find the silhouette of a woman's beautiful body in a sheer nightgown, standing in the doorway. He jumps up.

"Who's there? Who are you?" asks Mulder.

It is Agent Diana Fowley. She speaks to him as if she were comforting a young child, slowly advancing toward Mulder.

"Hundreds of little joys, to go to a door and have a woman beckon you in, to have her make a fire and lay the table for you, and when it's late, to feel her take you into her arms."

Fowley produces a key and unlocks his handcuffs. They kiss passionately. Mulder's hands wrap around her and pull Fowley to him.

•

Mrs. Mulder's voice comes from her answering machine. Scully leaves a message:

"This is Dana Scully. As before, you can reach me at your son's office at the FBI. Thank you."

Scully opens a package that has just been delivered to Mulder's desk and pulls out a book with symbols over the title: *Native American Beliefs & Practices*. She checks the unmarked interoffice envelope it came in. Then she notices the same symbols on the screen of her laptop computer. Scully opens the book and leafs through it, coming to a chapter headed "The Anasazi: An Entire Native American Indian Culture Vanishes without a Trace." Underneath is the subheading "History as Myth and End of the World Symbolism. Apocalypse and The Sixth Extinction." The words are familiar to her. She picks up the phone.

Skinner answers the ringing phone.

"Sir, did you send me this book?"

"Excuse me," says Skinner.

Scully says, "This book. It explains everything that I found in Africa, using the same symbols that I found on the ship."

"Agent Scully, I asked you not to involve me in this."

Scully says, "It's all here, sir. A foretelling of mass extinction. A myth about a man who can save us from it. That's why they took Mulder. They think that his illness is a gift. Protection against a coming plague."

Skinner hangs up on Scully.

•

Scully goes to FBI headquarters and into Skinner's outer office, where his secretary attempts to block her way. They hear a loud commotion coming from Skinner's office. There is a yell and the sound of a body hitting a wall. Scully rushes in.

Skinner is bent over his desk in pain with a long-haired man with a beard standing next to him. He immediately makes for the office's other door. Scully quickly goes to Skinner's side.

"Sir, are you hurt?" says Scully. "Are you cut?"

After instructing his secretary to call for help, Scully runs after the long-haired man. She spots him already at the other end of the hallway, moving through foot traffic.

"Hey, stop!" yells Scully. "Stop that man!"

The man places an electronic device in his pocket, then pulls the fire alarm, which causes a traffic jam in the hallway, allowing him to escape.

•

Mulder goes down the front walk for the morning newspaper, where he turns to stare at the house. Fowley walks out to join him with a cup of coffee.

"ONE WELL-PLACED BULLET, LIKE A PUNCTUATION MARK IN A MAN'S LIFE, AND YOU GET TO START A WHOLE NEW CHAPTER. I'M FINE, SON. ASIDE FROM A LITTLE TENNIS ELBOW."—Deep Throat

"What's wrong, Fox?"

"There's nothing wrong. Perfect. It's all perfect. What the hell am I doing here?"

"You just need some coffee," says Fowley.

"No. I'm serious. I have commitments to the X-Files, to Scully, to my sister."

Fowley says, "You think you know what that means. Commitment. It's all just childish, Fox."

"Childish?" he asks.

"Yes, you've been a child, with only the responsibility of a child, to your own dreams and fantasies. But you won't know the true joy of responsibility until you plant your feet in the world and become a father."

Mulder considers this. "Diana, you lay all this on me after I sleep with you one time. What's it gonna be like tomorrow?"

"You have to let go, Fox," says Fowley.

"Just like that. I'm just supposed to slip into domestic bliss, even after I was dropped off here by a man I have every reason to believe left here to carry on his dirty work?"

Fowley places her hand on his chest to calm him. "He lives the next block over. We'll go visit after breakfast."

•

A loud knocking on his apartment door brings Kritschgau to the peephole. He starts to open it when he is driven backward by the force of the door being forced inward. Scully storms in.

"You told someone, didn't you?" says Scully. "You let the information out."

"What are you talking about?"

She says, "A man attacked Skinner in his office."

"For what?" he asks.

"For what he knows about Mulder."

"I haven't told anyone," he says.

Scully's eyes are drawn to a computer screen. She recognizes the symbols from her work in Africa with the same lines and circles she had drawn in her research.

"What is this?" she says. "These are mine. You've hacked into my files! What are you doing with these?"

"I was having them analyzed."

"By who?" she says.

"The National Institutes of Health."

"What?"

"The material you have there . . . encrypted data that describes advanced human genetics. Where did you get it?"

Scully says, "This was not supposed to go public."

Scully types commands into the computer, deleting all the files that Kritschgau has stolen.

Kritschgau says, "Wherever you got it, that data supports what happened to Mulder. It proves what he's become . . . biologically alien."

Kritschgau is adamant in wanting to know what Scully is hiding. Scully says quite simply that it doesn't matter.

"It matters to someone," says Kritschgau. "And whoever it is, it sounds like they're looking for Mulder, too."

Scully leaves.

•

Mulder and Fowley arrive at CSM's house. Fowley knocks on the door, which opens to reveal a mellow CSM.

"I wasn't expecting you so soon. I thought you'd take a few days to settle in."

Fowley says, "I think you need to allay his unhappiness with things he perceives as left undone."

"Including why you live in a bigger house than I do," says Mulder.

"I've got quite a few mouths to feed," he says. "Three grandkids. And your sister."

Mulder turns at CSM's nod and is shocked to see his long-lost sister Samantha and three little kids in the street.

"She's been living here all along," says CSM. "Living a life you'd forsaken."

Samantha sees her older brother and breaks into a run. They hug. "He said you were coming."

The voice of CSM intones, "A father has high hopes for a son. But he never dreams his boy is gonna change the world."

The dream is over . . .

Mulder is splayed out on a medical table, arms outstretched and wrists, ankles, and head secured by metal bands, as CSM and Fowley observe.

"I'm so proud of this man," says CSM. "The depth of his capacity for suffering."

"Like father, like son," says Fowley.

Cigarette-Smoking Man says, "They think what he has is killing him, when in actuality he's never been more alive."

"Do you think he dreams?" she asks.

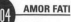

CSM says, "Oh, I'm sure he dreams."

"About what, I wonder."

"The dreams all men who are owned by the world have: of a simpler life full of small pleasures."

He looks down at Mulder with true pity. "Extraordinary men are always most tempted by the most ordinary things.

"Dreams are all he has now."

•

Fowley walks through the hallways of FBI headquarters. She is lost in thought and does not notice Scully walk up behind her at the elevator.

"Bum a cigarette, Agent Fowley?" says Scully.

"I don't smoke," she says.

Scully says, "Really? I could swear I smell cigarette smoke on you."

"Let's cut the crap, shall we," says Fowley.

"Yes. Let's."

The two women enter a stairwell where they continue their verbal war.

Scully demands to know where Mulder is.

Fowley says, "Maybe before you go around blaming everyone you can find for what's happened to Mulder, you could think about what you could have done to prevent it."

"I just want you to think," says Scully. "Think of Mulder when you met him, think of the promise and the life in front of him. Think of him now. And then try and stand there in front of me, look me in the eye, and tell me Mulder wouldn't bust his ass trying to save you."

Fowley replies, "I'm thinking, Agent Scully. I'm always thinking."

She leaves.

•

In the high-tech medical facility, Mulder is being observed by a project doctor and the Cigarette-Smoking Man. CSM is getting ready for an injection.

"It's a chance none of us ever expected, let alone hoped for," says the doctor as he rolls up CSM's sleeves. "After all these years trying to develop a compatible alien–human hybrid, to have one ready-made."

CSM says, "All these years, all the questioning why. Why keep Mulder alive, when it was so simple to remove the threat that he posed."

As he injects CSM with a syringe, the doctor comments, "There was no way you could have predicted this."

CSM says, "The fact remains, he's become our savior. He's immune to the coming viral apocalypse. He is the hero here."

The doctor warns, however, that Mulder may not survive the procedure.

CSM says, "Then he suffers a hero's fate."

•

Mulder is standing in a handsomely furnished room, wearing a tuxedo. He turns and sees Fowley looking radiant in a wedding gown. He lifts her veil. He turns to find Fowley walking toward him, in a nursery, obviously pregnant.

"Fox? I think it's time, honey," she says.

The dizzying dream takes Mulder through a pair of kids and the funeral of Fowley, where he is comforted by CSM. The dream gives way to reality as Fowley looks down at Mulder as he is being prepped for surgery. CSM sidles up beside her.

"Don't think of the man, think of the sacrifice he's making for all of us. For the world."

Fowley says, "It would have been nice to give him a choice."

"You don't think Mulder would've chosen this?" asks CSM as he circles to the other end of the exam table. "To become the thing he sought for so long, to feel what it's like? He is what he sought."

"We'll never know."

"Besides, his task is almost complete." He removes his jacket. "I'll carry the burden from here on in."

Fowley reaches down and touches Mulder's face as CSM begins to be prepped for surgery.

In Mulder's dream he is now a very old man, sleeping in the twilight of his years. He awakens to find CSM standing over him.

"I know about the boy. The boy on the beach," says CSM. "The vision you go to in your mind. We all have such places, born of memory and desire."

"I've seen him thousands of times and I've never seen what he wants me to see."

"Close your eyes," instructs CSM. "He's ready to show you. If you're ready to see."

Mulder closes his eyes and he is on the beach, where he sees the boy has created an alien spacecraft out of the sand. When the dream boy suddenly begins to destroy his creation, Mulder steps in, alarmed at what he's seeing.

"Why are you destroying your spaceship?"

"It's your spaceship," says the boy. "You're destroying it. You were supposed to help me."

Hosteen suggests that prayer might be the answer to her question. She is hesitant at first but, reluctantly, kneels with Hosteen in prayer.

"There are more worlds than the one you can hold in your hand," says Hosteen.

•

Cigarette-Smoking Man and Mulder have been laid out head-to-head for what appears to be some kind of genetic transplant procedure. A team of doctors is preparing for surgery.

"I hope you see the poetry in this, Diana," says CSM.

Fowley says, "You're removing genetic material that may kill your son."

CSM says, "We're forcing the next step in evolution, to save man. We're doing God's work, Diana. Without this immunity, everyone would die. This knowledge is God's blessing. I'll carry on for Mulder from here." He takes her hand and smiles.

•

Fowley is standing over Mulder, who is under anesthesia. Mulder's eyes open. Fowley notifies a doctor that he's awake, and he checks the settings on the equipment.

"I've got him topped off," says the anesthesiologist. "But he won't stay under. I don't think we can take him much further."

•

Scully enters her apartment, exhausted. A voice calls out to her from her living room, startling her. It is Albert Hosteen.

"You're running out of time," he says.

"Why do you come to me like this?" she asks. "Why? When I can't find him."

Hosteen tells Scully that she is not looking in the right place. Scully insists that she does not know where he is.

"Even if I did, I wouldn't know how to save him. The science makes no sense to me."

The project doctor wants to know if he's feeling any pain.

"Flat on the monitor," replies the anesthesiologist. "Any flatter he'd be circling the drain."

"Okay, let's do this thing," says the doctor.

The doctor shuts Mulder's eyes, but they immediately reopen, looking right at Fowley. Disturbed, Fowley leaves the OR. Mulder is back in the dream state as a very old man on his deathbed. Sitting next to him is the Cigarette-Smoking Man, who has not aged a day.

"Can you open the blinds?" asks Mulder. "I'd like to take a look outside."

"I wanted you to have peace," says CSM.

"Where's Samantha?"

"Your sister died five years ago."

"What about Deep Throat?"

CSM says, "We've been over this. He's dead. Diana is dead. And Scully."

"Scully's dead?" asks Mulder, distraught.

"She's dead," says CSM. "It's time for you to let go. They're waiting for you, if you let go. Close your eyes, Fox." He rises and walks toward the bed.

"We're the last?" sobs Mulder. "You and I?"

"The end," says CSM. "And the beginning. There's nothing to be done. Nothing at all."

Mulder closes his eyes. Cigarette-Smoking Man crosses to the window and opens the drapes to reveal a fiery, surreal end of the world. As spaceships soar through the sky and the world goes up in flames, CSM calmly takes out a pack of smokes and puts a cigarette in his mouth. A flame ignites its tip as he watches the alien attack.

•

In D.C., a pile of Kritschgau's notes are being set aflame by a mysterious man, who pulls off a long-haired wig and adds it to the fire. He then picks up Kritschgau's laptop computer and steps through the doorway of the apartment, over the dead body of Kritschgau, lying on the floor with a bullet hole in his forehead. As he leaves the apartment, his identity is revealed: Alex Krycek.

•

Scully comes out of a sound sleep on the floor of her apartment. Hosteen is nowhere to be found. She discovers that an envelope has just been pushed under her door. Inside is a key card from the Department of Defense. She races from her apartment.

•

The surgery on Mulder and CSM is proceeding. It is a bloody yet seemingly painless procedure in which doctors painstakingly work on their brains, apparently transferring genetic material.

•

Scully arrives at an undisclosed place where she swipes her card through a key reader. A door opens. She enters to find the room where the elderly dying Mulder lies. He reaches a hand out to her. "Scully, I knew you'd come. They told me you were dead."

"And you believed them. Traitor!" she shoots back.

"What?"

"Deserter! Coward!" Scully says.

"Scully, don't, I'm dying."

"You're not supposed to die, Mulder. Not here!" she speaks slowly and determinedly.

"What do you mean?"

"Not in a comfortable bed with the devil outside."

Mulder insists that CSM has taken care of him.

Scully says, "No, Mulder, he's lulled you to sleep. He's made you trade your true mission for creature comforts."

"There was no mission. There were no aliens."

"No aliens? Have you looked outside, Mulder?"

"I can't. I'm too tired."

"No, Mulder, you must get up. You must get up and fight. Especially you. This isn't your place. Get up, Mulder. Get up and fight the fight."

She is gone. "Scully . . . Scully," he calls.

Mulder lifts his head but then lies back down. "Scully."

•

A security card scanner grants access to someone on the other side of the door. The door opens to reveal Scully, who enters to find Mulder alone in the operating theater. A bandage has been applied to his head. Scully gently caresses his head.

"Mulder, you've got to wake up. I've got to get you out of here. Mulder, can you understand me?" Mulder sees a quick flash of his dream self and attempts to open his eyes.

"Mulder, you've got to get up. I don't know how much time we have. You've got to get up, Mulder. No one can do it but you, Mulder. Mulder, help me, please, Mulder." A tear drops as she rests her cheek against his.

Mulder's eyes flutter open. He asks her for help, and she hugs him tight.

•

One week later, Scully knocks on Mulder's apartment door. Mulder, in a dress shirt and a New York Yankees baseball cap on top of his bandages, answers.

"Scully, what are you doing here? Actually, I was just getting dressed to come see you, but I couldn't find a tie to go with my victory cap."

"Mulder, no work," says Scully, removing his cap. "You have to go back to bed." She tries to remove the tie as well, but he pulls it back.

"Wait! Tie goes to the winner. I was coming down to work to tell you that Albert Hosteen is dead. He died last night in New Mexico. He'd been in a coma for two weeks. There was no way he could have been in your apartment."

Scully insists that they'd prayed together. "Mulder, I don't believe that. I don't believe it. It's impossible."

"Is it any more impossible than what you saw in Africa? Or what you saw in me?"

Scully looks down for a moment. "I don't know what to believe anymore. I was so determined to find a cure, to save you, that I could deny what it was that I saw. And now I don't even know . . . I don't know what the truth is, I don't know who to listen to, I don't know who to trust." She struggles to control her tears. "Diana Fowley was found murdered this morning. I never trusted her, but she helped save your life, just as much as I did. She gave me that book. It was her key that led me to you. I'm sorry. I'm so sorry. I know she was your friend."

Crying, she hugs a stunned Mulder.

"Scully, I was like you once. I didn't know who to trust. And I chose another path, another life, another fate, where I found my sister. And even though my world was unrecognizable and upside down, there was one thing that remained the same." He pulls back and cups her face in his hands. "You were my friend, and you told me the truth. Even when the world was falling apart, you were my constant, my touchstone."

Scully replies through her tears, "And you were mine."

Mulder smiles and Scully kisses him on the forehead. She puts his cap back on and traces his face for a long moment with her fingers before turning and walking away.

Mulder is left to his thoughts and dreams of the dream boy on the beach, working together with Mulder on a sand sculpture of a gigantic spaceship.

"EVEN WHEN THE WORLD WAS FALLING APART, YOU WERE MY CONSTANT, MY TOUCHSTONE."—Mulder

BACK STORY:

David Duchovny has always had a warm spot in his heart for Nikos Kazantzakis's novel *The Last Temptation of Christ*. That it could be translated into a compelling *X-File* that he would cowrite with Chris Carter was an exciting possibility.

"For David, there was the strong desire to play something different as Mulder," explains Frank Spotnitz. "He saw a lot of parallels between *The X-Files* and *The Last Temptation of Christ* that he felt he could bring out."

" 'Amor Fati' was something very personal to these characters but, in particular, to Mulder," reflects Carter. "The big question was, had he made the right choice in deciding to pursue the aliens all these years through the X-Files? I think it had some very personal issues in it for David."

The story conferences were typical in that everybody fought hard for what they felt was important to the story. Particularly vocal in his defense of the storyline was Duchovny. "We all knew it was an important script and that a lot of the new mythology and the direction of the show for the rest of the season would hinge on it," says Spotnitz. "Everything about this story arc was a risk and 'Amor Fati' was quite possibly the riskiest element of the three episodes. As the cowriter, David had a particular stake in it being as good as it could possibly be."

The tight schedule would add additional challenges to the "Amor Fati" writing process.

"Chris had only just begun writing 'The Sixth Extinction,' " says Spotnitz. "David had written half the script for 'Amor Fati,' but there were blanks that Chris was supposed to come in and finish but couldn't because he was still writing 'The Sixth Extinction.' "

But enough of the "Amor Fati" script had been written to know that it was going to contain a who's who of *X-Files* episodes past.

Brought back for elements of Mulder's alternate future were Jerry Hardin as Deep Throat and Megan Leitch as Samantha Mulder. Also making appearances were Rebecca Toolan as Mrs. Mulder and Floyd Red Crow Westerman as the inscrutable Albert Hosteen. "It was like one big flashback," says casting director Rick Millikan.

Casting the little boy who appears to Mulder on the beach was perhaps the toughest part of the episode for Millikan. Originally, the son of a neighbor of producer Paul Rabwin came in, read for the part, and seemed perfect. But with the script and shooting schedule under time pressure, it was finally determined that all of the child's shots would have to be done in one day. This caused a problem in that child labor laws limit the number of hours a minor can work. Rabwin recalls that the problem was finally solved by going out and hiring twins.

William Davis was quite happy with the episode. "For me the episode was terrific to play because they ended up making Cigarette-Smoking Man a little tougher. We have seen so much softness in him; it was great to play that tough side."

But the down side for Davis turned out to be the sequence in which he and Duchovny were strapped down on adjoining gurneys for the transplant procedure. "I remember being totally uncomfortable lying on those tables. There was this metal strap that was pressing right into my shoulder blade. The only upside of that was that the author was lying right beside me, feeling equally uncomfortable. I wonder if David would have written it that way if he had known what he would have to go through."

"Amor Fati" worked as an X-File and Frank Spotnitz marvels at the fact that the underlying theme, aliens as God or as the creation of God, did not result in any flack from the religious community.

"We knew going into 'Amor Fati' that we would piss off some faction and we probably have but we haven't heard anything from anybody. Often in the past we've done stuff where I was sure we would get angry letters. But we rarely do. And the reason is because of the way we handle things. In 'Amor Fati' we treated the religious side with respect."

FACTS:

A scene that did not make the final cut of the episode had Mulder watching himself as he aged.

The sequence in which Mulder looks out a window and sees Armageddon was accomplished through the use of a matte painting and special effects explosions created behind the camera and reflected in the window.

Arlene Pileggi, who is married to Mitch Pileggi, has played Skinner's secretary for three seasons (including in "Amor Fati"). She would also appear as The Woman Who Looks Like Scully in the seventh season episode "Fight Club."

episode 7X01

HUNGRY

EPISODE: 7X01
FIRST AIRED: November 21, 1999
EDITOR: Heather MacDougall
WRITTEN BY: Vince Gilligan
DIRECTED BY: Kim Manners

Mulder and Scully come to sunny Southern California to investigate a mysterious killing at a drive-thru burger stand and find a tormented brain-eating mutant monster who constantly fights the urge to eat meat.

GUEST STARS:

Chasen Hampton (Hungry Guy)
Chad E. Donella (Rob Roberts)
Mark Pellegrino (Derwood Spinks)
Bill Lee Brown (Mr. Rice—Manager)
Kerry Zook (Lucy)
Steve Kiziak (Steve Kiziak)
Judith Hoag (Dr. Mindy Rinehart)
Kevin Porter (Motivational Speaker)
Lois Foraker (Sylvia Jassy)

PRINCIPAL SETTING:

Costa Mesa, California

A monster of a car, marked by the drone of heavy metal coming out of its radio, motors down the street, pulls into the empty parking lot of the 1950s-style fast food restaurant Lucky Boy, and makes its way to the drive-thru lane.

It pulls up to the outdoor menu and stops in front of the ordering speaker. Behind the wheel of the car sits a young Hungry Guy. He checks out the menu while bobbing his head to the music blasting from the car stereo. He waits for the expected "Can I help you?" But the speaker is silent. Finally he turns down the radio and leans out the window.

"Hello? Hello?"

The lighted OPEN sign suddenly goes dark. The lighted menu board clicks off. The Hungry Guy is pissed.

He yells, "Hey! I'm sitting here, dude!"

The angry Hungry Guy leans on the horn. Finally, a disembodied voice crackles through the ordering speaker.

"Sorry, we're closed."

"Uh-uh! I was here before you turned off the light! Grandfather clause, man! I need a Super Patty Double with Cheese . . ."

"The light was a mistake," says the drive-thru voice. "We're closed. Sorry."

The mike clicks off. The Hungry Guy is now the Angry Guy.

"The light was on! How bad do you want this job? 'Cause I'll call the head office right now! Super Patty Double with Cheese! Super-size fries! Super-size Diet Sprite!"

He leans on the horn.

The speaker voice comes to life. "Drive through, please."

Hungry Guy glides his car up to the order window. From his driver's seat, he can only see the ceiling inside. He waits and waits for his order. Fast food is now becoming slow food.

"What the hell is this? Customer service, man! Stop spanking it and gimme my food!"

The order window remains empty, but he hears the faint sounds of someone breathing. The Hungry Guy is becoming increasingly unnerved. He cranes his neck outside the car.

"Hey in there . . . guy?"

He maneuvers his body over the order window's ledge. The place is deserted. Hungry Guy eases his way farther into the window when a putty-white and hairless form with shark eyes and rows of razor-sharp teeth springs up and attacks the Hungry Guy. He is pulled violently through the order window.

The screams grow fainter and finally strangle off. The driverless car creeps away from the order window and to the curb. The Lucky Boy sign continues to glow against the night sky.

•

Three days later, the Lucky Boy restaurant appears busy. Everything is normal. A car pulls into the lot and out climbs Rob Roberts, a twentysomething, slim, and unassuming young man dressed in a Lucky Boy uniform. He puts on his uniform hat and checks himself in his car window.

"You are your own man," Rob tells his reflection, "and you control everything you do."

Rob walks through the restaurant carrying a register tray, exchanging greetings with other employees. He passes a particularly rough-looking character named Derwood, who is working the grill.

"Yo, Derwood."

"Hey, Rob."

Rob heads for the counter, passing his fortysomething manager, Mr. Rice.

"Hey, Mr. Rice."

"How's it going, Rob?"

Rob takes over for a female employee, politely wishing her a good day, and begins to count his change. He stares out the window as a police car pulls across the parking lot and blocks the restaurant entrance. He turns to see FBI agents Mulder and Scully and a couple of uniformed officers entering the restaurant and approaching the counter.

Lapsing instantly into Lucky Boy lingo, Rob says, "Welcome to Lucky Boy. May I take your order?"

Mulder smiles as he and Scully reach for their IDs.

"Yeah, we'll have it our way."

Scully adds, "FBI. Special Agents Scully and Mulder. We'd like a word with the manager, please."

Mr. Rice steps toward the agents.

"That's me," he says. "How can I help you?"

Scully says, "Sir, would you do us a favor and kindly gather your employees, please?"

Mr. Rice is visibly upset as he sees his customers being escorted from the restaurant by the police officers.

Mulder says, "We're investigating a murder. A car was found in a reservoir ten miles from here. A body was found in the trunk of that car."

The manager asks, "Well, what does that have to do with us?"

Scully says, "This was also found in the car."

Scully holds up an evidence bag. Inside is a round badge with two cartoon burgers on it and the caption FREE-FER FRIDAY on it. The badge is smeared with dried blood.

"It's a badge that's only given to employees. Is that correct?"

The manager examines the badge

"Yeah, 'Free-Fer Friday.' It's our promotion where you buy one Super Patty and get one free. But look, there's four Lucky Boys in Costa Mesa alone and something like thirty in Orange County."

"Thirty-two," corrects Scully.

Mulder says, "Long day. So let's make this quick. Does everybody *have* their button?"

The employees look at each other. None of them are wearing their badges.

"We only wear them on Fridays," says Rob. "Free-Fer Fridays."

"Yeah, but does everybody have their button?" asks Mulder.

One by one, the employees take out their badges and hold them up. Rob hesitates but shows the agents his badge. Mulder turns his attention away from Rob and to another worker in the background.

"Hey, you. What's your name?"

"Derwood Spinks."

"Derwood. Do you have your button, Derwood?"

Derwood pats himself down and comes up empty.

"I musta left it at home, on account of we're only supposed to wear them on Fridays. I sure as hell didn't leave it on no dead guy."

Scully glances suspiciously at Mulder. "I don't believe we ever said the victim was male."

Derwood's smile fades under their suspicious looks.

"We're going to ask everybody to step outside right now while we take a quick look around the premises," says Mulder.

Rob asks, "Who was the victim?"

"His name was Donald Edward Pankow," says Mulder. "Does that ring a bell?"

The employees shake their heads no. Mulder's gaze continues on Rob. The employees go into the parking lot. Derwood senses that their eyes are on him. To ease his discomfort, Derwood excuses himself to get some cigarettes as the manager calls up Lucky Boy corporate headquarters with the bad news.

•

Rob casually wanders over to the dining area window and listens as Mulder and Scully enter the kitchen area.

"Hey, Scully, check it out. You know how they always say you never wanna see the kitchens of your favorite restaurants?" says Mulder.

Scully says, "Somehow, I don't think Lucky Boy would make that list."

Scully's voice comes through in a staticky burst. "So what are you saying? That this place was scrubbed from top to bottom to cover up evidence?"

"Maybe," says Mulder. "Maybe I'm thinking this was the crime scene."

Rob listens as Mulder and Scully continue their inspection of the kitchen. Mulder offers a theory, but Scully is dubious.

"You're saying Mr. Pankow had his brain very neatly removed from his skull . . . right here, in this kitchen. But next to the shake machine, Mulder? I think we need to be checking employee lockers, and not entertaining the idea that ad hoc surgery was performed here."

"I wouldn't exactly call it surgery," says Mulder. "What if this man's brain was eaten?"

Outside, Rob shows no reaction to Mulder's statement. Mulder continues to speculate.

"It's sociologically not unheard of. There are some tribes in New Guinea that consider human brains a delicacy."

"YOU'RE SAYING MR. PANKOW HAD HIS BRAIN VERY NEATLY REMOVED FROM HIS SKULL . . . RIGHT HERE, IN THIS KITCHEN. BUT NEXT TO THE SHAKE MACHINE, MULDER?"—Scully

"My point being that this is a hell of a lot cleaner than all the others, don't you think?"

Rob makes a move to the order window and clicks on the intercom speaker. He moves to the back of the building, where he listens as Mulder and Scully's conversation comes through the speaker attached to the menu board.

"Yeah, but Mulder, we're in Orange County."

"Yeah, what's your point? There's nothing about the way the body was dumped which suggests a fetishistic killing. The brain wasn't removed intact. What if this man's brain was eaten right out of the skull?"

"Through an inch-and-a-half opening that looks like it was cut with a hole saw?" says Scully.

"Maybe it was cut, or maybe it was punched. What looks like tool marks to you looked to me like something organic. Like it was made from a tongue or a proboscis."

"The proboscis of what?"

Outside Rob strains to listen to the conversation. Mulder has no answer for Scully's question but continues to shine his flashlight into every corner of the kitchen. Suddenly he stops, moving his light under a counter. He pauses and looks at a few flecks of deep red color on the stainless steel counter.

"Does that look like blood to you?"

"Yes," says Scully. "Looks like it."

Mulder indicates another dab of dried blood on a lump of something nasty-looking.

"Oh, man, is that brain? Is that brain matter?"

"No, I'd say that's ground beef."

Rob is uncomfortable with this exchange.

•

Later that same day, Rob enters his modest studio apartment. It is the apartment of a loner, very clean and lacking a distinct personality. He takes off his Lucky Boy uniform and goes to the bathroom. Rob clicks on the light, kneels down, and reaches into a bathtub full of reddish water. Rob fishes another Lucky Boy uniform shirt out of the water and inspects it. He scrubs the bloodstained shirt with a nail brush before giving up. He tosses the shirt into the sink and pulls the plug on the tub. Rob jams the bloody shirt into a kitchen trash can. He is about to take it out when there is an unexpected knock on the door.

Rob freezes in terror but recovers his composure and goes to the front door. Looking through the peephole, he spies . . .

"Rob Roberts? It's Agent Mulder."

Trying to keep his panic at bay, Rob opens the door.

"Hello again. Sorry to bother you at home."

"No, no bother."

Mulder enters his apartment. He looks around the room, noticing how clean and in place everything is.

"You live here alone?"

"Yeah. Just me."

"Mom or girlfriend?" asks Mulder. "C'mon, man, who cleans up after you?"

"Just me. I live here alone."

"Bravo," says Mulder. "They say single guys are just bears who own furniture. I mean, my place . . . but here, I can smell the Pine Sol."

Rob is suspicious of Mulder's light, joking patter.

"Mr. Rice, your manager, he told me you stayed late on Friday night?"

"Uh . . . yeah. Friday. The freezer died on us. I stayed after to throw out the meat that was going bad."

Mulder takes out a notepad and begins to write on it as he interrogates Rob. Rob's calm demeanor falls apart as he stares at the kitchenette and the trash bag containing his bloody shirt, which is oozing pink water. He looks back at Mulder, who is glancing up from his notepad.

"The thirty-five pounds of ground chuck that Mr. Rice told you to throw away? What did you do with that?"

"I threw it out. In the Dumpster behind the restaurant."

"That's weird," says Mulder as he shuffles through his notes, "because that's what I figured you did. So I checked the Dumpster and it was empty. Which is weird, because it only gets cleaned out on Thursdays, and you only threw the meat out on Friday, so you'd expect the meat to be there.

"I don't see how that's relevant to our murder case, anyway. Lemme see if there's anything else I'm gonna ask you."

Mulder continues to pore over his notes. Rob is growing frantic as he watches the puddle at the base of the trash bag spread. He is jarred out of his thoughts when . . .

"Blood," says Mulder.

Rob freezes.

"You're bleeding," says Mulder, pointing to a dab of blood on Rob's face.

"I bit my lip."

Mulder stares at Rob. "I think that just about wraps it up for me," he says as he moves to the door.

Rob is relieved. "I hope you catch the guy."

"I already have a pretty good idea who it is."

As Mulder exits, Rob closes the door and gathers himself. Later, he literally trips out of the lobby door of his building as a garbage truck, having already emptied the cans in front of his building, is beginning to drive off. Rob just gets the bag in as the truck pulls away.

As the truck disappears with the incriminating evidence inside, Rob relaxes. As he dusts off his hands, he notices flecks of dried blood on his fingertips. He glances around, sees no one, and pops his fingertips into his mouth, sucking them clean.

As he turns to head back into his building, Rob notices a car parked at the curb. There is a man behind the wheel. Rob panics. He thinks Mulder saw him sucking blood. The driver's-side window rolls down, and it is not Mulder but rather a man known as Steve.

"What do you want?" asks Steve.

"N-nothing."

"So take a hike."

•

Rob returns to his apartment, where he continues to stare out the window at Steve, whose car remains parked at the curb. His thoughts are interrupted by the ringing of the phone. His answering machine clicks on. It is a greeting from Dr. Mindy Rinehart, a licensed mental health counselor with the Lucky Boy Corporation's Employee Assistance Program, who is speaking to all the Lucky Boy employees regarding their feelings about the murder at the restaurant.

As her message plays out, Rob notices his lip begins to bleed. He goes to the bathroom where he checks out his bloody lip as Dr. Rhinehart's message drones on.

"Rob, I want you to come down to my office at eleven A.M. tomorrow morning. As it is a requirement of your employer's insurance provider, this meeting is mandatory. I'm in the Irvine Medical Park, Suite Three-oh-Eight. Have a good evening."

Rob stares at his perfect teeth in the mirror. He takes a firm grip on the top row. There is the sucking-popping sound of something coming loose. There is the sound of something clinking into the sink. There are more clinks. Three tiny triangles, looking like tiny shark's teeth, lie in the sink. Rob closes his mouth. He continues to stare into the mirror.

Rob's stomach erupts in a deep growl. He instinctively touches his belly.

•

Later that evening, Rob slips a tape into his VCR and watches as an energetic motivational speaker extols the virtue of self-discipline. His hand reaches to a nearby table for a package of Slim-Chew Appetite Suppressant Gum. While the motivational speaker continues to do his thing, Rob opens the package, pops a Slim-Chew into his mouth, and begins to chew. But one is not enough, and so he pours a whole handful of Slim-Chews into his mouth, chewing them and hugging his stomach. The motivational speaker rattles off his tale of being overweight and living to eat as Rob goes to the window and peers out.

The car is still in the street. The man behind the wheel is still watching. An agitated Rob backs away from the window, his mouth working the Slim-Chew gum. He begins to mumble along with the motivational speaker: "You are your own man and you control everything that you do."

The mystery man continues to eye Rob's building as he blows cigarette smoke out an open window. Rob exits the building and walks toward the car, all the while checking the streets for possible witnesses. Seeing none, he continues to head for the car. As Rob approaches, the man in the car looks and seems to recognize Rob.

"What?" the man says, seemingly annoyed at the interruption.

Rob's jaw opens and two rows of needle-sharp teeth thrust into view. The eyes of the man behind the wheel widen in shock, but it is too late.

Rob lunges at the man. A muffled crunch cuts through the air.

•

The next morning Rob is fast asleep on his sofa. He is sleeping through the search of his apartment by an unknown intruder. Rob is awakened by a heavy boot coming to rest against his chest.

"What!" says Rob.

As his eyes focus, he sees Derwood staring down at him.

"Derwood. How'd you get in here?"

Derwood rolls a lockpick between two fingers.

"Just a little skill I picked up in Chino. I did a nickel for attempted murder. You didn't know I was an ex-con?"

Rob shakes his head no.

"Yeah, nobody at work did. Not till this FBI murder investigation whipped everybody up into a froth."

Derwood takes his foot off Rob's chest.

"Derwood, what can I do for you?"

"You know I got fired last night." Derwood wanders the room. "Plus, as far as that red-headed FBI agent is concerned, I'm the prime suspect in this murder."

Rob is surprised and relieved that Derwood is the prime suspect.

"But that's no skin off my nose, seeing as you did it."

Rob stares at him, trying to hide his fear. Derwood reaches into his pocket and pulls out a prescription bottle for something called phentermine made out to Rob.

"Diet pills," he says. "Yours, right?"

Rob remains tight-lipped and stone-faced.

"You see, I found 'em when I opened on Saturday morning. I didn't give 'em back 'cause I figured, 'Hey, free speed,' right? But then there's this whole flap about a murder and I notice this."

Derwood turns the bottle and points to a partial thumbprint of dried blood on the white plastic cap.

"That ain't ketchup, man."

Rob stares at the bottle. "What, what do you want, Derwood?"

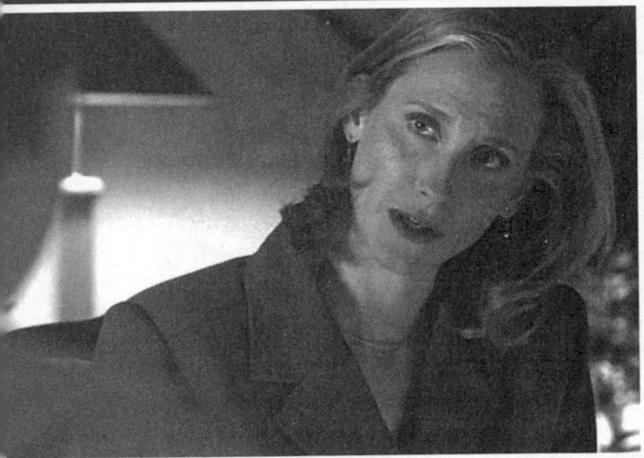

Derwood circles Rob's apartment, poking and peeking at Rob's stuff. "I dunno. What do you got? TV . . . VCR . . . nah, it's all crappy off-brand stuff. But I'll take that. And whatever money you got in the bank. And you get this and I keep my mouth shut. And just maybe you can blow town before the long arm of the law reaches out and grabs you by the gonads."

Derwood's blackmail plot is interrupted by a loud knock on the door. Rob rises to his feet as Derwood opens the door to Sylvia, Rob's fiftyish neighbor. She looks nervously at Derwood before noticing Rob. It turns out she also noticed the now deceased mystery man parked in the car across the street and wants to know if Rob knew anything about him. Rob feigns ignorance and Sylvia disappears down the hall. Derwood watches her leave, then turns his attention back to Rob.

"So, I'll call tonight and let you know where you can drop off my new VCR. And don't try skipping town. You won't get too far."

•

Rob exits his building and goes to his car.

"Hey, just the man I wanted to see," says Mulder as he walks up from behind. "How are you this morning, Rob?"

"Fine."

"I'm glad I caught you. Oh, hey, I was driving to your apartment just now and I saw Derwood Spinks not a block from here. He wasn't coming from your place, was he?"

"No, I haven't seen him."

Mulder warns Rob to stay away from him because he is the prime suspect in the Pankow murder. Rob wants to know if he thinks Derwood did it. Mulder offers that it is the opinion of the Costa Mesa Police and Agent Scully that Derwood is guilty, but that he believes the person they are looking for has a compulsion to kill, truly can't help himself.

"Oh, quick question. The meat that you threw in the Dumpster?"

"What about it?"

"That Dumpster has a padlock. Who would have the key?"

"We do," says Rob, "and the trucking company does."

Mulder thinks through Rob's explanation, is satisfied, and starts to walk away. Rob freaks.

"Hey, wait. What's your point?"

"I'm just tying up some loose ends."

•

Later that morning, Rob finds himself in the office of Dr. Mindy Rinehart, an attractive psychologist in her early thirties. Dr. Rinehart lays out the ground rules about "this being informal" and "feel free to just blurt out anything." Rob acknowledges her instructions with a forced smile. Dr. Rinehart talks him through the events of the murder and the FBI's suspicions. Rob agrees that it has been stressful but is really only half listening.

His stomach rumbles, scaring him back to full attention as Dr. Rinehart opens a file folder and questions him as to whether he has been suffering from bad dreams, insomnia, or nightmares. Rob shakes his head no as his stomach rumbles once again.

"Have you felt emotionally numb?" the doctor asks. "Do you ever see things that aren't there? Or hear voices?"

Rob blocks Dr. Rinehart out. His breathing is slow and deep. Rob stares intently at the shrink as she continues to ramble on.

"This, this murder that happened," he begins. "Yes?"

"What kind of a monster would do something like that?"

Dr. Rinehart sits back in her chair, digesting his comment.

"I don't believe in monsters. But I do believe in people. And sometimes they do terrible things, out of weakness or sickness or fear. But I do truly believe that deep down inside, even the very worst of us wants to be good."

Rob is listening intently. Dr. Rinehart asks if anything is bothering him. He finally summons up the courage to speak when the phone rings. She goes to answer it.

"Mindy Rinehart. Yes, Agent Mulder, what can I do for you?"

Rob is instantly on the alert as Dr. Rinehart listens silently to Mulder. She looks at Rob as Mulder continues to question her.

"No," she says. "I'm afraid I can't do that. I'm sorry, but that would violate patient confidentiality."

Rob panics. He gets up and heads for the door, tapping his watch to indicate he has to leave for work. Dr. Rinehart turns to Rob.

"Would you please call me later so we can finish our talk?"

Rob ducks out the door.

Later that day, Rob is doing grill duty at the Lucky Boy. He stares long and hard at the burgers sizzling on the grill, which to him look like human brains rimmed in red blood. His daymare is abruptly interrupted by the voice of his manager in a confrontation with Derwood.

"You shouldn't be here, Derwood. We would have mailed you your last check."

"Just gimme my money, Rice."

Rice disappears into his office. Derwood turns his attention to Rob.

"How you doing, killer? You better have some money for me, too, huh?"

Rob averts his eyes as Rice returns with Derwood's check. He turns and saunters out the door.

•

Rob goes to the ratty bungalow where Derwood lives and is going through it, looking for his prescription bottle. His search is interrupted by the sound of a motorcycle pulling into the driveway.

Derwood walks in and immediately realizes that his crib has been tossed. He picks up a menacing-looking baseball bat.

"If somebody's still in here, you're in for a world of hurt."

He steps on a plastic vial of prescription pills.

"Rob?" he says as he pulls out Rob's bottle of phentermine. "You looking for these? Deal's off, buddy."

Hiding in a closet, Rob's fear intensifies as his stomach begins to rumble.

"That guy you iced? Pankow? I just heard he didn't have any brain in his head. You are one sick little freak. You got a lot of problems."

Rob listens. The fear has left him. He has a look of regret. He puts a hand to his head and pulls off a toupee. Underneath he is completely bald. Derwood has zeroed in on the closet

"I DON'T BELIEVE IN MONSTERS. BUT I DO BELIEVE IN PEOPLE."
—Dr. Rhinehart

and inches closer to it. Inside the closet, Rob continues his nightmarish transformation. He reaches up and pulls off prosthetic ears. He removes his contact lenses as his stomach once again rumbles.

Derwood reaches the closet door and, holding the bat at the ready, yanks the closet door open. What he sees freezes him with terror. He drops the bat as the now fully transformed Rob eases out of the closet and into the light.

Rob is now a hairless, earless, shark-toothed, dark-eyed monster. The monster opens its mouth and a black lance of a tongue darts out and hits Derwood's forehead with a bone-crunching sound.

•

The next day, Dr. Rinehart is doing paperwork in her office when she is distracted by a faint rapping on the door. She goes to the door and opens it, revealing a tired, distracted Rob.

"Hi, you said we should finish talking . . ."

She ushers him into the office. There are tense moments of silence before Rob finally summons up the courage to talk.

"I think I need help."

"Tell me why you think that."

"I have compulsions . . . to eat. I get hungry."

Through Rinehart's gentle yet probing questioning, Rob confesses that he has compulsions to eat and that he puts it off as long as he can. But eventually he can't help himself and he must eat. He denies that his problem is binging and purging.

"No, I just eat," says Rob.

As the session continues, Rob couches his feelings in vague terms. He tells Rinehart that eating makes him feel like a bad person, and the doctor encourages him, citing many instances of low self-esteem being the cause of eating disorders.

She pauses for a moment, going to her desk to search for something. She finds a mirror and holds it up to him. Rob is touched by Dr. Rinehart's description of him as "a good person with a nice smile and soulful brown eyes." Feeling better about himself, he absently runs a hand through his hair, accidentally brushing it against his ear. It falls off. He panics, picks up the ear, and sticks it back on just as Dr. Rinehart returns to the chair.

"There's a meeting I'd like you to attend tonight," she says as she hands him a paper on Overeaters Anonymous. "You can talk to me anytime you want, but these people are the best. They can really help you."

"I have to go," says Rob.

"You always hurry away," says Dr. Rinehart.

"I appreciate it, and I want you to understand that I really am trying to do right."

•

Rob goes home. As he climbs the stairs to his apartment building, his stomach once again begins to rumble. He reaches for his bottle of phentermine and pops a capsule into his mouth. He passes Sylvia, who is coming down the stairs with a laundry basket. She stops and says to him, "Hey, Rob, you didn't tell me you had a friend in the FBI."

"Huh?"

"I just told him all about the strange man in the maroon car. He said he'd look into it."

Rob continues climbing the stairs. On the landing he sees Mulder at the far end of the hallway.

"Afternoon, Rob."

The lobby door opens below him and Scully appears at the foot of the stairs.

"Sir," says Scully, "may we speak with you?"

•

Inside Rob's apartment, Scully tells Rob that Derwood has disappeared. Mulder adds that Derwood's car and belongings are also missing.

"My partner saw Spinks in your neighborhood yesterday morning," says Scully. "At that time, you told Agent Mulder you hadn't seen Mr. Spinks. Is that correct?"

"I don't even know him that well. If he was going to leave town, he wouldn't come tell me about it."

Mulder says, "Who said he left town?"

"I don't know. Isn't that what you think happened?"

"No, personally I think he's dead. I can't speak for my partner, but I think that whatever it was that killed Donald Pankow got to Mr. Derwood Spinks."

"What do you mean, 'whatever it was'?"

Mulder presses his theory further.

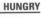

"Well, I'll let you in on a secret. We've been able to keep it pretty quiet up until now, but Donald Pankow's brain was missing from his skull. My partner found something that was previously undetected: the tip of what could only be described as a tiny shark's tooth, embedded deep in the bone. I think we're looking for some form of genetic freak. A carnivorous predator as yet unidentified. A monster, if you will."

"There's no such thing," says Rob.

"Don't you believe it," says Mulder. "This thing definitely qualifies. It has a biological imperative to eat. I think it even ate that ground chuck you threw away."

Mulder continues to lay out his monster theory.

"Because it can't kill with impunity and it knows it. It knows the more it feeds on humans, the closer it gets to getting caught. But the hunger is always there. And it satisfies it any way it can."

Rob wants to know why Mulder is telling him this.

"I think you know why."

Scully thanks Rob for his cooperation as she rises and heads for the door. Mulder follows, taking a parting shot.

"Watch out for that monster."

Rob sits motionless, then fumbles for the Overeaters Anonymous information in his pocket and stares at it.

•

Rob is seated in the back row of a meeting hall, where a meeting of Overeaters Anonymous is already underway. O.A. members are taking turns at the podium, declaring their triumphs and temptations. Rob's stomach once again rumbles. He grabs his knees and stares dejectedly at the floor. He is joined by his neighbor Sylvia, who is, coincidentally, also a member. At her insistence, Rob gamely agrees to take the stage and bare his soul.

"Hi, my name is Robert Roberts. I have an eating disorder. I'm definitely a meat eater—not a vegetarian."

The members respond with a "Hi, Rob!" and the troubled young man is off and running, explaining his addiction to food, his feeling of not being normal, and the lifelong cravings for meat that have become too powerful to resist. Rob warms to the support he's receiving and continues on with his love of meat.

"I guess it's the taste I respond to the most. Salty and juicy . . . kinda buttery. The texture

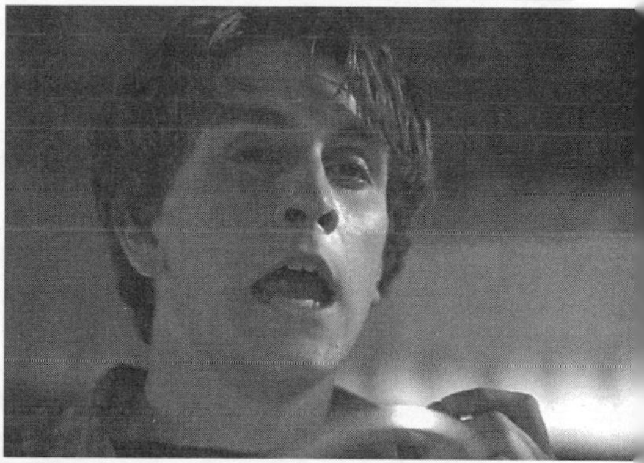

"I GUESS IT'S THE TASTE I RESPOND TO THE MOST. SALTY AND JUICY...KINDA BUTTERY. THE TEXTURE OF IT INSIDE OF YOUR MOUTH."—Rob

of it inside of your mouth. You know, your teeth just sink into it like this juicy cloud. And it tastes so good, you don't even wanna swallow it. You just wanna work it around your tastebuds until your eyes roll right back in your head."

The sympathetic response to his heartfelt confession has Rob in a comfortable place. He is also getting hungry. He stares out into the audience and at the back of a bald man's head, which transforms, in Rob's mind, into a human brain. Rob shuts his eyes and snaps back to reality.

"Anyway, it's a real problem."

•

Later that night, Rob and Sylvia enter their apartment building, giggling like a couple of kids.

"Your ex-husband did what?"

"He said I was too fat to ride in his sportscar, that I'd mess up the springs. So I sat on the hood and bounced. And I didn't stop until the police showed up. They sided with me."

Rob sees Sylvia to her door. He feels like a new person and he's made a friend. They say good night and Rob turns and walks down the hall toward his apartment. Suddenly his stomach begins to growl. He turns and walks back to Sylvia's door. He taps on it lightly.

"I'll be right there," says Sylvia from the other side of the door.

Rob removes his human teeth and waits for the door to open.

•

The next morning the garbage truck hisses down the street and up to Rob's apartment building. The hydraulic arm reaches down, grabs up a trash can, and lifts it into the air. Just as it reaches the apex of its arc, a flash of a woman falls from the can and into the truck.

Rob watches the scene from his apartment window. He picks up the baseball bat belonging to Derwood using a cloth, exits his apartment, and then suddenly kicks his door in. He re-enters like a wild man, screaming and bellowing with rage. He uses the bat to trash his apartment.

"Oh my God!" he yells. "Call the police!"

From off-screen, a neighbor's voice yells, "Are you okay?"

•

The police arrive on the scene. Mulder picks up the bat from the floor and speculates that the assailant was Derwood Spinks.

Rob sits shell-shocked on a sofa. "I lied to you before. Derwood was coming from my place the morning you saw him. He said if I spoke to you, he'd kill me."

Scully asks, "What didn't he want us to know?"

"Last Friday night, he hung out while I was cleaning out the freezer. He told me to go home, said he'd finish up. I didn't know why the hell he was being so nice to me, but then I got home and realized I had the key to the Dumpster. And when I drove back, I saw him cleaning up all this blood. I should have told the truth from the start."

Mulder reaches into his jacket and pulls out a brochure with a man's photo on it.

"Do you recognize this guy?"

Rob says no.

Mulder says, "He's a private eye. Sylvia Jassy's ex-husband hired him to spy on her. Now this Steve Kiziak has gone missing."

"He was last seen parked in front of your building," Scully adds. "You didn't notice him?"

Rob shakes his head no. Mulder suggests that maybe they should question Sylvia. Perhaps too quickly, Rob volunteers that he does not think she's home. Mulder starts to press Rob on where she might be but cuts it off. Mulder and Scully leave.

"Don't worry, Rob," says Mulder. "Won't be long now."

•

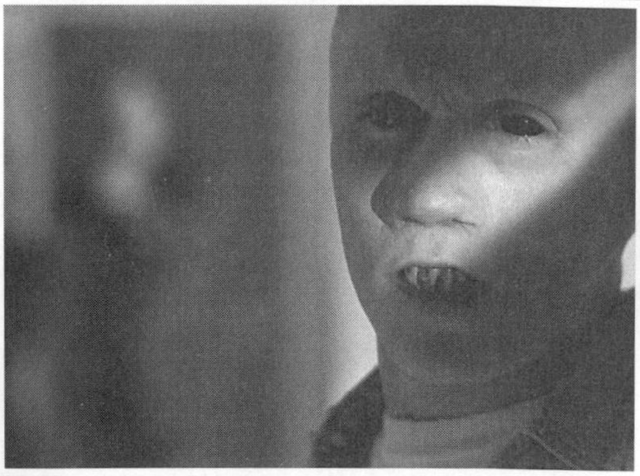

Minutes later, Rob is packing for a quick getaway. He grabs some clothes and jams them into the bag. Suddenly the door swings open to reveal Dr. Mindy Rinehart. Rinehart sees the trashed apartment.

"Oh my God! Rob, what happened?"

"It's a long story. What do you want?"

The flustered doctor explains that she was just in the neighborhood and wanted to say hi. Rob offers a curt "hi" and continues to pack. Rinehart asks if he's all right and what happened to the apartment.

"Derwood Spinks did this. You know, he's the one who . . . like I said, it's a long story."

Rob insists that he's going to a friend's house. Rinehart asks Rob if he's okay, if he's feeling any fear or anger.

"Look. Lemme stop you right there. You don't have to worry about me anymore. As of ten thirty-eight A.M., I am no longer employed by the Lucky Boy Corporation. I quit."

"Rob, I'm here as a friend."

"Well, then consider me cured. I had a breakthrough last night."

"Did you attend the O.A. meeting? How did it go?"

"It was a complete and utter waste of my time."

"I'm sorry you felt that way."

Rob's tirade continues. "So they're a bunch of fat people! So what? Maybe they've got what you call a biological imperative to eat too much! Did you ever think of that? Did you? Yeah, well, maybe I've got a biological imperative, too. So why is that such a bad thing? Like the world's gonna end? That is biology! You can't fight biology, you can't."

As he finishes packing his duffel bag Rob's anger subsides into self-consciousness.

"It sounds like you're saying that you're tired of feeling guilty," she says.

"Bingo. I'm sick and tired of pretending I'm something I'm not!"

Rob grabs his bag and starts for the door.

"You killed that man, didn't you?" asks Rinehart.

Rob stops dead in his tracks. He shuts the door and turns to face her.

"What did you just say?"

"That's why you feel so guilty, isn't it? Can you tell me why you did it?"

"You spoke to the FBI, didn't you?"

Rinehart insists she has told no one. She is equally insistent that Rob needs to get help.

The sound of sirens is heard, growing louder, coming closer. Rob goes to the window. Mulder's car speeds into view, followed by a pair of police cruisers. Anger is now coursing through his body. He turns on Dr. Rinehart.

"You don't know what the hell you're talking about."

"Yes, I do, Rob."

"No, you don't! You said you don't believe in monsters. Right?"

As if to finally drive his point home, Rob pulls off his toupee. Then he reaches up and pulls off his ears.

"How about now?"

Rob reaches for his false teeth and reveals his true nature to the paralyzed doctor.

"Do you believe in monsters?" he asks as he opens his mouth and his shark teeth extend.

"You poor man. What you must go through."

Rob is thrown by her sensitivity. Rinehart gingerly reaches a hand to his face. Just as she touches him the door explodes open and Mulder and Scully race in with guns drawn. They stare wide-eyed at the monster before them.

"Step away, Rob," says Mulder as he levels his piece on the Rob monster. "Step away."

Scully shouts, "Dr. Rinehart, step away from him!"

"Rob, we tracked Sylvia down on her way to the landfill," says Mulder. "You just can't stop yourself, can you?"

Mulder orders Rob to get on the floor. Concern etched into her face, Rinehart tells Rob to "be that good person I know you mean to be."

Rob realizes that his world and his torment are over. There is only one thing he can do. He turns and charges at Mulder, who fires twice. Rinehart screams as Rob falls. Rinehart, her eyes tearing up, goes to Rob as he breathes his last breath and asks, "Why?"

He painfully manages a final whisper.

"I can't be something I'm not."

BACK STORY:

An *X-Files* director since the second season, Kim Manners likes to sum up the general process of creating the show this way: "We're going to hell but we're having a great time."

Well, when it came to the episode "Hungry," the director had a lot of help in this down-and-dirty nightmare of the true terror that lurks behind the disembodied voice of your favorite fast food drive-thru restaurant, beginning with the story idea, courtesy of veteran cowriter and co-executive producer Vince Gilligan.

According to producer Frank Spotnitz, "Vince's career on *The X-Files* has always been about doing something different than what has been done before." It was that attitude that allowed for two great stand-alone episodes in Season 6, "Drive" and "Tithonus." Given his track record, it was not too far-fetched a notion when Gilligan brought his concept of a brain-eating monster behind a burger stand to the pitch meeting.

"I had always wanted to do a story where Mulder and Scully were the antagonists rather than the protagonists. The idea was that 'Hungry' would be solely from the monster's point of view and that the only time we would be aware of Mulder and Scully is when it was through the monster's eyes. I knew going in that this would be a real experimental type of episode. I wanted to take a bad guy and spend enough time with him to understand him so that he becomes sympathetic."

At the story meeting, Gilligan's gross-out concept, complete with a toothy, very sharklike monster, was an immediate hit. Spotnitz latched onto the basic intent of the idea. "The monster was sympathetic because he could not help himself. He didn't want to be a monster. He just was."

Chris Carter likewise applauded Gilligan's idea of a "really great monster show." "It was mentally scary and just a bottom-line quirky idea. It took the creep level to a new high."

"Hungry" would also prove to be a challenge on a number of fronts. Going into Season 7, *The X-Files*'s production company found itself with a bit of a scheduling problem. David Duchovny was putting the finishing touches on the motion picture *Return to Me* and Gillian Anderson was finishing up *The House of Mirth*. Consequently, neither would be available for the time required to work on the two-part season premiere, "The Sixth Extinction" and "Amor Fati."

But with plenty of experience in handling this kind of scheduling challenge already under their belts, The *X-Files*'s production company simply juggled the schedule so that "Hungry," which would ultimately be the third episode aired, was bumped to be the first episode filmed. Kim Manners, who always does well by the creepier outings, was a natural to direct the episode.

Behind the scenes, the detailed and seemingly rote elements of "Hungry" were being addressed by the costume designers, special effects department, and location manager.

The big set pieces for the production design department for "Hungry," specifically the design of the Lucky Boy restaurant and Rob Roberts's apartment, had the requisite challenges. Corey Kaplan found that making over the Lucky Boy, with its inherent retro-kitsch, was not too daunting. The apartment was a whole other matter.

"Doing the apartment interior was very complicated," explains Kaplan, "because Vince really didn't want to give us a thing in the script in terms of detailed explanation. So we went with a fairly stark, super-in-order look, and that seemed to work."

Monster shows are makeup coordinator John Vulich's favorite kind of show. Vulich, whose company, Optic Nerve, also provides alien images for *Buffy the Vampire Slayer*, *Angel*, and *Roswell*, found the challenge of turning put-upon Rob into a sharklike, brain-eating mutant complex on a number of fronts.

"The character had to be passable as a human being and the disguise had to look slapped together. The makeup was complicated in its level of subtlety. We had to get something that was a dynamic monster, but at the same time, we had to do a little tweaking so that he would look like a human being."

The job was accomplished with two basic prosthetic pieces, a forehead and a nose applied to the actor's features. Additional disguise bits, contact lenses, and ears applied to the main prosthetic appliances completed the looks. "Everything was very subtle and natural," explains Vulich.

Duchovny's relative absence from the show opened the door for his stand-in Steve Kiziak to make that rare on-camera appearance as a private detective who is tailing the monster Rob Roberts and meets a bloody demise at the business end of the monster's brain-sucking tongue.

"It was a lot of fun to be in front of the camera," says Kiziak. "I got to play this real hard-core private dick and it gave me some valuable screen time, which never hurts in this town."

Getting the most out of the limited availability of the show's stars proved an ongoing challenge during the filming of "Hungry," and producer Spotnitz relates that ingenuity was the watchword.

"There were some scenes where Mulder and Scully were together but were not even on the set the same day. But we made it look like they were together by the use of doubles. The main thing was that we knew we were taking a risk with this episode by giving the supporting actor the responsibility of carrying the show. Fortunately we had a very good actor in Chad Donella."

Casting director Rick Millikan adds that the choice of Donella, whom he describes as having "a subtle, interesting quality," was intregal to keeping viewers of this monster-intensive episode off-balance.

"Casting monster episodes can be tough because you don't want somebody who is going to jump out at viewers as the obvious bad guy. We always try to keep the true identity of the monster hidden as long as possible. And there was just something in Chad's eyes that was creepy but not in-your-face creepy."

The episode also turned out to have its share of stunts. The opening sequence in which Hungry Guy gets pulled through the drive-thru window was accomplished with a stuntman and high-speed cable rig. Doing the "blind driving" inside the car as it careened across the restaurant parking lot and into the tree was stunt coordinator Danny Weselis. A stuntman was also used in the sequence where the dead body dumped into a trash can is picked up by the garbage truck and dumped into the trash compactor.

Ultimately "Hungry" would typify the hard-core scares that would populate the first part of Season 7 and stands tall with the best of the stand-alone fright episodes of seasons gone by, including "The Host" and "Home." It would also signal *The X-Files*'s ability to conform to a season that found itself fraught with professional challenges and surprises that would bedevil the show through the entire season.

However, for the moment, Vince Gilligan could look back on a good idea thoughtfully executed. "My intention for the end of that episode was that at the end, when Mulder and Scully show up and kill the monster, to have the audience out there hoping that they would not show up."

FACTS:

For the obnoxious speed metal music playing in Hungry Guy's car in the opening sequence, producer Paul Rabwin went to his daughter for advice. She was dating a musician in a band called Unearthed, who were more than willing to allow the production to license their music.

The real Lucky Boy restaurant is located in Los Feliz, California, which substituted for the fictional drive-thru, which was located in Costa Mesa, California.

Actress Judith Hoag, who plays Dr. Mindy Rinehart, starred in the 1990 film *Teenage Mutant Ninja Turtles: The Movie*.

Ultimately, Duchovny and Anderson were available for only a combined two days of filming for "Hungry."

Originally the script called for the drive-thru to be called Burgerlishious. But the location department found a restaurant location that was ideal except for a big sign saying LUCKY BOY that couldn't be removed. So, ever flexible, *The X-Files* simply changed the fictional drive-thru's name to match.

episode 7X05

MILLENNIUM

EPISODE: 7X05
FIRST AIRED: November 28, 1999
EDITOR: Lynne Willingham
WRITTEN BY: Vince Gilligan & Frank Spotnitz
DIRECTED BY: Thomas Wright

Mulder and Scully enlist the aid of Frank Black to help prevent members of the Millennium Group from attaining an Armageddon New Year.

GUEST STARS:

Mitch Pileggi (A.D. Skinner)
Lance Henriksen (Frank Black)
Holmes Osborne (The Necromancer, AKA Mark Johnson)
Colby French (Deputy)
Marilyn McIntyre (Widow)
William Forward (Funeral Director)
Stephen Ramsey (First Agent)
Romy Walthall (Second Agent)
Michael Dempsey (Sheriff)
Eulan Middlebrooks (Young Cop)
Moné Walton (Female Coroner)
Octavia L. Spencer (Nurse)
Brittany Tiplady (Jordan Black)
Dick Clark (Himself)

PRINCIPAL SETTINGS:

Tallahassee, Florida; Woodbridge, Virginia; Rice County, Maryland

Tallahassee, Florida, on a sad day.

"Thank you. Thank you for coming," says a teary-eyed Mrs. Crouch as she sees the last of the mourners for the funeral of her husband off. She manages a brave smile as one final mourner approaches.

"Mrs. Crouch, I'm sorry for your loss," he says.

"Thank you, Mr. . . . ?"

"Johnson," says the man. "I worked briefly with your husband. I was impressed by him. Very much so."

After the man leaves, Mrs. Crouch goes to the casket and says a final good-bye to her husband.

"Hell of a Christmas, Raymond."

As she is escorted out by the funeral director, she adds, "Didn't even leave a note."

Mr. Johnson steps out from his hiding place and makes his way to the casket. He opens the casket and sees that Mr. Crouch's death was not a pretty one. Mr. Johnson begins to strip off his coat, tie, and shirt and does the same to the corpse. An FBI insignia tie clip is also removed from Crouch's tie.

"I am the resurrection and the life," says the man. "He that believeth in me, though I were dead, yet shall he live, and whosoever liveth and believeth in me shall never die."

He repeats the Burial Rite of the Dead over and over like a mantra as he completes the removal of Crouch's jacket, tie, and shirt, then produces a cell phone and carefully positions it so the corpse's thumb is over the CALL button. His work done, he extends the phone's antenna and shuts the lid of the casket.

•

A black car sits silently among the tombstones of a fog-shrouded cemetery. A heavy rain is falling. Behind the wheel is the man from the funeral parlor, now dressed in the corpse's jacket, shirt, and tie. A cell phone is positioned carefully on the car's dash. Suddenly it comes to life, the RECEIVE light glowing in the darkness. The phone begins to ring. The mysterious man does not answer it.

Finally the man exits the vehicle and begins walking toward a particular grave. He is dragging a shovel behind him as the cell phone continues to ring.

•

The next day, December 30, cops and crime technicians swarm the area and, in particular, a freshly dug grave. A car arrives on the scene, and Scully gets out and comes upon a clearly agitated funeral director.

"Are you with the FBI, too?" he asks. "Look, I know my job. The man was deceased."

"I'm sorry?" asks Scully.

The funeral director says, "I understand that he was one of your own, but these rumors I'm hearing, that I put a living human being into the ground? You people better get your facts straight—real fast."

The funeral director walks away, leaving Scully to wonder what the hell is going on. She walks over to the open grave. A ladder is sticking out of it. Scully looks down into the hole.

"Mulder? You been spreading rumors?"

"Why?" asks Mulder, on his hands and knees at the bottom of the grave. "Hear any good ones lately?"

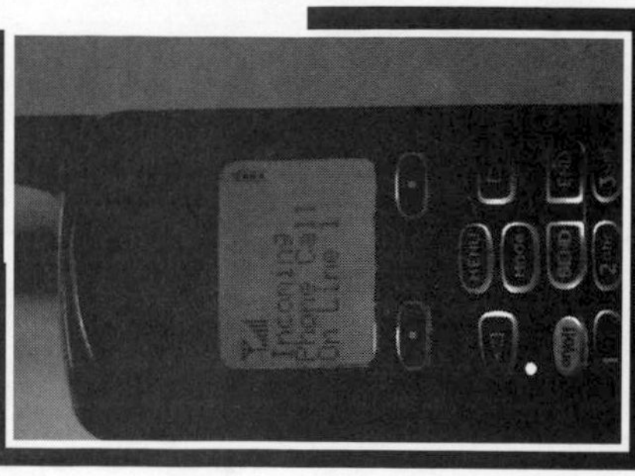

"Not particularly. So what do you have here?"

"Merry Christmas, by the way, Scully," says Mulder.

"Thank you. Merry Christmas to you."

"Grave robbery with a twist," says Mulder as he indicates the empty casket and the ripped and tattered lining.

"It looks like someone on the inside was trying to get out," states Scully.

"Indeed it does. To answer your question, no, I haven't been any spreading rumors. Local PD's done a pretty good job of that. Ever since they matched the fingerprints on the dead man to these and to those up there on that headstone."

He indicates fingerprints underneath the satin headliner, more on the casket lid, and a handprint on the tombstone. "There's a big, juicy handprint on the back."

"What about the person or persons who did the digging?" asks Scully.

"Well, we got one pile of dirt," says Mulder as he climbs out of the grave. "I'm guessing one man with a shovel. Other than that, last night's rain hasn't left us much to go on. Well, go ahead, Scully, naysay me. The body of an FBI agent gets disinterred, only to climb out on its own and disappear into the Yuletide night."

"See, you had me up until there. I think it's a grave robbery with a twist. You've got fingerprints, and the torn casket liner. Most likely, it's rigged evidence that was faked by whoever exhumed the body."

"Faked for what effect?" asks Mulder.

"Publicity, fear, rumors. I mean, I don't know what specific effect, but nonetheless . . . what?"

Mulder sees a dry reddish-black substance forming a trail in the blades of grass.

"Looks like blood," he says.

•

Mr. Johnson is driving his car along a lonely road. Two cell phones sit on the passenger seat. He continues to recite the Burial Rite of the Dead. Behind a steel barrier that separates the front and back seat, there is a creaking-scratching sound.

A withered, clawlike hand appears. The driver stares at the hand a moment, then turns his eyes back to the road, chanting the Burial Rite faster and faster as he drives along a highway in Georgia.

•

Scully and Mulder have gone to FBI headquarters in search of an answer and have found some clues in the dead man's personnel file, which is being passed around by A.D. Skinner to Mulder, Scully, and some other attending agents during a meeting in his office.

"Special Agent Raymond Crouch, age fifty-six," says Scully. "Married. No children. After a sterling twenty-one-year career with the Bureau, he retired in 1993."

Scully slides a grisly black-and-white crime scene photo out of the file and passes it to Skinner. "Earlier this month, he was found in the garage of his Tallahassee home, service weapon in hand."

"Definitely self-inflicted?" asks Skinner.

Scully says, "I read over the report and there's no indication otherwise."

Skinner goes around the room, looking for a possible motive for the grave robbery. Two of the attending agents give Crouch a clean personal and professional report.

"Nothing stands out," says Skinner.

"Should something stand out?" asks Mulder.

Skinner asks, "Agent Mulder, what's your take on this?"

"Only that I don't think it was grave robbery, per se," says Mulder. "It was necromancy: the summoning of the dead. It's a form of magic dating back to primitive shamanism, with a long tradition in the Christian church. Through it, the dead are brought back to life for the purpose of divulging arcane knowledge or performing ritual tasks."

One of the attending agents says, "So that's what this wacko thought he was doing, raising the dead?"

"That's what he was doing," says Mulder.

Mulder passes Skinner another photo, shot from above the open grave, surrounded by a thin circle of dried blood.

"This is a magic circle, drawn in goat's blood," says Mulder. "Rain washed most of it away."

Skinner passes this photo around.

Mulder explains, "The blood attracts the undead spirits while the circle focuses the necromancer's power while protecting him from the spirits that he's conjuring. He may also desire to wear the clothes of the dead man to create a bond between them. You would not want to be this man's dry cleaner."

The other agents are skeptical, to say the least.

Scully says, "Obviously, there's a clear ritualistic element to this crime. But the question is why were they directed at Raymond Crouch."

Says Mulder, "That is the question."

"Well, let's come up with an answer," says Skinner. He dismisses the meeting but asks Mulder and Scully to stay behind.

"Necromancy aside, this magic circle you mentioned. What if it looked something like this?" he asks.

From another file he produces a photocopy of a red Ourobouros, the symbol of a snake eating its own tail.

"An Ourobouros," Mulder says. "Possibly. Definitely a mystical symbol. Alchemists favored it. They believed that it represented all of existence."

"I'm thinking more of the Millennium Group," says Skinner. "It was their symbol as well."

There is recognition in Mulder's eyes at the mention of the Millennium Group. Scully is also somewhat familiar with the secret group.

She says, "They were a group of former FBI agents who offered consulting services to law enforcement. Somehow, they fell into disrepute."

"They operated in extreme secrecy," says Skinner. "Rumors abounded that they had their own agenda, which was less than altruistic, if not improper or illegal."

Mulder says, "That it was, in fact, a cult based upon Judeo-Christian 'Endtime' prophesies concerning the coming millennium. Was Raymond Crouch a member?"

"I can't seem to find out. Apparently, the group dissolved several months ago," Skinner replies. "They left no paper trail, nothing. However, I do have three other grave desecrations, all within the last six months."

Skinner lays out three more photos of open graves, all showing an Ourobouros outlined in blood.

He says, "Long Island, Northern California, Arizona. All three graves contained the bodies of former FBI agents. All three were recent suicides."

Mulder wants to know how long Skinner has been sitting on this information.

Skinner says, "Owing to the Millennium Group's former ties with the Bureau, this matter is sensitive, to say the least. Investigate them. Keep it low profile."

Mulder says, "I think I know where to start."

•

Mulder and Scully are buzzed through the security door of the Hartwell Psychiatric Hospital in Woodbridge, Virginia.

"How well do you know this man?" asks Scully.

"Only by reputation. He left VICAP before I got there. But he's been called the greatest criminal profiler that Quantico ever produced."

"What's he doing here?" asks Scully.

"Apparently checked himself in for a thirty-day observation. I gather the last few years haven't been kind to him. But if there's anybody can tell us about the Millennium Group, it's him. He used to consult for them. Later he fought to bring it down at the expense of his own career and reputation."

"Single-minded," says Scully. "Sounds like someone I know."

They arrive at the hospital's common room and approach a man who is sitting alone, watching a football game on television.

"Frank Black?" asks Mulder. The man turns around. "Hi, my name is Fox Mulder. This is my partner, Dana Scully. It's a pleasure to meet you. Do you mind if we sit down?"

Black rolls his eyes at the TV, unhappy with a play.

"Who's playing?" Mulder asks.

"Notre Dame and Boston College. What can I do for you, Agents?" he asks.

Mulder opens a file and produces the photos of the recently deceased agents.

Mulder says, "Well, we're working on a case I feel you might have some particular insight into. The deaths of four FBI agents. Do you recognize these men?"

Black glances at the photos and then turns back to the TV. "I do," he answers, not volunteering any more information.

Scully says, "All four committed suicide in the last six months." At hearing this, Black looks at Scully, then turns back to the game. "All were exhumed from their graves in a ritual desecration. They were members of the Millennium Group, is that correct?"

Black nods.

"Sir," she continues. "We've been having a hard time gleaning any information whatsoever about the group, about its membership, its practices. I believe you can help us."

Eyes still on the television, he replies, "No, thank you. I'm retired. I think you can tell by the circumstances, I'm trying to put my life back together. I can't get involved in this."

"We're not asking you to get involved," says Mulder. "I'm just asking you to take a look at the case file."

"No, thank you," repeats Black.

Mulder says, "Mr. Black, the day after tomorrow is January 1st, 2000. That's the significant date to these people, it doesn't give us much time. Don't you want to see them stopped?" At the lack of response, he declares, "Well, Mr. Black, you're not what I was expecting."

"Agent Mulder, it's first and eighteen. Just let me watch this game in peace."

Mulder glances at the television. "It's third and ten," he says. "Notre Dame."

"Happy New Year," says Black.

"Same to you," shoots back Mulder as he and Scully leave.

•

A police car is driving on a desolate Maryland road. The deputy spies a man changing a tire on the side of the road. He pulls to a stop behind him.

The deputy asks if he can use a hand. The mystery man nervously declines. The deputy flashes his flashlight on the tire. The deputy crinkles his eyes. He is smelling something nasty.

"Man. What is that?" asks the deputy. Flies buzz about.

"Oh, yeah," says the mystery man. "I'm thinking a deer maybe must have died in the woods."

"Sir, what's in the truck?" asks the deputy.

"Nothing."

"Mind if I take a look?" asks the deputy.

"There's, there's nothing in there. So . . ."

The deputy shines his flashlight on the rear of the truck. He notices the lug wrench still in the man's hand.

"Drop that," he says. "Take two steps back."

The man looks at the wrench, as if just noticing what he's holding.

"Drop it," the deputy repeats forcefully. The man obeys.

The deputy attempts to look into the rear window of the truck. The man uses the moment to reach into his coat pocket and withdraw a handful of salt. He is again chanting the Burial Rite. The deputy reaches for the rear door handle and opens it.

"Oh, lord," he gasps at the sight and the smell of the corpse of Raymond Crouch laying in the cargo section. The mystery man has encircled himself with the salt.

"Stand up there!" says the deputy. "Stand up! Lemme see your hands!"

The man is uttering something incomprehensible under his breath. As he gets closer, the deputy hears the words.

"Though he were dead, yet shall he live. Though he were dead, yet shall he live."

The deputy turns to see the rotting corpse of Raymond Crouch standing behind him. Before he can manage a yell, its hands shoot out and grab the deputy by the throat. The man inside the salt circle looks at the ensuing horror sadly as the deputy lets out a final scream and the sound of ripping flesh shatters the night.

•

Uniformed cops, FBI techs, and Mulder and Scully swarm around the police car.

"Hey, I've got the men concentrating on the woods," says Scully.

Mulder has found the circle of salt.

"Our necromancer was definitely here," says Mulder. "Salt. Heavy magic."

"If you're going to tell me he stopped by the side of the road to raise the dead, which I hope you're not, I've got two things to say to you: One is that his previous circles were made of blood, not salt. And two . . ."

"And they were large enough to contain a body. But this is a protective circle. It's just big enough for one man to stand inside."

Scully says, "Protecting himself? Against what?"

Mulder indicates a mess of dried blood nearby. "Whatever it was that did that."

Mulder's thoughts are interrupted by the voice of a sheriff's deputy. Mulder and Scully move through the underbrush to a group of cops staring down at something. They follow the stares to the dead deputy buried under a few inches of dirt. Only his face and neck are exposed. The wounds indicate his throat has been torn out.

"Bite marks," says Mulder. "They look human."

Scully notes that there is more salt here as well, and discovers that two staples have been shot through the dead man's lips. Mulder notices a tiny piece of paper sticking out from between the corpse's lips. He works the paper out, a bit of salt coming with it.

Mulder reads: "I am he that liveth, and was dead and behold, I am alive for evermore, Amen, and have the keys of hell and of death."

A young cop overhears Mulder and offers, "Book of Revelation. Chapter one, verse eighteen."

"Go Fighting Irish," Mulder adds.

•

Mulder is speaking with Frank Black in the psychiatric hospital. Mulder opens the evidence bag and slides the paper with the quote from Revelation toward him.

"First and eighteen," says Mulder. "Not football, it's Revelation. You wanted to tell us something, Frank. Why didn't you just come out and say it?"

Black says, "I don't know what you're talking about. I told you, I cannot get involved in this." He pushes the evidence bag back toward Mulder.

"Okay, so you'll occasionally drop the little arcane hint?" asks Mulder. "A police officer was murdered, Frank. Why do you want to play around? Your denials aside, you obviously know something about that. You knew we'd find this. What are you afraid of?"

Black won't answer.

Scully walks up. "Losing your daughter. You're in a custody battle with the parents of your late wife. I just spoke with your doctor, that's why you're here."

"They're claiming I'm an unfit father. That I was obsessed with conspiracies and the end of the world. That my work meant more to me than my daughter, Jordan. The thing is, they were right."

"So you retired," says Scully.

Black says, "I will sell insurance. I'll do whatever it takes. I'll 'get well' and jump through whatever hoops they want. But I will not mention the Millennium Group again."

"But you obviously want to help. You dropped that clue on us. Look, Frank, nobody needs to know about this. We're just three people sitting around talking," says Mulder. Black nods.

They move to a private room, where Mulder hands over a file. Black opens the file and begins to read.

Black says, "The Book of Revelation describes the end of the physical world in a battle between heaven and hell. Good against evil. The Millennium Group believed that time was upon us."

Black turns to the pictures of the four dead men whose graves were desecrated.

"These four represent a schism of the Group. They believe that for the Endtime to come, as it must, man must take an active hand in bringing it about."

Scully asks, "And to that end, they committed suicide?"

Mulder says, "For the express purpose of being brought back to life. The Four Horsemen of the Apocalypse. These four men—bringing with them war, pestilence, famine, and death."

"So that all the dead of the Earth will rise. Armageddon," says Black. "It must begin with the dawn of the millennium, or not at all. That's what they believe. The man you're looking for, your necromancer, he exhumed these men in accordance with their wishes."

Mulder asks, "So, he's a member of the Millennium Group as well?"

"No," says Black. "They sought him out. He believes he's doing God's work, but he's mistaken."

"Could you tell us a little more about this man?" Scully asks.

"White male, age forty-five to fifty. Religious man. No police record. No fulfilling relationships. You would pass him without giving him a glance."

Mulder asks, "So this is the one event that will give his life meaning?"

Black continues to paint a mental picture of the necromancer and his surroundings. There are fields, woods, and desolation.

"He needs privacy for this. He'll live alone, possibly in the house he grew up in. Most likely it's a large rural property, away from prying eyes. He'll own a truck or van. He needs it to transport the bodies."

As Black speaks, we see the man's house. It's just as he describes it.

The house is faded and antique in furniture and disposition. Outside is a tall stretch of chain-link fence. The necromancer works at his hobby, taxidermy. His current project is a snarling dog.

"There'll be high fences, no trespassing signs," Black says. "It's a solitary existence. He's worked around death all his life, in some capacity. A funeral parlor or a cemetery. Death comforts him. He took great care in burying the deputy. In preparing the body. Despite the fact that he feared being caught, he stapled the lips, sealed the mouth shut. It was to prevent the man from coming back to life."

Black says, "He believes, if disturbed, the deputy will rise from the dead. It's too soon for that. Which is why, when he realizes the deputy has been discovered, he'll feel a need to take action. He'll return to the body the first chance he gets."

•

At his secluded house, the man sees the news report regarding the discovery of the deputy's body.

"The Rice County Morgue," says Scully.

Black says, "I think you'll catch him there."

"These four members of the Millennium Group. The ones who truly 'liveth and were dead.' These are the ones we have to catch," says Mulder.

A look from Black tells Scully that even he does not ascribe to Mulder's theory. Their conversation is interrupted by a nurse who informs Black that his daughter is on the phone. Black smiles and excuses himself.

•

On the way out of the hospital, Scully plays devil's advocate with Mulder's theory.

"Mulder, you're telling me it's more important to track down four dead bodies than one live murderer?"

"He's not our murderer and those four dead bodies aren't dead," says Mulder as he checks his watch. "And the millennium is fourteen hours away."

"Mulder, these people, even when they were alive, mangled Biblical prophecy to the extent that it's unrecognizable. The year 2000 is just their artificial deadline. And besides, 2001 is actually the start of the new millennium."

"Nobody likes a math geek, Scully."

"Anyway, I think Frank's profile is sound," says Scully. Mulder agrees. "And I think with it, we have the best chance of catching this necromancer, as you call him. So I'm going down to the county morgue."

Mulder thinks that's a good idea.

"The deputy was killed on a road that connects from the north with no major highway," says Mulder. "I'm thinking our necromancer

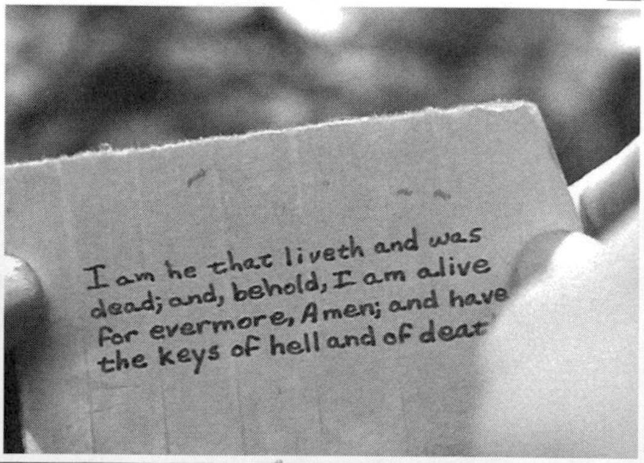

I am he that liveth and was
dead; and, behold, I am alive
for evermore, Amen; and have
the keys of hell and of deat

lives nearby. I'm gonna do a rundown on all single landowners in the area. See where all the bodies are buried."

Mulder has another thought.

"Scully, do me a favor? Don't let anybody remove the staples from the deputy's mouth, okay? Please, just humor me."

•

At the Rice County Morgue, a female coroner in a small autopsy room is removing the two staples and proceeding with a visual exam of the mouth. It is full of salt. The telephone rings and the coroner does not answer it. The coroner continues her work, removing the salt from the mouth of the dead deputy. The phone rings again, and the coroner stops and leaves the autopsy room to listen to the message. When the coroner plays the recorded message, Scully is heard warning that nobody should autopsy the murder victim and if they started, to stop immediately. Scully says she will explain when she arrives. A massive shadow falls over the coroner, who turns and screams.

Scully arrives at the morgue. She draws her service revolver as she passes sheeted bodies, then finds a desk disturbed, a telephone off the hook, and big droplets of blood on the floor. Scully follows the blood trail down the end of the hallway.

There she comes upon the body of the coroner, balled up behind a steel cabinet, a gout of blood around her throat. She appears dead. But at Scully's touch, the coroner turns to her, bloodied and unable to speak. Scully hears footsteps in the autopsy room and spins around to discover the necromancer staring at her from the far side of the autopsy bay. Before she can speak, Scully is distracted by a sound coming from across the room. Her eyes go wide at the sight of the dead deputy shuffling toward her.

Scully fires at the zombie. *Blam! Blam! Blam!* Three direct hits. The zombie keeps coming. The monster is on her and knocks her violently away, her gun skittering across the floor and stopping at the feet of the necromancer. He watches as a struggle between the living and the dead plays itself out.

•

Skinner arrives at the morgue. He passes a gurney upon which lies the unconscious but still alive coroner. He sees, lying under a sheet, the body of the dead deputy, who has a single gunshot wound to the head. Skinner is joined by a shaken Scully, who has gashes on her neck.

"How are you feeling?" asks Skinner.

"All things considered . . ." replies Scully.

"What the hell happened here?" asks Skinner. "Who is that man?"

Scully says, "The sheriff's deputy. The man we found this morning. He was dead. And then somehow he wasn't. He attacked me."

"You shot him?" asks Skinner.

"Three rounds," says Scully. "Center of mass, into his chest. No effect."

"There's a gunshot wound to the head, as well."

"Yeah, this man Mulder calls a necromancer, our suspect, he was here, too. He fired that shot from my gun. He saved me. I have no idea why. He got away, but I was in no shape to follow. Look, sir, I can't even begin to offer an explanation for what happened. But I have to say it is exactly what Mulder feared."

"Yeah, which is why I would like to talk to him," says Skinner. "Why isn't he answering his phone?"

•

Mulder's car pulls to a stop in front of a house fronted by a high chain-link fence. He checks a list of addresses in Rice County, Maryland. The next name on a printout reads MARK JOHNSON. Mulder tries to make a call on his cell phone, but gets a "no service" message. He gets out of the car and checks the padlock on the fence. He moves to a large trash can and begins checking the contents. It's the usual garbage . . . except for an empty fifty-pound bag of salt. On a hunch, Mulder reaches back in and pulls out a handful of salt, which he puts in his coat pocket, and then scales the outside fence.

Meanwhile, the necromancer is on his way home.

Mulder approaches the house, picks the lock, and goes inside. He wanders from room to room, encountering one of the necromancer's taxidermy projects, a snarling wolf. Mulder enters the kitchen and comes upon an ominous door that leads to the basement. It is heavily barred by two-by-fours set in heavy steel brackets.

As he removes the two-by-fours, Mulder is unaware that the necromancer has driven up.

Mulder removes the last two-by-four, clicks on his flashlight, and descends into the basement. There is little to see: some old furniture, a water heater. He leaves footprints behind in the soft earthen floor. The earth starts to shift and move.

A decayed hand silently rises out of the floor.

Mulder hears a sound. He turns in time to see more hands snaking up out of the earth. Mulder watches four undead creatures rise up out of the ground, reaching for him. He runs for the stairs and is about to break into the light.

Suddenly the necromancer appears in the doorway and slams the door shut.

"Open the door! Open the door!" screams Mulder. The necromancer hears gunfire behind the locked door.

•

Scully has returned to the psychiatric hospital and is talking with Frank Black.

Black says, "He didn't go to the morgue with you?"

"No, he went looking for our suspect's home. No one's been able to contact him since. I've got task force agents canvassing the northwestern Maryland area, but it's a large territory to cover and we're running out of time. Sir, I'm just afraid that Mulder may have found what he was looking for. I need your help in finding him."

"You've respected my reasons in the past, Agent Scully. Please respect them now."

Scully doubts how much Black really knows. She explains her own encounter with the undead. Black's facade of noninvolvement is beginning to crack.

Scully says, "Now, as crazy as it sounds, I have to ask: Do you believe the Millennium Group is actually capable of bringing about the Endtime? Armageddon?"

"I understand their beliefs," says Black. "I've spent years trying to unravel them, make sense of them. It doesn't mean I believe them myself."

"But what if it were true? Good and evil. Which would prevail?"

"I'm sorry," Black says.

Scully gives up and leaves. Black watches her exit. He makes a decision. Black goes to the on-call nurse.

"I'm going to check myself out," he says.

"You'd like a day pass?" she asks.

"I won't be coming back," he says.

•

Mulder, terrified, is standing in the middle of a circle he made from the salt he found in the trash can. His right arm is bloodied from a wound. Three of the creatures are staring at him.

The necromancer has taken up a vigil outside the house. Tears are streaming down his face. He is startled by the sound of someone walking swiftly through the grass. It is Frank Black. The necromancer is surprised to see him. Happily so.

"We'd given up on you," says the necromancer. "Thank God. Thank God.

"There's someone in the basement, a policeman. He killed one of the members. Shot him in the head. But you're here. Now we'll have four."

"I'm here," says Black.

Frank Black and the necromancer are inside the house.

"I can't tell you how happy I am," says the necromancer. "You were meant to be the fourth. I always knew that. I'd so hoped you'd come around."

"I didn't want to. The man in the basement. I told him how to find this place."

"Why?"

"I was trying to walk the straight and narrow. To leave the Millennium Group behind. I know that I can't do that anymore. Not now that I know you've succeeded."

"You didn't believe the dead would arise. You see what the future holds, Frank. You know you can't run from it."

"No, I can't run," Black agrees

"You paid so dearly," says the necromancer. "They've taken your daughter from you. Murdered your wife. There is no justice in this world." He takes a gun from a drawer. "But there will be in the next."

The necromancer looks at a clock. The time is 10:13.

"The hour's near," he says. "Are you ready, Frank?"

"I'm ready," says Black.

Black looks at the loaded revolver on the table in front of him. It is meant for his suicide. The necromancer begins his chant. Black finishes the chant, picks up the revolver, and aims it at the necromancer.

•

Scully is racing along a lonesome country road, a pile of maps and papers on the pas-

senger seat. Her cell phone rings. It is Skinner, pacing the room as other agents work through a massive paper trail.

"This is Skinner," he says. "We back-checked Frank Black as you asked."

"And?" asks Scully.

"He took no calls at Hartwell Psychiatric other than from his daughter. But the staff took messages, including one from a Rice County number."

"Rice County. That's where I am right now."

Skinner says, "We ran the phone records for Agent Crouch and the other desecration victims. All four received calls from this same number in the weeks before their deaths."

Scully says, "I'm going to need an address."

•

Frank Black is tying the man to a chair. Black removes the basement door barricades and then pulls open the door.

The necromancer says, "I'm begging you. Please. You know what the world is! Evil goes unpunished. The good suffer. There's no future here but uncertainty and pain. Let the Judgment come. You're damning yourself, Frank!"

Black descends the stairs.

"Agent Mulder? Can you hear me, Agent Mulder?" Black calls down into the basement.

Mulder replies from the darkness, "Yeah, I'm down here. They're all around."

Black pulls a road flare from his jacket, strikes it lit, and tosses it into the darkness. He sees Mulder and the dead creature. Black lights another flare as he steps toward the basement floor.

"You armed?" asks Mulder.

"Oh, yeah."

Mulder says, "Shoot for the head. That seems to stop them. There's three more of them."

"Where?" asks Black.

"I don't know. They're hiding."

Black is set upon by the monster that was once Raymond Crouch. Black fires. *Blam! Blam! Blam!* The creature falls to the ground.

"Mulder, can you get up?" asks Black.

Mulder begins to rise and shouts, "Look out!"

Another zombie attacks Black. The zombie hits him hard. The gun and flare go flying. Black and the creature crash into a pile of boxes, hands at each other's throats.

Scully has found the house. She jogs to the gate.

While Black is locked in a struggle with the zombie, his face scratched and bleeding, Mulder grabs the zombie by the hair, pulls its head back, and puts a bullet in its temple. Mulder fires again. The zombie falls to the ground. Mulder drops to his knees beside Black to help him up.

The last surviving zombie charges Mulder. Mulder raises his gun to fire. The gun is empty.

Boom! Boom! Boom!

Scully stands on the stairs. She has finished the job.

•

Frank Black is seeing in the millennium in front of a TV in the hospital waiting room. Black is stoic as he watches Dick Clark ring in the new year in Times Square. He is approached by Scully.

"Mr. Black, Mark Johnson is being taken for psychiatric evaluation. He'll be put under suicide watch, as you asked."

"Good," he responds.

"And there's someone here to see you," she adds with a small smile.

Scully steps aside to reveal Jordan Black, Frank Black's young daughter. She rushes to her father with tears in her eyes. They embrace. He kisses her on the cheek.

"I missed you, sweetheart," he says.

"I missed you, too, Daddy."

Scully is joined by Mulder, who has been treated for his wounds. Frank and his daughter rise to leave.

"Good luck," says Mulder. "With everything."

"Agent Mulder. Agent Scully. I guess this is it, huh?" He looks to the TV as the ball is dropping, the final minute in 1999. "Take care of yourselves."

"You're not gonna stay and watch?" Scully asks.

"No, I just want to go home."

They leave. Mulder and Scully turn to the TV as Dick Clark counts down the last ten seconds to the new year. The ball drops. The year "2000" lights up. Everybody is kissing. Mulder looks at Scully. She finally looks over at him. He leans down—

It is a sweet kiss. But longer, perhaps, than a kiss between friends should be. Their lips part. They share a tender look.

"The world didn't end," says Mulder.

"No, it didn't," says Scully.

"Happy New Year, Scully."

"Happy New Year, Mulder."

BACK STORY:

It took seven seasons, but *The X-Files* finally got around to doing a zombie episode. Yet there was much more to the episode "Millennium" than merely raising the dead.

"It was so hard because we were dealing with the mythology of *The X-Files*, the heroes of Mulder and Scully, the mythology of *Millennium*, and the hero of Frank Black," recalls Frank Spotnitz. "The question was how do you serve all those conflicting masters."

Millennium's three-year run on network television had been marked by critical acclaim, particularly for Lance Henriksen, and a group of viewers smaller than those for *The X-Files* but fanatically loyal. Initially a gritty, hardcore exercise in conspiracy and the impending apocalypse, the show transformed itself into a mythological exploration of fate during its second season before returning to a dark but straightforward voyage of discovery. The last episode of *Millennium* was shot before the show was officially canceled and so, according to Spotnitz, "there was never an end to the series proper."

Talk of doing an *X-Files–Millennium* crossover had begun while the show was still on the air. The biggest boosters were Frank Spotnitz and Vince Gilligan. "It suddenly became easier to do once *Millennium* went off the air," explains Gilligan. "From the beginning, the intention was not so much to wrap up *Millennium* as it was to answer the question of what would happen if Frank Black came into Mulder and Scully's world."

Spotnitz and Gilligan were tapped to script the story and, in conjunction with Chris Carter and writer-supervising producer John Shiban, set about crafting a story. Shiban recalled that those story sessions were difficult to start, "Until we realized that the story needed to be an X-File and that any *Millennium* ending we came up with had to come second. We needed to do what we always do, which is to follow Mulder and Scully through their case."

The resultant storyline, in which Mulder and Scully discover a zombie-infested plot to kill off the surviving members of the Millennium Group and bring them back to life as the harbinger of the final apocalypse, was a well-crafted and dark outing. While fundamentally an X-File, the story also skillfully incorporated Frank Black's heretofore untold fate as a reluctant hero on the eve of the millennium who has voluntarily institutionalized himself to regain custody of his daughter.

Shiban reflects that having the story was not the end of the odyssey. The Frank Black storyline did not always fit easily into *The X-Files* storyline.

"Our first responsibility was to *The X-Files*'s audience," remembers Spotnitz of the story sessions that produced "Millennium." "We couldn't bring anything over from *Millennium* that would confuse them. On the other hand, we didn't want to short people who were into *Millennium* and loved Frank Black."

It was during the story sessions that Shiban came up with the idea of the millennium kiss between Mulder and Scully. "It just felt like the logical culmination of their relationship. They had been heading toward the kiss for years and they almost did it in *The X-Files* movie. It was actually Frank [Spotnitz] who suggested that it was New Year's Eve and somebody has to kiss somebody."

Series creator Chris Carter notes that there were still some potential obstacles as the "Millennium" script rounded into shape. "We knew the zombie angle was going to be tricky because so much had already been done with zombies. I knew the degree of difficulty was going to be high. I also knew we wanted to make sure we made the inclusion of Frank Black in the show as interesting as possible, not just for the character but for Lance Henriksen as well. Lance was doing us a favor by coming back."

To make Henriksen feel comfortable, Thomas Wright, who had directed a number of *Millennium* episodes, was picked to direct this proper ending to the *Millennium* odyssey. Spotnitz also reveals that there was some "nervousness" at the prospect of the star of one series coming over and working with the stars of another. But the concerns were unfounded.

"There were no problems working with Lance," reports Gillian Anderson. "I think everybody connected with the show appreciated having him come over and be a part of our series. Plus he was a real professional and quite easy to work with."

Predictably, some of the toughest challenges faced in "Millennium" centered on the antics of the zombies and, in particular, the sequence in which the zombies are seen climbing out of shallow graves in the basement.

"We did that on Stage 5," recalls stunt coordinator Danny Weselis. "We buried the four stunt guys in shallow graves up to their heads, put a snorkel in their mouths, covered their heads, and then removed the snorkels. Then the director yelled action and they began to dig themselves out."

The climactic sequence of "Millennium," in which the case is wrapped up just in time to witness that time-honored television tradition, watching the ball drop in Times Square to the enthusiastic refrains of *Dick Clark's New Year's Rockin' Eve*, also necessitated special effects intervention.

"The problem was, we were shooting in October," explains producer Rabwin, "and so obviously we had no footage of the coming event. At the time, the only picture of what the Millennium Ball would look like was on the Internet. From that photo, Bill Millar digitally created a copy of the year 2000 ball. We then took footage of Dick Clark's 1998 New Year's Eve show and inserted the new ball digitally into the old footage. Finally, we hired Dick Clark to come in and do a year 2000 bit of voiceover work and we had what we needed."

But in the end, for most of the fans at least, "Millennium" was always about the kiss.

"David and I knew the kiss was coming," relates Anderson. "I felt the editors of that episode milked it in a very effective way. When we were shooting the scene, the director slowed everything down and changed the camera angles. That scene was made to last a lot longer than it actually was."

Carter agrees that the final scene was something of a present for the fans. "It's something they've been waiting a long time for. And I'm glad we did not cheapen the gesture for the sake of a ratings grabber. It came about in such a natural way."

FACTS:

Lance Henriksen appeared in James Cameron's directorial debut, *Piranha 2: The Spawning*. He also appeared in the Cameron-directed *The Terminator* and *Aliens*.

Hidden deep in Dick Clark's filmography is a role in the 1978 biopic of surf music singers Jan and Dean called *Deadman's Curve*.

Romy Walthall appeared in the fourth and seventh films of *The Howling* series under the name Romy Windsor.

episode 7X06

RUSH

EPISODE: 7X06
FIRST AIRED: December 5, 1999
EDITOR: Louise A. Innes
WRITTEN BY: David Amann
DIRECTED BY: Rob Lieberman

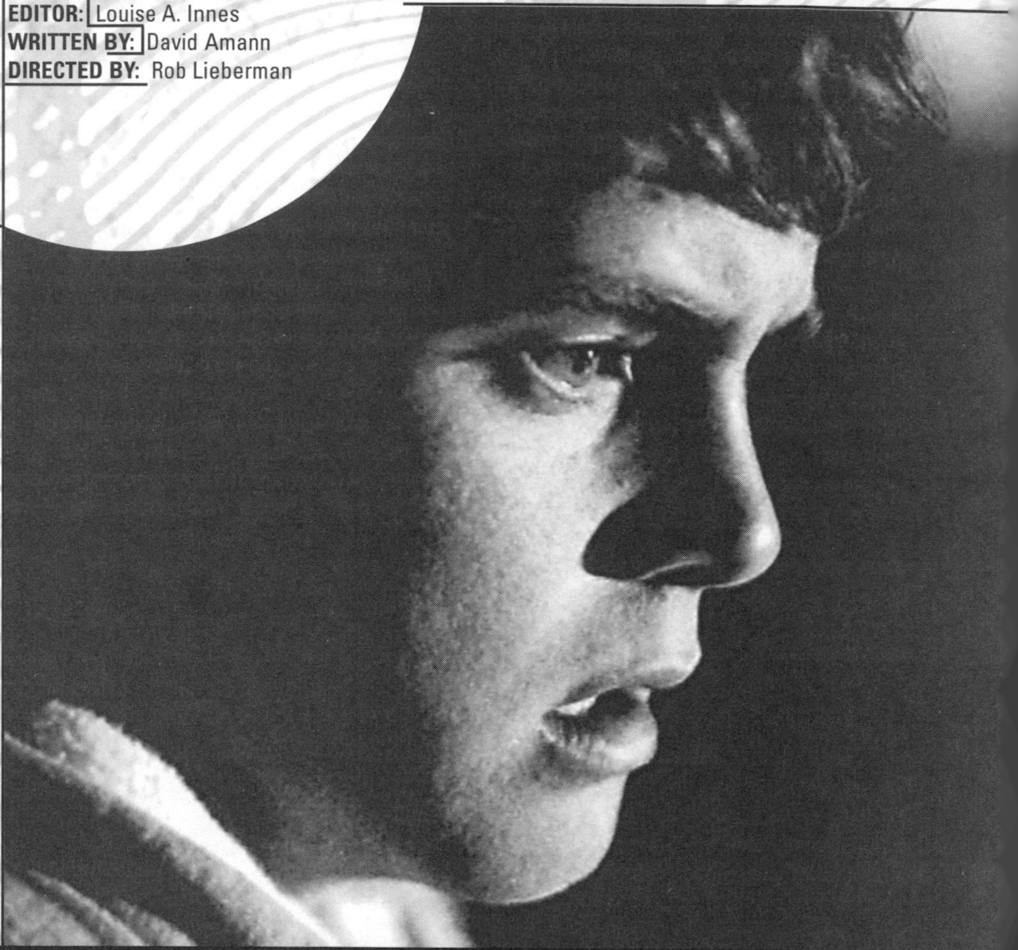

A teenage killer eludes Mulder and Scully by moving too fast for the human eye.

GUEST STARS:

Rodney Scott (Tony Reed)
Scott Cooper (Max Harden)
Nicki Aycox (Chastity Raines)
Les Lannom (Deputy Foster)
Tom Bower (Sheriff Harden)
David Wells (Mr. Babbitt)
Ann Dowd (Mrs. Reed)
Bill Dow (Charles Burks)
Rachel Winfree (Nurse)
Christopher Wynne (Deputy)

PRINCIPAL SETTING:

Pittsfield, Virginia

A car lurches down a desolate dirt road in Pittsfield, Virginia. The car pulls over and Tony, a skinny, sweet-faced sixteen-year-old, steps out. He walks past a NO TRESPASSING sign, into a stand of trees, and down a narrow path.

"Max? Max, are you there?" asks Tony.

A flaring match startles Tony, who whips back around to discover Max, a dangerous-looking seventeen-year-old, and Chastity eyeing him.

"You're late, kid," says Max as he lights up a cigarette. "You get lost?"

Tony says, "Sorry, I had to wait till my mom took off."

"It's way past his bedtime, Max," says Chastity. "He's not cut out for this."

"Cut out for what?" asks Tony.

"Oh, there's more here than just trees," Max tells Tony. "Before you can find out what, I gotta know you're not gonna tell anyone about this place."

"I won't," says Tony. "I swear."

Max says, "It's a vow, Tony. Don't make it if you're gonna break it."

"I won't break it, man. Not ever."

"No matter what? Even if someone dies tonight?"

Before Tony can answer, a blinding flash of light slices through the trees. The blast of a siren follows.

Tony turns back to find that Max and Chastity are gone. Deputy Foster, in aviator glasses and a no-bull attitude, is in his face.

Foster scans Tony's driver's license.

"Anthony Reed. Got any outstanding warrants, Anthony?"

Tony says, "Well, no, of course not."

"Well, I'll have to check that out for myself. So put your hands on the vehicle."

Tony protests his innocence and claims to have been out for a walk. Foster is not convinced as he returns to his cruiser to check for priors.

"Oh, man!" says Tony. "Come on, I didn't do anything."

"I wish I had a nickel for each time I had to drag you kids out of these woods. That'd be a lot of nickels."

Suddenly a blur rushes through the trees and brush toward Tony and Deputy Foster. There is an agonized gasp and a metallic thud.

Then there is silence.

Tony moves cautiously toward the patrol car. Through the headlights' glare, he sees a figure in the driver's seat. He spots the patrolman's flashlight lying on the ground. Tony picks it up and immediately drops it.

His hand is smeared with blood.

His heart pounding, Tony inches toward the driver's-side door, where he sees Deputy Foster—his face obliterated by blood and tissue.

•

Scully steps out of a basement elevator at St. Jude's Memorial Hospital. A folder of pages is clutched in her hand. She looks down the hall and . . .

"There you are," says Mulder. "Heavy traffic?"

"Slow going. Let's just say I had ample time to read the police report that you faxed me."

"Thoughtfully provided by local authorities," says Mulder, "even though it doesn't begin to tell the whole story."

"A sheriff's deputy was slain during a routine patrol. It's a tragic occurrence. But I don't see the mystery here, Mulder."

"Except that the deputy was beaten to death by an invisible assailant."

Scully says, "Yes, but that's according to the young man accused of his murder."

Mulder puts a name to the perp, one Tony Reed.

"He's an A student," he says. "Moved here a few months ago from Philadelphia. Never been in trouble in his life."

They enter the morgue and look at the body of Deputy Foster.

"Mulder, tell me you have more than good SAT scores to show that this Tony Reed didn't commit this crime."

"Maybe. Take a look at the body." Scully pulls back the sheet. "The former Deputy Ronald Foster. As you can see, the report doesn't quite do it justice."

Scully says, "Oh my God! It looks like he was hit with a sledgehammer."

"A police flashlight," says Mulder. "One blow."

Scully looks at the caved-in skull of Deputy Foster. She says the damage was consistent with blunt-force trauma.

"I'd say that Tony eats his Wheaties," she comments.

Mulder says, "Check out the back of his head."

"His eyeglasses."

Mulder says, "Penetrated to the back of his skull. Babe Ruth couldn't hit this hard, let alone a high school sophomore."

"Well, maybe, if he were under the influence of PCP or some kind of stimulant."

"His tox screen came back negative," says Mulder.

"Even so," adds Scully, "stress and fear might've triggered an adrenaline response, which is known to enable feats of near-superhuman strength."

Sheriff Earl Harden enters. He averts his eyes from the body of Foster.

"I'd like Ron left in peace," he says. "I don't know what there is to see, anyway. We got the kid who did this."

Scully says, "Sheriff, we don't mean to second-guess you. We're just hoping to be of some assistance."

"I don't need it," says Harden. "I've got a murder weapon with bloody fingerprints. And once the state crime lab matches them to Tony Reed, it's open and shut."

Mulder says, "Well, we're done here. But Sheriff Harden, you don't mind if I talk to Tony Reed, do you? It won't hurt your case. If he did it, you'll want to know why."

Harden grudgingly agrees to let them talk to Tony.

Mulder and Scully are soon walking down the hallway of the Warren County Sheriff's Station. As they reach a room marked INTERVIEW 1, Chastity steps out and walks past Mulder, flashing him a flirtatious smile. Mulder watches Chastity walk away. They step into the interview room, where they find a very scared Tony.

"Well, Tony, must be your lucky day for visitors," says Mulder. "This is Agent Scully with the FBI, I'm—"

Tony interrupts, "Look, I'm not talking anymore, okay?"

"Well, that might make things worse," says Scully. "And they seem pretty bad already."

Tony is unresponsive.

"In your statement," Scully continues, "you say that Deputy Foster stopped you, but you don't say why."

Mulder adds, "Come on, you were cruising, right? In a small town like this, you're not exactly living *la vida loca*. I know, I grew up in Dullsville, too, you know, nothing to do but drive and park."

Tony says, "How long ago was that? Look, don't you think I know what you're doing?

You're like the tenth cop that's come in trying to relate to me till I confess."

"If you didn't do it, it's all the more reason to clear it up," says Scully.

Tony says, "Everything I know is in my statement."

"Okay, but bear with us because we're old and stupid," says Mulder. "How long was it from the time you heard the scream until you found Deputy Foster?"

Tony estimates ten to fifteen seconds.

"Okay, but you didn't see anyone near the patrol car," says Mulder. "And you're still going to stick to your story that you were the only one there?"

Tony says, "I want to go back to my cell."

Mulder and Scully watch as Tony is taken back to his cell.

"Sixteen years old and his life is over unless he starts telling the truth," says Scully.

Mulder says, "If you really think he's guilty, Scully, ask yourself this. Why wouldn't he make up a more plausible cover story? Why didn't he say a pickup full of hillbillies drove by, clobbered the deputy, and ran away?"

"I'm not saying he's guilty, Mulder," she says. "I'm inclined to agree that Tony Reed did not commit murder. But I think he saw the person who did and he may be covering up for it."

"I think there was a force at work here," says Mulder.

Scully wants to know what kind of force.

Mulder says, "I don't know. Some sort of territorial or spiritual entity, maybe. Poltergeists have long been associated with violent acts like this. They also tend to manifest around young people. They seem to be drawn to the turmoil of adolescence."

"Mulder, rather than spirits, can we at least start with Tony's friends? Please, just for me? I can think of one person in particular I would like to talk to."

•

Chastity is in her science class at Adams High School, bored with her science midterm. The classroom door opens and Max swaggers in. He is immediately set upon by science teacher Mr. Babbitt.

"There goes half your grade, Max," says Babbitt. "You missed the midterm."

"Mind if I take it right now?" asks Max.

"In one minute?" asks Babbitt.

"Oh, I've been studying," says Max.

"I don't care who your father is. If you fail my test, it sticks."

"I guess I better ace it, huh?"

Max takes the exam, skims it briefly, and slams it down on the teacher's desk.

"Piece of cake," says Max.

"It is when you mark them at random," says Babbitt.

"Go ahead, check it."

Babbitt lays Max's test sheet over the clear plastic answer sheet. They line up perfectly. He looks at Max.

"Maybe I got more going on than people know," says Max as the bell rings.

•

Chastity leaves the classroom and finds Mulder and Scully waiting for her in the hall.

"Chastity, what did you and Tony talk about this morning?" asks Mulder.

"He didn't kill that cop," says Chastity.

Mulder asks, "How can you be so sure?"

"Tony just doesn't have it in him," she says.

"Do you?" asks Scully.

"Look, I gotta go," says Chastity.

"Do you realize Tony could go to prison for the rest of his life?" asks Scully.

"Chastity, if you know something, now is the time to mention it," says Mulder.

Max wanders over.

"Unless they got a warrant, you don't have to say nothing," says Max.

"Wow. You must be her lawyer," Mulder says.

"Come on, let's go," says Max.

"Gee. Butting into our investigation. What would your father, the sheriff, think?" says Mulder.

"How do you know who my dad is?" asks Max.

"You have the same last name," says Mulder as he points to an ink-marked binder Max is holding.

Max shines Mulder on as he looks Scully up and down.

"You must have been a Betty back in the day," he says.

"A Betty?" asks Scully.

"Back in the day," says Mulder.

Scully's cell phone rings. "Scully. What about the murder weapon?"

•

Mulder and Scully go to the sheriff's station, where they find Sheriff Harden in the evidence room.

He says, "All I know is, we put the flashlight in here, and now it's gone. It's like it just disappeared into thin air."

Scully eyes an empty evidence locker and the video camera mounted on the ceiling.

"What does the tape show?" asks Mulder.

"That no unauthorized persons came in, and no one went anywhere near this locker," Harden says.

Mulder looks down and prods a gumlike blob stuck to the floor. The blob is black, swirled with veins of gold and red. Several others dot the floor.

"Was this here before?" asks Mulder.

"I don't know," says Harden.

Scully insists on seeing the surveillance tape. They see the image of Sheriff Harden handing the flashlight to the evidence deputy, who places it in a locker.

"You can see that the flashlight was properly secured," says Harden. "It's not like we're running some kind of half-assed operation here."

"No one is saying that you are, Sheriff," says Scully.

The tape is fast-forwarded to reveal the state police officer showing up to take the flashlight to the crime lab and Sheriff Harden opening the locker to an empty interior.

Harden says, "I maybe didn't give y'all the warmest welcome, but if you have any ideas."

"May I?" asks Mulder, reaching for the remote.

"I watched it a dozen times," Harden says.

Scully says that there might have been a malfunction in the VCR as Mulder runs through the tape yet again.

"The murder weapon was the only hard evidence we had," Harden points out. "Without it we got no case. Know what I gotta do now? I gotta call Ron Foster's widow and tell her I gotta turn his killer loose." He leaves.

"Scully, check this out," says Mulder as he slowly advances the tape to a seemingly static series of shots of the empty evidence room.

"Here it comes," says Mulder. "Now you see it . . ."

Mulder slowly advances a frame and a thick, blurry band smears across the frame and the locker. Mulder advances one more frame.

"What do you make of that, Scully? Take another look. Now it's here, now it's not," says Mulder.

•

Tony Reed returns to his home, a modest house in a working-class neighborhood. His mother, fresh off her shift as a waitress at the local diner, comes in right behind him.

"Are you ready to be straight with me?" she asks.

Tony says, "Leave me alone, Mom. Would you just leave me alone? I'm tired."

"This isn't like a bad report card, Anthony. A man is dead," says his mother.

"I told you I didn't do it!"

"It's just that what you say happened doesn't make sense. There's gotta be more to it."

"Well, there isn't, okay?" says Tony.

Mrs. Reed senses that Tony was not alone in this situation.

"Are those kids involved in this? That boy Max?" asks Mrs. Reed.

"No. Mom, they're the only friends I have here."

"Well, you're done seeing them!"

Tony says his mother does not even know them.

"I know them," says his mother. "I was your age once. Tony, we came here to get a fresh start. Get away from them bad schools, the wrong crowd. You're doing so well here."

Tony accuses his mother of not knowing his friends because she is never around.

Mrs. Reed says, "You think it's my dream to work two jobs? I'm doing it for you, Tony."

Tony says, "I just wanna get some sleep. That's all I want."

Mrs. Reed says, "You got a chance at a good life. A real future. We didn't come all this way so you could throw it away."

His mother walks out. Tony's attention is drawn to a light tap on his bedroom window. He hears it again, a pebble bouncing off the glass. Tony looks out the window and sees Max standing in the yard.

Tony joins Max behind the wheel of a Jaguar.

"Chastity told you to shut up, sit tight, and things'd be fine," says Max. "You did that. It tells me a lot."

"It's not fine!" Tony says. "We're in a stolen car. A cop is dead."

"Calm down, man. He'd been snooping around. He had to go."

"What do you mean he had to go? What happened out there?"

"You gotta learn not to ask so many questions," says Max as the car roars off into the night. Tony freaks as the speedometer climbs past 100 miles per hour.

"Slow the hell down, man. You're freaking me out!"

Max says, "You ain't seen nothing yet."

The car careens off the road onto the shoulder.

"Max, look out!" says Tony as he turns to Max.

Instead he finds the driver's seat is empty.

The car bounces violently as Tony grabs for the wheel in a futile attempt to get it under control. Through the windshield he sees that he is on a collision course with a utility pole. Tony braces for impact.

The Jag hits the pole with a deafening crash. The car is totaled, but Tony has survived the impact—and even more amazingly, finds himself on the road, some thirty feet away from the crash. He turns and finds himself face-to-face with Max.

figures. Whatever this is, it's not a ghost."

"Especially since ghosts don't go around leaving synthetic polymers in their wake," adds Scully.

Mulder says, "That's what the gunk on the floor turned out to be. Chuck, I get the feeling you don't know what the hell this is."

"I cross-referenced the shape's silhouette against every organic and inorganic object in the Library of Congress database," explains Burks. "The closest match was a Soviet Akula-class submarine."

"I think we can rule that out," says Scully.

Burks looks back to the monitor and enlarges the mystery tape.

"Then there's this weirdness. My enhancement brought out this dark edge around the anomaly," says Burks.

"A shadow?" asks Mulder.

"That would fit with the lighting in the room. The problem is, it can't be throwing a shadow unless—" says Burks.

"Unless this is a solid object," says Mulder.

Scully says, "Which is not possible, because it only appears for a single frame."

"I'M GOING TO MAKE YOU ONE OF US. BUT I CALL THE SHOTS. ALWAYS REMEMBER THAT."—Max

"I'm going to make you one of us," says Max. "But I call the shots. Always remember that."

•

Dr. Charles Burks is seated at a desk in Mulder's office, staring at the high-resolution video monitor feed of the evidence room. Mulder and Scully enter.

Scully says, "Sorry to make you trek over here for what's probably a glitch."

"What did you come up with, Chuck?" asks Mulder.

"Nothing but eyestrain, at first," says Burks. "Then I ran it through my imaging software. I'm here to tell you it's not a glitch. It's what the camera saw."

Mulder says, "Buckle up, Scully. I believe Chuck's about to take us on a ride through the paranormal."

Burks says, "Yes and no. Initially, I was thinking spectral manifestation. But with spirit activity, you'd expect to see light streaks, auras, atmospheric disturbances, translucent

Or a mere one-thirtieth of a second, offers Burks, who indicates that SCAG (Spectrographic Color Attribute Generator) might give them a clearer picture.

Burks applies dime-sized dots of color to the image. "Still in the tweaking phase, but here's the basic idea. I assign known color values onto the black-and-white image. Then, SCAG assigns chromatic values throughout the frame, in effect making an educated guess at what all the colors might be," says Burks.

Burks introduces a wash of color over the black-and-white image. The shape is now purple.

Mulder says, "Recognize these colors, Scully?"

They are the colors of Adams High School.

•

Tony is walking down the hallway, hearing the whispers, feeling the stares. He approaches Chastity.

"Everyone's looking at me like I'm a criminal," he says.

"I'm not," says Chastity. "I heard you took a ride."

Tony asks, "What was that? How did he do it?"

"You'll find out," says Chastity.

"Maybe you were right. About me not being cut out for this."

"It's a little late for second thoughts," she says.

Max's hand falls heavily on Chastity's shoulder. "You trying to move in on my girl?" asks Max, as the bell rings for class.

"Saved by the bell," Max says with a smile as he and Chastity walk away. Tony enters science class, where he is once again the target of gawkers. Max leaps to his defense.

"You want to stare at someone, stare at me," says Max.

Mr. Babbitt enters the room and hands back the previous day's tests.

Babbitt says, "Welcome back, Mr. Reed. Expect to make up the test tomorrow. Mr. Hart, you're here on time for a change."

He reaches Max's desk and hands him his test. Max looks at an F marked on the cover of the test booklet.

"What's this?" asks Max.

"Self-explanatory, isn't it?" says the teacher.

"I got every answer right," says Max.

Babbitt says, "Not because you knew the material."

"You saying I cheated? How?"

"I have no idea how. But you did, and I won't tolerate it."

Max storms out of the classroom.

"Back to business, people," says Babbitt.

Tony asks Chastity, "How do I tell Max I want out?"

"I wish I could help you, Tony," she says. "I can't even help myself."

•

Tony is eating lunch in the cafeteria when he sees Mr. Babbitt walking down the aisle with a tray of food. He trips and falls. Applause, laughs, and cheers erupt. Tony looks around the cafeteria and spots Max leaning against a wall. Max seems to subtly vibrate.

Babbitt cleans up the mess from the floor. Suddenly he yells in pain. His face is badly bruised, with cuts and welts. He looks up at Max in terror. An empty dining table suddenly swerves into the teacher's path. He is folded over the table, which immediately rockets across the floor and into a wall with bone-crushing force. A chair comes to life and flies straight toward him.

•

Mulder, Scully, and local authorities go over the grisly remains of the teacher, whose head was crushed by the impact of the chair.

"I'll show you my theory if you show me yours," Mulder says.

Scully says, "Based on the eyewitness accounts of the students I spoke to, at this moment I'd have to say that I don't have one."

Mulder gestures to the floor and a half-dozen gumlike streaks, similar to those found in the evidence room. Mulder thinks that Max Harden knows how they got there.

"You think Max did this?" asks Scully. "Based on what?"

"I spoke to a few students myself. Apparently, Max was angry at Mr. Babbitt because he failed him on his midterm exam. So he had motive."

Scully says, "He may have had motive, but he didn't have opportunity. Nobody here saw him go near the victim."

Mulder produces a file on Max that indicates recent attendance and discipline problems. Scully thumbs through it.

"Look at his transcripts," Mulder tells her. "As his behavior got worse, his grades went through the roof. This kid has changed, Scully."

"Well, Mulder, he's a teenager," says Scully. "Everything about him's changing. His brain and body chemistry are in a state of unparalleled upheaval. Plus there's peer pressure and substance abuse. Any one of these factors could alter his behavior radically."

"But what if it's also given him a kind of psychokinetic or paranormal ability that allows him to exert force over a victim without ever laying a finger on him?"

"Is that your theory?"

"Yes, it is. Soon to be proven," says Mulder, "as soon as we get Max in for questioning."

A deputy delivers the news that Max was taken to the hospital after he collapsed in the school parking lot.

•

The death of Mr. Babbitt and the news of Max's collapse are playing on Tony's mind as he runs into Chastity.

"You hear about Max?" he asks her. "You okay? Where are you going?"

"Tony, the less you know, the better, all right?" says Chastity.

•

A car pulls to a stop on an isolated dirt road. Chastity sits behind the wheel. Chastity gets out of the car and races into the woods. Tony jogs after her, rounds a curve in the path, and is surprised to see that Chastity is nowhere in sight. What he does see is a huge boulder, with a vertical fissure in it. He squeezes through the fissure and into the darkness of a cave. Walking a short distance, Tony comes upon a small chamber.

Tony circles the chamber, noticing a small depression in the middle of the floor. He steps into it and his shoulder suddenly begins to twitch and vibrate. He steps out and the vibrating stops. Tony steps into the depression again. His hand begins to vibrate at a blur of speed. His head starts to vibrate. Tony feels a change coming over him.

His entire body vibrates inside the depression in the cave floor, where a strange beam of light is illuminating the center.

•

Max is laying in a hospital bed, his father standing nearby, when Mulder and Scully enter.

"What? No candy? No flowers?"

Harden says, "My deputy told me you were coming and why. So you can turn right around. Whatever the hell happened at that school, my son didn't do it."

"Sheriff, we'd just like to ask your son a few questions, if that's okay," says Scully.

"The boy is sick! The doctors can't even say what's wrong with him," Harden says.

Mulder says, "Max could tell them. You know why you collapsed, don't you, Max?"

"Yeah, too much teen spirit," says Max.

"You think?" says Mulder. "It smells like murder to me."

Harden interrupts, demanding to know who they think they're talking to.

"Yeah," says Max. "It's not like you got a damn thing on me."

Harden is startled by his son's remark.

"You've got a problem with authority figures, don't you, Max?" Mulder asks.

Max counters, "If I wasted Babbitt, how'd I do it? Am I Carrie or something? I used some kind of mental powers?"

Mulder says, "No, something else. You've figured out how to tap into something that gives you superhuman powers. It comes in handy with Mr. Babbitt and Deputy Foster." But Max denies this.

Scully scans the medical chart at the foot of his bed.

"High temperature and heart rate, low blood sugar," she reads. "Electrolytes show acidosis. All these symptoms are consistent with extreme exertion and withdrawal."

"Withdrawal from what?" asks Harden.

"The rush," says Mulder. "I think whatever it is that gives you the power to rearrange furniture and turn a flashlight into a battering ram also gives you quite a buzz."

Max says, "Well, if I can do all that, what's stopping me from doing it to you?"

"I don't know. Maybe the effect's worn off," says Mulder. "Maybe you need another fix."

"Soon as I blow out of here I'll be sure to get one."

"Well, that's not going to happen anytime soon," says Scully. "Your condition's getting worse. We're not going to be able to help you unless you can tell us what's going on."

Harden asks, "Boy? Is any of this true?"

Max answers, "No."

"You'd better pray I don't find out that it is," his father warns.

Mulder motions the father out into the hallway. Harden is distracted and doubtful but continues to defend Max to the agent. Mulder asks the sheriff for permission to search his home for clues. Harden refuses, walking off in a huff. Scully has been going over Max's chart.

"Some test results are missing from Max's chart. I think we should track them down," she tells him.

Mulder and Scully head off. They are being watched by Chastity, who is hiding in an intersecting hallway.

•

Mulder and Scully are in a hospital viewing room, where MRIs of Max's skull and spine are up on a light box.

"Hot off the presses," says Scully.

Mulder asks, "Anything interesting?"

Scully looks long and hard at them. She's puzzled.

Scully says, "This can't be right. Evidence of cerebral lesions from repeated concussions. Arthritis in the spine and major joints. Stress fractures, numerous muscle and ligament microtears."

Mulder asks, "What would cause all this?"

"In a teenager? I can't even imagine. This is the kind of thing you'd see in someone who's crashed race cars or played pro football fifteen years. Whatever Max is doing, it's killing him."

"I think I'm starting to get it."

•

A floor nurse is working at the nurses' station. Suddenly an alarm beeps. The nurse looks on the monitor into Max's room and sees Chastity disconnecting his IV and monitor leads. She rushes to Max's room, where she sees Max alone.

"I thought I saw a young lady come in here," says the nurse.

"I wish," says Max.

The nurse leaves. Chastity looks after her.

•

Mulder and Scully are in a hospital viewing room, checking the contents of a plastic bag—Max Harden's personal effects. Mulder goes straight for a pair of running shoes and checks the soles.

"This is it," says Mulder.

He exposes a congealed melted patty of multicolored rubber.

"Those blobs we found? This is where they come from. Speed, Scully. Somehow Max Harden has found a way to move faster than the eye can see. That would explain how Babbitt was killed. It would also explain how a chair and table appeared on their own, with enough force to penetrate a wall. Force equals mass times acceleration, isn't that right?"

"Yes, Mulder, but it's impossible. The human body just isn't designed to move like that."

"Exactly. That is why his is falling apart," says Mulder.

The agents are approached by the flustered floor nurse and taken back to Max's room . . . which is now empty.

•

Max and Chastity have gone to the woods. Max, showing signs of withdrawal, is preparing to go down to the cave and get his speed fix.

Chastity says, "Max, please don't do this. You can stop."

"Sure," says Max. "Just like you can."

"I mean hurting people," she says. "Haven't enough people already been hurt? This is not why I got you out. Look, let's just leave here."

"And do what?" asks Max.

"Let's just go away. Find a place to get some help."

"Help for what? This is the best thing that ever happened to me. I can't go back to things standing still. Neither can you."

Max goes down the path. Chastity is about to join him when she is surprised to see Tony, dazed and a bit unsteady, approaching.

Chastity says, "Tony, what are you doing here? You went to the cave, didn't you? You shouldn't have done that."

Tony admits that it was a rush moving that fast.

"I didn't want this for you," she says. "How did you find it?"

"I followed you. I was worried about you."

Chastity says, "That's so sweet. I wish things were different than how they are."

"Maybe they can be. With Max in the hospital, we could go to the cops."

"He's out," she says.

•

Harden enters his house and goes to his son's room, looking for a clue. He finds the expected dirty laundry and unmade bed but is thrown by the dozen pairs of running shoes he discovers when he opens the closet. Harden moves to the dresser and opens the drawers. Under some clothes, he finds a gun.

Harden realizes that his son is the killer.

There is a disturbance downstairs. Someone has entered the house. Harden races downstairs but sees nothing. The front door slams shut by itself.

"Boo," says Max, suddenly appearing right behind his father, the flashlight now in his hand.

"You killed Ron Foster," says Harden.

"Yeah. I did," says Max.

"Why?" asks his father.

"I don't know. You want some great reason?"

"You little son of a bitch."

Harden doubles over and drops like a stone. Max is standing over him, the flashlight clenched in his fist.

"He thought he was really something," says Max. "Always liked to push people around. Same as Babbitt. Same as you. I'm not afraid of you anymore."

Suddenly the front door slams open. Max looks down. The flashlight is gone. Tony is in the room, holding Sheriff Harden's pistol to Max's temple and the flashlight in the other hand.

"I can't let you do this, Max," says Tony.

•

Mulder catches up with Scully as they walk through the hospital at the news that Sheriff Harden has been brought in. He is wheeled in, eyes shut, an oxygen mask over his face.

"How bad are his injuries?" asks Mulder.

Scully says, "It's too soon to tell. He's unconscious and bleeding internally, apparently from a blow to his abdomen."

"Delivered with this," says Mulder, holding up the flashlight. "Max's weapon of choice against cops."

"Why would he leave it behind?" asks Scully. "Do you think he's doing it to taunt the police?"

"No, I think somebody intervened. I think that's why the sheriff is still alive. And why his gun is missing," says Mulder.

Scully is at a loss as to who could have intervened. Mulder says that it would be someone who knows exactly how Max does what he does—and who is finally standing up to him.

"Tony," states Scully. "How do we find him?"

"I would guess the source where Max gets his power from."

"The woods near where the deputy was killed. You know, Tony never came clean as to what he was doing out there."

"Maybe that's why the deputy was killed. Maybe he got too close to the truth," says Mulder.

•

Tony and Chastity speed down the road in her car.

Tony says, "Chastity, we don't have to be doing this. I told you, I took care of things with Max."

"No, you didn't, and you shouldn't have tried," Chastity says.

"He was gonna kill his father. I had to stop him."

"You stopped him because he let you. He was slowing down. Tony, you've slowed down, too. If we don't get to the cave before Max does, we're history."

In a matter of minutes, Chastity's car skids to a stop in the woods. They get out of the car and start running to the cave. Tony trips and falls. Chastity races on ahead and into the crevice in the rock. Tony catches up and enters the cave. He goes into the main chamber, where he sees Chastity sprawled on the ground near the depression. Tony rushes to her.

"Chastity, are . . ." he begins. When suddenly he is paralyzed by the presence of a speeding entity. After a moment, his universe returns to normal speed and he completes his sentence.

". . . you okay?"

He turns to find Max standing behind him.

"What did you do to her?" he asks.

"She took a swing at me," says Max. "You believe that? You got her all turned around."

Before Tony can respond, he is flung backward against a cave wall by an invisible force. Tony slumps to the ground. He reaches for Sheriff Harden's pistol, which he had tucked

into his waistband, only to find that the gun is gone.

It is now in Max's hand.

"Come on, man, who do you think you're dealing with?" asks Max, as he tosses the gun on the ground. "All I ever wanted was for you to be my friend, Tony. You stuck a knife in my back. Now I'm gonna mess you up."

Before Max can move, Chastity fires a bullet into his back. Time seems to slow down as the bullet tears out the front of Max's chest.

"I'm sorry, Tony," says Chastity. "I can't go back."

Using her ability to move in a flash, she positions herself in the path of the bullet and it tears into her, too.

Max and Chastity crumple to the ground.

Mulder and Scully arrive on the scene just as the fatal gunshot is fired. They race to the cave where they find Tony bent over the lifeless Chastity, cradling her body.

•

Tony is recovering in his hospital room as his mother sits next to him. Mulder and Scully are in the hallway.

"Did the USGS show up?" asks Scully.

Mulder says, "Eighteen geologists and three semis full of gear. They covered every inch of that cave."

"And what did they come up with?" asks Scully.

"Nothing. Bat guano and above-normal magnetic field readings, but nothing that would cause a physiological effect."

"What did you expect them to find, Mulder?"

"I don't know. A vortex, like the one in Oregon. Gravitational aberrations, unique chemical compositions, relics that would indicate that the cave was a sacred site. Something, anything. I don't know."

"You and I, we were both in there and nothing happened to us. We're still slowpoking around."

"What if we're too old?" says Mulder. "You said teenagers differ from adults chemically and psychologically. What if whatever's in that cave affects only them?"

"It's doubtful. But no more so than any other theory. It's worth checking out."

"Oh, yeah? Well, we can't. As of an hour ago, they pumped concrete in the cave and sealed it. For precautionary reasons. We'll never know."

The agents look at Tony.

"Bruises and muscle strains," says Scully. "He'll recover. Go back to being a normal kid."

•

Tony is staring at the slowly moving minute hand of the clock as he lies in bed. Tony realizes the truth . . .

He will be trapped forever in a slowed-down world.

BACK STORY:

X-Files episodes that focus on people with supernatural abilities have always had a certain subversive "wish-fulfillment" charm. "Rush" extrapolated on the conceit by putting a powerful force in the hands of angst-ridden teenagers.

Even by the standards of *The X-Files* writing staff, who were accustomed to extended script development schedules, the David Amann script was a long time in coming together. As early as the beginning of Season 6, the idea of putting a druglike addiction to super speed in the hands of hormone-raging teenagers had surfaced, according to Chris Carter.

"How to do it was going to be tricky. It had been a long time since we had dealt with teenage angst. [But] it was being done everywhere else and we wanted to take a run at it."

Amann appreciated the thematic development that occurred during the writing of the script. "The initial idea for the story was what effect having the power of super speed would have on troubled teens. But it became much deeper than that. I loved the way the paranormal aspect of the show dovetails with the thematic aspect of the show, which was the impatience and impetuousness of youth."

Frank Spotnitz adds, "The story had a real strong emotional focus, which was this kid who wants to belong to the cool group. The speed kills thing and how it related to drug abuse and the general boredom that most teenagers experience just fit right in."

Casting teen leads for the episode appeared on the surface to be an easy job, given the number of aspiring young actors in Los Angeles. But Rick Millikan recalls that "Rush" was actually one of the tougher episodes of the seventh season to cast. "It was all teenagers, but this being *The X-Files* we were looking for something other than the typical *90210*-type kids. There were specific qualities that these kids had to have. They had to have a subtle kind of evil about them as well as arrogance and vulnerability. What was tough about casting that age group is that all the good ones were already working. We had to find somebody who was between gigs or wasn't working at the time."

"Rush" was very much a special effects episode, but rather than immediately turning to computer-generated images, director Rob Lieberman was able to capture the all-important speed imagery by filming the sequences at different film speeds. Stunt coordinator Danny Wesiles was a key part of creating the speed-related killings.

"I doubled the teacher who gets killed by the table flying across the gymnasium floor," he explains. "We rigged a cable to the table and pulled it across the gym floor. Then we cut, put a dummy on the table, and rammed it into a concrete wall. For the speed sequences inside the cave, we put a stuntman in a harness and air-ratched him across a cave wall. For the car crash sequence we cabled a car and ran it at fifty miles an hour into a telephone pole."

Producer Harry Bring says that "everything about filming 'Rush' was difficult because everything had to be so precise." He remembers that the climactic scene in the cave was easily their hardest day. "We had to figure out how this girl could shoot the gun, rush around the guy she shot at, and end up taking the bullet herself. The scene ended up being a complex mixture of different camera speeds and blue screen work that was composited together."

Frank Spotnitz remembers that the scene where the teacher is killed by the flying table was the subject of much discussion even while it was being filmed. "That was probably one of the most horrific things we've ever done. There were a lot of questions about how long we could linger on the shot and what sounds we could make."

And sure enough, John Shiban recalls that when "Rush" was in the editing stage, he began to receive calls from network Standards and Practices. "Their big problem was that in the original cut, you actually saw the impact between the table and the man. Standards and Practices did not want to see the impact. So we took out the actual impact.

"But what they did not realize is that when you take out the impact, the audience's imagination is ten times worse."

FACTS:

Rob Lieberman directed the alien abduction movie *Fire in the Sky* in 1993, which starred D.B. Sweeney, who would go on to be one of the stars of Chris Carter's short-lived series *Harsh Realm*.

Rodney Scott, who played Tony Reed, played the recurring character of Will on *Dawson's Creek*, as well as David Cassidy in the 1999 TV movie *Come On, Get Happy: The Partridge Family Story*.

The role of Max Harden was played by Scott Cooper, whose credits prior to *The X-Files* include parts in the Mike Myers comedy *Austin Powers: The Spy Who Shagged Me* and *Takedown*, a film about the capture of infamous computer hacker Kevin Mitnick.

In addition to Chastity Raines, Nicki Aycox's roles include the recurring character of Lily on *Providence*, and the part of Cecil in the 1999 film *Crime + Punishment in Suburbia*.

episode 7X02

THE GOLDBERG VARIATION

EPISODE: 7X02
FIRST AIRED: December 12, 1999
EDITOR: Lynne Willingham
WRITTEN BY: Jeffrey Bell
DIRECTED BY: Thomas J. Wright

Henry Weems is the luckiest man in the world. But as Mulder and Scully investigate his near-death experience, they discover that Henry's attempts to do a good deed may result in his luck running out.

GUEST STARS:

Willie Garson (Henry Weems)
Ramy Zada (Jimmy Cutrona)
Alyson Reed (Maggie Lupone)
Shia La Beouf (Richie Lupone)
Tony Longo (Dominic)
Ernie Lee Banks (Maurice)
Chip Fogleman (Billy)
Marshall Manesh (Mr. Jank)
Dom Magwili (Mr. Ng)
Nicholas Worth (Mr. Haas)
Dominique Di Prima (Megan McLean)

PRINCIPAL SETTING:

Chicago, Illinois

A high-stakes card game is unfolding in a private room of a Chicago high-rise. A pair of kings, a seven, a two, and a four go to Jimmy Cutrona, a John Gotti–like thug complete with sharkskin suit and a pinky ring.

"Three," says Cutrona as he discards.

To Cutrona's left, Mr. Jank discards two cards and jabs two new cards into his hand. Mr. Ng, an expensively dressed Vietnamese man, discards two cards.

Henry Weems, a nondescript middle-class man, seems out of place with the other card players, but the huge stack of chips in front of him indicates he is having good luck. His hand includes three tens. So it is a surprise when Henry says:

"Can I have five cards, please?"

Mr. Haas, the dealer, is irritated at the request.

"Five?" he asks. "What, are you serious? Four's the limit. Let's see your ace."

Cutrona, who is running the show, says, "If Mr. Weems wants five, give him five."

Haas deals Weems five cards and takes two for himself. Watching the game unfold with only marginal interest is a swarthy knuckle-dragger named Dominic. Cutrona smiles as he checks his cards and finds he now has four kings. He tosses two gold chips into the pile. Mr. Jank shakes his head in disgust and folds. Mr. Ng sees Cutrona's two chips and raises two more.

"How much is that?" asks Weems.

"Four grand keeps you in," says Haas. "You and your five shiny new cards."

Henry slides four gold chips into the pot. "Here's four thousand and four more."

Too rich for Haas. He folds.

"Let's make this interesting," says Cutrona. "I'm raising you fifteen large."

He slides another tall stack of chips into the pot.

"I wouldn't do that," says Henry. "This is all I need."

Cutrona stares hard at Henry. He thinks he might be bluffing, but he's not sure.

Cutrona says, "You're gonna need Depends after you see this hand."

Mr. Ng folds. Henry counts off fifteen chips and slides them into the pot.

"Now we show each other our cards?" asks Henry.

Cutrona smiles as he reveals his four kings. All eyes are on Henry as he lays his cards on the table. It's a straight flush in spades. Cutrona is in shock.

"Beginner's luck," says Henry as he stands up, pulling his winnings toward him.

"What the hell do you think you're doing?" asks Cutrona.

"Going home," says Henry.

"No. Not so fast. We expect a chance to win some of our money back."

Henry meekly responds, "Guys . . . there's over a hundred thousand dollars there."

"You're damn right there's over a hundred thousand dollars there," says Cutrona.

"Hundred thousand's all I need," says Henry as he scoops his winnings into a plastic shopping bag. "Sorry. I had fun, though. Where can I cash out?"

Cutrona glares at Dominic.

•

Henry, flanked by two goons, soon finds himself in an elevator going up. The elevator doors clang open on the rooftop. Henry is marched out, a firm hand under each arm. He drops his shopping bag.

Henry says, "Guys, this is not what I meant by cashing out."

The goons push Henry toward the roof's edge and toss him off.

The sidewalk and street rush up to meet Henry as he plummets, flailing wildly through space. He disappears through an open sidewalk service elevator and lands with a thud. Moments later a hand reaches out of the shaft, then another. Henry drags himself out of the opening, seemingly unharmed, scrambles to his feet, and hurries off.

•

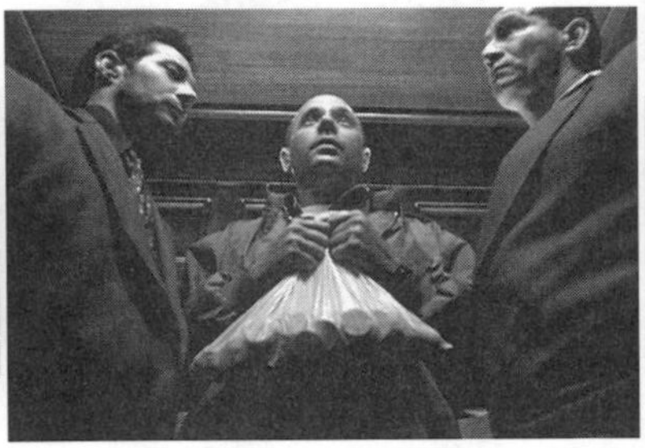

The next day a cab pulls to the curb in downtown Chicago. Scully gets out and is standing alone on the sidewalk. She takes out her cell phone and speed-dials.

"Hey, Mulder, it's me," she says into the phone as she strolls along the street. "What now?"

"Are you in Chicago?" asks Mulder.

"Yes. I'm in Chicago. I'm on the northeast corner of Seventh and Hunter, just like you asked. Only you're not here."

She crosses the steel doors of a sidewalk service elevator. The doors open behind her and the elevator begins to rise up.

"So where are you?" asks Scully, unaware that Mulder is on the rising elevator.

"Oh, around," he says. "Hey, nice outfit."

Scully looks behind her. She is not amused. She looks down at the elevator.

"Hey, what's down there?"

"Before you check out down there, check out up there," he says, pointing skyward to the skyscraper. "The top two floors are leased by one Jimmy Cutrona, whose name you might be familiar with."

"Organized crime," Scully says. "The Bureau's been trying to build a racketeering case against him for the past few years. Gambling, extortion, murder."

"Which is why last night, there were two agents parked across the street on surveillance. They witnessed a man being thrown from Cutrona's roof at ten-forty P.M. This man fell thirty floors plus the distance down this shaft because these doors just happened to be open. Straight through. Nothing but net."

"Ouch," says Scully.

"I'm guessing that's what he said. After he got up, climbed out of here, and scampered off into the night."

They step into the elevator and descend below the street. Scully asks the identity of the man as they step out into the dark basement. Mulder says that the two agents chased him but he got away and they did not get a clear description.

"Was this basement thoroughly searched?" asks Scully.

"No. Technically, falling three hundred feet and surviving isn't a crime."

"And your theory is?"

He says, "What if this man had some kind of special capability? Some kind of genetic predisposition toward rapid healing or tissue regeneration?"

"Basically, what if we're looking for Wile E. Coyote? You're saying that he's invulnerable," says Scully.

Mulder responds by giving her a look like it could be possible.

She continues, "You know, in 1998 there was a British soldier who plummeted forty-five hundred feet when his parachute failed. And he walked away with a broken rib."

"What's your point?" Mulder asks.

"My point is that if there's a wind gust, a sudden updraft, plus if he landed in exactly the right way, I mean, I don't know. Maybe he just got lucky."

"What if he got really, really lucky? That's your big scientific explanation, Scully? I mean, how many thousands of variables would have to convene in just the right mixture for that theory to hold water?"

"I don't know."

"Thousands."

Scully shines her light around the basement and on to some laundry carts. She notices that one cart, piled high with towels, has four flattened wheels.

Scully says, "If this cart were on the platform when he hit, that would explain the condition of these wheels. And what if this whole thing had just enough give to save his life?"

"We'd have to find him to ask."

"Yeah, we have to find him."

Mulder is looking through the cart's towels. He pulls one loose and a small round object flies out. When Mulder retrieves it and turns it around, he sees an iris and a pupil. It is an artificial eye.

Says Mulder, "Looks like maybe we found part of him already."

•

Mulder and Scully are standing in front of the tenant directory of a brownstone in the solid working-class community of Melrose Park. Mulder runs his finger down the tenant list and stops at WEEMS, H. BUILDING SUPER #313. He presses button number 313.

"Think you're taking a flyer here, Mulder. There's got to be at least six hundred people with prosthetic eyes in the greater Chicago area."

"Yeah, but only this one, Henry Weems, made an appointment this morning to get a new one," says Mulder.

Mulder buzzes again. Still no answer.

"Maybe he can't see his way to the door," says Scully.

A woman walks out of the building. Mulder grabs the door before it can close.

"Come on, Scully. I feel lucky."

An elevator opens on the top floor. Mulder and Scully exit and head down the hallway. A woman in her early thirties named Maggie Lupone dashes around the corner, straight at the agents.

"Can you help me?" asks Maggie. "It's an emergency!"

She turns and rushes away. Mulder and Scully race after her. They enter Maggie's apartment only to find that the emergency is water shooting out of a busted tap.

"Ma'am?" says Scully. "We're not plumbers."

"I didn't say you were," says Maggie. "I just want the damn water turned off so that I can go to work! Look, you've got to be stronger than me, right? Valve's under the sink."

"BASICALLY, WHAT IF WE'RE LOOKING FOR WILE E. COYOTE?"
—Scully

Maggie shoves a crescent wrench at Mulder. He shrugs, sloshes across the flooded floor, and squats down under the sink.

As he struggles with the valve, Mulder asks Maggie, "Your building super, Henry Weems, isn't around?"

"Mr. Dependable?" scoffs Maggie. "I might as well wait for Jimmy Hoffa to show up."

Richie, Maggie's frail ten-year-old son, pads into the room. He tells Mulder he's turning the valve the wrong way. Maggie sends her son back to his room. Mulder strains as he doubles his efforts to turn the valve. The valve snaps off, soaking Mulder in a geyser of water. He stands up and the flooded floorboards let out a creak under his feet. He looks from his feet to Scully and Maggie . . .

. . . just as the floor gives way under him and he drops through to the vacant apartment below. Scully approaches the hole and clicks on her flashlight. She spots Mulder lying atop a pile of debris on the floor of the empty apartment.

"My ass broke the fall," he says. "Guess who I found?"

Scully angles her flashlight to reveal Henry Weems, with a black patch in place of his missing eye.

Mulder says, "Henry Weems, I presume?"

•

Henry leads Mulder and Scully inside his modest apartment, past an elaborate sculpture of Rube Goldberg proportions, into the living

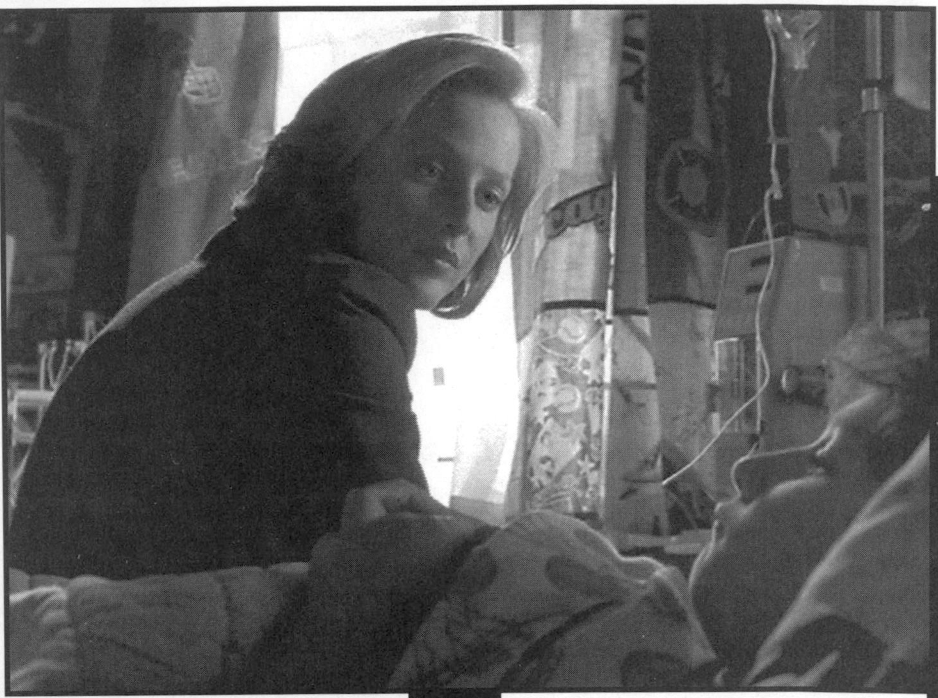

room. Mulder towels himself off, reaches into his pocket, and produces the glass eye.

"Next time leave the plumbing to a professional," says Henry.

"You wanna try this on for size, Cinderella?" asks Mulder.

Henry takes the eye and retrieves a special cloth to clean it.

Scully says, "Mr. Weems, why were you hiding in a vacant apartment?"

"Not hiding," says Henry. "Avoiding."

"Avoiding whom?" she asks.

"You people. Now that you found me, let's just get it over with. No way am I testifying against Jimmy Cutrona."

"Last night, Cutrona had you thrown off the roof of 1107 Hunter Avenue. Is that correct?"

Henry says, "You didn't hear it from me. I'm not letting you people move me to Muncie, Indiana, to milk cows."

Henry removes his eye patch and inserts his artificial eye.

"More to the point," says Mulder, "you survived a three-hundred-foot fall, essentially unharmed."

"I don't know," says Henry. "Maybe the wind was just right and I landed on a bunch of towels. No biggie."

Says Scully, "You got lucky."

"Yeah, I guess, except you should look at my bruise," Henry says. "Plus, I didn't get to keep my poker winnings."

"So that's what you were doing there last night?" asks Scully. "Playing poker?"

"Cutrona thought I was cheating. I wasn't. But like I said, you didn't hear it from me."

Mulder speculates that it was a high-stakes game and that Henry must have won a lot of money. Mulder wanders over to Henry's bookshelf and pulls out *Poker for Dummies*, indicating that Henry must have been lucky.

Mulder goes to the mousetrap contraption. He studies it for a moment, then sets it in motion. A dominolike piece knocks over several others that trigger a ball, which in turn sets off a number of cause-and-effect reactions that result in hanging a hand-carved wooden man standing on a gallows.

"That's craftsmanship," says Mulder. "What does it mean?"

Henry says, "What do you mean, 'what does it mean?' Doesn't mean anything. I just sorta . . . I dunno . . ."

"Cause and effect," says Mulder.

"So are we done here?" asks Henry.

Scully says, "Mr. Weems, can we ask you to reconsider testifying against Cutrona?"

"Nope. No way, Jose."

"It would be in your best interest," Scully advises. "He's tried to kill you once. And he will undoubtedly do it again."

Mulder adds that they can protect him if he testifies. Henry says he will take his chances. Mulder and Scully give up trying to convince him and leave.

"So here's the plan, as I see it," says Scully. "We inform the Chicago field office about Weems, leaving it to them to secure his testimony. You change your clothes, we fly back to D.C. by sunset, and all's right with the world."

"Come on, Scully. You're gonna dump this case just as it's getting interesting?"

"Interesting, Mulder, was when we were looking for Wile E. Coyote. Come on, Mulder, this guy just got lucky. There's no X-File here."

"Maybe his luck is the X-File."

They get tired of waiting for the elevator and decide to take the stairs. Just as they leave, the elevator finally arrives and opens to reveal one of Cutrona's hired enforcers, Angelo. He goes to Henry's apartment, drawing a .38, and kicks in the door.

Mulder and Scully exit the front door and start down the steps. Mulder reaches into his pocket and pulls up short.

"The car keys," he says. "I must have lost them when I fell."

He buzzes Henry's apartment. Back at the apartment Angelo kicks in the door, aims his gun at Henry, and is about to fire when the buzzer buzzes, startling him. Mulder and Scully hear a gunshot ring out. Mulder forces open the front door and they race back into the building and upstairs, guns drawn. In the meantime, a struggle is taking place, furniture and bodies flying everywhere. Mulder and Scully reach Henry's door. They burst in.

Angelo the enforcer is hanging upside down, his shoelaces tangled in one of the fan blades. He is dead. The room is trashed.

Henry is nowhere to be found.

•

Mulder and Scully are soon joined by feds, uniforms, and a lot of crime-scene types.

"So, you get many of these?" Mulder asks a crime-scene photographer.

Scully says, "They've searched the entire building, and there's no sign of Henry Weems. I'm guessing that he's on the run."

"Our dead man's name was Angelo Bellini, AKA 'Angie the Animal,' " Mulder says. "He's an enforcer for the Cutrona family. I don't think his visit was friendly."

Scully asks, "Do you think that Weems could have killed him in self-defense?"

"A skinny guy with no depth perception against a man nicknamed 'the Animal'? I don't think so. You and I both know that Weems didn't kill anybody. Besides, we were just gone for two minutes. This guy doesn't have a scratch on him. I'm thinking it was a heart attack."

"What the hell happened here, Mulder?"

"Cause and effect," he mutters.

"Meaning?"

He looks around the room at all the randomly upset furniture and Angelo dangling upside down from the fan.

"Okay," he says. "Watch. Bellini kicks down the door, poised to kill Weems. But just as he's about to pull the trigger, a noise startles him. The buzzer, when I buzzed to be let back in the apartment. So when he does pull the trigger, his aim is off. Right? And he hits this lamp, which falls over and knocks over the ironing board. So as the bullet ricochets, Weems dives over the sofa. Now when Bellini goes for him, he trips over the ironing board, bounces off the chair, flips end over end, and his shoelace gets caught in the fan. QED."

The fan blade gives way and Angelo hits the floor.

"Cause and effect. Seemingly unrelated and unconnected events and occurrences that appear unrelated and random beforehand but which seem to chain-react in Henry Weems's favor."

"Dumb luck," says Scully,

Mulder agrees. "He's tapped into it somehow. He won big at poker, he survived getting thrown off a skyscraper, and now this."

Richie, Maggie's little boy, wanders into the apartment. As Scully stoops to shield him from seeing the dead body, she notices his skin is jaundiced. She ushers him back to his room. It is a typical little boy's room, complete with sports posters and team logos on just about everything. She can't help but notice an IV stand, assorted medical paraphernalia, and a Rube Goldberg–like contraption.

"Did Henry make this for you?" she asks as she sets the basketball-themed toy into motion. "That's pretty neat."

"He made it for me when I was in the hospital," says Richie. "He says it's because everything happens for a reason. Only just sometimes it's hard for us to see it."

Scully asks, "You went to the hospital because of your liver?"

"It doesn't work so good," says Richie. "Are the police looking for Henry?"

"Yeah," says Scully. "They just want to talk to him. Do you have any idea where he might have gone?"

Richie says, "Uh-uh. Since I got sick, he hardly ever goes out."

Mulder and Scully meet up outside Henry's front door.

"Mulder, as to your theory: Why would the world's most supernaturally lucky man work as a building superintendent? Why doesn't he just run down to the Illinois State Lottery, enter, and, you know, he'd win automatically?"

Inside an air vent, Henry watches and listens as the agents disappear down the hallway.

•

Richie is dozing inside his darkened bedroom when he is awakened by a figure sitting on his bed. It is Henry. Henry asks how Richie is feeling. Richie asks Henry why the police are looking for him.

Henry says, "Aah, you know. You do folks a favor, wire the joint for free cable. Don't worry about it. You gonna be okay by yourself for a while?"

Richie nods. "Where you going?"

"Something I gotta do I've been putting off. You get some rest."

Mulder and Scully are parked outside Henry's building. Scully is on her cell phone. She hangs up and gets inside the car, where Mulder is flipping through a file.

Mulder says, "Henry Weems has no police record, I assume."

"He has no record of any kind, Mulder," says Scully. "He doesn't earn enough in a year to file tax returns, he has no savings accounts, no checking accounts, no insurance. He doesn't even have a video rental card, for that matter. He doesn't even have a driver's license. It's like he's intentionally stayed off the radar. He's retired from the world."

"Ever since December of 1989. A commuter jet crashed into Lake Michigan carrying twenty-one passengers. There was one survivor."

Mulder holds up a newspaper clipping with the headline LOCAL MAN SURVIVES CRASH. It was Henry. Scully reads the clip.

"That was how he lost his eye," says Mulder. "Snowy night, Christmas rush. He had been bumped from three previous flights before they finally found a seat for him on the fateful plane. Guess what seat number?"

Reading the particulars, Scully says, "Thirteen?"

"Of Flight Seven."

"More good luck, you're saying,"

"Well, call it good or bad, but maybe that's where it all started," says Mulder. "What if a brand-new Henry Weems was plucked from the wreckage? One whose fortunes had been irrecovably, permanently changed? Before 1989, Henry worked a job for nine years in the train yards. After the accident, as you said, it's like he just disappeared off the face of the earth. He severed ties with all of his friends and moved out to Melrose Park."

Scully says, "There are millions of reasons for that, including survivor's guilt. But what doesn't track for me is why Henry Weems would drop off the map just because he suddenly became incredibly lucky."

"What doesn't track for me is why he's resurfaced after all these years. Why he's suddenly decided to use his luck in this way."

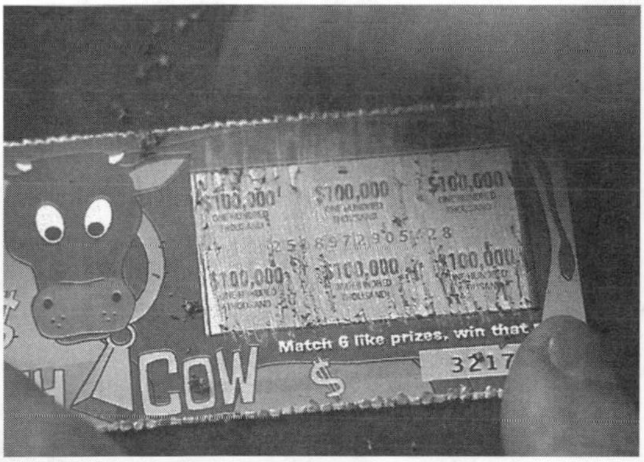

•

Henry enters Felicity's Mini-Mart, a small mom-and-pop store. He walks up to the checkout where Maurice Albert is working.

Henry asks what the lottery is up to. He is disappointed when Maurice tells him twenty-eight million.

"I don't need that much," he says.

"You don't need that much?" asks Maurice. "How much you need, Rockefeller?"

Henry says, "More like a hundred grand."

Maurice reaches over and tears off a brightly colored scratcher that promises WIN $100,000 INSTANTLY. Henry gives Maurice a dollar and takes his ticket over to a counter where a guy named Billy is having no luck scratching off his pile of tickets. Henry has never done this before and so he watches Billy to figure out what to do. He does not have a coin to rub off the ticket so he reaches for one of his tools and uses the bottle opener attachment to scratch. He scratches off the first spot and $100,000 is revealed. They all reveal the same amount. One more to go.

As he scratches the last spot, Henry's eyes travel to a TV news report. A news reporter is standing in front of his apartment building, reporting on the death of Angelo Bellini and saying that the police are looking for Henry Weems in connection with the vicious gangland slaying.

Henry continues to scratch. Suddenly . . .

"You did it!" says Billy. "You won a hundred grand!"

"Where do I collect the money?" asks Henry.

"They mail it to you. Eighty-two hundred dollars a month for twelve months," Maurice says.

"That's too long," Henry says.

He drops the winning ticket into the trash can. Billy and Maurice watch in disbelief. Billy dives head first into the can and comes up with the ticket. Maurice and Billy squabble momentarily about who owns the ticket.

"No, please, I wouldn't do that," says Henry. "Just throw it away. Something bad is gonna happen."

Billy says, "So long, suckers!"

Billy dashes out into the street, triumphantly turns to face Henry and Maurice, and is run over by a bakery truck.

•

Mulder, Scully, and the cops have arrived. Billy, miraculously still alive, is taken away in an ambulance. Scully is showing a picture of Henry to Maurice, who identifies him as the man who initially had the winning ticket.

Scully says, "And once you and he ascertained that the accident victim was still alive, this man fled on foot. After which, the man who was hit by the truck handed you the lottery card and said . . ."

"'Maurice, I want you to have this,'" finishes Maurice.

Maurice heads back into the store as Scully joins Mulder, who has been questioning the bakery truck driver.

Scully says, "For such a fortunate man, a lot of unfortunate things happen in Henry Weems's wake."

"Maybe that's all part of the package," says Mulder. "You can't have one without the other."

Scully says, "So, Mulder, Henry Weems came here to buy a lottery ticket. Why?"

"Maybe it's like you said. Why wouldn't the luckiest man in the world enter the lottery? Actually, that's exactly what you said about an hour after you said it."

•

Mulder and Scully are back at the apartment building and have discovered Henry's air vent hiding place. They determine that by using the air vent, Henry could be anywhere in the building. Scully heads off to start with the roof, while Mulder decides to start in the basement. They disappear into the stairwell.

Just then Sal, another of Jimmy Cutrona's toughs, wanders into the hallway. He draws his gun and pushes open the door to Henry's apartment. Finding nobody, he returns to the hallway, where he notices the air vent cover laying on the floor. He peers inside for a closer look.

Henry, who has taken refuge in a vacant apartment, wiles away his time carving a wooden figure with his leatherman's tool. He starts at the sound of a faint rattle of the doorknob and hides as the door opens. Mulder, lockpick in hand, walks in. He passes an air vent set low in the wall. Mulder pauses a moment, then drops down, yanks loose the air vent cover, and reaches into the duct, pulling Henry out by his ankles.

"Hey, hey, hey!" says Henry. "Watch the rough stuff!"

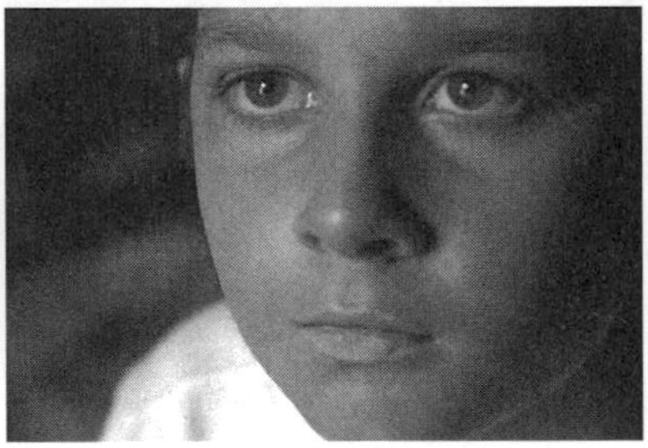

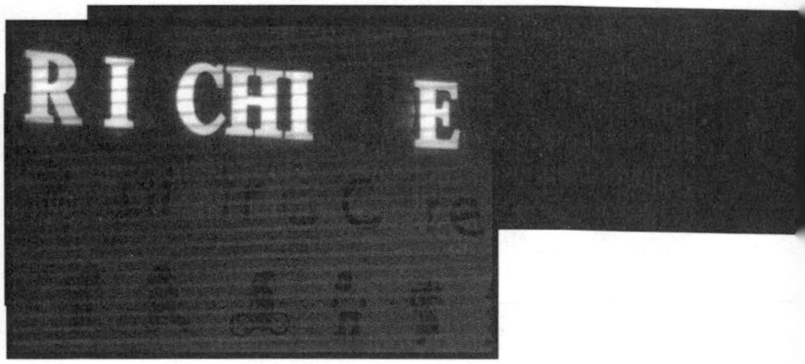

"Henry Weems," says Mulder, "you're a hard man to track down."

"I'm working here!"

"You and I are gonna have a talk. You sit right here and don't move, okay?"

Suddenly Henry's eyes widen.

"Oh crap," he says. "Not again."

Sal appears in the doorway and rushes in, his 9mm pointing directly at Henry. Sal aims at Henry and fires.

The bullet strikes Henry in the chest, ricochets, grazes Mulder's arm, sparks off the steel leg of a piece of furniture, bounces off the steel doorframe behind Sal, and changes direction one last time. Sal's expression changes as he drops his pistol and pitches forward. A small circle of blood begins to expand from his back.

Scully races into the apartment. She goes to Sal's body, feels for a pulse, and finds a faint one. Mulder is holding his arm. He stares at Henry, still on his feet, and the bloodless bullet hole in his work shirt. Henry reaches into his breast pocket and pulls out the bullet-dinged leatherman tool. He holds it up to Mulder and Scully.

•

Sal has been taken to St. Patricia's Hospital and is being brought to surgery. Mulder is having his flesh wound dressed by a nurse.

"Does it hurt?" asks Henry.

"Stings a bit," says Mulder. "But I'll live."

Scully enters, carrying an unopened pack of playing cards. Mulder opens the pack and gives the deck a quick shuffle. He rolls an instrument table between Henry and him, cuts the cards, and shows the nine of clubs.

"Nine of clubs," says Mulder, as he restacks the deck. "You go."

"It's a nightmare," says Henry. "You have no idea."

Mulder says, "I do. Because when you get lucky—really, really lucky—people around you tend to suffer. Is that right?"

"I think it's a balance thing," says Henry. "Something good happens to me, and everybody else has to take it in the keister."

"So you stay close to home mostly, keep a low profile," says Mulder. "But recently, you've been venturing out a little further. You've played poker with those mobsters."

Henry says, "I figure they could stand the trimming. Buncha goombah jerks. They got issues, man!"

"You don't mind so much if a few criminals get hurt," Mulder says. "But then you played the lottery."

"I knew I shouldn't have done that. I needed the money."

Mulder wants to know for what but Henry suddenly clams up.

"For Richie, right?" asks Scully.

"It's the complications from his hepatitis," says Henry. "He's on every donor list they got, but he's got a rare blood type, B negative. And he's CN something."

Scully says, "CMV negative. Cytomegalovirus."

"There's no way they're gonna find a donor in time," says Henry. "There's a treatment program in England. A hundred grand gets him in. It's experimental, but it's the best chance he's got now."

"I THINK IT'S A BALANCE THING. SOMETHING GOOD HAPPENS TO ME, AND EVERYBODY ELSE HAS TO TAKE IT IN THE KEISTER."
—Henry Weems

"What for?" Henry asks.

"I think you know."

Henry cuts the cards and holds up the ten of clubs.

"You win," says Mulder. "Double or nothing."

Mulder cuts to the king of diamonds. Henry hesitates, then cuts to the ace of spades.

"Mulder, what does that prove?" asks Scully.

"I think it proves that if we played this ten thousand times in a row, he would win ten thousand times in a row. He's incapable of losing. How does it feel to be the luckiest man in the universe, Henry?"

Henry asks the agents if he's under arrest. Mulder says no.

"However," says Scully, "you will need protection from Cutrona and his men."

Henry cuts the deck of cards and flips over a king of hearts. "I'd say they need protection from me."

Henry walks off. Scully is angry—at Mulder.

"I'm sorry, Mulder, that was utterly irresponsible," she says. "You're feeding the delusions of a man who's had three attempts made upon his life. We're supposed to be talking him into protective custody, not out of it."

"I'd agree with you," says Mulder, "if I thought his life was in danger."

Henry walks out of the hospital and past a town car that is pulling to the curb. Out of the car step Cutrona and his muscle Dominic. The mob boss stares after Henry and gives a nod to Dominic, who takes off on foot after the man.

•

Mulder is pulling on his jacket, getting ready to leave, when Scully restacks the deck of cards and cuts them in an attempt to beat Henry's king of hearts. Up comes the ace of hearts. Scully wins.

"Luckiest man in the world?" she says. "Hell, Mulder, *I* just beat him."

Mulder stares at the ace. He realizes something is wrong and runs after Henry.

Henry is standing on the corner, waiting for the light to change. He is unaware that Dominic, a switchblade in his hand, is closing in from behind.

"Henry!"

Henry turns to see Mulder rushing toward him. Dominic is only a few yards away. Henry takes a step off the curb and into oncoming traffic. The sound of air horns mixes with the sound of brakes locking up. There is a loud, sickening thump. As Dominic slinks away, mission accomplished, Mulder sprints to the aftermath of the accident. He is joined by Scully. Henry is on the ground. It doesn't look good.

•

Maggie walks into Richie's room and finds him sprawled out on the floor, playing with Henry's toy contraption. She tells him to get back in bed. The frail boy struggles to his feet as his mother helps him. She picks up the toy and sets it on a nearby toy chest.

"Don't you ever get tired of this thing?" she asks.

Richie says, "Henry says it's educational."

"Yeah, well, I don't want you believing everything Henry says," says Maggie. "Did you know the police are looking for him?"

"He said it is no big deal."

Maggie's voice fails her. Maggie's worst fears are magnified as she stares into the sickeningly yellow, jaundiced eyes of her son.

•

Henry is back at St. Patricia's Hospital, laying in an emergency room exam bed. He has a black eye and a few cuts but otherwise appears okay. Scully is standing over him, but he is in no mood to talk. Mulder heads her way as she draws the curtain around his trauma bay.

"How's he doing?" asks Mulder.

"Bruised ribs, a black eye. It certainly could have been worse," says Scully. "Don't tell me he just got lucky."

Mulder says, "Far from it. I guess what you said about streaks was right. Looks like his has just about run its course."

Scully says, "I don't mean to make light of his misfortune, but I may have knocked some sense into his head. He's agreed to testify against Cutrona."

•

Jimmy Cutrona is sitting in his favorite poker parlor when he is approached by Dominic.

Dominic says, "Our guy from the Justice Department just called. They're filing a federal warrant this afternoon. This mook Weems . . ."

"This mook Weems was street pizza last I heard from you!"

"He was," says Dominic. "I don't know what it is. Maybe he has some special ability. He's impervious or something. Anyway, we can't get to him. They got cops all over the hospital."

"Who says we have to get to *him*?"

•

Maggie has called the paramedics in the face of Richie's worsening condition, and he is on his way to the hospital. She is packing an overnight bag and Richie's toys and is about to follow him when Dominic suddenly appears.

•

Richie is in the hospital, sleeping as monitors keep tabs on his vital signs. Henry is standing over the boy, on fire with panic. The door opens behind him and Mulder and Scully enter.

"Did you find her?" asks Henry of Maggie's sudden disappearance.

Mulder shakes his head no.

Henry says, "You know Cutrona took her! He did it to keep me from testifying!"

Mulder says, "And he's who we're focused on. But there's no sign of a kidnapping, no ransom note."

"He's too smart for that," Henry points out. "It makes it very hard for us to obtain a search warrant."

Scully says that they will get it. But Henry rages that there is not enough time. He grabs his jacket and heads for the door. Mulder attempts to stop him.

"What if what I said before wasn't true, that your luck hasn't changed? Maybe all of this is happening for a reason."

"You're saying that Maggie getting taken is a good thing?"

"I'm saying what looks like it might be bad luck may not be bad luck. We can't tell yet. We're not in that position. We can't see the forest for the trees."

Henry storms out, leaving Mulder and Scully with Richie. Scully's dire prognosis for Richie is that if a donor isn't found in the next few hours it will be too late.

"Scully, what if everybody who gets involved with Henry Weems's life becomes an intregal part of his luck? Including you and I?"

"Mulder, you're speaking as if we're all trapped in one of those contraptions he builds," she says. Mulder pulls out a telephone book. Scully asks what he's doing. Mulder says that he's looking for Maggie Lupone.

"Luck is the overreaching force in this investigation. I say roll with it," he says.

He closes his eyes and stabs his finger into the book. It lands on a listing for THE MUHAYIM DAY CARE CENTER—NURTURING THE CHILDREN OF ISLAM SINCE 1983. Mulder sheepishly calls that a practice run, riffles through the pages again, and once again stabs his finger to the page. This time his finger lands on an ad for the GRAYSON LINEN SERVICE.

•

Elevator doors slide open to reveal Henry, flanked by Dominic.

"Look who came calling," says Dominic, as they walk down the corridor and up to Jimmy Cutrona.

"I wanted to tell you personally that there's no hard feelings," Henry says. "I'm not testifying against you. Just let Maggie Lupone go."

Cutrona tells Henry he doesn't know what he's talking about. Henry says not to jerk him around.

Cutrona says, "Jerk *you* around? You try to cheat me out of a hundred large, you kill Angie, you put Sal in the hospital, and I'm jerking you around?"

"I apologize for my choice of words. Please. Just let her go. Her kid's really sick. I don't care what happens to me."

"You'll care," says Cutrona. "By the time I'm finished, you'll definitely care."

•

His hands tied in front, Henry is roughly pushed through a doorway and down stairs to the Grayson Linen Service, where he sees Maggie unharmed but locked in a large chain-link cage. Dominic shoves Henry under a tall rolling ladder and against a table, which knocks an electric iron into a bucket of liquid. Dominic grabs Henry's bound hands and slips them over a floor-mounted electric winch crane. Dominic throws the switch and all the electrical equipment, including the iron in the bucket, begin to spark and zap.

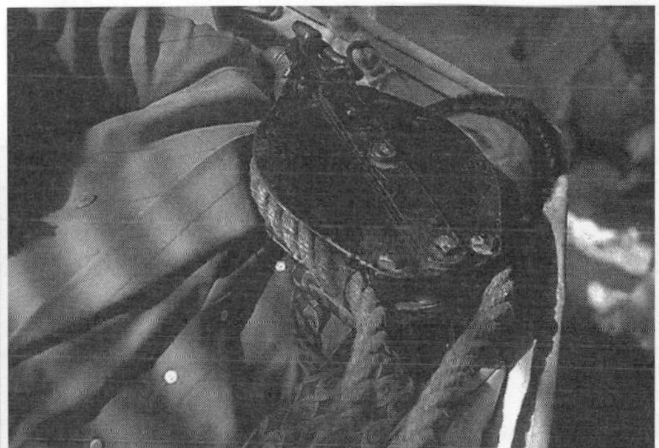

Cutrona hits the switch on the control box to raise Henry off the ground.

"Don't you hurt him, you sonofabitch!" screams Maggie.

Cutrona orders Dominic to get her out of the cage. The tough guy pulls the key out and jams the key into the lock. Just as Dominic grabs the door, the conduit cable from a lamp drops on the cage.

Dominic, shaking violently and smoking from the electric jolt, is thrown back into Henry, knocking him in an arc on the long crane arm. Cutrona tries to stop the winch but accidentally releases Henry, who falls onto a small folding table that contains a container of dry-cleaning fluid. The container catapults into the air and hits a block and tackle, which begins swinging. Cutrona sees the block and tackle heading straight for his head.

But it is too late.

Henry rushes to the cage and lets Maggie out. They go to the laundry cart, where they find what's left of Cutrona buried under the massive block and tackle. A door at the top of the stairs bursts open and Mulder leads a group of Chicago's finest and the FBI belatedly into the fray.

•

Meanwhile, Scully's vigil over Richie at the R. I. Childes Pediatric Care wing of the hospital is interrupted by a sudden brownout in the city. Lights dim and surge while the emergency power kicks in. As the brownout stabilizes, Scully happens to glance out into the corridor as the letters of the name of the wing have reilluminated to spell R I CHI E.

•

The luck continues back at the scene of the crime, where we discover that the now very deceased Cutrona is wearing a medic alert bracelet that indicates his blood type is B negative, the same as Richie's.

•

Cutrona's blood saves the day. The next day Richie is weak but smiling in the wake of his life-saving operation. Maggie is sitting next to him on his bed. She turns to Henry, Mulder, and Scully, who are standing behind the recovery room window. Henry stares in, and at the Goldberg-like contraption he had built for Richie.

"What are the odds of Cutrona being the perfect match?" asks Mulder. "A thousand to one? A million to one?"

"Maybe higher," says Scully. "Maybe everything does happen for a reason, whether we see it or not."

Maggie motions for Henry to come into the room.

Mulder says, "Maybe your luck is changing."

"Maybe," says Henry.

Henry steps into the room but can't resist setting the Goldberg-like toy into motion and watching as a tiny basketball drops into the hoop.

BACK STORY:

"The Goldberg Variation" was the brainchild of staff writer Jeffrey Bell. The writer had always wanted to do a story about the luckiest guy in the world, with luck being the titular X-File.

Bell explains, "I pitched the episode as a teaser of a guy falling thirty thousand feet out of an airplane into the ground and walking away unharmed. I wanted the whole thing to be about good luck and bad luck. From the beginning I saw the whole plot functioning as a Rube Goldberg device, with luck centering around the kid he's trying to help. I knew that the bad guy would die at the end and that his organs would be a perfect match for the kid. When you already have an ending, it helps."

Frank Spotnitz recalls that Bell's pitch was met with a lot of enthusiasm. But it was enthusiasm tempered with a certain amount of caution. "The episode had a lot of humorous moments that we were afraid of doing because as many people who like the funny ones hate the funny ones. But the idea seemed so strong to us that we decided to push it to later in the season because we wanted to scare the hell out of everybody during the first few episodes."

With the extra time, Bell set to writing the script, goosing up the "life as a Rube Goldberg machine" with an ersatz Mafia storyline and replacing the fall from an airplane idea with a more budget-friendly fall from the top of a hotel. It was quickly apparent to Bell that the Rube Goldberg–like devices would be the biggest production challenge and, potentially, the biggest headache, embodied in his quirky script. Bell consulted early on with Corey Kaplan and the rest of the art department to give them a head start on constructing both the toys and the real-life set pieces that triggered various elements of the storyline.

Rick Millikan remembers that casting the episode was relatively easy. He found the perfect thug types in Ramy Zada and Tony Longo. Casting the lucky guy, Henry Weems, caused Millikan to break a long-standing rule for the first time. "We don't like to repeat people on this show. But Willie Garston, who appeared previously as Quinton 'Roach' Freely in the third season episode 'The Walk,' was literally the best person for the job."

Filming "The Goldberg Variation" at various downtown Los Angeles locations was a welcome change of pace. The stunts, which included a sixty-foot fall from a building, a trampoline jump flying by the camera, and hanging a man from a ceiling fan blade by his shoelaces, were appropriately low-key and consistent with the comic proceedings.

Anderson recalls that working with the Rube Goldberg contraptions often required a lot of patience. "We loved working with the machines, but because they were machines, we ended up doing a lot of takes to make sure they would do what they were supposed to do."

While on the surface "The Goldberg Variation" was a rather uneventful shoot, behind the scenes there was a growing tension that something was not quite right with the execution of the promising idea. "We were biting our nails as we were watching the dailies," recalls Spotnitz. "In the back of our minds, there was the question of whether this was going to work."

"When they were first cutting the show together, there was an element of disappointment," says Chris Carter. "I kept hearing that the episode wasn't cutting together well and that there were things that just didn't work. Too many alarms were being sounded throughout the post process, which was lengthy. I started getting nervous because it was looking like we were in trouble and that we were coming out of the gate with a limp."

Paul Rabwin remembers that the episode had to be reedited "so that it would move like we wanted it to."

"Unfortunately," Rabwin said ruefully, "when we finally came up with a cut of the episode we liked, we discovered that it came up four minutes short of the running time of a one-hour episode."

Fortunately the schedule allowed time to bring the episode up to the demanding standards of *The X-Files*. Additional insert shots of the Rube Goldberg devices were shot. An additional scene was also written and shot for Act 2 in which Mulder and Scully are sitting in a car, discussing the back story. Finally, many months after its inception, "The Goldberg Variation" aired, an alternately heartwarming and provocative fantasy along the lines of last season's "The Rain King," that connected with audiences along primarily emotional rather than paranormal lines.

Carter's confidence in the idea of luck as an X-File was ultimately rewarded. "It was tight, funny, touching, and quirky."

Spotnitz was also satisfied. "We really had to reach to find the X-File in the story and, when all is said and done, there is nothing paranormal about it. What I tried to say with the story was that coincidences in life may not be coincidences at all but rather hidden forces and that luck may have a design all its own."

FACTS:

By the time the additional scene of Mulder and Scully talking in the car was shot, it was months later and Gillian Anderson had changed her hairstyle. For the reshoot, she wore a wig.

Ramy Zada, who portrays thug Joe Cutrona, played a college professor in the horror anthology film *After Midnight* and an unscrupulous doctor in the fright film *Two Evil Eyes*.

Nicholas Worth, the high-stakes card-playing Mr. Haas, has also appeared in a number of horror films, including *Don't Answer the Phone, Swamp Thing, Darkman,* and *Dark Angel*.

Willie Garson, the "lucky" Henry Weems, also plays recurring character Stanford Blanche on HBO's *Sex and the City*.

Bystanders watching the sixty-foot fall from the hotel were shocked when the stunt man hit the side of the building before crashing to the ground. They were relieved when they discovered it was only a dummy.

episode 7X07

ORISON

EPISODE: 7X07
FIRST AIRED: January 9, 2000
EDITOR: Heather MacDougall
WRITTEN BY: Chip Johannessen
DIRECTED BY: Rob Bowman

Scully's sense of right and wrong are put to the test as the agents track down an escaped Donnie Pfaster.

[redacted]

GUEST STARS:

Nick Chinlund (Donnie Pfaster)
Scott Wilson (Orison)
Steve Rankin (U.S. Marshal Joseph Daddo)
Irene Muzzy (Waitress)
Tara Buck (Runaway)
Lisa Kushell (Lady in Red)
Rick Cramer (Guard)
Emilio Rivera (Brigham)
Eric Buker (U.S. Marshal)

PRINCIPAL SETTINGS:

Marion, Illinois; Harrisburg, Illinois; Equality, Illinois; Washington, D.C.

"God's love will set us free," says Orison, an intense, passionate prison preacher, as he addresses a captive audience during services in the prison chapel of a maximum security prison in Marion, Illinois.

"And I believe if I pray for that love, if I get down on my knees and allow God to enter my hardened, lonely, miserable heart and change me through and through, that miracle will come. Now who here believes that with me?"

He moves among his flock, asking if they believe. Most of the convicts say they do believe. Except for one, who meets the preacher's exhortations with a mocking stare.

He is Donnie Pfaster.

Orison continues his preaching, growing more and more passionate. "Let God's love free you from your prison and deliver you to his side in heaven."

Orison moves through the crowd again, dipping his fingers in a glass of water and sprinkling a few drops on each man.

"Praise his holy name," says Orison. The men, getting into the spirit, recite back "Glory. Amen." over and over. "Glory. Amen. Glory," he says as he stands in front of Pfaster and sprinkles water on his face.

Pfaster sits unmoved.

•

Pfaster is walking through the prison uniform shop. He approaches a prison guard with a completed pair of pants for inspection.

"You believe that, Donnie?" asks the guard. "God loves a sack of crap like you?"

"Bible says," replies Pfaster.

"Bible says you kill women, cut their pinkies, you're gonna burn in hell."

Pfaster is fixated on Inmate Brigham, who is working at a blade-driven machine used for cutting shoe leather. His Bible rests nearby. The guard pulls a seam out of the pair of pants.

"Sorry," says the guard. "Just not good enough for the Illinois penal system."

The anguished cries of Inmate Brigham are heard. He holds up both hands to reveal that he has cut off his fingers. The guard talking with Donnie rushes to the injured inmate. Other guards unsheath riot sticks and advance on the cons, who are gathering to see what happened.

Donnie Pfaster sees everybody suddenly moving in super slow motion . . . except him. Pfaster moves through the guards and the mayhem toward an exit. He is amazed at what is happening to him. He looks back one more time and walks calmly through the exit.

•

A weird sound, symphonic, musical in a creepy sort of way, wells up over Scully's sleeping form. A gust of wind begins to play at her face. She sits up as if from a bad dream.

The wind is now stronger, blowing through her bedroom and disturbing the contents on her bureau, except for her gun and a Bible, which sit side by side. Scully closes the open window and turns to her clock radio.

It displays 6:66. She picks up the clock, puzzled. The power flickers off for a moment, then comes back on. She looks at the time on the clock again. It now reads 6:06.

•

U.S. Marshal Joseph Daddo is reciting the criminal record of Donnie Pfaster to Mulder and Scully and a group of marshals.

Daddo says, "Life without chance of parole. For the premeditated and sadistic sexual murders of five Twin Cities women in 1994. Donald Addie Pfaster. You two put this man

away." He hands a file to Scully, who appears somewhat shaken.

"Someone forgot to throw away the key," says Mulder.

"Well, that's another story," says Daddo. "Right now we have to apprehend this man. We'd use all the help you can give us in understanding exactly who it is we're after."

Mulder speaks to the room: "Donnie Pfaster is a death fetishist. A collector of bone and dead flesh. Of toenails and hair. It's what floats his boat. What gets him off."

"He's a sick man," says Daddo.

"Sick would describe him," agrees Mulder. "We found women's fingers in his freezer. He liked to eat them with his peas and carrots."

"So it's just women he's after?" Daddo clarifies.

"Just women," Mulder reminds him. "He spent five years in here thinking about only that. I'm sure he's worked up quite an appetite."

Scully hands the file back to Daddo.

"I happen to know you two agents have a particular forte," Daddo says. "A thing for, what is it called, the supernatural. Now, the circumstances of the escape—"

"I promise you there's nothing supernatural about this man," says Scully, cutting him off. "Donnie Pfaster is just plain evil."

Scully walks out of the room.

•

Scully has entered the prison chapel. She hears the sound of music, the haunting refrain of the oldies song "Don't Look Any Further." Scully is having a very private reaction to the song. She turns to find Mulder standing behind her.

"Case closed. Didn't look at the file, did you?" he asks.

"A man escaped from prison," says Scully.

"Not a man," says Mulder. "Donnie Pfaster. And he didn't just escape, he walked out. Walked out of a maximum security facility, and no one seems to know how he did it."

"Isn't that why we're here?"

"It's why I'm here. I don't know about you. Why are you here?"

Scully can't form an answer.

Mulder picks up on her discomfort.

"Go home, Scully."

"Mulder, this case doesn't bother me."

"The man abducted you," Mulder reminds her gently. "Donnie Pfaster did a number on your head like I've never seen. It's okay to walk away."

"Mulder, that man does things to people no one should ever have to think about. It's not a question of if I should stay. I don't have a choice. So let's get to work."

"This isn't the first incident. Two prisoners have escaped from maximum security facilities in neighboring states over the past year. At 6:06 yesterday morning, Donnie Pfaster made it three."

Scully pauses in hearing it happened at 6:06.

"And what's so supernatural about that?" she asks.

"Dozens of witnesses, guards, and staff, and no one seems to remember anything. For a while they didn't even know these guys were missing."

"Have they been apprehended?" asks Scully.

"No. Neither of the men have ever been seen again."

•

Mulder and Scully interrogate Inmate Brigham, who, miraculously, still has all ten fingers. Brigham says he has no idea how Pfaster broke out. Mulder reminds the prisoner that he was in the garment shop with Pfaster. Brigham still claims he doesn't know anything about what happened.

"But you had something happen, you had an incident," says Mulder.

"Yeah. Something like that."

"You cried out to the guards. That you'd cut your hands."

"My fingers, man," says Brigham as he holds his hands out to Mulder. "I saw 'em all cut off."

"Others say they saw them, too," says Mulder.

"No, but I felt them cut off," says Brigham.

"How do you explain that?" asks Mulder.

Brigham smiles. "God works in mysterious ways, brother."

Mulder tries an experiment. He raises his forearm off the table, palm open. In response, Brigham raises and lowers his foot while repeating, "Glory. Amen."

•

"Posthypnotic suggestion. Did you see him?" Mulder asks Scully later when they are alone.

Scully says, "You mean did I see him raise his foot? Yes, I saw that."

"A programmed behavior prompted and manifested by suggestion. In this case a rhythmic motion of the hands." He demonstrates, raising his arm. "Producing an unconscious act in a conscious state. It doesn't work on you," Mulder adds.

"I know what hypnosis is, Mulder."

"Group hypnosis."

"If you're suggesting that Donnie Pfaster escaped from prison using a technique from a Vegas lounge act, I'd think again."

"Mesmer was able to hypnotize and command entire audiences," says Mulder.

"So how would Donnie acquire this amazing ability?"

"I'm not saying that it was Donnie."

"Well, then who?"

Mulder says, "Three inmates are missing from three separate prisons. One man has had possible contact with each of those cons. The prison chaplain. Glory. Amen. Not God. The chaplain."

Scully looks in the direction of a ceiling air vent from which she again hears the song "Don't Look Any Further."

"Scully. What?" asks Mulder.

"That song," says Scully. "Can you hear that?"

They walk to the vent.

"Barely," he says.

"I haven't heard that song since high school," she says. "That's the second time I've heard it in the last hour."

"If it was a makeout song, I think it would be ruined forever now, huh?"

Scully ignores the joke, lost in her own thoughts.

•

A waitress is working the counter inside a Harrisburg, Illinois, bus station diner. The door opens and Donnie Pfaster, now in civilian clothes, walks in and takes a booth at the back of the restaurant. He stares at the waitress, not at her ample cleavage but rather her overly red fingernails.

"Looking for something to eat?" asks a seductive voiced teenage runaway with red hair who looks to be in need of a bath.

"Me?" asks Pfaster.

"How about today's special?" she asks, suggestively.

Pfaster looks at her hands. Her nails are raw and dirty. A distinctive tattoo is on her ring finger. She is nervous at Pfaster's attention to her hands and pulls them off the table. She asks if he's a narc. He assures her he's not.

"You're looking at my hands," she says.

"You could use a buff and polish," says Pfaster.

"What are you, a freak?"

"I just got out of prison."

The waitress walks over and yells at her to leave the customers alone.

"I'll do it for free," Pfaster says.

"You just got out of prison and you want to give me a manicure?" asks the runaway.

"I'll even do your cuticles," he says.

Pfaster is distracted by a familiar fire-and-brimstone voice.

"You receive the Lord's grace and this is your thanks?"

It is Orison standing behind him.

"Who do you think got you out of prison?" asks Orison.

"I don't care," says Pfaster. "I'm busy right now."

"The grace of God got you out. And it's the only thing that will keep you out."

The runaway looks at Donnie. "I thought you were kidding."

Orison says, "He's chosen you, Donnie."

Pfaster looks out the window as U.S. Marshals in unmarked cars pull up and walk toward the counter. Leading them is Marshal John Daddo. Pfaster is worried. The girl splits.

Pfaster rises from his seat.

"You called them on me," says Pfaster.

"No."

"Then do something!"

"I have a car," says Orison.

"We're aren't going to make it to the car."

Orison takes out the car keys and swings them back and forth. "It's within His power." Daddo and the other policeman walk into the diner, heading down the aisle toward Donnie and Orison. "Glory. Glory. Amen," Orison begins to chant.

Everything goes into slow motion except Pfaster and Orison. The waitress screams as one of the customers reaches over and rips her blouse. She reaches for a pot of hot coffee to throw in his face.

Pfaster looks at the thrown coffee in mid-flight and the marshals ever so slowly drawing their guns. The marshals' attention is totally on the waitress. Everything suddenly returns to real time. The marshals have their guns drawn on an empty asile. Donnie and Orison have dissapeared. Daddo and the rest of the marshals stare in confusion at what just happened.

Orison looks for Pfaster in the parking lot. Pfaster, at the wheel of an old car, careens out of the parking lot and races toward Orison. The car, with the runaway in the passenger seat, runs down Orison, knocking him onto the hood, and then he falls to the ground. The car slams on the brakes and reverses straight for him. Orison manages to roll out of the way.

At the last possible moment, the car reverses again and heads out, leaving Orison lying in the dust.

•

Mulder and Scully pull up and make their way to the restaurant, where they find Daddo.

"Was he here?" asks Mulder.

"We're trying to determine that," says Daddo, still shaken from earlier.

"Did you see him?" asks Scully.

"Well, that's a good question," Daddo says. "We thought we saw something but apparently we didn't."

"We got a call about a possible sighting of the suspect," says Mulder. Daddo nods. "Well, something happened here."

The waitress volunteers that some guy got hit by a car. Daddo offers up an ID that describes Orison as a prison chaplain. Scully again hears the song "Don't Look Any Further" coming from somewhere. She finds it being played on a radio behind the counter, where she asks the waitress to turn up the volume. She listens intently.

"COME WITH ME, SCOUT. I'LL SHOW YOU HOW THE REVEREND TALKS TO GOD."—Mulder

•

Scully has gone to the hospital where Orison has been taken and is there when he opens his eyes. He asks who she is.

Orison says, "Believe in the Lord, Agent Scully. He believes in you."

"That's nice, but my partner and I are more concerned with several disappearances from maximum security facilities that seem to involve you."

"Don't be concerned," says Orison. "God has them."

Scully does not know what he means.

"You're a believer, aren't you?" asks Orison.

"This has nothing to do with me, sir."

"It has everything to do with you. You have faith. Have had faith. You hear Him calling you but you're unsure what to do."

Scully holds out the cross around her neck. "That's not exactly a long shot, sir."

"You stand as you do now. Neither here, nor there. Longing but afraid. Waiting for a sign. When the signs are everywhere."

Scully asks, "What happened to the inmates, sir?"

"Everything has a reason, Scout." Scully freezes at this. "Everything on God's earth.

Every moment of every day, the Devil waits for but an instant. As it is, it has always been. The Devil's instant is our eternity."

Mulder enters the room, carrying an envelope. He asks Orison about how he does it, whatever it is.

"His is the word," says Orison. "I am but the messenger who delivers it."

Mulder opens the envelope and hands Orison some photos.

Mulder says, "Well, this delivery arrived a little late and a little cold, as a matter of fact. I thought you'd want to see it."

The gory photo shows the runaway from the restaurant laying dead in a bathtub, her hair shorn in ragged clumps and the fingers cut off one hand.

"What is this?" Orison asks, shaken by the photo.

"Blood of the lamb, Reverend. Handiwork of Mr. Donnie Pfaster."

"Where is he, Reverend?" asks Mulder.

"He took my car," says Orison, his bravado gone. "She wasn't supposed to die."

"No. Donnie was supposed to die. You were supposed to kill him. That's why you freed him. God knows you're capable of it." Mulder tells Scully, "The Reverend Orison is really Robert Gailen Orison, convicted in 1959 of first degree murder. Served twenty-two years in Soledad."

"God spoke to me. He told me to look after Donnie."

"When God spoke to you, Reverend, did he happen to mention where Donnie was headed?"

•

Mulder and Scully leave Orison. Mulder starts to go. Scully wants to know where he's going.

"To prove this guy's a liar," he says.

"How do you prove someone isn't being directed by God? You don't believe that it happens?" Scully demands.

"God's a spectator, Scully. He just reads the box scores."

"I don't believe that," says Scully.

"You think God directs that man? You think he directs him to kill?"

Scully says she thinks Pfaster is not dead and that the other escaped convicts may not be dead.

"So what, you think God directs him to let the prisoners out to kill?"

"No. But I believe that the reverend believes what he's saying. That it's God working through him."

"Plenty of nut bags do." Scully doesn't respond. "Has he ever spoken to you?"

"I'm trying not to take offense," says Scully evenly.

"What did he say?" asks Mulder.

"Mulder, I've heard that song three times now. That might not mean anything to you, but it means something to me."

Mulder wants to know what it means.

Scully says, "I never thought about it before. It never meant anything to me until yesterday when it made me remember something. When I was thirteen, my father was stationed in San Diego. I was listening to the radio, to that song, when my mother came in and told me that my Sunday school teacher'd been killed. He'd been murdered in his front yard. And that's the first time that I ever felt there was real evil in the world. Mulder, Reverend Orison called me Scout. That's the same name my Sunday school teacher called me. Donnie Pfaster escaped from prison at 6:06 A.M. That's exactly the same time I woke up yesterday morning when my power went out."

"So what do you think that God is telling you?" asks Mulder.

Scully doesn't know.

Mulder says, "Come with me, Scout. I'll show you how the reverend talks to God."

•

A car radio broadcasts the news about a manhunt for Donnie Pfaster and a description of the car he's driving. Pfaster opens the driver's-side door and begins to rip the vinyl top off in an attempt to disguise his vehicle. He goes to the trunk and opens it. Inside are bloody prison uniforms with different names on them. Pfaster shoves them back into the trunk. He rummages inside a duffel bag and finds Orison's wallet and a different set of keys.

•

Mulder and Scully are in the hospital neurology lab.

"It's a cerebral edema," says Mulder as they look at a 3-D computer image of the brain.

"A swelling of the brain," says Scully. "A trauma not uncommon with this kind of head injury or accident."

"Except this isn't accidental," says Mulder, pointing to a particular spot on the 3-D image.

"The cause, in fact, as it was stated to me, is self-inflicted. There's a small hole here in the skull which allows oxygen into the brain cavity. The result of which is the Reverend Orison has three times the normal blood volume pumping through his brain."

"And he did this himself?" asks Scully.

"My guess is he probably did it when he first got into prison, when he first learned how to use its powers."

Scully is confused.

Mulder says, "There's a theory that at this point in human evolution, our mental capabilities are limited only by inadequate blood supply. In fact, centuries ago, in the Peruvian Andes, holy men used to physically remove parts of their skulls in order to increase blood volume. Or drill small holes."

"So this hole in his head enables Reverend Orison to help these prisoners escape."

"The practitioners of this found that they could perform certain mental tricks, one of which they called 'stopping the world.' "

"Well, nobody can stop the world, Mulder. I don't care how many holes they have in their head."

"Yeah, but maybe they can alter the perception of it. Creating a disparate version of reality, which they can then project through hypnosis."

"But why? I mean, even if he could . . . why?" asks Scully.

"Donnie Pfaster is serving a life sentence without the possibility of parole. That's the final judgment as far as society is concerned. But not in the eyes of God. Or in the eyes of a man who thinks he's God's tool."

Scully asks if Reverend Orison meant to kill Pfaster, why he is still alive.

Mulder says, "I don't know. Maybe he unleashed something that he couldn't control. Maybe he thought he was opening the door of perception but then unwittingly he opened the gates of hell."

•

Orison is being watched by a marshal. The marshal reads a newspaper. Suddenly he hears a low whisper seemingly coming from the direction of Orison. Orison is mumbling the mantra, "Glory. Amen. Glory. Amen." over and over.

The real world lapses into super slow motion. The deputy sits zombielike, his paper moving ever so slowly. Orison slides out of bed, pulls out his IV, and takes the marshal's gun.

•

In a shabby one-bedroom apartment in Equality, Illinois, Donnie Pfaster, clad only in underwear, has just finished putting four amputated fingers inside a Ziploc bag, which he puts inside the freezer compartment of the kitchen's refrigerator.

There is a knock on the door. Pfaster opens it to reveal an overly made up and dressed woman.

"Are you Donald?" she asks. "I'm from Tip Top Gentlemen's Service."

She enters the apartment.

"This isn't your place, is it?" she asks.

"No," says Pfaster. "Why?"

The hooker says, " 'Cause I was coming up the stairs and got stopped by the landlord, like it's any of his business. He told me that some Reverend Orison lives here. Now you ain't no preacher, are you?"

"No."

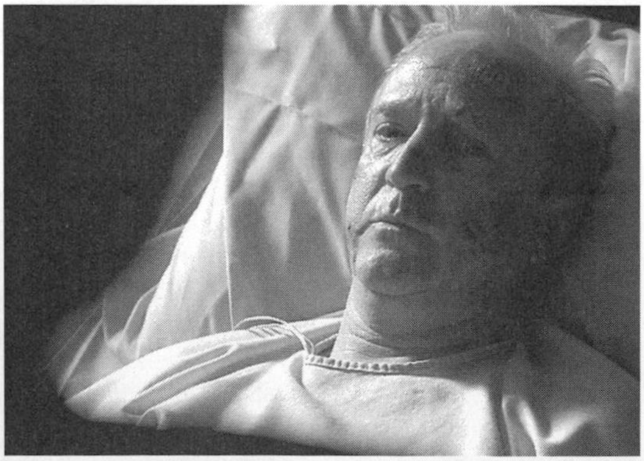

"Good, 'cause they always like the weirdest things," she says, smiling.

She moves into the living room and begins to take off her sweater. Pfaster is eyeing her fingers and her red hair. The hooker notices Pfaster's look.

"You okay?" she asks.

"Yes."

"Something you wanna say?"

"Love your hair," says Pfaster.

•

The hooker has no problem with Pfaster's suggesting that she take a bubble bath. But she gets a little spooked when Pfaster comes into the bathroom carrying an armful of shampoos and conditioners.

"What are you doing?" she asks.

"Is your hair chemically treated?" he asks.

"My hair?" she asks.

"I don't know which product to use."

"You're not using no product," she insists. "I'm clean, my hair's clean. If you're gonna be that weird about it, I oughta just leave."

"I'm being a gentleman," he says.

The hooker is no longer amused, "Well, be a gentleman and get me a towel. I'm gonna get outta here."

As he is wrapping the towel around her, he notices that the red-headed hooker he was promised is wearing a wig. In a rage, Pfaster grabs it off her head and flings it across the room.

"They lied to me," he says. "You lied to me!"

Pfaster steps toward the woman. The hooker grabs a lighted candle off the windowsill and flings it at Pfaster's face, blinding him with hot wax. She punches him and he falls back, hitting his head on the edge of a sink.

•

Mulder and Scully enter Orison's hospital room. They see that he is missing. The marshal still sits frozen, holding the newspaper. Mulder gently slaps his face, waking him from the trance. The marshal looks dazed and confused.

"The prisoner," says Scully. "The man you were guarding in this room. What happened to him?"

Mulder says, "He's gone, Scully. So's the marshal's gun."

Scully asks, "You didn't see him?" The marshal begins to look around the room, confused.

"Let's go, Scully," Mulder says.

Scully notices a notepad on the night table next to the bed and picks it up. The name of the song that's been haunting Scully, "Don't Look Any Further," is on it.

"What does this mean?" asks Scully.

"Did you tell him?" asks Mulder.

"No. I only told you."

Mulder suggests that Orison must have heard them discussing it in the hallway. They argue about whether either of them mentioned the song title.

"Then maybe this was meant for you. Don't look any further."

Mulder walks away, leaving Scully confused.

•

Pfaster comes to, blood running down his face. He is woozy. He slowly rises and looks at himself in the bathroom mirror.

Staring back at him is Orison, a gun pointed at Pfaster.

"Whosoever sheddeth man's blood, by man shall his blood be shed," says Orison.

"What are you doing?" asks Pfaster.

"Taking you home," says Orison. Pfaster slowly turns to face him. "The wicked will be punished."

•

It's night. Orison digs a shallow grave in a deserted ravine. Pfaster stands watching, hands tied behind his back. Orison, emotional to the point of madness, spouts scripture. Orison points the gun at Pfaster and asks if he's sorry. Pfaster mumbles something, unintelligible through his sobbing.

Orison steps closer and asks why he's crying.

Orison insists, his gun touching Pfaster's chest, "Beg His forgiveness for what you did to those girls. For what you did to all those poor, helpless girls."

"My violence is always waiting," says Pfaster. "For an instant. For when His back is turned. You can see it now."

The reverend asks, "Are you crying for your sins or for yourself?"

Pfaster stops crying. "No, Reverend, I cry for you. Because you cannot kill me." He raises his head.

Orison's eyes go wide with fear—for he is now staring into the face of the Devil.

•

The next morning, Mulder and Scully join a group of marshals at the ravine, where they

find three completed graves and the partially buried body of Orison.

"It's funny," says Mulder. "When all is said and done, there's not much mystery in murder."

"For that I owe you an apology, Mulder," says Scully.

"What do you mean?" asks Mulder.

"You were right. I was looking too hard for connections that weren't there. Orison was a murderer, plain and simple. He liberated those prisoners so that he could bring them out here and pass judgment on them."

"In his own twisted way, he was making good with his God. Glory. Amen. Let's go home, Scully."

"You know, Donnie Pfaster placed the call to the police that led us out here. It's almost like he's begging us to hunt him down."

"This X-File is over. Lying dead there in a grave he dug himself. Let's let the U.S. Marshals take over from here. Don't look any further, Scully."

•

The door to Scully's apartment opens. It is Donnie Pfaster. He walks through Scully's apartment and into her bedroom. He spots her Bible at the foot of her bed. He opens a bureau drawer and puts it away.

Scully enters her apartment. Turning on the lights, she heads for her bedroom. She sets her gun on her dresser and starts to undress.

Inside a darkened closet, Pfaster is watching her every move.

Scully finishes buttoning her flannel pajamas. She picks up her clothes and carries them toward the closet. Just as she is about to open the closet, she notices that her clock radio is once again displaying 6:66. The power goes out and the lights go off. Scully looks around nervously.

Pfaster bursts out of the closet and attacks.

•

Mulder's apartment is empty. The phone begins to ring. The answering machine picks up.

"Agent Mulder, Marshal Joe Daddo in Marion. Just talked to a call girl who ID'd Donnie Pfaster as an attacker. Claims Pfaster got real upset when she was wearing a red wig. Upset she wasn't a redhead. This mean anything to you? Appreciate a call back."

Mulder enters his apartment. He ignores the red blinking message light as Scully and Pfaster are in a violent hand-to-hand confrontation. Scully gouges his eyes. She lunges for her gun, but just as she grabs it, Pfaster slams her repeatedly into her mirror, shattering it. She hits him viciously in the head, bringing him down. She then pulls her bookcase down on top of him and runs to the phone. Pfaster recovers and follows, knocking Scully to the ground face first. He straddles her, grabbing her hands and twisting them behind her.

"Go back to hell," yells Scully.

Pfaster responds by yanking her hands upward. He examines Scully's fingers and nails.

"Who does your nails, Girly Girl?" asks Pfaster as he ties Scully's hands with her nylons.

"Let me go. The only reason why you're alive is because I asked the judge for your life. And the only reason why you're alive is because we didn't kill you when we could."

"You're the one that got away," says Pfaster. "You're all I think about."

"I'm a federal agent," she says. "You do anything to me, they will not give you a break this time."

"I'm going to run you a bath," he says.

Scully starts to scream. Pfaster covers her mouth with his hand.

•

Mulder is brushing his teeth, getting ready for bed. He picks up the clock radio to change the setting, accidentally hitting the radio PLAY button. He sets the radio down as he continues to brush his teeth. The station is playing "Don't Look Any Further."

•

Pfaster drags a bound and gagged Scully back to the closet and pushes her down on the floor.

"Now be good and don't cause me any problems," he says as he shuts the door on her.

The phone rings as Pfaster passes through the living room. He ignores it and turns on Scully's stereo. Strains of the song "Don't Look Any Further" begin to fill the room.

•

Mulder is in bed, the phone to his ear, waiting for Scully to pick up. When she doesn't, he hangs up.

•

Pfaster is filling Scully's tub with hot water.

Scully is trying to work her hands free while peering under the closet door, where she spots her holstered gun lying on the floor. She works the closet door open. As Donnie finishes preparing for her bath, she begins to scoot across the floor on her stomach. Pfaster leaves the bathroom, not noticing Scully hiding on the floor under her bed. He continues into the kitchen, and she struggles toward her gun.

In the kitchen, Pfaster searches for candles, matches, and knives. He brings out a tray of sharp knives. He rummages around and finds a pair of kitchen shears, which he takes, with the candles, back to the bathroom. All the while, the song "Don't Look Any Further" continues to play in the background.

Scully has almost made it to her gun. Pfaster reenters the bedroom and Scully freezes in fear. Pfaster doesn't notice and moves into the bathroom, beginning to light candles for Scully's bath. Scully manages to get her hands in front of her and begins crawling forward.

Time slows again as Mulder slams through Scully's door, his gun at the ready. He pushes Pfaster, yelling at him to get his hands in the air. Pfaster's eyes move to Scully standing in the doorway, who has untied herself and pulled the gag out of her mouth.

There is intensity in her eyes. A war is being waged behind those eyes, her sense of morality and religion struggling with a primitive sense of justice. Pfaster stares at Scully. The maniacal music sound wells up. The madness is shattered by a single gunshot. Scully, holding her gun, looks down at it in horror.

•

Washington, D.C., police and a number of technical support have swarmed into Scully's apartment. A body bag is being wheeled out.

The bathroom door opens. Scully exits, goes directly to her bedroom, and closes the door behind her. Mulder enters, finding Scully looking out the window, lost in thought.

"You want to pack some things, we can get out of here."

Scully opens her bureau drawer. She sees her Bible and takes it out.

"You can't judge yourself," Mulder says.

Scully sits down on the bed. Mulder attempts to console her.

"Maybe I don't have to," she says.

"The Bible allows for vengeance."

"But the law doesn't," says Scully.

"The way I see it, he didn't give you a choice. And my report will reflect that, in case you're worried. Donnie Pfaster would've surely killed again if given the chance."

"He was evil, Mulder. I'm sure about that without a doubt. But there's one thing that I'm not sure of."

"What's that?" asks Mulder.

"Who was at work in me. Or what. What made me pull the trigger."

"You mean, if it was God?"

"I mean, what if it wasn't?" she says.

BACK STORY:

Two of the most memorable *X-Files* episodes, "Beyond the Sea" and "Irresistible," had one thing in common. They both featured a psychologically tormented Scully in a torturous cat-and-mouse emotional game with the personification of pure evil. Those episodes were the stuff of pure, primordial horror and the idea was most certainly worth visiting again.

But the road to "Orison" would not be a smooth one.

Chip Johanessen, who had been an executive producer on *Millennium*, had an idea about a prisoner with the ability to stop time. An intriguing secondary story involved the strange effect this prisoner would have on Scully through a mysterious song from her childhood. Carter, Spotnitz, and Shiban immediately saw the possibilities in "Orison." For Carter it was the eerie similarity to "Beyond the Sea" that was appealing.

After reading Johanessen's original draft of the script, Carter and Spotnitz came up with the idea of bringing back Donnie Pfaster, the nail and hair fetishist and serial killer from the Season 2 episode "Irresistible."

Carter says, "We had talked about possibly revisiting some old monsters this season, and this seemed like the perfect opportunity. We knew that Donnie had some history with Scully from 'Irresistible' and that bringing him back would set up all sorts of possibilities with Scully."

Spotnitz was likewise enthused at the idea of bringing an old *X-Files* nemesis back. "For me, what really justified bringing Donnie back was the final act of the script when Donnie comes for Scully and she ends up shooting him full of holes. Once we decided to bring Donnie back, we all started to get excited by the script."

John Shiban relates that one of the key decisions around this time was to make Donnie Pfaster bigger than life. "We decided late in the process to turn him into this totally demonic character, essentially evil as an entity."

Casting "Orison" was both easy and difficult. Easy because Nick Chinlund, whose intensity as Pfaster had helped make "Irresistible" a standout episode, was naturally brought back. But finding the right actor to portray the dual nature of Orison was a tougher task. Casting director Rick Millikan finally settled on veteran character actor Scott Wilson.

On the production side, "Orison" was shaping up as one of the most physically and visually demanding stand-alone episodes of the season. Stunt coordinator Danny Weselis took one look at the stunt list, which had the stunt people being tossed through mirrors and bodies bouncing off moving cars, and proclaimed "Orison" "the most violent show I've done in two years."

Rob Bowman was brought in for what would be one of only two episodes he would direct this season. His first piece of homework was to revisit "Irresistible" and reacquaint himself with the haunting rhythms of this death fetishist and, in particular, the psychological interaction between Pfaster and Scully.

Spotnitz remembers that going back to the original Pfaster story was intregal to giving "Orison" a substantial new direction. "The problem with doing this was that ninety percent of the good stuff was done the first time in 'Irresistible.' That story was terrifying and scary. It was going to be tough to compete with that. But what the script for 'Orison' was giving us was another bad guy who was attempting to serve God by liberating prisoners and then killing them. We also knew the intensity between Scully and Pfaster would be deeper and more involved. And that it would end up taking Scully someplace she had never been before."

Anderson had long ago proclaimed "Irresistible" one of her all-time favorite episodes. But reuniting with actor Chinlund and the Donnie Pfaster character brought back memories. "Working with Nick Chinlund again was freaky. I had almost forgotten how intense he was."

Easily one of the most technically complex sequences in the episode was the opening scene in which Pfaster stops time and walks out of the prison. Bowman shot multiple takes using different film speeds. The most challenging element of this scene fell to actor Chinlund, who had to zigzag around actors with the aid of a motion control camera. Bowman blocked out numerous actors who would be composited digitally into the scene in postproduction.

The "Orison" demon was a classic example of recycling at its finest. Effects man John Vulich wanted to pay homage to the makeup design of "Irresistible." While waiting for the official makeup shots from that episode's makeup man, Toby Landella, to show up, Vulich turned to *X-Files* fan sites on the Internet and found a number of photos he was able to use as models to get started. One of Vulich's employees, Brian Blair, was the perfect fit for actor Nick Chinlund, and so served as the demonic stand-in for the actor.

The fight between Scully and Pfaster in Scully's apartment was a knockdown-dragout sequence that took a day and a half to film. Stunt doubles for Anderson and Chinlund took the hardest hits, but Anderson recalls that she came by her many bumps and bruises honestly.

"Some of the stunts I had to do," she says, remembering the discomfort. "I had to crawl under the bed with my legs and hands tied. It was take after take of having to crawl like a worm. I got bruised and swollen."

The song from her childhood that haunts Scully, "Don't Look Any Further," is a minor classic of sorts, originally recorded by the Temptations and covered by a half dozen other performers. Unfortunately, what producer Paul Rabwin found when he went looking for just the right version for the episode was "that none of them really worked."

Rabwin adds, "We felt we needed someone to record an original version of the song. We approached Lyle Lovett but he wasn't available. But a lot of us admired singer-songwriter John Hiatt and so we called him. He was really up for it and he sent us a demo of the song. It was chilling, eerie, and soulful . . .

"It was perfect."

FACTS:

Nick Chinlund and David Duchovny had crossed paths once before *The X-Files* when the actor appeared in an episode of the erotic anthology series *Red Shoe Diaries*, which was hosted by Duchovny.

Scott Wilson's acting résumé includes the films *In Cold Blood, The Ninth Configuration*, and *The Exorcist III*.

Chris Carter came up with the idea of having Scully's bedside clock read 666.

Set costume designer Nancy Collini reports that Gillian Anderson required ten pairs of pajamas for her fight sequence.

episode 7X08

THE AMAZING MALEENI

EPISODE: 7X08
FIRST AIRED: January 16, 2000
EDITOR: Lynne Willingham
WRITTEN BY: Vince Gilligan, John Shiban, & Frank Spotnitz
DIRECTED BY: Thomas J. Wright

When a magic trick goes very wrong, Mulder and Scully are drawn into the world of small-time hoods and big-time illusions, where seeing is not necessarily believing.

GUEST STARS:

Ricky Jay (The Amazing Maleeni/ Albert Pinchbeck)
Jonathan Levit (Dude/Billy LaBonge)
Robert LaSardo (Cissy Alvarez)
Jim Maniaci (Bullethead)
Rick Marzan (Holding Cell Officer)
Mark Chaet (Bank Officer)
Dennis Keiffer (Bullethead)
Dan Rice (Uniform Cop)
Sherri Howard (Female Employee)
J. David (Young Boss)
Steven Barr (Courier Guard)
Adam Vernier (Driver)

PRINCIPAL SETTING:

Los Angeles, California

An old utility van is parked in an alley behind an out-of-service merry-go-round on the Santa Monica Pier, overlooking the Pacific Ocean. On the side of the van is painted:

THE AMAZING MALEENI

Maleeni sits on the van's rear bumper, dressed in a traditional magician's tuxedo, hands on his knees, deep in concentration. He is interrupted by a young kid with a T-shirt with the word STAFF emblazoned on it and a microphone at his neck.

"Mr. Maleeni. Hey, guy," says the young MC. "Ready to rumble?"

"By rumble if you mean perform, yes I am."

"Cool. Oh, you know how they said you'd get one hundred and twenty-five for the day? Gonna be seventy-five instead. The gate's for crap. But hey, the show's gotta go on, right?"

Maleeni says, "This will be my greatest show ever."

"Right on," says the young MC.

The Amazing Maleeni strides up to the stage. He opens with a long-winded dissertation on the history of magic that is over the head of his audience, except for a dangerous-looking dude who is growing impatient with the lecture.

"Get on with it!" he yells.

Maleeni ignores the heckler and begins with a simple trick involving cups and traveling balls. The audience is impressed. Except for the heckler.

"Yo, can't you do anything that ain't a hundred years old? That ain't old school. That's decrepit."

"Young man, shall I come heckle you on your job? Make sure you count out the requisite number of McNuggets?"

The heckler says, "Show me something. C'mon, show me something!"

Maleeni is determined not to be upstaged by this punk.

"A callow challenge to be met by experience and skill. To wit: the Egyptian Dedi, whose most celebrated feat was to reattach a recently severed head, reuniting it with a still warm body, and no harm done. Western history knows three previous attempts at recreating this Noachian feat, each of the three ending in tragedy. This will be the fourth. May I have complete silence, please."

The small crowd watches intently. Maleeni concentrates, and his head turns completely around. The audience freaks. They love it. Maleeni recovers and smiles out at the appreciative audience, giving the heckler a nod. The heckler walks away.

Maleeni and the young MC head back to the van.

"Guy, you rock! That kicked ass! I mean, it looked completely real. How'd you do that?"

Maleeni fixes him with a dramatic look as he climbs behind the wheel of his van.

"Oh yeah, right. Magic. Oh, hey, your money! Hold up!"

The kid dashes back for the cash. The young MC reappears with the money. He finds the magician sitting motionless with his eyes closed, not responding to his words. He reaches into the van and pokes Maleeni. He pokes a little harder.

Maleeni's head falls off and out the open window, where it thunks to a stop at the young man's feet.

•

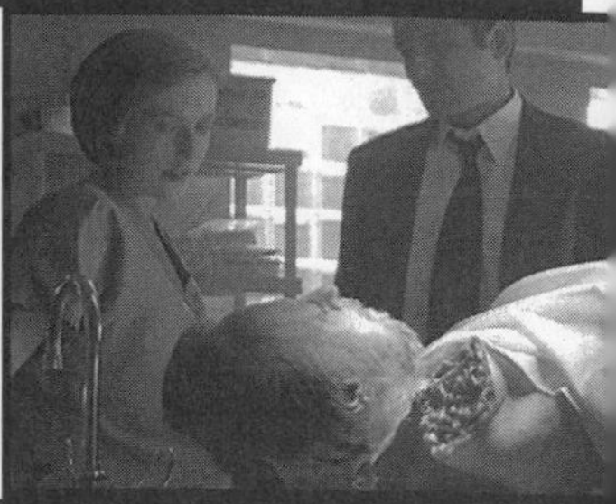

Mulder and Scully arrive at the scene. The police are still there, as is the Amazing Maleeni's van, but the body and head have been taken away.

"Neat trick, huh?" says Mulder.

"I can think of a neater one. How you convinced me to drop everything and get on the first plane to Los Angeles."

"Come on, Scully. This isn't intriguing enough for you? A magician turns his head completely around three hundred and sixty degrees to the delight of young and old alike, after which it plops unceremoniously onto the pier? See the picture?" he says, holding up a crime-scene photo which shows Maleeni's head resting by the front tire.

"Yeah, I saw the picture. And as for this Amazing Maleeni turning his head all the way around: like you said, neat trick. But I'd guess this was an event completely removed from his subsequent murder."

"You think this was a murder?" asks Mulder.

"Don't you? Mulder, his head was cut off."

"Observe the nearly complete absence of blood. Observe the paucity of fingerprints, as evidenced by the LAPD's liberal use of lycopodium powder."

"Why are you talking like Tony Randall?" asks Scully.

"Know that the Amazing Maleeni was alive one moment and expired the next, and also that no one saw his fleeing attacker, nor heard the dying man's cries."

Scully admits she doesn't know how the man died, but she still believes he was murdered. She asks Mulder what his theory is.

"A magic trick gone horribly wrong. One that claims the lives of all who attempt it," says Mulder, who then asks a policeman to look at the camcorder retrieved as evidence.

"A tourist videotaped Maleeni's performance."

Scully looks at Maleeni's final show. She notices the heckler. "That heckler's pretty hard to impress, wouldn't you say? Look. And then he just takes off in a huff."

"You think he's a murderer?" asks Mulder.

"It's worth checking out, don't you think?" responds Scully.

Mulder thinks that might be tough, since his face is not visible on the video. Scully says, "Ah, but observe his discarded soda cup. The hand may be quicker than the eye, but it still leaves fingerprints."

"Provided they haven't dumped the trash," says Mulder.

"Skeptic," says Scully.

•

Scully and Mulder make their way to a small theater where, according to the marquee, the heckler AKA magician Billy LaBonge is headlining. They enter the theater, where they discover LaBonge rehearsing card tricks onstage.

"Mr. LaBonge?" asks Scully. "We're Agents Mulder and Scully from the FBI."

LaBonge doesn't respond.

"Were you at the Santa Monica Pier yesterday morning?" asks Scully.

"Yeah."

"You attended a magic show? The Amazing Maleeni?"

"Yeah. He sucks. Why?"

Says Scully, "He's dead. Under extremely suspicious circumstances."

"He still sucks. How'd you find me?"

"Your fingerprints. You have a criminal record."

Adds Mulder, "A conviction for pickpocketing."

"Man, that was performance art! And besides, that's ancient history. What are you saying, you think I killed him?"

They inform him that they have him on tape heckling the deceased and want to know what he had against Maleeni. LaBonge explains that Maleeni is the name of a turn-of-the-century "real" magician named Max Malini.

"Anyway, he steals the name, spells it a little differently, then does some tired crap that wouldn't cut it at a kid's birthday party."

"What about the trick where he turns his head completely around?" asks Mulder.

LaBonge takes Mulder's question as a challenge. He lays the palm of his hand flat on the floor and rotates his wrist a full 360 degrees. "No problem," he says. He continues by showing Mulder and Scully a handful of impressive follow-up tricks.

"Those are great," says Mulder. "But I don't see they're any different or better than the ones Maleeni did."

"Mozart and Salieri. They sound pretty much the same—to a layman. But they ain't. You know what I'm saying?" says LaBonge, continuing to perform magic trick as he talks. "It's about originality and style. And more than anything else, soul. Because that's what separates the great ones from the hacks. You can't do this halfway. We're dealing with powerful forces at work here, energies far beyond our mere mortal understanding."

Mulder asks, "Enough to make a magician lose his head?"

"Could be. That and I hear Maleeni racked up some pretty big gambling debts. Who knows who he might have pissed off."

"Thank you, Mr. LaBonge," says Scully. "We'll be in touch."

LaBonge calls after them. They turn and see LaBonge holding up Mulder's and Scully's IDs, which he has pickpocketed from them.

•

"Mulder, I think professional jealousy's as good a motive for murder as any," says Scully, as they walk away from LaBonge.

"If it was a murder. I'm not convinced."

"Well, if I can get Mr. Maleeni into an autopsy bay, hopefully we'll put this issue to rest as soon as possible," says Scully.

•

Scully is at the city morgue, hard at work on the two distinct pieces of Maleeni as Mulder watches.

"All right," says Scully. "I'm stumped. And I think I'm supposed to be."

"What do you think?"

Scully moves the head away from the rest of the body. "Well, first of all, and I'm sorry to disappoint you, but Maleeni's head didn't just magically fall off. It was very carefully sawed. Very slow, exacting work. Probably with a fine-toothed meat saw. And check out this little detail."

Scully points to traces of a substance inside the wound. "Spirit gum, Mulder. It held the head to the body. Just barely, of course."

"So he was murdered."

"Well, no. As far as I can tell, this man died of advanced coronary disease."

Mulder says, "So basically he died of a heart attack. Someone crept up, sawed his head off, and glued it back on, all in a space of thirty seconds. So does that make sense to you?"

"No. Which makes it even stranger still. Because as far as I can tell, this body has been dead for over a month. I see signs of refrigeration."

Mulder says, "And yet he performed yesterday. What a trouper."

"Well, somebody performed yesterday," says Scully.

•

Billy LaBonge enters a pool hall and goes up to a mean-looking guy with many tattoos.

"Cissy Alvarez," says LaBonge.

"Who are you?" asks Cissy, barely glancing up from the notepad he's writing in.

"You don't remember me. Ain't that a bitch. My name's LaBonge. I did time with you about eight years ago. You were in for bank robbery."

"The name doesn't mean anything. What do you want?"

"I hear you're a poker player. You won big off a guy who calls himself the Amazing Maleeni? Also goes by the name of Herman Pinchbeck." Now he has Alvarez's attention. "He's dead," says LaBonge.

"Yeah, I saw in the paper. Sumthin' about his head fell off. What's it to you?"

"I'm the guy that made his head fall off," says LaBonge.

A couple of Cissy's goons are shooting pool nearby, paying close attention to the conversation.

"You took his marker, right? What'd he owe you? Fifteen grand?"

"Twenty," says Cissy.

"I don't think he was ever going to pay you back," says LaBonge.

"You wanna cut to the chase? Get a little more of your story out before we stomp you to death?"

"How would you like to get back what you're owed, times ten?"

"Two hundred thousand. How?"

"Helping me."

"Do what?"

"Magic."

Cissy signals the two thugs to mess LaBonge up. LaBonge holds his right hand up in front of his face and waves it once.

It bursts into flames. He waves it again. Cissy's notepad magically appears in his firey hand. LaBonge waves his hand once more and the flames disappear.

"Wanna hear more?" he says, as he hands a shocked Cissy his notepad.

•

Mulder and Scully enter the lobby of the Cradock Marine Bank. Mulder stops a passing female employee.

"Excuse me. I'm looking for a Mr. Albert Pinchbeck?"

"He's right over there. The poor man."

Mulder and Scully walk toward an office. They stop, surprised.

"He look familiar to you, Scully?"

"He certainly does."

They are staring through a glass wall into a small office where a man is working. The man is the spitting image of the Amazing Maleeni, and he is wearing a neck brace.

"The plot thickens," says Mulder.

"He might try to run," adds Scully.

They move to the office and knock on the door. Pitchbeck invites them in. He does not rise to greet them. They flash their IDs.

"You're not here for a home loan, I take it."

Scully says, "No. We are investigating the death of a magician who called himself the Amazing Maleeni."

"Herman Pinchbeck. My twin brother."

"Yes, we know," says Scully. "We checked his next of kin."

"What happened to your neck?" asks Mulder.

"I was in a car accident."

Mulder is skeptical of the car accident story. "So your injured neck has nothing to do with a magic trick you performed at the Santa Monica Pier two days ago? One which involved you turning your head around three hundred and sixty degrees?"

"Uh, no. That wasn't me. I was in a bad car accident in Mexico."

"Do you know magic, Mr. Pinchbeck?" says Scully.

"Yes, I do. Back in the seventies, my brother and I performed together."

Mulder asks why he stopped.

"You never really stop."

He pulls a deck of cards out of his desk and performs a card trick that involves Mulder pulling a card out of a deck, replacing the card, and Pinchbeck finding it.

"Very impressive," says Mulder.

"My brother and I both wanted to do the absolute best magic the world had ever seen. The difference was, I knew we'd never get there. But he always believed we would. We didn't talk much after I quit the act."

Mulder says, "I have a theory, Mr. Pinchbeck, and I'm going to tell you how it goes. I think your brother, Herman, died of heart disease, having never made it as the world's greatest magician, and I think that hurts you, just as your estrangement from him hurt you. And what I think you did was perform his last act for him. One last act for which he'd always be remembered. One last act that would end with such a shock, such a denouement, as would forever be remembered in the annals of magic. That's what I think."

"I so wish that were true," Pinchbeck replies as he rolls back from his desk to reveal a wheelchair and the fact that he does not have any legs.

"It was a very bad car accident in Mexico," he says.

The agents excuse themselves.

•

"Oy," says Mulder.

"No kidding," adds Scully. "What now?"

"A guy's head falls off. It's the greatest trick in the world. Only there's no discernible point to it. What's the point for doing it in the first place?"

"Well, why do people do magic?" asks Scully. "To impress, to delight, to gain attention."

"This one's gained mostly police attention. Or maybe that's the point."

Scully suggests they consult an expert. "Someone who knows magic, who's seen the greatest trick in the world. Maybe he can help us figure it out."

•

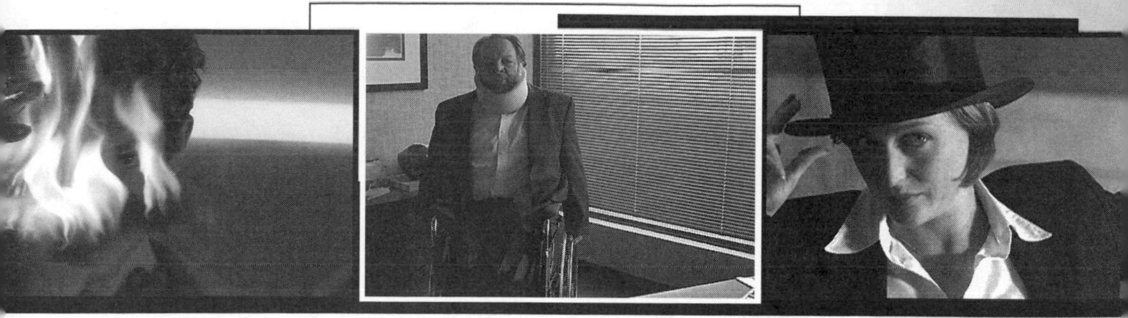

Billy LaBonge meets Mulder and Scully in a deserted police evidence garage. They have brought a large object, covered by a tarp, with them.

"What's in it for me? Let's say I help you out," he asks. "What do I get in return?"

Scully says, "The feeling of pride that comes from performing your civic duty."

"How about the chance to root through the professional secrets of your least-favorite magician?" says Mulder.

"Good for a laugh, I guess."

Mulder pulls the tarp off Maleeni's van.

LaBonge opens the van and rummages through the props.

"Man, it's worse than I thought." LaBonge lifts up a top hat and doves fly out. "You gotta feed those things, ya know?" He places the hat on Scully's head as he continues, "So, Maleeni wasn't murdered. So someone impersonated him and his crappy act. It's impressive. I'd say the twin brother did it. But I don't think he's any better a magician than Maleeni was."

Says Mulder, "There's that and he's got no legs."

LaBonge says, "Yeah, whatever. Anyway, we're looking for a magician with the same height and build. A good makeup job, and the right wig, and no one would know the difference."

Mulder asks LaBonge how the impersonator would have switched the dead body.

"With ease," says LaBonge, as he begins to empty the van. "You're gonna kick yourselves when I show you how he did this, it's so simple. Because magic is all about misdirection. Your impersonator simply made sure everyone was looking the other way when he pulled Maleeni's body from its secret hiding place, underneath the floor."

LaBonge makes his point by pulling up the plywood panels on the van floor. He discovers only a steel van floor and no secret compartment.

"Man. This guy's good."

"Well, thanks for your expert opinion," Scully says. "I guess we're right back where we started."

Mulder looks down at the pile of magic stuff at his feet. He bends down and picks up a folded piece of paper.

"Maybe not. You said the Amazing Maleeni had some gambling debts?" asks Mulder.

"That's what I heard."

Mulder turns to Scully. "Well, check this out. Looks like a marker. Twenty thousand dollars. 'Pinchbeck.'"

Scully asks, "What would this be doing in Maleeni's van?"

•

Pinchbeck and a pair of armed courier guards, Anthony and Marvin, are in the bank vault area. Pinchbeck asks Anthony what type of gun he carries. "A Glock-17," says Anthony.

"I've been thinking about maybe buying one since my accident."

Anthony takes his gun out of its holster and lets Pinchbeck handle it. He even offers to take him to the shooting range sometime. Pinchbeck returns the gun, wishing the guards a good day. He goes back to his office. Cissy Alvarez walks in and shuts the door.

"May I help you?"

"Damn, you look just like him," says Cissy, sitting down.

"I'm sorry?"

"Your no good, *malapaga* brother died owing me money. A lotta money. You gonna make good."

"I'm sorry, but my brother's debts are his own."

Pinchbeck makes a subtle move toward the phone when Alvarez's hand comes down on his, pinning it to the desk.

"I said you gonna make good. 'Cause me and my friends, we know where you live."

Pinchbeck looks down at Cissy's tattooed hands covering his.

•

The armored truck leaves the bank and rounds a corner. Suddenly a loud *thump, thump* is heard from behind the driver's cab. The armored truck pulls over and Anthony climbs out to investigate while Marvin radios in their situation and location. Anthony approaches the rear door with his gun drawn, unlatches the door, and swings it open. He notices a pair of feet sticking out from behind some canvas bags.

"You in the truck! Get up where I can see you!"

A man wearing a windbreaker and a black stocking mask rises up from behind the bags. He has his back to us.

"Hands up where I can see them. Up! Hands up!"

The man raises his hands, exposing the tattoos on his hands. Anthony orders the crook out of the truck. The man suddenly reaches into his waist, as if reaching for a gun.

Anthony opens fire. *Blam-blam-blam-blam!* The masked man pitches forward. Anthony races around to the driver's side. Marvin is already there with his gun drawn. They both hurry back to the rear of the truck to discover the man is gone.

The guard is incredulous. "It was a guy with tattoos. I shot him four times. I don't understand."

Magically, the dead man is now very much alive, standing behind a Dumpster across the street watching the guards. He pulls off his mask and begins to rub off the tattoos on his hand.

It is Billy LaBonge.

•

Mulder and Scully have tracked Cissy Alvarez to the pool hall, where they drop Pinchbeck's gambling marker on a pool table.

"It's your handwriting, is it not?" asks Scully. "Mr. Alvarez, please answer the question."

"That ain't mine. And I don't know where you got that."

Mulder says, "Interesting. Yours are the only fingerprints on it."

"We ran them through the California Criminal History database, to which you seem to be quite well known," says Scully.

"So it's my marker. So Pinchbeck owed me money. It was a friendly game of poker."

"Very friendly. Twenty thousand dollars friendly," says Mulder.

"Where did you find that?"

"In Herman Pinchbeck's van," says Scully.

"What is it you think I did to Pinchbeck? What's in it for me? If I kill him, he ain't gonna pay me."

"Why did you play poker with him in the first place?" Mulder asks. "You knew he was a professional magician."

"I didn't know what he was," says Alvarez. "And he sure as hell couldn't play worth a damn."

Scully warns Alvarez not to leave town. Outside the pool hall they consider the problem.

"Don't you find it odd that the Amazing Maleeni is a lousy poker player? This is a guy who's adept at manipulating cards," says Mulder.

"Maybe he wasn't so adept. LaBonge certainly doesn't have a high opinion of his skills."

"There's another possibility," says Mulder.

"Which is?"

As Scully watches, Mulder performs a simple sleight-of-hand trick involving a coin passing from one hand to another. Scully follows

the trick to its successful conclusion, in which the coin magically drops out of Scully's nose.

"Amazing," she says.

"The Great Maleeni."

"And what's the point?"

"Misdirection," says Mulder. "It's the heart of magic. Just like LaBonge said. I made you look in one direction, the quarter went in the other."

"And that's what you think is happening in this case."

"I think we're being led around by our noses."

"By whom? Maleeni is already dead."

"It certainly would appear so," says Mulder. "But then again, you thought the quarter was in my right hand."

•

LaBonge is standing by a pay phone across the street as he watches Mulder and Scully drive away. He picks up the phone and dials 911. And, in a disguised whisper, says, "Yeah, hello? I wanna report a man with a gun. He's threatening to kill somebody. I can't speak up. I can't."

He lets the receiver drop and walks toward the pool hall, where we find Cissy Alvarez frantically going through his marker notebook and finding that one page has been torn out. His goons are standing by.

"Son of a bitch," curses Alvarez, as LaBonge strolls in.

"Hi, partner," he says. "Hey, guys."

"You son of a bitch. You try to frame me? *Hijo de tu.*"

Alvarez and his goons advance on LaBonge.

"Guys," he says. "I didn't. Guys, wait. We've got a deal!"

"We got no deal," says Alvarez. "I'm gonna bleed you, you little bitch!"

"Back off." LaBonge whips a pistol out of his windbreaker and waves it in the faces of Alvarez and his men.

"You're dead!" says Alvarez, as LaBonge races out the door, just as an LAPD cruiser screeches to a stop. The cops draw their weapons. LaBonge raises his hands.

"Drop your weapon!" yells a cop.

The gun hits the ground and a goofy flag pops out of the barrel. It says BANG! A smirking LaBonge is taken into custody.

•

Mulder and Scully are back in the bank, looking for Albert Pinchbeck. They find him in his office.

"Agents. What an unexpected surprise. Good afternoon."

"We'd like a word with you, Mr. Pinchbeck," says Scully.

"I'm fairly busy, actually."

"I'll bet," says Mulder.

Mulder moves behind Pinchbeck's wheelchair and wheels the legless man out of the office and into a deserted room. Pinchbeck wants to know what Mulder is up to.

"It's about misdirection, Mr. Pinchbeck. Or should I say, the Amazing Maleeni."

Mulder pushes the wheelchair forward, tipping it over and sending Pinchbeck toppling to the floor. Scully is shocked by this unprovoked act of cruelty. Until she sees that Albert Pinchbeck has legs. They see the cut pantlegs, a false bottom, and the mirrors that have combined to create the illusion.

"It's a trick, Scully."

"Had you fooled," says Pinchbeck.

Scully says, "You're Maleeni?"

"Call me Herman."

Maleeni plays with a deck of cards as his story unfolds.

"I was afraid for my life. That's why I did what I did. I'm not proud of that. But I owe a lot of money that I can't possibly pay back."

"We know," says Scully. "Gambling debts to a man named Alvarez."

"Yeah, that tattooed psychopath. I've since heard terrible stories about him. Things he did in prison to fellow inmates."

Scully says, "So, why play poker with him?"

"He runs a good game. I gamble to supplement my income. God knows magic barely pays."

Scully wants to know why he did not use his ability to manipulate cards to cheat.

"You could, right?" she says.

"Of course I could. But how would I live with myself? Who raised you?"

"IT'S MISDIRECTION. IT'S THE HEART OF MAGIC."—Mulder

Scully says, "Well, sir, what does any of this have to do with your twin brother being found decapitated at the Santa Monica Pier?"

"I went to my brother for a loan. Just my luck and his . . ."

"You found him dead of a heart attack," Scully says.

"His body was still warm. Looking at him, lifeless, I saw myself. My own eventual mortality. I saw all of the things I meant to accomplish, but didn't. It was an opportunity to vanish, to become someone else. Like I said, I'm not proud of what I did."

Scully guesses that he refrigerated the body.

"I needed time to figure out how to pull it all off. Impersonating my brother, I called the bank, told them I needed a vacation week, a trip to Mexico. Then they received word I'd been in a terrible accident. It gave me plenty of time away from work."

"And you posed as an amputee to allay suspicion that you weren't your brother."

"That and I rather enjoyed the sympathy, especially from the women in our office."

"You still haven't explained why you left your brother's body at the pier. Or why you arranged to have his head fall off," says Scully.

Maleeni turns to Mulder.

"He explained it. He put it so elegantly when we last spoke. It was my final performance. I wanted to go out with such a shock, such a denouement, as would forever be remembered in the annals of magic."

"That was your last performance," says Mulder, as he takes out a pair of handcuffs and locks Maleeni's hands in front of him.

"I still think you've got a few tricks up your sleeve," says Mulder.

•

Maleeni stands in the doorway of his office in cuffs. Bank employees are shocked at the notion that he has legs. Mulder turns to the bank officer.

"Did he have access to the vaults?" asks Mulder.

"Well, yes," he says. "He has a key to the day gate. Several of us do."

"What are you looking for, Mulder?" asks Scully.

"Any hint at all as to why Maleeni here is really impersonating his brother."

"What about this?" he asks, pointing to a computer monitor. "Could he remove the funds electronically?"

The bank officer indicates that Maleeni/Pinchbeck did not have security clearance for EFTs—electronic funds transfers. The bank officer checks a transactional list and discovers everything is in order.

Maleeni gives his handcuffs a gentle tug and they magically fall off his wrists. Maleeni holds them up with a smile. Scully picks up a clipboard lying on the desk.

"Mulder, it says here something about a robbery attempt yesterday."

The bank officer says, "Yeah. That wasn't against us, but the armored transport service we deal with. No money was taken and no suspects were caught."

Scully says, "Yeah, well, Mr. Pinchbeck was the employee who signed out the truck. He knew their schedule."

"I had nothing to do with that!" says Maleeni.

"Maybe. Maybe not," says Scully.

Mulder says, "We'll hold you 'til we find out. Make sure you don't pull a vanishing act."

•

A police officer escorts Maleeni into a dark cellblock at the North Hollywood police station.

"Wait, don't I get a phone call? Sir? Sir?"

He is left alone in the cell. There is a faint rapping on the cell block wall. He returns the tapping.

It's LaBonge.

"How'd it go?" he asks.

Maleeni says, "Swimmingly."

"Abracadabra, man," replies LaBonge.

•

Cradock Marine Bank opens on schedule. The bank officer opens the door and escorts the armored truck guards, Anthony and Marvin, into the bank.

"Oh, damn," says the bank officer.

The vault has been cleaned out.

•

Police and crime scene techs arrive. Fingerprints are lifted from the vault. Mulder surveys the crime scene as Scully finishes up a phone conversation.

"Maleeni?" asks Mulder.

Scully says, "He's still in city lockup, where he's been since we arrested him last night. It certainly doesn't look like he did this . . . lots of fingerprints."

"Yeah, I guarantee you none of them match our thieves. They're too clever to leave clues. Except for the ones they want us to find."

The bank officer leads them to security monitors. He theorizes that the security camera footage might show the robbers. Unfortunately there is a twenty-minute blank spot on the tape from 3:00 A.M. to 3:20 A.M., the time of the robbery. Anthony points to a freeze frame from two days earlier. He presses PLAY and they see Cissy Alvarez walk into the bank. The armored truck guard is surprised when Mulder and Scully recognize the man as Alvarez.

"I know those tattoos," says Anthony. "That's the man who tried to rob my truck."

•

"What the hell? What did I do?" says Cissy, as an officer pushes him onto the pool table and cuffs him.

"Yo, FBI!" yells Alvarez when he spots the agents. "What's up with this? Can't just come busting in here. I got civil rights! Gonna call my lawyer! Then we're going to see what's what!"

The search of the pool hall turns up nothing. Mulder's gaze goes to the ceiling and a noticeable bulge. He picks up a pool cue and pokes at it. The ceiling gives way and canvas moneybags come raining down.

Scully says, "Well, saving up for a rainy day?"

"We got framed!" screams Alvarez. "This is a frame-up! It was the magician!"

"The magician. Maleeni?" asks Mulder.

"No, not the dead one! That little *cabrón*, LaBonge! LaBonge set me up!"

"Billy LaBonge," says Scully.

"And the Amazing Maleeni," adds Mulder. "That's a double bill I wouldn't want to miss."

•

Inside the jail, Maleeni and LaBonge are all smiles as they step out of their cells. They have made bail. They head for the exit when Mulder and Scully appear on the cellblock.

"I think releasing these two may be a bit premature," Scully says to the guard.

"Give us a minute, would you?" asks Mulder as the guard leaves.

"Good morning, gentlemen," says Mulder. "Sleep well?"

"Agent Mulder, Agent Scully," says Maleeni.

"Bravo. Really," says Mulder.

"Last night, the Cradock Marine Bank was robbed of one-point-eight million dollars. This morning that entire amount was found in the possession of Mr. Cissy Alvarez," says Scully.

"Wow," says Maleeni. "I told you he was bad news. Bravo to you. That was expeditious police work."

Mulder says, "It was, wasn't it? It's only that Alvarez was so obviously guilty. A convicted bank robber, caught red-handed. Witnessed trying to rob an armored car just days earlier. He's up a creek. Just like you two want him."

The magicians feign innocence.

Mulder says, "I have no evidence, but I have a theory, Mr. Maleeni. And I'll tell you how it goes. I think your twin brother, Albert, died of a heart attack, at which point you and your young protégé saw a golden opportunity."

"Protégé?" says Maleeni. "I hate this guy's guts."

"That's what you wanted us to think," Scully says.

Mulder turns to LaBonge. "You wanted revenge on the man who made your life in prison a living hell. Alvarez. You and he were on the same cell block eight years ago."

Scully says to Maleeni, "It was a setup from the start. You played poker with him and you made sure you lost big."

"Which," says Mulder, "gave LaBonge an in with Alvarez, once everybody thought you were dead."

"LaBonge planted Maleeni's marker in the van and made sure we found it," says Scully. "Then you used Alvarez's greed to ensnare him and then orchestrated that attempted robbery in order to implicate him."

"Yeah, and that was you in the armored car, disguised as Alvarez," says Mulder to LaBonge. "Somehow Mr. Pinchbeck got hold of the guard's gun and switched the clip. The guard didn't know it, but he was firing blanks."

Scully turns the screws a little tighter. "Then last night you two robbed the bank and planted the money at Alvarez's place."

"Don't you think we have pretty good alibis?" says LaBonge.

"You have great alibis," Mulder says. "You have the best alibis in the world, which is why I think you two got arrested in the first place."

"With your expertise in sleight of hand, pickpocketing, and escapology, I think you

were able to get out of here by pilfering a guard's key," says Scully.

Mulder says, "You could have escaped, stolen the money, framed Alvarez, and been back here in time for breakfast."

"Scrambled eggs and sausage. That would be the world's greatest trick, wouldn't it?" asks Maleeni.

"One that would be forever remembered in the annals of magic," says Mulder.

Maleeni and LaBonge know they've been busted.

LaBonge asks, "What happens to us?"

"You go free," Mulder says. "Provided the magic is over."

Maleeni says, "The great ones always know when to leave the stage. Billy, let's get the hell outta here."

The two magicians walk out the door to freedom.

"They are the world's greatest."

"We saw through their magic."

"There's more," says Mulder as he magically produces a large billfold. "Behold. The Amazing Maleeni's wallet."

"You picked his pocket?"

"No. I pilfered it from the evidence room to prevent them from completing their final act of prestidigitation."

"What are you talking about?"

Mulder begins to search its contents.

"I began to wonder: Why did they need so elaborate a setup? Why so high-profile? Why draw the attention of the FBI in the first place?"

"We were the last piece of the puzzle."

"Framing Alvarez was another misdirection," he says. "This trick was about EFTs—electronic funds transfers at the bank. Maleeni—Pinchbeck—he didn't have security clearance for them. So he needed a little federal law enforcement intervention. Specifically my badge number and thumbprint."

Mulder flashes back to the moment when LaBonge pickpocketed his badge and the time at the bank when Maleeni had him participate in a card trick.

"With those two items, they could pull off an EFT and steal enough electronically to make the one-point-eight million look like cigar-lighting money. But they can't do it without this."

Mulder holds up a piece of folded plastic. It's a Ziploc bag containing the playing card.

"Pick a card, Scully, any card."

The two agents leave the jail.

"You know, Mulder, there's one thing you haven't explained."

"What's that?"

"How the Amazing Maleeni was able to turn his head completely around."

"I don't know how to do that," says Mulder.

"I do. Observe."

Scully crouches down and presses the palm of her hand against the floor. As Mulder watches, Scully rotates her hand a full 360 degrees.

"Very nice. How'd you do that?" asks an impressed Mulder.

"Magic," says Scully.

Scully begins to walk away.

"No, seriously. Scully, how'd you do it? Well, it's not the same thing, it's different with the head," says Mulder, as he follows her out the door.

He follows, doing the old disconnecting-thumb trick.

BACK STORY:

Frank Spotnitz was not the most popular guy around the day he suggested the story that would ultimately become "The Amazing Maleeni." "Vince was ready to kill me," says Spotnitz. "He wanted to know why I wanted to do a story about magic. For him, this was agony."

Gilligan can laugh about it now, but he was not laughing when Spotnitz was laying down his ideas for the show. "Frank wanted to do this stand-alone episode about a magician. But he did not want to have anything even remotely paranormal in it. He wanted it to be totally about magic and illusion."

Spotnitz's love of magic had translated into an ongoing campaign for an *X-Files* magic episode since season two. Ricky Jay was his favorite magician, and so a magic show starring Jay was his dream project. Spotnitz's persistence eventually led to a green light and the collaboration between Spotnitz, Gilligan, and John Shiban in which magic and a heist plot reminescent of *The Sting* unfolds in Los Angeles. Even though they had not even begun to cast the show, Ricky Jay was very much on everyone's mind, so much so that Gilligan went out of his way to incorporate many of Jay's trademark tricks into the script.

While the script for "The Amazing Maleeni" was being fashioned, the casting department began what Chris Carter described as "a delicate courtship" to land Ricky Jay for the episode. Rick Millikan called his agency and the response was that he might be available. For the young punk magician who challenges him, the show cast its net for magician David Blaine, who had come to some notoriety by burying himself alive. Things were looking promising. Then the roof fell in.

Spotnitz recalls, "We found out that the agency had never even informed Ricky Jay that we wanted him. We found out that Ricky Jay couldn't do it. Then we found out that David Blaine couldn't do it. We had the script all ready to go and all of a sudden we had no magicians. We were ready to shoot ourselves."

The agency finally admitted that they had not broached *The X-Files* episode to Ricky Jay because they knew he was very busy and very tired. But Chris Carter was not going to take no for an answer. "We got on the phone with him," says Carter. "He agreed to come to our offices to talk about the script and ended up doing some card tricks for us that reduced Frank and I to being six-year-olds again."

Jay was agreeable to doing the part but requested that he stick to the tricks he normally does onstage rather than performing new ones. John Shiban relates that the scene in which Maleeni talks to Mulder and Scully in the bank office underwent a slight change when Jay argued that the scripted trick of tossing a playing card into a bulletin board was not in character. A more traditional card trick in which he locates a card selected by Mulder was substituted.

"The Amazing Maleeni" proved to be an interesting travelogue of Los Angeles, from the famous downtown to less well known East Los Angeles. For the truly amazing opening sequence in which a down-and-out Maleeni plies his craft for chump change, the Santa Monica Pier was utilized.

The actors enjoyed the "amusement park" nature of the episode but were constantly on the alert not to forget that there was an X-File at the core of all the smoke and mirrors.

"Because of all the magic, I was constantly being entertained," says Gillian Anderson. "The difficulty with something like this is you have a tendency to forget that people are still having bad things happen to them. It was tough because a lot of the lines were being written tongue-in-cheek and David and I were constantly playing to the comedic side of the script. We had to keep reminding ourselves that we were dealing with murder."

A constant challenge on the special effects front during the making of "The Amazing Maleeni" was to keep things as camera-real as possible, in keeping with a show about magic and illusion. Which meant that during the sequence in which Billy LaBonge impresses crime boss Cissy Alvarez by having his hand burst into flame, a stuntman was brought in rather than relying on a more time-consuming and ultimately less convincing visual effect.

FACT:

The superrealistic prosthetic head was supplied by John Vulich's Optic Nerve.

episode 7X09

SIGNS & WONDERS

EPISODE: 7X09
FIRST AIRED: January 23, 2000
EDITOR: Louise A. Innes
WRITTEN BY: Jeffrey Bell
DIRECTED BY: Kim Manners

A back woods cult of snake worshippers leads Mulder and Scully to a confrontation with genuine satanic forces.

GUEST STARS:

Randy Oglesby (Reverend Samuel Mackey)
Michael Childers (Reverend Enoch O'Connor)
Tracy Middendorf (Gracie)
Beth Grant (Iris Finster)
Eric Nenninger (Jared Chirp)
Elyse Donalson (Elderly Woman)
Phyllis Franklin (Middle-Aged Woman)
Dan Manning (Deputy)
Steve Johnson (EMT)
Philip Lenkowsky (Holy Spirit Man #1)
Clement E. Blake (Holy Spirit Man #2)
Donna May (Holy Spirit Woman #1)

PRINCIPAL SETTINGS:

Blessing, Tennessee; Hamden, Connecticut

Lightning cracks and thunder rumbles outside a small clapboard house in McMinn County, Tennessee. Inside, a young man in his early twenties moves his hand past a rattlesnake rattle, which sits atop a printout with the heading MEDICAL TEST RESULTS. He grabs the printout, tears it in half, and drops the pieces near the trash can. He is packing a suitcase for a quick getaway.

"Holy Ghost, come to me," he says. "Praise God . . . praise God. Move up on me, Holy Ghost."

He opens a nightstand drawer and grabs up a Bible. A photo of a young woman is inside.

"Praise God, this here sinner repents. Holy Ghost, move up on me, protect me and mine with your quick'ning power," he says.

A lightning flash illuminates a figure standing out in the night. With the next flash, the figure is gone.

The man reaches for one last item, a long-barreled revolver. Hearing a rattler's sound, he snaps the suitcase shut and races through the rain for an old car parked outside the house. The figure once again appears and watches as the man jumps into the car. The young man locks the car as he fumbles with the ignition key. The key slips out of his hand and drops to the car floor. He bends to pick up the key.

A huge rattlesnake eases out from under the driver's seat.

The horrified man slowly eases his hand back and reaches for the revolver.

A second rattlesnake glides into view over the edge of the suitcase and curves around the gun.

The man's other hand reaches for the door. The door will not open. He looks over and sees that the dashboard and interior of the car are suddenly covered with snakes.

"Help me, Jesus! Help me, Jesus! Help me, Jesus!"

He reaches for the revolver. He grabs the gun and fires in every direction until he caps on an empty chamber. The car rocks with his death spasms.

•

Mulder is in his office, watching a rattlesnake documentary on a computer monitor while talking on the phone.

"Not this time of year. All right, thank you, doctor."

Scully enters. Mulder turns the computer screen so she can see it.

"Snakes?" asks Scully.

"Lots and lots of snakes," says Mulder, as he hands Scully a file. "Very pissed off ones by the looks of it."

Scully winces at a gruesome photo of a bloated and blackened body, dotted with hundreds of fang marks.

Mulder says, "That's the former Mr. Jared Chirp of McMinn County, Tennessee. One hundred and sixteen separate bite marks. Judging by wound measurements, there were fifty different snakes involved, mostly copperheads and rattlers."

Scully reads the police report.

"But it says here he was found dead in his car," she says.

"Yeah, with a pistol in his hand. He fired six shots into the floorboards, the passenger seat, even his own right kneecap. And the windows were shut and the doors were locked."

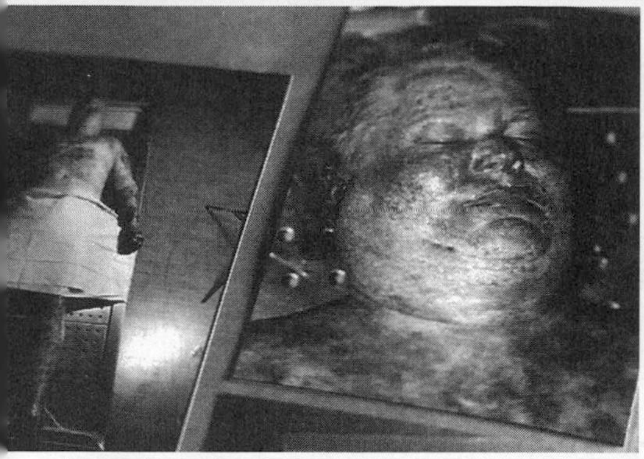

"What happened to all the snakes?" Scully asks.

"No one seems to know that. There was not a scale found. I just got off the phone with a herpetologist with the Smithsonian. He's stumped. Especially because these rattlesnakes tend to hibernate in winter."

"So you think that Mr. Chirp was murdered?" asks Scully.

"It certainly would appear that way. The question is how. No physical evidence at all. No tire tracks, no footprints."

"Maybe it's symbolic. I mean, serpents and religion have gone hand in hand. They've represented the temptation of Eve, Original Sin. They've been feared and hated throughout history as they were thought to embody Satan. To serve evil itself."

"Maybe these ones actually do," Mulder suggests.

"THESE PARTICULAR SERPENTS ACTUALLY WERE SERVING EVIL? ARE YOU GONNA TYPE THAT ON OUR TRAVEL REQUEST?"—Scully

"Are you gonna type that on our travel request?" Scully asks.

"No, but at the very least, this case does seem to center on religion. And you're not the only one who thinks that, by the way."

•

The Reverend Samuel Mackey is concluding a funeral service for the departed Jared Chirp in the Blessing Community Church. Among his parishioners is Iris, a woman in her mid-fifties, and her friend, Gracie, a nineteen-year-old and very pregnant woman.

"Jared is in a better place now, Gracie," says the reverend. "He's at peace."

Gracie nods as she and Iris head up the aisle out of the church. But she gives one lingering look back at the reverend. Mulder and Scully arrive as the mourners leave the church.

"Reverend Samuel Mackey? My name is Fox Mulder, this is Dana Scully. We're with the FBI. May we speak with you, sir? I apologize for our timing. We'd like to ask you a few questions about Jared Chirp."

"I've already spoken to the sheriff about it," says Mackey, "though I'm not sure that was a good idea."

Mulder says, "Specifically, you said you had suspicions about the manner in which he died."

"I should be the last one to point a finger or say a harsh word," explains Mackey. "Our church is founded on acceptance and tolerance of all people, all beliefs. Before Jared joined us, he belonged to a fundamentalist congregation outside of town. The Church of God with Signs and Wonders. It practices snake handling."

Mulder says, "As a sign of faith, worshippers handle deadly snakes and drink poison."

Mackey continues, "They believe the Holy Spirit protects the righteous. Jared grew up in that church. But it's very difficult to walk away from a belief system one was raised in. It takes great courage."

Mulder asks, "Why did he walk away?"

"He and Gracie, his girlfriend, left it together. They found that a rigid interpretation of the Bible was not for them. Especially when it involves risking life and limb in the act of worship. But again . . . it's not for me to judge. I will say, however, that both Jared and Gracie were persecuted by the members of their former church. All this animus stems from their church leader, Enoch O'Connor."

"Animus enough to motivate a murder?" asks Scully.

•

Mulder and Scully drive up to a tumble-down building at the end of a dirt road. A plywood sign reads CHURCH OF GOD WITH SIGNS & WONDERS. They approach the front door, over which an eight-foot rattlesnake skin is tacked.

"Snake handling. We didn't learn that in catechism class," comments Scully.

Mulder says, "Funny, I knew a couple of Catholic school girls who were experts at it."

Mulder knocks on the door, the force of his rap causing the door to inch open.

"Enoch O'Connor? Federal agents," says Mulder.

There is no answer. They walk into a room dotted with plain wooden pews.

Mulder asks, "Where's the light switch?"

Says Scully, "The nearest one? Probably ten miles from here."

The door closes behind them. They turn on their flashlights and continue into the church. Scully shines her light on a nearby wall, where a disturbing print of a painting by Hieronymus Bosch is tacked.

Scully says, "Rattlesnakes and medieval visions of damnation. Well, I for one feel a whole lot closer to God."

"I don't know, Scully," says Mulder. "When you get right down to it, is snake handling any harder to buy into than communion wafers and transubstantiation?"

"Or believing in flying saucers, for that matter," says Scully.

"I'm just saying your faith and O'Connor's seem to be based on the same book."

A rattlesnake slithers out of a rotted section of baseboard. Scully just misses stepping on it. Mulder's flashlight shines on a closed box, half wood and half screen, resting on a chair.

"Uh-oh. Scully? What do you think O'Connor keeps in here?" asks Mulder.

Scully instinctively takes a step back. Mulder edges forward and peers inside the box. He reaches out and gives it a shake.

"It's all right. It's empty."

Scully asks, "Why is it empty?"

The sound of a rattlesnake rattle is heard by the pews. Mulder and Scully shine their lights around the room. They see nothing, but the rattling is growing louder and close. They draw their pistols. The look on their faces tells it all.

Suddenly a shaft of light blasts into the room, revealing the stern face of Enoch O'Connor in the doorway and four huge rattlers on the floor around them.

"By what right are you here?" asks O'Connor.

Scully says, "Reverend Enoch O'Connor, we're federal agents. We're with the . . . the FBI!"

Adds Mulder, "Reverend, do something about these snakes!"

"You've got nothin' to fear if you're righteous people," says O'Connor.

Mulder trains his pistol on a snake that is getting a bit too close. "Just in case we're not, we could use a little righteous help here."

O'Connor wades into this den of vipers and slowly begins to pick them up, one by one, and drop them into a burlap sack.

"What do you want?" asks O'Connor.

Scully says, "We're here to ask you questions about a former member of your church, Jared Chirp."

"That boy strayed from the path and was lost to the dark one. I'm sorry for his soul. There ain't much else to say."

Mulder says, "He died from multiple snake bites. We thought you might have some special insight into that."

"I do," says the preacher, picking up another snake. "It was a test."

"A test," says Scully. "What do you mean?"

"A test of faith. A test of righteousness. When the Devil aims to test you, you best be ready . . . and you sure better know which side you're on."

O'Connor puts the last snake into the bag and cinches it shut.

Scully says, "Are you speaking about the Devil's test or your test?"

"I don't think you people realize which side you're on. I do. You can leave now," says O'Connor.

They walk out the door.

Scully says, "Tennessee. Snakes. Thank you, Mulder. Thank you so much. I say we arrest him and catch the first flight out of here."

"He does seem a likely suspect," says Mulder. "Only the local sheriff's office ruled him out. Apparently he was in Kentucky the night Jared Chirp died."

Scully reminds her partner that there are others in his congregation.

"Jared Chirp died with a packed suitcase by his side. There's got to be somebody who knew where he was headed," says Mulder.

•

A Bible study class is taking place in the Blessing Community Church. Everyone seems open and friendly, except Gracie, who is sitting off by herself. Gracie is joined by her friend Iris. Reverend Mackey enters, smiling to his flock. Iris approaches him.

She confides, "Jared called the boardinghouse late the night he died. He wanted to talk to Gracie. I didn't let him. It was after two, she was sound asleep, and it sounded to me like the boy'd been drinkin'. He just wasn't makin' any sense. Rantin' about seein' the Devil and payin' for his sins."

Reverend Mackey asks, "Why didn't you tell the police?"

"I don't know how to tell Gracie. I kept her from speaking to Jared his last night on earth. I couldn't have known, though. I couldn't . . ."

Mackey comforts her, insisting it is not her fault but that she should talk to the FBI agents about the incident.

"You and I will see this through, Iris," says the reverend. "Right after study group."

•

In another part of the county, the Church of God with Signs and Wonders is holding a prayer meeting. Its attendees are enraptured in the music, the prayers, and the fervent voice of Enoch O'Connor.

His words are greeted by shouts of "amen" and "thank you, Jesus."

O'Connor says, "Revelation Three, the sixteenth verse. It is better to be hot or cold than lukewarm. God says if you're lukewarm he will vomit you outta his mouth. You hear what I said? God hates the lukewarm!"

•

Back at the Blessing Community Church, the Reverend Mackey is delivering a more sedate version of the same words to his study group.

"So 'because you are lukewarm . . . I am about to spit you out of my mouth.' That could sound pretty harsh, couldn't it? Depending on how one reads it."

Meanwhile, the reading at the Church of God with Signs and Wonders is a sweating, fiery experience for those in attendance.

"God wants you hot, he wants you on fire, he wants you to put your money where your mouth is!" says O'Connor.

He picks up a serpent box off the floor. Two rattlesnakes coil inside.

"People ask me why I handle snakes and I tell 'em it's because Scripture tells me to. And if there's one thing I obey, it's the word o' God!"

He opens the serpent box, jams his hand inside, yanks the snakes out, and holds them aloft.

"Hallelujah!" says O'Connor. "Thank you, God!"

Back at the Blessing Community Church, Iris is busying herself, pulling staples from collated papers with a staple remover. Suddenly the staple remover turns into a rattlesnake that bites her hand. Iris drops the snake in horror. But it is a staple remover that lands on the desk.

The Church of Signs and Wonders has turned into a very heathen vision. A half dozen snakes twist and coil on the floor, driven by tambourine rhythms. A woman picks some of them up and jerks around with them. One parishioner has a seizure.

O'Connor says, "Witness the power! Witness the awesome power of God as he blesses his people and destroys his enemies! Thank you, God!"

Iris is in the bathroom, cleaning her wound over a sink, the blood drops mixing with the water as they swirl down the drain. She is putting a bandage on when something catches her eye.

A rattlesnake crawling out of the sink's drain.

She backs away and sees more snakes coiling on the floor. Hearing a loud rattle above her, she looks up just as the snake strikes.

•

Reverend Mackey is shaken as he watches Iris's body being taken away by the coroner's men. The churchyard is empty except for Mulder.

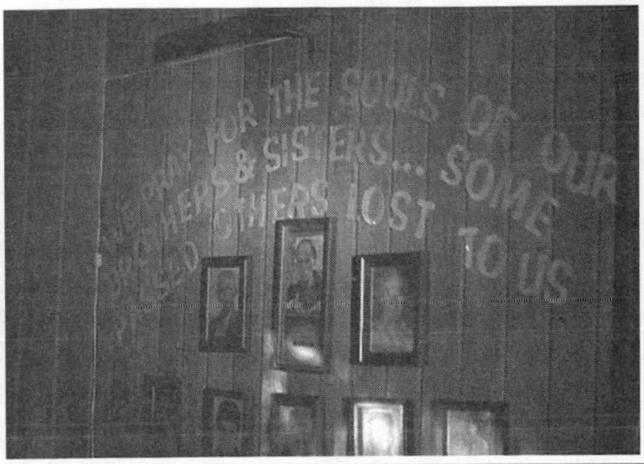

"I don't understand it," says Mackey. "None of us saw or heard anything. Just her scream. When we ran in, she was lying on the floor. I cleared everybody out of the building once I saw all the bite marks."

"Reverend, how close was Iris to Jared Chirp?" asks Mulder.

"Not particularly close. But I had spoken to her not fifteen minutes earlier about him."

"What did you talk about?"

Mackey says, "She was upset. Something about Jared calling her the night he died, looking for Gracie. Something about him paying for his sins. But I don't know. We didn't get to finish our conversation."

"Maybe that was the point."

Inside the church office, Scully is talking to Gracie.

"Why Iris?" Gracie asks as Mulder and Mackey enter. "Why is this happening?"

Scully says, "Gracie, we're investigating the leader of your former church, Enoch O'Connor. We believe he may have had something to do with what happened here tonight."

"No, he didn't do this," says Gracie. "No. He didn't do this. This is Satan's work, not man's."

"That sounds a little like what Reverend O'Connor might say," Scully remarks. "Now, you're not a member of his congregation anymore . . . and I understand that's because you're someone who thinks for herself."

Adds Mulder, "Keeping an open mind, Gracie, is it conceivable that O'Connor could have done any of this?"

"No!" says Gracie. "Don't you think I would know, me of all people? He couldn't have done this. He couldn't . . ."

Mackey says, "Gracie might be biased."

She turns to the reverend for help.

"O'Connor is your father," says Mulder.

To Mulder and Scully, Mackey says, "When Gracie got pregnant . . ."

"O'Connor barred her from his church," says Mulder. "She and Jared Chirp."

Mackey says, "His church and his home."

•

A flashlight flares as the door to the Church of God with Signs and Wonders creaks open. Mulder enters and turns on the lights. He turns to Scully, who is hanging back.

"You coming?" he asks.

"I think I'll check around back."

Mulder moves through the sanctuary. He comes upon a wall of photos of past church members. Among the photos he notices one of Jared Chirp. Nearby is a photo of Gracie O'Connor, and finally a photo whose label reads ALICE O'CONNOR.

Scully is checking the outside of the building when she comes upon an old dilapidated trailer. She approaches, gun drawn. Inside, her flashlight plays over junk, cages of mice, and a stack of serpent boxes. Hearing a chorus of rattles rising from them, Scully turns and runs into Enoch O'Connor, standing silently in the darkness.

Before she can react, O'Connor knocks the pistol from Scully's hand, grabs her wrists, and walks her back toward the serpent boxes. O'Connor pushes Scully down toward the mesh screen of one of the boxes.

"You must be judged," says O'Connor, as he forces her hand into a box with a snake. "Pray for the Lord's quickening power. Into the hands of God."

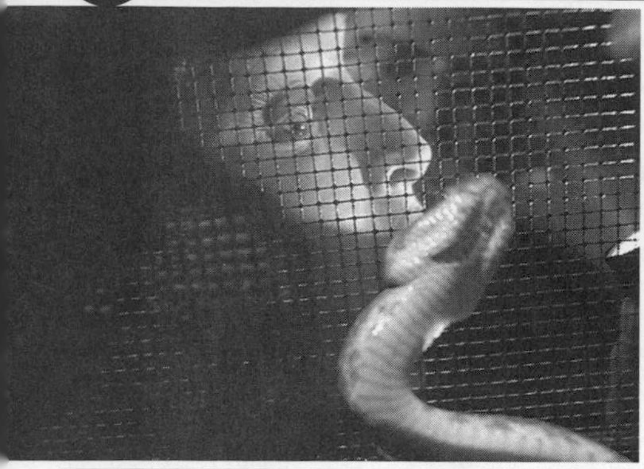
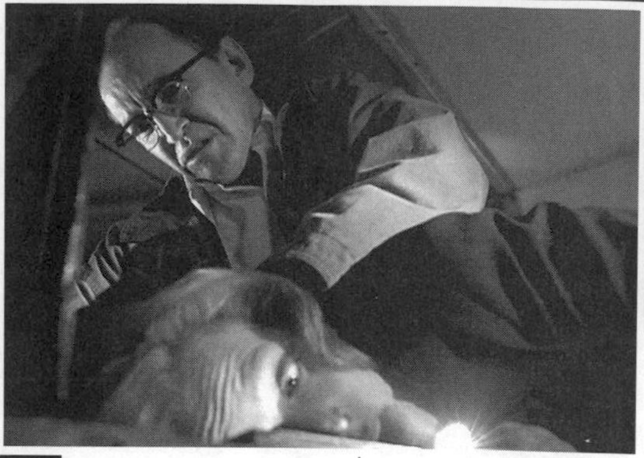

Scully's hand is inches from a coiling snake.

"Let her go!" yells Mulder, as he comes up behind O'Connor, gun drawn.

•

O'Connor is hustled off to the sheriff's station, where he is interrogated by Mulder.

"Your FBI partner could've learned something 'bout herself, you hadn't stopped me. Some powerful good news, maybe," O'Connor says.

Mulder says, "I'd say it's good news for you she's not in here right now, considering what you tried to do to her. . . . Is that what you did to your wife?"

Mulder slides the photo of Alice O'Connor toward him. "Alice O'Connor. Succumbed to multiple snakebites in June 1994. It happened during a church service . . . or at least that's what you told local police. You got away with it. Almost. What was the problem with your wife? Was she not righteous enough for you? Just like your daughter's boyfriend or Iris Finster?"

"Educated man. Too smart to know any better," O'Connor says.

"Smart enough to know you're a murderer."

"Satan is near and you don't even have eyes. You're just proud and fancy free."

Mulder replies, "No one quite passes muster with you. You feel the need to exact some kind of Old Testament revenge. What about your daughter? What were your plans for her?"

"I pray for her soul," says O'Connor. "I pray and I pray, because she's lost."

"Because she no longer believes as you do?"

"You think 'cause you're educated, you're better'n most. You ain't. Unless you're smart down here"—O'Connor points to his heart—"the Devil's gonna make a fool of you and you ain't even gonna know it."

•

Gracie is talking to Scully in the hallway.

"I changed my mind," she says. "I don't want to see him. Besides, I won't do any better'n you people in getting him to talk."

"Gracie, you still don't believe your father did it?"

"It don't matter what I believe. He'll be judged as he deserves. Can't nobody avoid it," says Gracie.

•

Enoch O'Connor lies sleeping on a cot in his jail cell. Suddenly he opens his eyes, feeling a presence in the room. O'Connor walks to the center of his cell, kneels down, and begins to pray. The sound of rattlesnakes buzzes through the cell. A snake slithers out of the darkness. Then another . . . and another . . . and another.

Until O'Connor is surrounded by snakes.

•

Enoch O'Connor lies in the ICU of the McMinn County Hospital, swollen and scarred from a hundred snakebites. Mulder and Scully are standing over him.

"A deputy found him about an hour ago," Mulder says.

Scully says, "I guess it's looking less and less like he's a suspect."

"Unless he somehow managed to do this to himself . . . as a test of his own righteousness."

"If so, the jury's still out," says Scully. "I just spoke to his doctors. It's a tossup whether he'll pull through."

Mulder suggests antivenom treatment. Scully reports that he's not receiving it.

"PEOPLE THINK OF THE DEVIL WITH HORNS AND A TAIL...THEY'RE NOT USED TO LOOKING FOR THE KINDLY MAN WHO TELLS YOU WHAT YOU WANT TO HEAR."—Mulder

"Gracie has stepped in," she says, "she's trying to forbid treatment on religious grounds. It's not clear whether she has a legal claim to do it. But she says it's up to God as to whether he lives or dies."

"And you're thinking that her actions may not be entirely motivated by a concern for her father's eternal soul?"

"Well, more to the point, Mulder, what if she did this? She told me that her father would be judged as he deserves."

"So you think this is what she meant?"

"Well, she grew up around snakes, Mulder. Who's to say she's not every bit as adept at handling them as he is?"

"I can see her being angry at her father to attack him. But what about the others?"

•

Mulder and Scully are at the late Jared Chirp's house, going over his bedroom for clues.

"He left in a hurry," says Mulder as he rummages through dresser drawers. "Packed one suitcase and a gun. Earlier that night, he calls Gracie. He gets Iris instead and starts rambling to her about paying for his sins. He's frightened and wants to leave town. Presumably with Gracie."

"So what's he scared of?" asks Scully. "Although I don't understand it, O'Connor's church exerts a strong pull on these people."

"That's not so hard to understand," counters Mulder. "It's a culture with a very well-defined set of rules."

"It's an intolerant culture," says Scully.

Mulder talks about how some people appreciate the appeal of everything being black and white, right and wrong.

"So you're saying you, Fox Mulder, would welcome someone telling you what to believe?"

"I'm just saying that somebody offering you all the answers can be a very powerful thing."

Mulder notices a piece of paper crumpled near a wastebasket. He pulls the paper out and reads. It is lab results.

"Am I reading this right?" he asks. "That Jared Chirp had himself tested for sterility?"

"Which turns out to be more or less the case," adds Scully. "Based on this, Jared can't be the father of Gracie's baby."

"It's dated the day he died."

"So maybe he was killed because he discovered the truth."

•

Gracie is standing over the still body of her father. Standing next to her is the Reverend Mackey.

"Gracie, I'd like to ask you to reconsider," says Mackey.

"No. This is what he'd want," she says.

"He may die without medical treatment."

Gracie says, "I've seen him bit a dozen times. He always said it was up to God whether he lives or dies. Said it was the worst sin not to trust God."

"There are many ways to trust God, Gracie. One of them is to trust in the miracles of doctors and medicine. In your heart, do you really not want him to get better?" asks Mackey.

"It ain't for me. I can't risk his soul."

Mackey puts his hand on her arm.

"When you first came to me, you said you wanted to think for yourself . . . to live your life as you saw fit. If you stand here and let your father die, whose beliefs are you living? Yours? Or his?" Gracie nods her head. "You're doing the right thing. I'll go tell the doctor, okay?"

Mackey leaves the room. The heart monitor begins to beep faster and faster. A straw-colored fluid begins to seep through his many wounds. The heart monitor is racing. Gracie turns to get help when O'Connor's eyes suddenly snap open and his hand rises up and grabs Gracie's wrist.

•

Mulder and Scully enter the hospital and go to O'Connor's room, where they find Reverend Mackey, a doctor, and a couple of nurses standing over an empty bed.

"Agents, Enoch O'Connor is gone," says Mackey. "I was away five minutes . . . his bed's empty. Gracie's gone, too."

Scully asks how Gracie managed to get O'Connor out of the hospital. Mulder says that maybe O'Connor took her.

"Mulder, he was on his deathbed. That's impossible and besides, what's his motivation?"

Mackey says, "I may be able to answer that. Jared Chirp wasn't the father of Gracie's child."

Adds Mulder, "We know. What about it?"

"Enoch O'Connor is," says Scully.

Mulder and Scully are looking ill.

"That's why she wanted to get away from him and his church as fast as she could. And I tried to teach her to forgive him," says Mackey.

•

The door to the Church of God with Signs and Wonders opens and Enoch O'Connor enters, dragging Gracie into the midst of a group of congregation members.

"I'm bringin' you home," says O'Connor.

"Somebody help me!" cries Gracie.

O'Connor and a second man pick Gracie up and place her in a tub of water. The congregation begins to speak in tongues as O'Connor pushes her head under water.

"In the name of our holy and most fearsome God," says O'Connor. "Resist the Devil and he will flee. Resist him."

Gracie doubles over in pain, wrapping her arms around her belly.

"Something's wrong," she screams. "Something's wrong with my baby!"

Gracie is lifted out of the tub and laid out on the floor. O'Connor kneels down and lays his hand on Gracie's belly. The congregation surrounds her and begins to pray. An elderly woman bends down and puts her in a birthing position. Gracie's belly is illuminated by candlelight. We see something squirming beneath her skin. She screams in pain as her water breaks. Blood-tinged amniotic fluid gushes out onto the floor, and with it a half dozen baby rattlesnakes!

They slither and squirm on the floor among the shocked congregation as O'Connor continues to pray.

•

Mulder and Scully arrive at the church, where they find an ambulance and sheriff's cars sitting outside the church. Gracie, on a gurney, is being administered to by a pair of emergency medical technicians.

"How is she?" Scully asks.

The EMT says, "Deep shock, some loss of blood."

Inside the church, a few members of the congregation are standing to one side. O'Connor is nowhere to be seen.

"What happened here?" asks Scully. "Where's the baby?"

"These folks aren't talking," says a deputy.

"Scully, take a look at this." Mulder is looking at the floor. He spots the trails made by the baby snakes and a shed skin.

"Snakes. She gave birth to snakes?" he asks the members of the congregation.

"The Devil has been cast out," says an elderly woman.

Mulder tells Scully to stay with the woman. She wants to know where he is going.

"To find her father. He's gonna want to tie up some loose ends," says Mulder.

•

Inside the Blessing Community Church, the Reverend Mackey is setting hymnals on seats. He is startled by Enoch O'Connor standing behind him.

"You stole what was most precious to me," says O'Connor.

"Gracie? She came to me on her own."

O'Connor begins to pray in tongues.

Mackey says, "She wanted to escape a life of fear and judgment. Of intolerance. She fled a harsh and vengeful God. And you."

O'Connor pulls a long hunting knife from under his coat and steps toward Mackey. The door bursts open and Mulder races in, drawing his weapon.

"Drop the knife!" he yells.

O'Connor raises the knife. Mulder fires. O'Connor drops the knife and collapses, blood pooling from underneath his shoulder.

•

Gracie is in the ambulance, rocking as it speeds along. She asks for her daddy. Scully, sitting beside her, leans in closer.

"Gracie, it's Agent Scully. We're taking you to the doctor right now, okay? Can you tell me what happened?"

Gracie asks, "Where's my daddy?"

"You're safe. My partner's gone after him. Gracie, you're going to be okay. He can't hurt you anymore."

"You don't understand! He saved me!"

•

Mulder is attending to O'Connor's wound. He is staring intently at Mackey, who returns the gaze. Mackey goes to call for an ambulance, leaving Mulder alone with O'Connor, who tries to get up. Mulder pushes him back down, assuring him that help is on its way.

O'Connor says, "No, it's not. I told you, boy . . . you still don't know which side you're on. Be smart down here."

Mulder considers the ravings of this mad preacher. He goes to the office, where Mackey is apparently asking for an ambulance. He draws his gun and points it at Mackey.

"Agent?" says Mackey.

Mulder says, "It wasn't O'Connor. It was you. You killed Jared Chirp."

"You're joking."

"No. I'm just beginning to see it now. Jared must have come to understand that he wasn't the father of Gracie's baby . . . that you were. Did he confront you earlier that night, only to see you for who you really are?"

"Just who is it you think I am?" asks Mackey.

"Is that what happened to Iris Finster? She was beginning to catch on, is that why you killed her? Or is it just to further frame Enoch O'Connor? Is that what this is really about? Ruining O'Connor? Seducing his daughter? Destroying him by any conceivable means?"

Mackey begins to ease toward Mulder.

"Are you a righteous man, Agent Mulder?"

"Stay where you are."

"It's just a simple question. Most people believe they're on the side of angels. But are they? If you were put to the test, how would you do?"

Mulder raises his pistol a bit higher. He is suddenly distracted by the ominous sound of doors slamming. He lowers the pistol, then brings it back up.

He's holding a rattlesnake in his hands. He drops the snake, now transformed back into his gun. He looks down as another snake slithers out of his pant leg. He stumbles back. A number of snakes are now crawling over his body.

Scully rushes into the church. Spotting O'Connor lying wounded on the ground, she rushes to him.

"Where's Mulder?" she asks.

"You can't help him," says O'Connor.

Before Scully can answer, she hears Mulder call for help. She starts to go to him when O'Connor tries to stop her, saying, "This is his alone."

She goes to the office door, finding it locked. As she starts kicking it in, Mulder lies inside, fang marks on his shirt, crawling away from the snakes. Mackey looks down on him as one large snake, poised to attack, bites Mulder.

Eventually Scully bursts through the door and sees Mulder on the ground, unconscious and alone, as one giant snake slithers out the door. His gun is by his side. She begins helping her partner as O'Connor steps into the doorway.

•

Mulder is in his hospital bed, recovering from what have turned out to be minor wounds. He looks up as Scully enters the room.

"Mackey?" asks Mulder.

"Still no trace, even though every law enforcement agency in Tennessee's out looking for him."

"They won't find him. People think the Devil has horns and a tail. They're not used to looking for the kindly man who tells you what you want to hear."

"He's just a man, Mulder. Just like O'Connor."

"Not like O'Connor. If this really was some kind of test, looks like I failed."

Scully says, "I'd say if it was, you passed with flying colors. You're alive, aren't you?"

"Proud and fancy-free," he says.

•

A middle-aged woman is sitting in the office of a church in Hamden, Connecticut. She is meeting with the new minister, Reverend Winston Wells.

"Reverend Wells, it's a real joy to have a man in the pulpit who has such an open and modern way of looking at God."

"Bless you for saying so," says the reverend.

"Well, I won't keep you. I just wanted to welcome you to Hamden."

"Thank you," says the reverend. "I look forward to seeing you on Sunday." Reverend Wells is, in fact, Reverend Mackey.

The woman leaves. Closing the door behind her, Mackey/Wells plops back down in his leather chair. He opens his desk drawer and takes the lid off a small box, revealing a white mouse inside.

He grabs the mouse by the tail, lifts it high above his head, and opens his mouth wide. A bulge begins to rise in Mackey's throat.

The bulge is a rattlesnake, which rises out of Mackey's mouth, swallows the mouse in a single gulp, and slips back down inside Mackey, content and well fed.

BACK STORY:

Kim Manners is deathly afraid of snakes. So is David Duchovny. John Shiban would not go near the set when the episode was being filmed.

"Signs & Wonders" was looking promising. On the surface primarily an exercise in pure horror playing to people's very real fear of serpents, "Signs & Wonders" also worked as a religious allegory, in which the concept of good and evil, in a classic *X-Files* twist, was stood on its head.

"Signs & Wonders" was the brainchild of *X-Files* staff writer Jeffrey Bell, who was dying to do a down-and-dirty *X-Files* horror episode and who had also long been an informal student of Appalachian snake handling religious practices. "I thought anything involving snakes would be scary and I saw the church stuff as something that would be really fascinating," says Bell, who also wrote the Season 6 animal attack episode "Alpha." "I wanted the snake church people to end up being the good guys. The big trick was going to be how we were going to hide the real bad guys. The way the shows usually work out, Mulder is the one to figure out who the bad guys are. So I went into the story meeting with the idea of having Mulder being wrong. Because Mulder believes so strongly it's the other guy, it helped to hide the true identity of the bad guy from the audience."

As Bell worked to complete the "Signs & Wonders" script against the typical short deadline, the *X-Files* production staff turned to casting the backwoods population of the fictional Blessing, Tennessee. And the specter of live rattlesnakes slithering around the actors was a major consideration.

Frank Spotnitz remembers the rather unorthodox casting process. "Kim Manners told me, 'When we cast this thing, I don't want the actors to say they're not afraid of snakes, get to the set, and then find out that they are.' So we had a snake wrangler come into the casting office the day actors were reading and, after they read, he would take a rattlesnake out of its cage and the actors would have to hold the rattlesnake as part of their audition. And the funny thing was that the actors couldn't wait to hold the rattlesnake. They were thrilled at the idea . . . but we were still nervous."

And so a series of safety meetings was set up prior to the start of filming. Among the items on the agenda, according to makeup effects coordinator John Vulich, was the distance to the nearest hospital in case somebody was bitten. During one of those meetings, the production company's collective snake phobia was accidentally tested. John Shiban remembered, "When we were prepping the show, the snake wrangler brought his snakes to Kim Manners's office and they were talking and showing the snakes to everybody. At one point, the snake wrangler said, 'Hold on, everybody, one of the snakes is not in the box.' One of the snakes had gotten loose in Kim's office."

The snake was eventually found, coiled behind Manners's desk, but the incident served to emphasize the fact that rattlesnakes would be a constant potential threat on the "Signs &

Wonders" set. However, using the snakes was critical to the verisimilitude of the episode. The snakes' lips were sutured shut so that they could effectively perform while cutting down the chance of the unexpected happening.

"But the thread on those sutures could break," cautions Spotnitz, "and we had to be very careful how the actors held them because if they got agitated, they might get loose."

Not surprisingly, the tension was thick as the actors and reptiles began filming the episode. Snake jokes were not tolerated on the set. And despite assurances that all the human actors had passed snake muster, a Gillian Anderson stunt double panicked during the shooting of an insert scene in which Anderson's hand was thrust into a box of snakes. The on-set snake wrangler had to step in and do the shot.

A potential problem developed midway through the filming over a scene where a rattlesnake is thrust into the camera frame as part of an attack sequence. Paul Rabwin recalled that the production people were at a loss as to how to shoot the sequence until visual effects coordinator Bill Millar stepped forward with the creative suggestion that they reverse the sequence on a fiber optic camera. "So we shot the scene with the snake's mouth on a fiber optic camera and rolled the camera on the snake snapping back from the camera, reversed the shot, and we had our snake attack," explains Rabwin.

According to stunt coordinator Danny Weselis, there were anywhere between six and fifty snakes on the set at any one time. Fifteen snakes were involved in the truly horrifying sequence when Mulder is attacked by an army of rattlers who crawl inside his clothes. Duchovny was not within blocks of that scene. "We doubled David," reveals Weselis with an evil grin. "We just dumped fifteen snakes down the stunt double's pants and had them crawl out of his pant legs. It was disgusting, but it turned out to be a great shot."

Separate body parts were a definite part of the "Signs & Wonders" equation. John Vulich relates that his company brought to the table a number of silicone arms that the snakes would attack and, in the sequence where Gracie gives birth to snakes, a false stomach whose mechanics simulated the disgusting vision of live snakes wriggling around inside her stomach.

"Signs & Wonders" turned out to be easily one of the most viscerally horrifying episodes of the season. The primary expected response from viewers was one of true, nightmare-inducing terror. However, executive producer Spotnitz hopes that audiences got the underlying theme of the episode, which, he claims, is scary in its own way.

"The theme of the episode was that intolerance can be good. That the snake charmer-preacher turned out to be the good guy turned the expectations totally on their head."

The general impression in the production company was that network Standards and Practices would be all over this snake-infested episode. However, Spotnitz laughingly recalls that just the opposite was true.

"We thought we'd get all kinds of notes but we didn't. Ironically, the only thing they objected to was in the very last scene of the show. In the background of the preacher's office was a very famous painting of Adam and Eve being cast out of the Garden of Eden. The only note we got was that they could see the genitalia on the figures in the painting."

FACTS:

Actor Michael Childers, who plays the snake preacher Reverend Enoch O'Connor, is actually the father of a real-life snake preacher.

Not all the snakes in "Signs & Wonders" were real. A puppet snake was used for some of the tight closeup scenes.

When he could not find an appropriate gospel song for the snake-handling sequence, producer Paul Rabwin wrote the song "Sweet Lord Protect Me and Take Me to the Light."

A fake Mulder snake-bite arm was recycled from the sixth season episode "Dreamland."

episode 7X10

SEIN UND ZEIT

EPISODE: 7X10
FIRST AIRED: February 6, 2000
EDITOR: Heather MacDougall
WRITTEN BY: Chris Carter & Frank Spotnitz
DIRECTED BY: Michael Watkins

The kidnapping of a little girl brings Mulder and Scully face-to-face with a decades-old spectre of evil.

GUEST STARS:

Mitch Pileggi (A.D. Skinner)
Megan Corletto (Amber Lynn LaPierre)
Shareen Mitchell (Billie LaPierre)
Mark Rolston (Bud LaPierre)
Spencer Garrett (Harry Bring)
Rebecca Toolan (Mrs. Mulder)
Martin Grey (Agent Flagler)
Kim Darby (Kathy Lee Tencate)
Randall Bosley (Paunchy Man, AKA Ed Truelove)
Marie Chambers (Guard)
John Harnagel (World-Weary Dad)
Dylan St. Jepovic (Dean Tencate)
Nancy Tiballi (News Anchor #1)
John Bisom (News Anchor #2)
Nick Lashaway (Young Mulder)
Ashlynn Rose (Young Samantha)

PRINCIPAL SETTINGS:

Sacramento, California; Greenwich, Connecticut; Redding, California

"Now I lay me down to sleep. I pray the Lord my soul to keep. If I die before I wake, I pray the Lord my soul to take."

Amber Lynn LaPierre is kneeling by her bed, saying her prayers, as her parents, Bud and Billie LaPierre, watch with affection. As Amber finishes, Billie pulls up the covers on her bed while Bud locks the open window.

"Night-night, Little," says Bud, kissing his daughter on her forehead.

"Headlights out, Amber Lynn," says Billie, as she turns off the light.

Bud and Billie exit the room, leaving the door partway open.

Bud is in the living room watching television. In the master bedroom, Billie comes out of the bathroom, dressed for bed. She pauses a moment, goes to her closet, and emerges with a piece of clothing on a hanger, encased in dry cleaner's plastic. Billie rips off a piece of paper from the hanger, takes out a red felt-tip pen from a drawer, and scribbles something onto the paper.

Bud hears the sound of a shutting drawer. He calls for his wife, gets no answer, and goes to the bedroom, where he sees his wife writing what the camera shows to be a ransom note:

Mr. and Mrs. LaPierre, Listen carefully: I have kidnapped your daughter and will kill her unless you do exactly as I say!

Bud goes to his daughter's room. He looks in and sees his daughter sound asleep in her bed. He pushes open the door and quietly goes to her bed. Meanwhile, Billie continues to write her ransom note:

Any deviation from my instructions will result in the execution of Amber Lynn. Go to the police and I will strangle her and send her body parts one by one!

Bud reaches down to turn his sleeping daughter over. Amber Lynn's face is covered in bruises and she has been strangled. He gasps in horror and reaches back to his daughter, only to discover that she is sleeping soundly—and very much alive.

And his wife continues writing her note:

Talk to anyone and I will behead Amber Lynn. Tell a stray dog and you will never see her alive again. So don't do anything dumb. No one shoots at Santa Claus!

Bud covers his daughter up and leaves the room. He starts down the hall when Amber Lynn's door suddenly slams shut behind him. Bud races back to the door and tries to open it. It won't open.

A pool of blood oozes under her door.

Bud screams, "Billie! Amber Lynn! Oh my God!"

Bud repeatedly slams his shoulder against the door and it busts open. He bursts into the room.

His daughter is gone.

•

Mulder walks briskly down a hallway and into A.D. Skinner's office, where he finds his boss surrounded by agents, speaking anxiously into the phone.

"Amber Lynn LaPierre, that's right. A federal investigation is under way of a kidnapping in Sacramento, California," says Skinner.

Mulder is greeted by a strange look from Skinner as he puts down the phone receiver.

"Why are you here, Agent Mulder?" asks Skinner.

"I want this case," says Mulder.

Skinner says, "I'm fairly certain I've got more than enough competent agents here. This is a kidnapping, Agent Mulder. A little girl snatched from her bedroom. Basic missionary-style FBI work. Not an X-File."

"I'm aware of the facts."

"We're trying to rule out all possibilities before we start making any statements."

"That's what I'm talking about. Ruling out other possibilities."

"I can't just give you the case. I have to follow protocol. Behavioral has first crack, then the people down at NCMEC."

Mulder says, "Two, three, four hours, this case's going to be a circus. Every starstruck attorney in America is gonna want to represent these people for free. If somebody doesn't ask the right questions right now, they may never get asked."

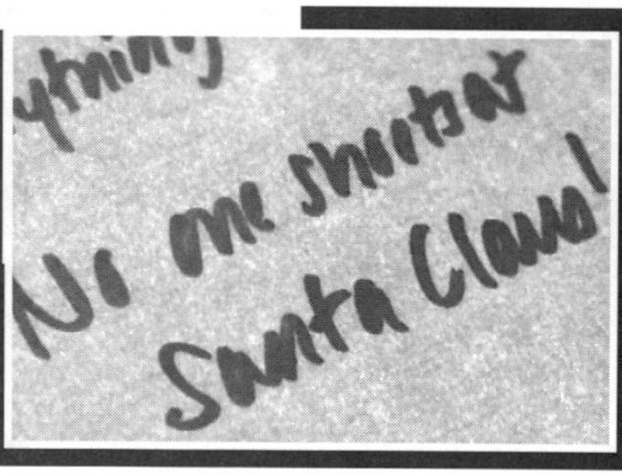

Skinner looks at his watch.

"You've got 'til noon," he says.

Mulder nods and turns to leave.

Skinner says, "Mulder. The agents in my office . . . they have a pool going."

Mulder understands what Skinner is trying to say. "They think she's dead. Don't bet on it."

•

Mulder's car pulls to a stop in front of the LaPierre residence. A group of news crews and deputies swarm around the front lawn of the modest home. He flashes his FBI badge and is immediately surrounded by reporters shouting questions. Mulder ignores them and makes his way into the house, where he is confronted by the LaPierres' lawyer, Harry Bring. Bud and Billie sit on a coach in the background.

"Sorry. No press allowed inside," says the lawyer.

"Special Agent Fox Mulder, FBI. I'd like to speak with Mr. and Mrs. LaPierre if I may."

Bring produces a business card. "My clients have nothing to say. Harry Bring. How can I help you?"

Mulder checks out the card. "Mr. Bring, your card says real estate law and conveyances. Have you ever handled a murder case?"

"This isn't a murder case," says Bring.

"It might as well be once the facts about Amber Lynn's disappearance get out. If you want to help your clients, Mr. Bring, get them a real lawyer."

Bud LaPierre overhears the conversation.

"It's okay, Harry. Billie and I got nothing to hide," says Bud as he comforts his crying wife.

Mulder introduces himself to the couple

"Mr. and Mrs. LaPierre, I'm a special agent with the FBI and I've had a lot of experience with crimes like the one that took place here," says Mulder. "Now, I know you've made a statement to the police, but I'd like to ask you some questions about that and I'd like you to answer in as much detail as both you and your lawyer are comfortable with. I want to ask you about the note you found. Where did you find it?"

Bud says, "In my daughter's bedroom."

"When?"

"When I went to check on her. It was nine-thirty, I think. It was right about then. I was watching TV in here."

"What were you watching?" asks Mulder.

"I've never heard of it before," says Bud. "It was good."

"What about you, Mrs. LaPierre?" asks Mulder.

Billie has clearly been crying nonstop. She hesitates, looks at Bud, then answers, "I was in bed already."

"Were you asleep?"

"Half."

"Is that Amber Lynn's bedroom that I saw down the hallway there?" asks Mulder.

"Yes."

"Do you always lock your doors at night, even if you're at home?"

"Yes." She nods again, trying not to cry.

Mulder says, "You know most of your neighbors, I bet. Up and down the street. You're on good terms with them?"

"Most of them, yes," says Bud, also holding back tears.

"Can you think of anyone who might have wanted to hurt Amber Lynn?"

The mother breaks down crying. "That's enough questions," says Bring.

"Mr. and Mrs. LaPierre," Mulder says. "I want you to understand something, because it's all going to get very confusing from here on in. But whatever else the FBI says or does, they're going to try their damnedest to find your little girl."

"Thank you," manages Billie.

Bring asks, "Agent Mulder, do you think they will? Find her?"

"I hope so," says Mulder. "Yeah, I really do."

•

That night a car pulls into the parking lot of the May Lane Motel. Scully gets out and goes to a room. It is dark except for a faint light from the television. Scully knocks on the door.

"It's open," says Mulder.

He is lying on the bed, staring silently at the ceiling.

"What are you doing?" she asks.

"Thinking."

"About?"

"Amber Lynn LaPierre," he says.

"Mind if I turn on a light?"

"Yeah, I do."

The TV silently blares out a news report about the LaPierre disappearance.

Scully leaves the room dark and says, "Skinner is royally pissed. At you."

"I'm sure he is." Mulder's eyes never leave the television.

"He expected a report at noon. He waited. Now he sent me to find you, to get it."

"I don't have a report."

"They had to move on the case," reports Scully. "The media got wind of the police findings and they're going to broadcast them. The parents are being held for further questioning."

"They're not guilty, Scully."

"The facts would state otherwise. There's no sign of a break-in. Both the parents were at home at the time the girl disappeared."

"They lied about where they found the note."

"Why?" asks Scully.

"That's what I've been thinking about," he says, looking at her for the first time.

Scully looks at the television, which now shows photos of other notorious kidnap cases. "Is it the media, or just our own morbid fascination with the killing of an innocent?"

"She's not dead, Scully," says Mulder.

Mulder's cell phone rings before Scully can respond. It is Mulder's mother, who is watching the same television news coverage.

"Fox, it's me. I'm watching the news. That little girl in California. You're out there, aren't you?"

"Yes, I am. Are you okay, Mom?"

"When are you coming back here?" asks his mother.

"Well, I'm not sure. I don't know."

"Call when you get back, Fox."

"Okay, I will. You take care, Mom."

He hangs up, as does Mrs. Mulder, who nervously fingers a photo of Mulder and his sister, Samantha.

•

Skinner and a group of agents are going over the evidence during a late-night meeting in his office. Of particular interest is the ransom note, which has been projected onto a screen.

"From the note we can and have determined several facts," says Skinner. "There is the threat of physical violence, but no demand for money or a ransom. The note is short and written on a torn piece of paper, suggesting haste and little or no planning."

Mulder and Scully enter.

Skinner continues, "The paper is a type used by dry cleaners to protect laundered garments. The torn piece the note was found on matches exactly a piece that was found in the garbage of the LaPierre home. The ink matches a felt-tip pen also found in the garbage. One set of prints were found on it. Billie LaPierre's prints."

"Is it her handwriting?" Mulder asks.

Agent Flagler, a handwriting expert, steps forward and enlightens the group. While it is difficult to say for sure, and despite the apparent attempts to disguise the writing, when compared to another writing sample, there are strong similarities to Mrs. LaPierre's handwriting. "Enough to make a connection."

Mulder disagrees with the conclusion that this solves the case.

Skinner asks, "Do you have information you'd like to share with us, Agent Mulder?"

Mulder says, "Bud LaPierre says he'd been watching television and had gotten up to go to bed when he found Amber Lynn missing. But according to the police report, the TV set was still on when the first officers arrived on the scene. By his own account, both mother and father put Amber Lynn to bed and were never more than twenty feet from her room during the period in which she was abducted."

The word *abducted* does not sit well with the assembled agents.

Mulder says, "The LaPierres know all their neighbors, are on good terms with them, but no one saw a stranger on a Friday, at a fairly early hour, enter into a locked and lighted house and remove this little girl undetected."

"Husband's lying for his wife," says Flagler.

"I don't think so," says Mulder.

Skinner wants to know why.

"Because that doesn't explain what happened to this little girl."

Mulder looks at the projected ransom note and focuses on the line "No one shoots at Santa Claus!" He abruptly walks out.

Scully follows and enters Mulder's office to find him intensely going through a file cabinet.

"What are you doing, Mulder?" asks Scully.

"There's something in that abduction note that I've seen before."

"That's not what I mean," says Scully. "You're personalizing this case. Identifying with your sister."

"My sister was taken by aliens. Did I say anything about aliens, Scully?"

"There are a lot of good agents up there in Skinner's office who do not have the patience for this."

"What did I do?" asks Mulder. "I provided a logical counterpoint."

"You told them that they were wrong, Mulder."

"But they are," says Mulder, opening a file and showing Scully: "1987—Pocatello, Idaho." Inside is a photocopy of a ransom note that ends with the sentence "Nobody shoots at Santa Claus!"

"Look familiar?"

•

A car sits on a residential street in Redding, California, in front of a home where children are playing on the front lawn. In the front seat, a man holds a video camera, taping the children at play. Inside the car, a Santa Claus ornament dangles from a rearview mirror.

•

Mulder and Scully are escorted through the cell block at Idaho Women's State Prison to a particular cell.

"Kathy Lee?" says the guard. "Visitors are here."

Kathy Lee Tencate, a slight, mousy woman, puts down the book she's reading, *Strangers Among Us*.

"Can you let them in, please?" she says. Mulder introduces himself and Scully and asks if they may have a seat. "It's not the Ritz," she replies.

Mulder sits down with a smile. "We just have a few questions," he begins. "We've reviewed the facts of your case and the facts seem to speak for themselves. Your six-year-old son, Dean, was taken from his bed while he slept. A note found threatening his life, was later determined to be written by you. You pled innocent at trial, but you were convicted and given twelve years, even though your son's body was never found."

Kathy Lee says, "Yes, that's right."

"Your story," Mulder continues, "is that on the night your son disappeared you had a vision of him dead. That you thought it was your mind playing tricks on you, but when you got up to check on him, he was missing from his bed. Is that accurate?"

"Yes."

"Now, three years ago, after seven years of incarceration, you changed your story and confessed to the murder of your son in a fit of insanity. A psychotic break."

"Yes, that's right," she says.

"Why did you do it?" asks Scully.

"I don't know. I was full of rage."

Mulder says, "I have a copy of the note that you wrote. Do you mind if I show it to you? Now, there's a phrase down here at the bottom: 'No one shoots at Santa Claus!' Can you explain what that means to me?"

"It means . . . that when someone promises you something . . . a gift . . . like Santa Claus, that no one would do anything for fear of not getting the gift."

Mulder hands Kathy Lee another piece of paper. "A little girl disappeared from her bed three days ago. This was a note that was left at the scene. Could you take a look at that and tell me what it says at the bottom?"

She stares at the LaPierre note. "The same thing," she says softly.

"Neither note has a specific demand," says Mulder. "In both cases, there's no evidence of foul play or a break-in. And, as in your son's case, there's no body to be found."

Kathy Lee claims she told investigators where her son's body was, while Mulder insists the body was never found. The argument turns loud, with Kathy Lee insisting she can't explain it.

Mulder says, urgently, "You can't explain it because you didn't do anything." Kathy Lee stays silent. "You didn't kill your son, you didn't bury him. You're not guilty of anything other than a lie, just like these people. The only reason you changed your story was to get out of here. Because you know the parole board might buy the story of a psychotic break and of your terrible remorse. But they would never ever let a woman out of jail who claimed her son just disappeared into thin air. They need someone to tell them it's okay. Someone to corroborate their story."

"I'm not that person," says Kathy Lee, unable to look at Mulder.

"They need your help," says Mulder. Kathy Lee does not respond.

The guard arrives, signaling it's time to leave.

"That was utterly irresponsible, Mulder. It was out of line and without any basis in reality," Scully comments as they leave the cell.

"Do you think that woman could've killed her son?" asks Mulder.

"She was convicted in a court of law."

"So how do you explain those two notes, written over ten years apart, could contain the same obscure phrase?"

Scully accuses Mulder of personalizing the case.

Mulder says, "No, I'm gonna to solve this case. I'm going to solve it."

"How?" asks Scully.

"I'm going to find those kids."

"What if they're dead, Mulder? Don't go looking for something you don't want to find."

•

Kathy Lee is in emotional turmoil as the result of Mulder and Scully's visit. Curled up on her cot in her cell, she looks up to see a ghostly apparition of her son standing silently in her cell, then he is gone. Kathy Lee rushes to the cell door and calls, "Guard! Guard, can you please get them back? Guard, I need to talk!"

•

Mrs. Mulder is once again on the phone to her son. She picks up the photo of Fox and

Samantha Mulder. She hears an answering machine beep.

"Fox, it's your mother. I'd hoped you'd call upon your return, but I haven't heard from you. I'm sure you're busy. There are so many emotions in me I wouldn't know where to start."

As she speaks, Mrs. Mulder takes the photo from the frame and drops it into a flaming wastebasket in which other photos are being consumed.

"There's so much that I've left unsaid for reasons I hope one day you'll understand."

•

Mulder, a videocassette in hand, enters an interrogation room to meet with Mr. and Mrs. LaPierre and their lawyer, Harry Bring, who demands to know why this meeting was called.

"I have something I'd like your clients to see," says Mulder.

The lawyer says, "I want to know what it is first."

know you're afraid of the truth because I saw things I was afraid of, too. And I can't explain all of it, except to say that I don't remember ever thinking those words that I wrote, let alone writing them. It was like they wrote themselves using my hand. But what I know for sure, because I feel it in my heart, is that my son is safe and protected. And in a better place."

The video screen fades to black. Tears continue to roll down Billie's face.

•

A television news report announces that the parents of Amber Lynn LaPierre were released for lack of evidence after giving a new statement to the Sacramento police. Over footage of the LaPierres returning to their home, the news announcer continues . . .

". . . recounting a detailed story that claims supernatural forces were at work when their daughter was abducted. The LaPierres, seen here returning to their home, declined comment."

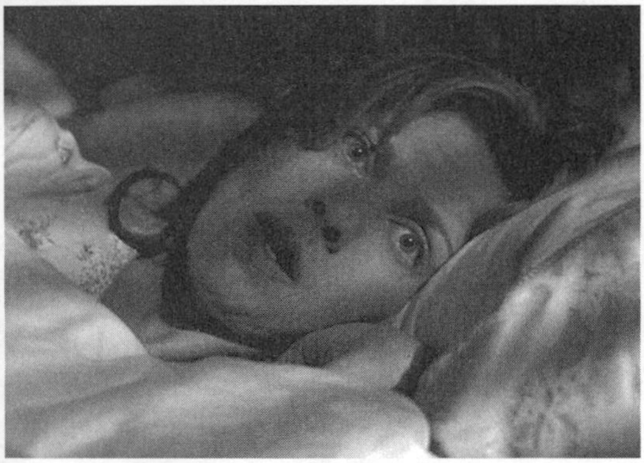

Mulder says, "Don't shoot at Santa Claus, Mr. Bring. You're gonna want to see this, too."

He pops the videocassette into a TV monitor. On screen appears Kathy Lee Tencate, who has been videotaped in her cell. "I believe you share a secret," says Mulder, with a look at Billie.

Kathy Lee begins, "I'm doing this because I feel it's the right thing to do and because I know what you're going through. And I wouldn't want to happen to you what happened to me. I just want to tell you that your little girl is okay." Billie begins to sob. "And I

The mysterious videotaper is viewing a bank of monitors, among them the news report and one showing a tape of Amber Lynn LaPierre. On other monitors are videos of different children, some playing in the yard, some sitting on Santa Claus's lap.

The mystery man returns to the news report with renewed interest as Mulder appears onscreen, giving a statement.

Mulder says, "Federal investigation of the case will continue, but will no longer focus on the LaPierres as primary suspects. We will intensify our search for Amber Lynn and we will remain hopeful of her eventual safe return."

•

Skinner is watching the news broadcast in his office. Mulder is seated nearby. Skinner, not happy, turns off the television.

Skinner says, "Intensify our search where? The Twilight Zone?"

"I have a corroborating witness," says Mulder.

"In state prison."

"There's a material connection between these two women."

Skinner says, "The only connection, Agent Mulder, is you. I've got people busting their butts on this thing, Agent Mulder. Putting together hard evidence, real evidence, while you're out gathering Grimm's fairy tales from convicted murderers."

Mulder says, "It doesn't make sense. It's incomprehensible in any kind of real-world way."

Scully enters the room.

"I deal in the real world, Agent Mulder. You begged on to this case as part of the solution. All you've done is hand our only suspects the Twinkie Defense."

Scully timidly interrupts.

"What? What is it, Agent Scully?" asks Skinner.

"I need to have a word with Agent Mulder."

"It can wait," insists Skinner.

"No, it can't, sir."

"What is it, Scully?" asks Mulder.

"Mulder. Your mom's dead."

•

In Greenwich, Connecticut, local police and coroner's assistants gather evidence as Mulder and Scully push through the front door. Mulder moves to talk with the coroner. An open oven door and masking tape over cracks beneath doors and windows are evidence that Mrs. Mulder took her own life. The coroner hands Mulder an empty pill bottle. Scully hangs back at a discreet distance. Mulder comes out of the bathroom holding three empty medicine bottles.

"What is it?" asks Scully.

"Diazepam," he says. "She used them to sleep."

Scully asks if there was a note. Mulder shakes his head no.

He says, "She called me when I was in California. She'd wanted to talk but I never called her back. Why would she do this? It just doesn't make any sense."

"We never truly know why," says Scully.

"No. She wouldn't kill herself," says Mulder. He crosses to her dresser and notices the empty frames. "Why are the pictures gone? There were photos of my sister and I. This is all that she had left of us and they're missing. Why would . . . ?" Mulder, realizing something, takes a deep breath. "She saw me on the news, she wanted to talk about the missing girl, Amber Lynn. She wanted to tell me something about her. Maybe she couldn't tell me over the phone because she was afraid that they would do something like this to her."

"Who?" asks Scully.

"THERE'S SO MUCH THAT I'VE LEFT UNSAID FOR REASONS I HOPE ONE DAY YOU'LL UNDERSTAND."— Mrs. Mulder

"Whoever took my sister. Look at this place, it's like, it's all staged. The pills, the oven, the tape. It's like a bad movie script. They would've come here and they would've threatened her. She would be upset. They had to sedate her. I would look for a needle puncture mark or something else in her system besides these pills."

Mulder stares hard at Scully. She senses what he wants.

She says, "No, Mulder, please don't ask me to do this."

"Scully, who else can I ask?"

"Mulder, an autopsy? It's one thing on a stranger, but you're my friend. And she's your mother."

Mulder insists, "I know, but if you don't do it, then I might never know the truth."

•

Kathy Lee is laying on her bunk when she hears the sound of approaching footsteps. She sits up and sees Mulder standing on the other side of the cell door.

"You've seen things," he says. "I need to understand them."

"Something happened to you?" she asks, approaching him.

"My mother is dead. You know why." She shakes her head no.

"Look, I can help you," says Mulder. "I can talk to the parole board for you. But right now I need you to help me."

She says, "I don't understand what you want."

"I'm not here by accident. My sister was taken away from me. When she was eight years old. Like your son was taken away from you."

"Where is your sister now?" she asks.

"I don't know."

"Your mother knew, didn't she?"

Mulder senses the tone of certainty in her voice.

"Why do you say that?" asks Mulder.

"She was trying to tell you."

"Tell me what?"

"She'd seen them," says Kathy Lee.

"Who?"

"The Walk-ins," she says, calmly. "Old souls looking for new homes. Your sister is among them."

"THE WALK INS. OLD SOULS LOOKING FOR NEW HOMES. YOUR SISTER IS AMONG THEM."—Kathy Lee

Mulder tires to process this. "You can see them?" he asks.

She smiles. "Yes. But sometimes it's very difficult because they live in starlight."

Mulder gets up the courage to ask. "Is my sister dead?"

Kathy Lee says, "They took her. To protect her soul from the great harm it would've suffered in her life. Just like they did my little boy."

"Where do they take them?" asks Mulder. "Your boy, this little girl, Amber Lynn LaPierre?"

"I don't know," she says. "But they're okay. I'm sure your sister's there, too."

•

Santa's North Pole Village is a deserted throwback to another time. A Volvo wagon pulls into the empty parking lot. The doors open and a bunch of kids, followed by their weary parents, scramble out. The kids race through the petting zoo, looking at deer standing sedately in the sun.

A man dressed in work clothes comes out from a building, looking and smiling at the children. He appears to be a caretaker.

"Hey, buddy, kids just want to see Santa. What about it?" asks the father.

"He's just flying in," says the man. The kids cheer at the impending visit from Santa.

The man walks away and into Santa's Workshop, a room full of toys, workbenches, and all kinds of Christmas stuff. He takes out a key and opens an adjoining room. Inside the room, a group of monitors take in the various locations of the park. The videotaper takes off his clothes and prepares to put on a Santa Claus suit.

Mulder is sitting alone in his apartment, listening intently, over and over, to his mother's final phone message when there is a knock on the door. Mulder opens the door and lets Scully in.

"Glad you're here."

He says, "My mom was trying to tell me something." He returns to the answering machine and rewinds the message once again. "I think I figured it out. Something about my sister, she was never able to tell me." He plays part of her message. "She knew what I'd find with this case out in California."

"How could she know that, Mulder?"

"A child disappearing without a trace. Without evidence. In defiance of all logical explanation." Scully can tell where Mulder's going with this. "She knew because of what's driven me. What I've always believed, Scully, these parents who've lost their children, they've had visions of their sons and daughters. In scenarios that never happened, but which they described in notes that came through them as automatic writing and words that came through them psychically from old souls protecting the children. My mother must've written a note like that herself. Describing the scenario of my sister's disappearance. Of her abduction by aliens. Don't you see, Scully? It never happened. All these visions that I've had have been to help me to cope, to help me deal with the loss. But I've been looking for my sister in the wrong place. That's what my mother was trying to tell me. That's what she was trying to warn me about. That's why they killed her."

"Your mother killed herself, Mulder," Scully says, gently with concern. "I conducted the autopsy. She was dying of an incurable disease. An untreatable and horribly disfiguring disease called Paget's carcinoma. She knew it, there were doctor's records. She didn't want to live."

Mulder stares at Scully, unable to respond. He suddenly jumps up and shakes his work table in frustration. Tears begin to flood into his eyes. "She was trying to tell me something. She was trying to tell me something." Mulder curls up on the chair, crying.

"She was trying to tell you to stop. To stop looking for your sister. She was just trying to take away your pain."

Scully takes Mulder in her arms as he cries on her shoulder.

•

The LaPierres have come to the end of another bad day. Bud climbs into bed next to his wife. Billie is in a sad state. As she lays in bed, her eyes are wide open, staring up and out. Suddenly she gasps and tries to sit up.

Amber Lynn is standing in front of her, her nightgown blowing gently in the night breeze. Her lips are moving.

But nothing is heard.

•

Scully has spent the night comforting Mulder. She answers a knock on Mulder's door. It is Assistant Director Skinner.

"How's he doing?" he asks.

Scully says, "It's been a hard night for him."

Skinner nods. "Billie LaPierre is asking for him," he tells her. "She's got something to say, and she'll only talk to Mulder."

Scully quietly argues that it is not a good time for Mulder to be pursuing this case. An emotionally drained Mulder appears behind Scully, wanting to know what is going on.

Skinner says, "This case has heated up. I've booked two flights for us."

Mulder nods and leaves to get his things. Scully looks at Skinner. "Well, then you better book three."

•

Bud LaPierre walks into his bedroom, where he finds his wife, Billie, still in bed, sleeping.

"Honey, wake up. He's here."

She sits up and sees Mulder standing in the doorway of the bedroom. She tells Mulder to come in, but is taken aback when she sees Scully standing behind him.

"It's okay," says Mulder. "She's here to help. What happened here, Billie?"

Billie says, "I saw my daughter. Right in this room. Standing right there. I swear to God, she was right over there. In the pajamas her Gramma gave her. Saying something to me."

Mulder asks, "What was she saying?"

"I don't know. Her lips were moving but I couldn't hear." Billie fights her tears. "I thought she was saying 'seventy-four,' " says Billie, who is overwhelmed with emotion.

" 'Seventy-four'? Does that mean anything to you?" Mulder asks.

They shake their heads no. Scully slips from the room. Mulder stays with the couple for a few moments, then joins Scully and Skinner outside the house.

"Let's go home," Mulder says.

Scully says, "Mulder, we just got here."

"We're not going to find these people's daughter alive."

"How do you know that?" she asks.

"What we're hearing . . . it's the delusional talk of people that don't want to accept the truth."

"Do you think they know what's happened to the child?" asks Skinner.

"Maybe, maybe not. But she can't see a ghost and still hope to find her alive. Both things can't be true, and if that little girl's spirit really did appear to her mother, then there's probably only one explanation," Mulder says, grimly.

"You think the daughter's dead," says Skinner. Mulder nods.

Scully broaches the question of the mysterious handwritten note.

"I don't know what that means," Mulder admits. "I don't know what is the truth and what isn't anymore. I'm way too close to this case to make any kind of sound judgment. In fact, I'd like to ask for you to let me off this case and I'd like to take some time off."

Mulder walks to the car, leaving Scully and Skinner to ponder their friend and colleague's state of mind.

•

Skinner, Scully, and Mulder are driving. Inside the car it is dead silent. Scully turns to the backseat, where Mulder is staring vacantly out the window. She turns to the front just as a Highway 74 road marker whizzes by. Scully opens the car's glove box and removes a map, opens it, and runs her finger to Highway 74.

Skinner asks, "What is it?"

Scully follows Highway 74 on the map to a maker for Santa's North Pole Village. "Santa Claus," she says.

Mulder hears Scully's words and is jarred out of his private thoughts.

"What?"

Scully says, "Stop. Turn around."

The car pulls into the Santa's North Pole Village parking lot. The three agents jump out. Skinner is moving swiftly through the petting zoo and other sections of the park. Mulder and Scully enter the workshop and see the door to the video room. Mulder opens it and he and Scully enter the video monitor room. The monitors, showing parts of the park, are on. They see stacks of videocassette recorders, videocassettes, eight-millimeter film reels, and Super-8 cartridges. Mulder inspects these, looking closely at their crudely handwritten labels.

"Some of these tapes go back to the sixties," he says.

Scully picks out a tape and pushes it into the VCR.

Mulder says, "I think I know what we're going to find here. It's what my mother was afraid of. My sister."

An image pops on the monitor. It is footage of Amber Lynn LaPierre dated two days before her disappearance. As they watch, something on another monitor draws their attention. It is a live feed from the next room. They realize that what they are seeing is right behind them. Mulder turns around just as the videotaper slams the door closed. Mulder and Scully race to the door. They are locked in.

Skinner is moving through the park when he catches sight of the man running. Skinner yells for him to stop, but the man runs into a building and out the other side. Skinner gives chase.

Mulder slams his shoulder against the door, busting it open. They race through the workshop and out into the park, guns drawn. Now on the outskirts of the park, Skinner is closing the gap on the man. He yells at him to stop. When he doesn't, Skinner fires his gun into the air. The man thrusts his hands in the air.

"Keep your hands up!" Skinner yells.

Mulder and Scully race up to Skinner. Scully demands, "What's your name?" as she handcuffs him.

"Ed Truelove," he says.

Scully says, "I'm putting you under arrest. You have the right to remain . . ."

As she continues to read him his rights, Mulder moves to a spot where there is freshly turned earth, about the size of a child's grave. Mulder scans the area. "Scully." She sees what Mulder is looking at, horror all over his face as he surveys dozens of child-sized graves in the clearing.

TO BE CONTINUED

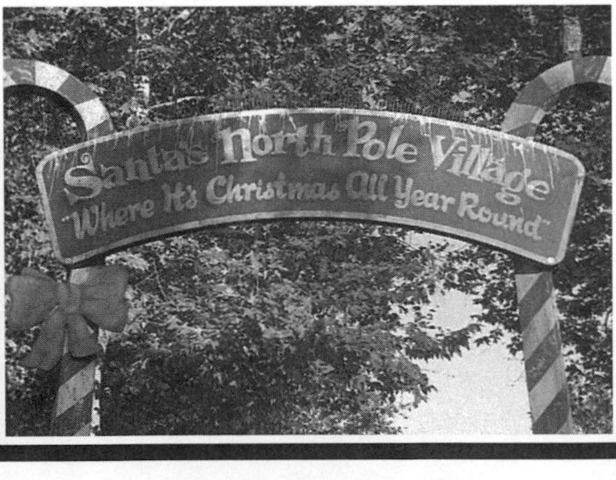

BACK STORY:

"Paper Hearts" toyed with the idea of Samantha Mulder's fate. So did "Redux II." But when it came down to plotting the storyline for the midseason two-part story arc "Sein Und Zeit" and "Closure," Chris Carter decided that with the strong possibility that this would be the final season, it was time to throw the audience a curve.

"The expectation was that if this were going to be the final season, that the finale would be about Mulder's sister," says Carter. "We wanted to deal with that sooner rather than later. We wanted to wrap up Mulder's emotional story with his sister and do it in such a way that would emphasize David's dramatic abilities."

Carter and Frank Spotnitz set to work, crafting "Sein Und Zeit" as a gradually unfolding mystery that begins with Mulder and Scully investigating a child's disappearance. The case quickly turns into a chase after a serial killer who has been active for decades and a personal torment for Mulder as clues begin to be uncovered that link the case to the disappearance of his sister. The unexpected death of Mulder's mother only deepens his depression and desperation.

Frank Spotnitz remembers, "It's similar to the episode 'Paper Hearts' in the sense that what you always thought happened to Samantha may not have actually happened. 'Paper Hearts' never ultimately answered the question. We've had people come up to us and say, 'Okay, so we know she's really dead, so what happened?' So we decided in this one to answer the question."

"Sein Und Zeit," which inevitably and chillingly evoked the real-life Jon Benet Ramsey case, fell to director Michael Watkins, whose experience as the director of previous episodes was an asset for this episode, which included an unusually large number of outdoor locations around Southern California. John Shiban recalls that filming was highlighted by one particularly dramatic misunderstanding. "The prop department had created a fake photo and a ransom note for a scene. A crew member was assigned to take them to one of our locations. On the way up, he stopped at a phone booth and made a call. When he left the phone booth, he left the folder with the photo and the note. What he did not realize was that somebody had been watching him from a nearby house, got suspicious, and called the police. The crew member realized he had left the folder and turned around and went back. In the meantime, the police showed up, looked in the folder, and found the note that said 'Don't do anything or we'll kill your baby.' When the crew member showed up, he was arrested. It took an awful lot of explaining to get him out of that mess."

Near the end of production on "Sein Und Zeit," producer-troubleshooter Paul Rabwin discovered that there was no money left in the budget for a small but necessary sequence in which a TV news anchor gives a news report. Rather than request extra funds, Rabwin overcame the problem creatively by tracking down an Australian TV correspondent based in Los Angeles who was happy to "donate" the needed news report for the chance to be on *The X-Files*. "We went to his studio setup, inserted a visual of a busy newsroom behind the correspondent, added some photos of the kidnapped children, and we had our scene."

Ultimately, "Sein Und Zeit" not only proved to be a strong introduction to the critical revelations that would unfold in the aptly named "Closure," but stood on its own as a creepy, atmospheric addition to *The X-Files*'s powerful oeuvre of serial killer episodes.

FACTS:

Kim Darby's long and distinguished career includes roles in the films *True Grit, The Strawberry Statement, The Grissom Gang,* and the TV series *The Streets of San Francisco.*

Rich Millikan recalls breaking the unwritten rule of casting an actor a second time by using Mark Rolston as Bud LaPierre. "He had appeared in the second season episode 'Red Museum,' but he was so good an actor that we had to use him again."

"Sein Und Zeit" is German for *Being and Time*—the title of Martin Heidegger's best-known work.

episode 7X11

CLOSURE

EPISODE: 7X11
FIRST AIRED: February 13, 2000
EDITOR: Lynne Willingham
WRITTEN BY: Chris Carter & Frank Spotnitz
DIRECTED BY: Kim Manners

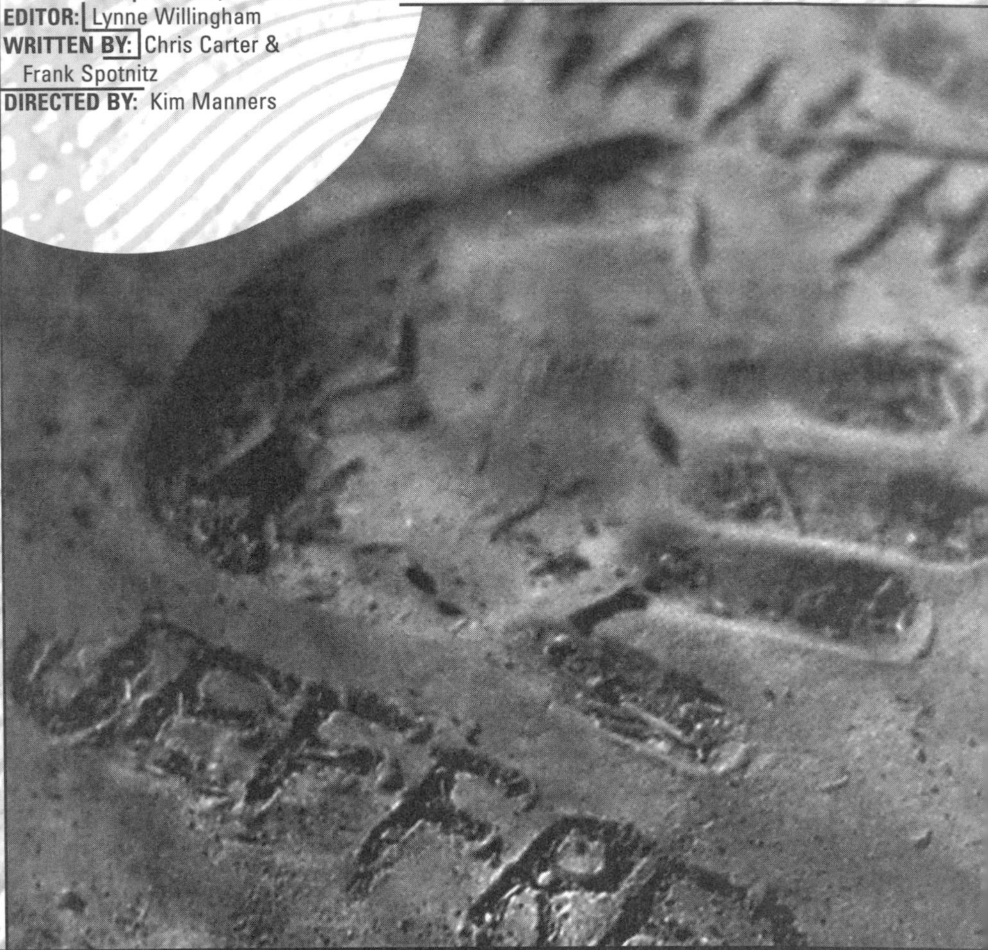

Mulder continues to search for the truth behind the disappearance of his sister, Samantha, with the aid of a psychic. Scully discovers the true involvement of the Cigarette-Smoking Man and Mulder finally finds the secret that sets him free.

[redacted]

GUEST STARS:

William B. Davis (The Cigarette-Smoking Man)
Mitch Pileggi (A.D. Skinner)
Anthony Heald (Harold Piller)
Stanley Anderson (Agent Schoniger)
Rebecca Toolan (Mrs. Mulder)
Patience Cleveland (Arbutus Ray)
Megan Corletto (Amber Lynn LaPierre)
Ed Beechner (Deputy)
Christopher Wynne (Base Cop)
Lillian Adams (Hospital Administrator)
Nicholas Stratton (Appearing Boy)
Mimi Paley (Young Samantha Mulder)
Fort Atkinson (Detective #1)
Jeff Xander (Detective #2)
Norman Smith (Detective #3)

PRINCIPAL SETTINGS:

Sacramento, California; Victorville, California

"They said the birds refused to sing and the thermometer fell suddenly, as if God himself had his breath stolen away."

Mulder's thoughts are sad as he watches cops, detectives, and coroner's assistants poring over the clearing and the child-sized graves behind Santa's North Pole Village, exposing rotten clothes and bodies in various stages of decomposition to the light.

"No one there dared speak aloud, as much in shame as in sorrow. They uncovered the bodies one by one. The eyes of the dead were closed, as if waiting for permission to open them."

More small bodies are revealed.

"Were they still dreaming of ice cream and monkey bars, of birthday cake and no future but the afternoon? Or had their innocence been taken along with their lives?"

Shovels lift the cold, dark earth.

A plastic-wrapped body is placed in a body bag.

Mulder thinks. "Buried in the cold earth so long ago. These fates seem too cruel even for God to allow."

Mulder's sadness is unfettered.

The grim business continues. A breeze rustles dirt, crime scene tape.

"Or are the tragic young born again when the world's not looking?

"I want to believe so badly in a truth beyond our own, hidden and obscured from all but the most sensitive eyes."

The ghostly figures of the dead children rise out of the grave. They gather in the clearing, forming a circle, holding hands and looking skyward. Amid a wash of Mulder's thoughts, the focus shifts to the night sky, dense with stars.

"In the endless procession of souls. In what cannot and will not be destroyed. I want to believe we are unaware of God's eternal recompense and sadness. That we cannot see his truth. That that which is born still lives and cannot be buried in the cold earth. But only waits to be born again at God's behest. Where in ancient starlight we lay in repose."

•

At the Sacramento police station, a group of detectives are watching a video of Amber Lynn LaPierre. Scully enters. Mulder is sitting nearby, hunched over a light table examining brittle strips of decades-old Super-8 film.

"Ed Truelove was nineteen when he committed his first murder," she tells him. "He was working as a janitor at an elementary school and they needed someone to play Santa Claus. He never got over the feelings it aroused. He's admitted to all of it, Mulder. Twenty-four separate murders. But he refuses to take blame for Amber Lynn LaPierre. I was just handed the preliminary forensics report. Her body was not among those found in the graves." Mulder continues to examine the film strips. "Mulder, I know you wanted to find her out there."

Mulder says, "He had hours of video of her."

"I'm talking about your sister. I know that's who you're looking for."

"You know how badly I wanted for her to be in one of those graves," he sadly confesses. "As hard as it is to admit, I wanted to find her here riding her bike like all these other kids. I guess I just wanted it to be over."

A deputy enters the room and tells the agents that there is a Harold Piller to see them. They go outside, where they find Harold Piller looking at and touching missing persons posters.

Scully asks, "Do we know each other?"

"Not personally," says Piller. "I'm happy to meet you. Hi, Harold Piller."

"Are you part of this investigation?" asks Scully.

"I hope to be."

"How can we help you?" asks Mulder.

"I was hoping to help you," says Piller, as he hands Scully his business card, which describes him as a police psychic.

"My references are on the back. I've gotten some strong hits off this case. You're looking for a little girl, but she's not among the dead. Your suspect is going to say he didn't kill her."

"Did he?" asks Mulder.

"No. I think I can help find her."

"Mr. Piller, you have some interesting references here," says Scully. "You've worked with law enforcement in Kashmir, India. Myanmar. Afghanistan. Pakistan. Khyber Pass . . ."

"That was a train wreck. A horrible tragedy. They called me in to locate the bodies of seven children who were unrecovered."

"And did you recover them?" asks Scully.

"I didn't recover them, no. But I explained what happened."

Mulder asks, "What happened?"

"The children's bodies were transported from the accident site via spiritual intervention. What are known as Walk-ins." This phrase captures Mulder's attention.

Scully says, "Thank you, Mr. Piller, but we have real work to be done."

Scully turns to leave, but Mulder lingers.

Piller says, "I've studied this phenomenon the world over. Mudslides in Peru, earthquakes in Uzbekistan. Kids' bodies never found, never accounted for in any other way."

"What happened to them?" asks Mulder.

"The bodies were transported from the various sites . . . in starlight."

Scully senses that Mulder is vulnerable to Piller's theories. She leads Mulder down the hallway, away from Piller.

•

"Mulder, you've been through so much in such a short time. The death of your mother and the feelings it's brought up for your sister. You're vulnerable right now."

"We still have a missing a body. Amber Lynn LaPierre. She may be alive. We don't know."

Scully says, "This man isn't going to help us find her. By his own admission."

"It's not the first time I've heard what he's saying. About the intervention of these Walk-in spirits. Kathy Lee Tencate mentioned it to me in prison. She said that's who took her son."

"Because it's foolproof, Mulder. Nobody's going to disprove it if there's no body. It's exactly what this man does. He gives a comforting explanation at a train wreck or an earthquake that everybody can live with. But the fact is the bodies are still buried."

"Or maybe they are somewhere else," says Mulder.

"Like your sister?" she asks. "Mulder, you told me all you wanted was for this to be over."

"I do. I do."

"Well, then, I'm going back to Washington. There's nothing more to be done here," Scully says.

•

Mulder is soon at the mass gravesite with Harold Piller, watching as the psychic surveys the area.

"How long have you been doing this?" asks Mulder.

"A few years. I had a son who disappeared under strange circumstances. He's never been found. And then one day, I just . . . started to see them."

Mulder asks, "These Walk-ins? You say they come and take these children. Why?"

"In almost every case the parents had a precognitive image of their child dead. Horrible visions. I believe what this is is the work of good spirits, foretelling their fates. A fate the child was about to meet. A particularly violent fate that wasn't meant to be. Which is why the spirits intervene, transforming matter into pure energy. Starlight. But it's not what happened here."

"How do you know that?" asks Mulder.

"Because these children all died suffering. Pleading innocently for their lives. These beautiful children, so trusting and pure." He appears to be getting more and more upset. "I see them. My God, why? Why must some suffer and not others?"

Tears well up in Piller's eyes. Mulder asks the psychic if he's seen Amber Lynn LaPierre.

"She wasn't here," says Piller. "She never was. But I'm sensing a connection with her to this place. It's . . . no. It's a connection . . . it's a connection to you."

Mulder's head snaps up at this. "How's that?" Piller reaches out and touches Mulder's chest, over his heart.

"You lost someone close to you. A young girl. It happened a long time ago. A sister. There's a connection between these girls, isn't there? Between her and Amber Lynn."

"What is the connection?" asks Mulder.

"I don't know. But we're going to find them. I'm sure of it."

•

A tape is playing on a video monitor. Its date is 6/16/89. It is footage of Mulder undergoing regression hypnosis.

The hypnotist says, "I'm going to count backwards now, Fox, and you'll fall into a deep relaxed state," as Mulder, reclining in an easy chair, begins to relax. "So you can remember all about your sister and what happened."

Mulder falls quickly under the spell.

"Where are you now, Fox?"

"We're at home. We're at my mom and dad's . . . we're in the den . . . playing a game."

"Who are you there with?"

"Samantha."

Scully and veteran FBI agent Lewis Schoniger are watching the tape. The hypnotist asks Mulder if he feels any danger.

"No. We're arguing, you know, but not really. We're just playing the game."

Schoniger, an expert in matters of hypnosis, tells Scully that Mulder appears to be in a legitimate hypnotic state. Mulder's words continue to tumble out.

". . . pieces of the board are falling off. Samantha!"

Schoniger reaches for the PAUSE button. "But here I become suspicious."

"Suspicious of what?" asks Scully.

"In thirty years with the FBI you'd think you'd see it all. I sometimes think I have, but this is just garden-variety compensatory abduction fantasy."

Scully says, "Compensatory for what?"

"His guilt. His fear. Everything that's preventing Agent Mulder from remembering the truth about what really happened that night."

"You mean his sister wasn't abducted?"

Schoniger explains, "His sister definitely went missing in 1973. That's not in dispute. Agent Mulder, however, wasn't regressed until 1989. See, his delusion is playing into his unconscious hope that his sister is still alive. And if you think about it, his delusion has the effect of giving him reason to pursue her."

"But why alien abduction?" asks Scully.

"*Close Encounters, E.T.*, who knows? But there was probably a lot of imagery collecting in his head in those sixteen years. Then he comes down here and he finds the X-Files."

Scully stresses that something did happen to Mulder's sister.

"Well, in 1973 we were pretty damned unsophisticated about violent, predatory crime. My guess is she was kidnapped in the house, her body was disposed of, never found."

"You think that his sister's dead?" Scully asks.

Schoniger looks through Mulder's file. "Have you seen this file? There was an extraordinary amount of effort put into finding his sister. Even the Treasury Department got involved. His father worked at a high level in the government. But they found nothing."

Schoniger is curious as to why Scully is digging up this case now after all these years. "A word of advice? Me to you? Let it be. You know there are some wounds that are just too painful ever to be reopened."

Scully says, "Well, this particular wound has never healed. Mulder deserves closure, just like anyone."

•

After an emotionally trying day, Mulder is trying to sleep in a room in the Red Carriage Motel, staring blankly at a television showing a *Planet of the Apes* movie. There is a persistent knock on the door. He opens the door to reveal a troubled Harold Piller. Mulder wants to know what Piller is doing here.

"I'm picking up something," says the psychic, looking past Mulder into the room.

"It's three in the morning."

"There's someone here."

"The TV is on."

"No. A visitor."

Mulder lets Piller in. Piller closes his eyes, sensing something.

"They want to speak," says Piller, eyes closed, concentrating. "They want to tell us something." Mulder is not convinced. "Get a piece of paper and a pen."

Mulder does as told. "Shoot," he says, wryly, pen poised to transcribe.

"It's your mother," says Piller. "She's here in the room with us. She's trying to speak to you."

Mulder considers this. "What does she say?"

"She wants to tell you about your sister. Where she is."

A ghostly apparition of Mulder's mother, which Mulder does not see, appears behind him. Her lips are moving, but she is saying nothing.

"What's she saying, Harold?"

"I don't know," says Piller, as the vision of Mrs. Mulder fades away. "I . . . she's gone. I lost her."

Mulder says, "That's crap. You're full of crap. Get out of here."

"I'm telling you," says Piller.

"No. I'm telling you. I never should have listened to you."

Piller insists, "She was here. She had a message."

"Please go."

Piller's eyes go to the desk, where the pen and paper sit.

"Look," says Piller, grabbing the paper.

Something has been written on the paper: the words APRIL BASE.

"Who wrote that?" asks Mulder.

"You did," Piller replies.

•

Scully has returned to Mrs. Mulder's house, the case file folder in hand. She opens drawers and checks a desk, looking for something. She notices the wastebasket that Mrs. Mulder had used to burn old photos. Reaching into the char-red remnants, she notices a small piece of paper that has lodged in the lip of the container. Scully looks closely at the scrap with interest.

•

Mulder and Piller are driving in Mulder's car when his cell phone rings.

Scully says, "Mulder, it's me. I've found something. I'm standing here not quite believing what it is."

"What is it?"

"I don't know if you know this, but there was a special Treasury Department investigation into Samantha's disappearance."

Mulder says, "In 1973, I know all about that."

"Well, I'm in your mother's house," she says. "I found a piece of a document that she burned. A document that matches one that I found in the Treasury investigation file. But she had the original, Mulder."

"I don't see where you're going with this, Scully," he says.

Scully has matched the scrap of paper to a photocopy in the file folder, completing the document.

"This is the document that effectively calls off the search for your sister, Mulder. And signed with the initials CGBS. C.G.B. Spender. The Smoking Man. He was involved with this back in '73."

"That's not exactly a revelation, Scully. He was a friend of my father's."

"Mulder, you told me you believe that he's the man that killed your father. That he's the man who's done nothing but confound your work. Who's come close to killing you! And here he's ordering people to stop looking for your sister."

"I don't see what you think this proves. Or how it's going to help me find her now."

Scully asks, "You don't want to press him?"

"It's a dead end. He's never been of any help and he's not going to be of any help now. Look, I'm pursuing this my own way. I gotta go." Mulder hangs up.

•

Mulder and Piller pull up to the unmanned gate of April Air Force Base. Mulder takes a cursory look, shakes his head, and after a brief exchange with Piller, starts back toward the car. Pillar insists there is something there.

"What are you afraid of?" asks Piller. "That you'll really find her? That you'd have to deal with it?"

"There's nothing here, Harold," says Mulder. "It's a decommissioned base."

"You wrote the name down yourself," Piller says.

"Why do you care so much about what I feel? Why's this so important to you?"

Before he can answer, a military police cruiser pulls up. An MP informs them that there's nothing for them to see and that they'd better leave.

As they head back to the car, Piller says, "There is something to see here, Agent Mulder. I'm sure of it."

•

Scully opens the door to her apartment just as her telephone rings. She picks it up just in time to hear the clicking sound of someone hanging up.

"I should have grabbed it for you," says a very familiar voice from somewhere in the room.

Scully looks up and discovers the Cigarette-Smoking Man sitting in a chair in the dark.

"I like to make myself useful."

"You can start by putting out that cigarette," says Scully. He doesn't.

"You've got it all figured out, don't you, Agent Scully?"

"All but why you can't just come to the door and knock."

"I did that, no one answered."

The CSM rises out of his chair and steps into the light. Scully notices how sickly and gray he looks.

"You're sick."

"I had an operation."

Scully demands to know what he wants. The CSM responds by saying that he wants her to stop looking.

"You've wanted that since 1973. When you ordered an end to the search for Agent Mulder's sister. Your initials are on that document."

"Yes, I signed that order," says the CSM. "Because I knew then what I know now. No one's going to find her."

"Why not?"

"Because I believe she's dead. No reason to believe otherwise."

"You're a liar. If you knew she was dead, why didn't you say something earlier? Why now?"

"There was so much to protect before. But it's all gone now."

"So you just let Mulder believe that she was alive for all these years?"

"Out of kindness, Agent Scully. Allow him his ignorance," says the CSM. "It's what gives him hope." He let himself out of the apartment.

•

Mulder and Piller drive up to the fence of April Air Force Base at night. They go to the gate, climb the fence, and make their way across open ground to a group of buildings within the base. Mulder and Piller's search brings them to base housing, deserted streets, empty houses. The psychic tells the agent that indeed, Samantha was here.

Mulder asks, "Which house, Harold? Where?"

"I don't know."

"Harold, we don't have all night. Which house was it?"

A military police cruiser rounds onto the street, heading toward them. They duck into the shadows behind some garbage cans as the cruiser rolls past. They move out of the shadows and start to jog away when something catches Mulder's eye.

"You were right," says Mulder. "This was the house."

Mulder points to two handprints set in the concrete. Under one of them, written in a child's scrawl, is the name SAMANTHA. Piller looks at the handprints.

"I told you. What did I tell you," says Piller.

"You told me she was here," says Mulder. "But you didn't say with who."

JEFFREY is written under the other print.

•

Scully has traveled to Sacramento and hooked up with Mulder at the Red Carriage Motel, where they are filling each other in on their respective investigations.

"When did you come up with this story, Mulder? Because yesterday when I spoke to you, you said the Smoking Man wasn't involved."

"It turns out you were right, Scully. He had every reason to call off the hunt for my sister. After her abduction she was returned to him. Then he raised her at the military base, along with his son, Jeffrey Spender."

He continues, "I saw her name in the cement. Her handprints right next to his."

"Mulder, I spoke to him," says Scully. "The Smoking Man. C.G.B. Spender, or whatever his name really is."

"You went to him?" Mulder asks, incredulous.

"He came to me. He told me that she was dead."

"Well, he's a liar."

Scully says, "Mulder, why would he lie now? I mean, think about it. It hurts me to tell you this."

"The handprints prove he's a liar," says Mulder. "I saw her handprints in the cement. Her name, *Samantha*, right underneath them. How more obvious can it be? Harold Piller led me right to them."

"Oh, he led you, Mulder. He led you from the moment that he met you."

•

Harold Piller is sitting at a table at a coffee shop when he looks up and sees Mulder and Scully entering the restaurant. He starts to get up but Mulder stops him with a gesture. He sits down at the table while Scully remains standing.

Mulder says, "Agent Scully has informed me that you failed to mention something to me when we first met. That you're currently the subject of a criminal investigation into the murder of your son."

"My son was taken from me. The police need someone to blame."

"That's not all, Harold," says Scully. "Your history of mental illness. You were institutionalized, diagnosed with schizophrenia."

"I've got that under control. You wouldn't have believed me if I told you any of that. Look what I've shown you."

"You only tell me what you see."

"I came to you because I want to help. You think I'm a fraud. What do I have to gain from this? How am I any different from you? All I want is to find my son. I just want my little boy back. I see these things. I don't know how, but there has got to be a reason. If it's not to help, what is it? I know your sister is out there."

Piller says, "Maybe I can prove it to you." Mulder looks from Piller to Scully.

•

That night, Mulder, Scully, and Piller return to April Air Force Base. They go to the house with the handprints in the driveway, go inside, and find the house completely bare.

Harold looks around the empty house.

"We're going to need to hold hands," says Piller.

Scully asks, "What do you mean?"

"I'm going to try and summon their presence. Into the house."

Scully says, "Oh, yay. A séance. I haven't done that since high school." She puts her hand out for Mulder.

Adds Mulder, "Afterwards we can play postman and spin the bottle."

They all join hands.

"I'm not going to say anything," says Piller. "I'm just going to be very quiet and still. That's how it seems to work best. You might experience a sudden chill or feel pressure in your ears. That means they're here. And if they need to, they'll let themselves be seen."

There is disbelief in Scully's eyes. Mulder's eyes are closed.

Piller says, "Close your eyes and let them come to you. They will come to you, if you're ready to see."

"How will we know?" asks Scully, her eyes now closed.

Piller says, "Stay quiet. You'll know."

The room around them slowly begins to take on a ghostly glow. A panorama of ghostly figures stand around the edges of the room: men in military haircuts, mothers and housewives, the former residents of this house through the decades. The ghostly figure of a young boy steps from their midst and up to Mulder. Mulder opens his eyes to discover his hand in that of the young boy, who takes him from the circle and leads him to a darkened room at the rear of the house.

Scully opens her eyes to find Mulder missing. The room is back to normal. She walks to the back of the home and finds Mulder standing alone.

"Mulder, what are you doing?" she asks.

Mulder says, "It's here. There was a boy. He led me into this room."

Mulder pries open a piece of wood from the back of an old bookcase and pulls out a moldy leatherbound book. As Scully comes to take a closer look, Piller appears in the doorway.

Piller says, "It's a diary. It's your sister's."

•

At a table in a restaurant, Mulder opens the

diary to pages written in a young girl's hand. Mulder begins to read out loud, Scully listening:

> *They did more tests today, but not the horrible kind. I was awake and they made me lay still while they shined lights in my eyes. They ask me questions, but I always lie now and tell them what they want to hear just to make them stop. I hate them and I hate the way they treat me like I'm an old suitcase they can just drag around and open up whenever they want to. They know I hate them but they don't even care.*

"This is 1979. She's fourteen years old here," Mulder says to Scully.

Mulder turns the page and reads another passage.

> *Sometimes I think my memories were taken by the doctors, but not all of them. I remember faces. I think I had a brother with brown hair who used to tease me. I hope someday he reads this and knows I wish I could see his face for real.*

Mulder's eyes begin to tear up as he flips through more entries. "And then she's talking about running away. She wants to run away so that they stop doing the tests. And then it just stops."

Scully, full of concern, takes Mulder's hand.

"Let's get out of here."

Outside the restaurant, Mulder stares up into a clear, starry night.

"You know, I never stopped to think that the light is billions of years old by the time we see it. From the beginning of time right past us into the future, nothing as ancient in the universe. Maybe they are souls, Scully. Traveling through time as starlight, looking for homes. I wonder what my mother saw. And I wonder what she was trying to tell me."

Scully regards Mulder a moment. "Get some sleep," she says.

Mulder chuckles at this, and as Scully walks away, he again looks at the starry sky.

•

Mulder is asleep in the hotel bed. Suddenly the ghostly figure of Mrs. Mulder appears. She bends close to her still sleeping son and whispers a message to him.

The next morning Mulder is awakened by a knocking on the door. He opens the door to find Scully standing there.

"I got it, Mulder. I couldn't believe it when I saw it, it was like it was looking for me. The sergeant's blotter, 1979."

"What are you talking about?"

She hands Mulder a photocopy of a police blotter in which a fourteen-year-old girl had been picked up on I–5, claiming she had been held hostage. The item indicates that the girl was taken to a hospital for an exam. "The description matches your sister."

The pair goes to the hospital listed in the report and soon they are up to their necks in file folders. There is nothing listed under SAMANTHA MULDER. At one point, Mulder fixes on a particular file.

"Read this," says Mulder. "The medical report."

Scully goes through the report. Mulder says that nobody could get the mystery girl to give up her name.

Scully reads from the file. "Her medical examination is normal, her mental state . . . it says here she was exhibiting signs of paranoia."

Mulder says, "There was evidence of probable self-inflicted abuse, including small crescent-shaped scars on her knees, wrists, and chest. Those are from the tests, Scully. That's her. She was here. Fourteen years old, in this hospital."

Scully notes the fact that there was no diagnosis of her condition and that test results were unavailable.

"He knew. He lied. He knew she was alive and the only reason he's lying now is because she's still alive."

Mulder grabs the files and turns to leave. Scully hurries after him.

"I know. You don't want me to get my hopes up. I understand that."

Scully says, "This was 1979. It was twenty-one years ago. I don't even know where to begin. And we don't even have a record here of a doctor signing her out."

"But we have an ER nurse who signed her in."

•

Mulder and Scully's car pulls up to an old farmhouse in Victorville, California. Harold Piller is with them. As they head for the door, Mulder hesitates.

"I have this powerful feeling, and I can't explain it," Mulder says. "That this is the end of the road. That I've been brought here to learn the truth."

Scully says, "Are you ready for it?" Mulder nods. "Do you want me to talk to her myself?" He nods again.

Scully and Piller go up to the door. Arbutus Ray, the now elderly nurse, answers.

Mulder watches as Scully introduces herself and verifies that Ray used to be a nurse at the hospital. Scully explains why they are here, and Ray's response can be faintly heard by Mulder: "I remember. She was such a pretty young girl. You couldn't forget someone like her. Or how frightened she was. Scared for her sweet life. Deputy brought her in, she was shaking like a leaf. Wouldn't let anyone touch her but me. Then the strangest thing happened."

Piller breaks in. "You had a vision of her. Dead. Like the parents of Amber Lynn LaPierre."

Arbutus Ray says, "No one believed me. Honestly, you're the first person."

"So, you saw her dead?" asks Scully.

"That night, in her bed. I blinked and it was gone. She was sleeping sound as could be. I don't know why, but it made some kind of strange sense. There were men. They came to pick her up late that night. I assumed the one was her father, but he gave me such a chill when he looked at me. When I asked him would he please put out his cigarette . . ."

Scully pauses at this, then asks, "So they took her?"

"They meant to, but when I took them to her room, she was gone. She disappeared out of a locked room. Just vanished."

Scully is shocked by this revelation. She looks to Piller, then back to the street.

Mulder is gone.

He is walking into darkness. The sky is clear and starry. His pace is slowed by the appearance of the ghost image of the young boy he met during the Piller séance. He raises his hand to Mulder and leads him to a clearing where the phantom figures of children run and play. It is a blissful image of a much better time. Mulder takes in the ghostly children at play with a sense of pure wonder. Mulder sees Amber Lynn LaPierre, quite happy as she plays with other little girls. Suddenly his thoughts are distracted.

"Samantha?" he asks, as a ghostly vision of the fourteen-year-old girl runs toward him and hugs him tight. For Mulder the reunion is joyous rather than sad.

•

Scully and Piller are standing near the car, wondering where Mulder has gone. Suddenly he appears from the nearby woods.

"Mulder, where'd you go?" asks Scully.

"End of the road."

He walks up to Piller. "He's okay. It's okay."

"My son? You saw my son?" he asks, eagerly.

"He's dead. They're all dead, Harold. Your

son, Amber Lynn, my sister. Harold, you see so much, but you refuse to see him. You refuse to let him go. But you have to let him go. Now, Harold, he's protected. He's in a better place. They're all in a better place. We both have to let go."

Piller insists, "You're wrong. I'm going to find him. I don't believe you." He's now almost shouting in denial.

Piller turns away from the agents and stalks off. Scully is looking at Mulder.

"Mulder, what happened? Are you sure you're all right?"

Tears glisten in Mulder's eyes.

"I'm fine. I'm free," he says, as he looks toward the heavens.

BACK STORY:

The disappearance of Samantha Mulder and Fox Mulder's constant search for her has been a major component of the emotional backbone of *The X-Files* since its inception. And so when it was decided that "Closure," the conclusion of the two-parter that began with "Sein Und Zeit," would resolve the question of Samantha's final fate, the reaction around the production office was inevitably mixed.

"I think David grew tired of playing the man who is missing his sister," reflects Frank Spotnitz. "So when it came time to shoot 'Closure,' I told him, 'This is going to be the last time you're going to have to play that.' "

Paul Rabwin offers, "It's been seven years. I don't think any of us are going to miss Samantha Mulder. That device and motivation were very strong in the early years of the show. But as the years have gone by, the speculation kind of melted away."

The script, coauthored by Chris Carter and Frank Spotnitz, picked up the intensity of "Sein Und Zeit" and made a smooth transition from the horror of the Santa serial killer into the realm of the supernatural. Carter, in looking at the relationship between the two parts of the story arc, saw a definite evolution.

"Emotionally it was heavy stuff for everybody, but necessarily so," says Carter. "These episodes involved two very personal cases, the search for a serial killer and the search for Mulder's sister."

From a visual perspective, "Closure" was a delight. Abrupt camera angles and alternating shades of light and dark provided a surreal, diffused visual tableau over which the powerful tale unfolded. Performances were uniformly first-rate. Duchovny, as the emotionally distraught Mulder, favored controlled pathos and anguish over obvious histrionics as he dealt with the final answer to the disappearance of Samantha. Gillian Anderson, in an equally understated performance, provided believable strength and support for her suffering partner. As the emotionally damaged psychic, Anthony Heald turned in a potent guest star turn.

And while the script's main intent was to lay the long-standing question of Samantha's disappearance to rest, "Closure" is also very much a Cigarette-Smoking Man episode. It is a somewhat foreshadowed but nonetheless effective revelation that CSM was deeply involved in Samantha's abduction. Even more surprising and well executed was the moment, while seemingly in passing, it is revealed that CSM is ill, a storyline that will take center stage by the end of the season.

The concept of the "Walk-ins" was a daring move, deftly exploring the concept of the afterlife and spirituality and casting the preconceived notion of an X-File as something paranormal or otherworldly in a different light. In Kim Manners's hands, "Closure" proved a big imagery episode in which emotion and visual magic combined to finally put Samantha Mulder to rest. Or did it?

Frank Spotnitz teases, "Just because Samantha was taken to starlight does not mean that she's necessarily gone. It doesn't mean that there are not clones out there and that tissue samples weren't taken."

FACTS:

This episode's title sequence tag line was changed to "Believe to Understand."

Ⓧ

The haunting background music was "My Weakness" by the techno musician Moby.

Ⓧ

Anthony Heald, who plays troubled psychic Harold Piller, has also appeared in the films *The Silence of the Lambs* and *Deep Rising* and is now playing Vice Principal Scott Gruber on *Boston Public*.

episode 7X12

X-COPS

EPISODE: 7X12
FIRST AIRED: February 20, 2000
EDITOR: Louise A. Innes
WRITTEN BY: Vince Gilligan
DIRECTED BY: Michael Watkins

A mysterious monster is terrorizing a crime-ridden Los Angeles community. For Mulder and Scully, it is an X-File. For the *Cops* TV crew following them, it's ratings in the making.

GUEST STARS:

Judson Mills (Deputy Keith Wetzel)
Perla Walter (Mrs. Guerrero)
Dee Freeman (Sergeant Paula Duthie)
Lombardo Boyar (Deputy Juan Molina)
Solomon Eversol (Sketch Artist Ricky)
J. W. Smith (Steve)
Curtis C. (Edy)
Maria Celedonio (Chantara Gomez)
Frankie Ray (Crackhead)
Tara Karsian (Coroner's Assistant)
Daniel Emmett (Cameraman)
John Michael Vaughn (Soundman)

PRINCIPAL SETTING:

Willow Park, California

The episode opens with a Fox preshow warning voiceover and graphic: *The following is a special episode of* The X-Files. *Viewer discretion is advised.*

We hear the familiar *Cops* theme song "Bad Boys" over a montage of clips from an upcoming *Cops* episode that features Agents Mulder and Scully in a number of shots.

A voice-over informs us that *Cops* is filmed on location with the men and women of law enforcement, and that all subjects are innocent until proven guilty.

"I don't know what it is about a full moon," says sheriff's deputy Ken Wetzel as his cruiser passes through the mean streets of Willow Park, California. "Something about it. People just go off the wall."

Officer Wetzel, a barrel-chested rookie officer in his mid-twenties, looks back into the lens of the *Cops* camera held by the crew riding with him this night in Los Angeles County.

"I mean, these are some scary neighborhoods to begin with," he says. "I haven't been on the job all that long myself, but I've already seen more than my fair share of crazy stuff. And when the moon is full, it's like, times ten. I don't know. Maybe it's the tides or something."

The camera turns to focus out the front windshield at the city streets. The Willow Park neighborhood is full of hourly-rate motels and rundown houses with bars on the windows. The focus returns to Wetzel as he continues to address the camera.

"But irregardless, we're on the job. And if that makes people breathe a little easier, knowing we're out there, and are a little less nervous walking the streets at night—that's a good feeling."

Wetzel's radio squawks to life.

"Got a report of someone lurking around the neighborhood," says the officer, "and making noise."

The full report comes across Wetzel's mobile data terminal.

"Actually, I take that back. We've got a report of—what? A monster? Lurking around the neighborhood? What the—"

Wetzel shrugs. "Hey, full moon." He steps on the gas.

Neighborhood houses slide past the patrol car.

"Lotta drug activity in this district," he says. "We're probably looking at somebody rattling doorknobs, trying to steal some money for a quick fix. They're usually not the stealthiest of criminals . . . so maybe we'll get lucky. Sneak up on 'em."

Wetzel says a crisp "212 Adam is 10-97" to dispatch as he pulls the patrol car to the curb. He exits the vehicle, followed by the *Cops* crew. Wetzel shines his flashlight up and down the street, then over the fence of a house.

"212 Adam to dispatch. I don't see anything. Could you let the lady inside her house know I'm out here?"

Wetzel climbs the steps and shines his flashlight at the windows and the doorknob. He notices five deep parallel scratches in the wood just below the doorknob.

"Lotta scratches," says Wetzel. "Maybe a big dog. That's probably what she saw."

He knocks on the door with his flashlight. "Sheriff's Department," he calls.

An older Mexican lady, Mrs. Guerrero, peers out. She is upset as she rattles off something in Spanish. The literal translation:

"The Claw Monster is out there! He's trying to get in my house! You have to shoot him! Don't let him get into my house!"

Wetzel says, "Whoa, whoa . . . usted cálmate . . . No monstruo . . ."

Mrs. Guerrero continues to talk hysterically, finally slamming the door in Wetzel's face.

"Man. Scared of something."

Wetzel draws his gun and moves around to the side of the house. Strange noises—*Bam! Bump! Bump!*—come from somewhere behind the home.

"Hey! You there! Freeze! Sheriff's Department!"

Trash cans are knocked over. Wetzel takes off in pursuit. The *Cops* crew follows but loses sight of the officer. They pan the junk-filled yard, looking for action.

Suddenly, Wetzel appears, racing toward the *Cops* cameramen.

"Run!" he screams, almost knocking over a cameraman. "Run! Back to the car! Back to the car. Now! Run, goddamnit, run! Get in the car."

They turn tail and run. Wetzel is right behind them as they move back out into the street. All goes black for a moment as the cameraman falls in his haste to get back to the car. Wetzel continues to yell to keep moving. "Run, run—get in the car!"

Wetzel and the *Cops* team reach the patrol car and jump in. The frightened officer starts the car as he fumbles, with the radio.

"212 Adam is 1097!" he shouts into the mike as he starts the car and squeals away. "Requesting backup!"

The car is under attack. The windows smash and spiderweb. The car is jarred from side to side. "I need backup at the 500 block of Prince!" he yells to dispatch. The car begins to shift. Something is lifting the side of the car. Wetzel screams into the radio mike.

"999! 999!"

The patrol car tumbles sideways, upside down once or twice, and comes to rest with a loud crash.

•

Sheriff's cruisers arrive on the scene as Wetzel and the *Cops* crew climb out of the demolished car. Wetzel, bleeding from a cut over his eye, is stunned. He is approached by Sergeant Paula Duthie.

"Everybody all right? Hey—you all right? Keith . . . what was this?"

"I was responding to a 921 at this house right here. It was a prowler call."

Duthie looks at the flipped patrol car.

"You flipped it?"

"No, no, hell no, I didn't flip it. It was parked! It was . . . We were attacked."

"Was it gangbangers?" she asks. Wetzel hesitates. "Keith?"

"Yeah," says Wetzel. "I guess. Yeah. Gangbangers."

Duthie deploys other deputies to search the area.

"You should double everybody up," says Wetzel.

"How many?"

Wetzel still seems shaken as he notices he's bleeding.

"I didn't get a good look—"

Duthie's thoughts are interrupted by a radio message.

"Two 417 suspects on foot, one block north on Holly."

A deputy cries out, "Over here!"

Sergeant Duthie orders, "Armed suspects! Somebody bring a unit around! Holly Street!"

The cops all take off at a run down the street as police cruisers converge on the suspects. They run through an alley, past darkened houses, to a weed-filled lot where they see officers drawing down on two figures standing with their backs to the deputies. "FBI," they are insisting. The man and woman carefully raise their hands. Everyone is yelling at once.

It is Mulder and Scully.

"We're FBI," Mulder says. "I've got ID in my back pocket."

Pinning his hands behind his head, Duthie checks Mulder's wallet and badge and sees that they're okay. As she gives him back his gun, words appear on the *Cops* broadcast: SPECIAL AGENT FOX MULDER.

"We're investigating a case," says Scully.

"What case?" asks Duthie.

As Scully steps closer, another caption appears: SPECIAL AGENT DANA SCULLY.

"Same case you're working on," says Mulder.

"So, who are you looking for?" asks Duthie.

"Not who," says Mulder. "What."

Mulder and Scully realize they're being taped by the *Cops* crew. They are uncomfortable with having a video camera in their faces.

Scully does not like the camera crew documenting their every move.

"Mulder, what the hell is going on here?" she asks.

Mulder shrugs.

•

The deputies, along with Mulder and Scully, arrive at the home of Mrs. Guerrero. Mulder is examining the scratches on the door while Scully attempts to keep her back to the *Cops* camera.

"See the claw marks here," says Mulder. "Something tried to get in."

He walks over to a nearby ambulance, where Wetzel is being treated by an EMT.

"Deputy, can you describe for me what you saw?"

"It was pretty dark. I didn't really see, uh . . . I don't know. I don't know."

"You had to have seen something in order to run from it. You were responding to the same call we were . . . a monster prowling the neighborhood."

Sergeant Duthie joins them at the side of the ambulance.

"We've been to this house before," she says to Mulder. "The lady has a history of medication, you know what I mean?" As the *Cops* camera turns to get Duthie, Scully is seen as well—before she quickly ducks back behind the ambulance doors.

"Maybe, but she's not the only one seeing monsters," says Mulder. "There's been half a dozen such sightings in this area in the past sixty days. Are you aware of that?" There is a long pause. "No," Wetzel finally answers. Duthie appears incredulous at Mulder's speech. "Also, these sightings only occur on nights when there's a full moon . . . which tells me something. What you saw was large, right? . . . Maybe seven to eight feet tall when it stood up on its two legs. It was covered with fur and had glowing red eyes and claws . . . claws sharp enough to gouge the wood of that front door."

"You're not serious?" asks Duthie. The camera pans to Duthie, and again Scully steps out of view of the camera.

"And dare I forget teeth."

Mulder takes hold of the deputy's wrist. He sees a bite mark on his wrist. "It bit you, didn't it? Look at this. Deputy, how long were you going to hide that from the EMTs?"

Wetzel stammers.

"Where'd you get this, Keith?" asks Duthie.

"I didn't even know where it came from."

Scully leans into check out the bite marks.

Duthie turns to Mulder.

"Big teeth, eight feet tall. What the hell are you describing?"

"A werewolf."

"Excuse me?"

"It's what did that," says Mulder, indicating the totaled police car. "It also attacked

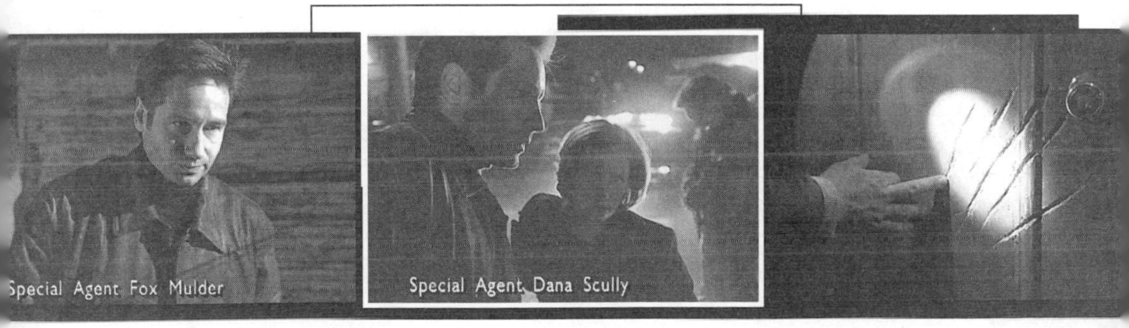

one Hyman Escalara twenty-nine days ago during the last full moon. Hyman died of his wounds in Compton General Hospital but not before giving a detailed description of what attacked him. My partner and I are here to catch it." Mulder points to Scully, who turns away.

Scully cringes and puts her hand to her face as Mulder grills Wetzel.

"Unfortunately, Deputy, you've been bitten. The skin is broken. Werewolf lore pretty much universally holds that someone who's been bitten by such a creature becomes a creature himself."

"But that's not what really happened," says the officer.

"I'm sorry," says Mulder, "but you need to be isolated and kept under guard."

Duthie says, "With all due respect . . . what the (bleep) are you talking about?"

"I'm talking about preventing this man from becoming a danger to himself and others."

Wetzel stands, dumbfounded.

Duthie asks if she can see Mulder's badge again. Scully notices the camera crew taking all of this in.

"Agent Mulder? Can I have a word a second?"

"What is it?"

Scully takes Mulder aside. The *Cops* crew follows at a distance.

"What is it?" repeats Mulder.

"What is it? Mulder, have you noticed we're on television?"

"I don't think it's live television, Scully. She just said (bleep)."

"But it's a camera and it's recording!" They notice the camera is again right there. Scully pulls Mulder away. "It's recording everything that you are saying. Do you understand? I just want to make sure you're clear on that."

"Sure. I'm clear on that, Scully."

"My point being, Mulder, that we are on the case . . ."

"And this presents an opportunity," says Mulder. "I feel we're very close here. The possibility of capturing concrete proof of the paranormal, of a werewolf? In front of a national audience, even international audience? What's not to love?"

The camera is just a few feet away. With a glance back, Scully pulls Mulder and continues to walk away from the camera—which follows.

"Look, Mulder. You wanna talk about werewolves to me? Knock yourself out. I may not agree with you, but at least I'm not going to hold it against you. But this . . . Mulder, this could ruin your career."

Mulder laughs. "What career? Scully, I appreciate it. You don't want me looking foolish. I appreciate it."

She says, "I don't want *me* looking foolish, Mulder."

Mulder looks into the camera. "Okay, fine." Back to Scully. "Do me a favor then. Would you please escort Deputy Wetzel to the hospital and keep an eye on him? In case I'm right? Thank you." Mulder walks back to the house.

"I'm going to call Skinner, Mulder," Scully shouts after him. "I'm sure he's going to want to say a couple of words about this."

Scully dials her cell phone. The *Cops* camera is on her.

"Guys, give it a rest, huh?" They don't move.

Scully puts her hand over the camera lens.

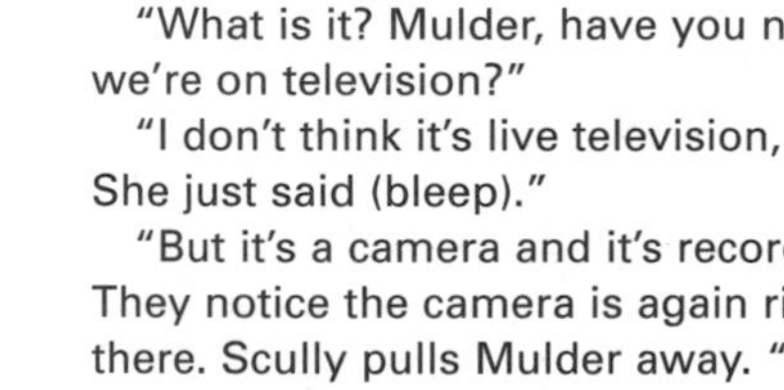

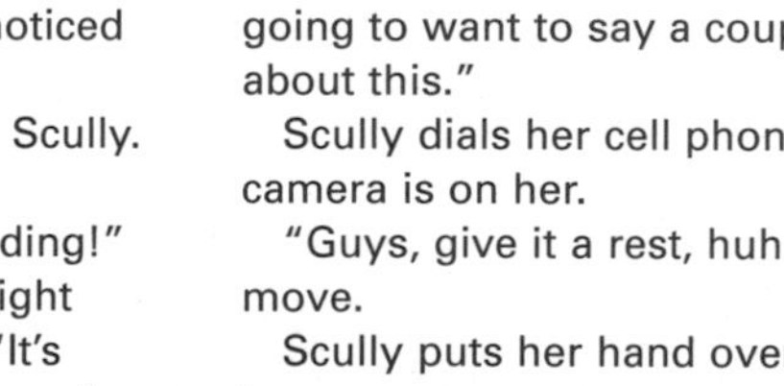

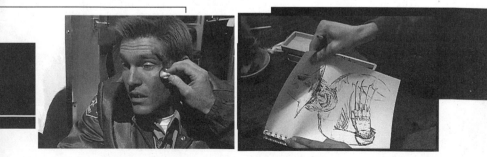

•

Mrs. Guerrero is in the living room speaking excitedly with Spanish-speaking Deputy Juan Molina. Molina explains to Sergeant Duthie and Mulder that she said that a claw monster tried to get into her house. Also present is a fragile-looking police sketch artist named Ricky, who wears a bulletproof vest. Mulder asks if Mrs. Guerrero can describe it in detail to the sketch artist.

"Claw monster?" asks Ricky.

"Just do it, Ricky," says Duthie.

Ricky moves off with Mrs. Guerrero and Deputy Molina to work on the drawing. Mulder takes another look at the scratches in the door.

"Looks like five claw marks. Just like the human hand has five fingers. Pretty much the same spread, too."

Duthie says, "Agent, you seriously believe we're looking for some kind of . . . ?"

"I'll show you," Mulder says.

Mulder reaches into his jacket pocket and pulls out a copy of a police sketch. He shows it to Duthie. It is the classic werewolf: all teeth, claws, and glowing eyes.

"This is what Hyman Escalara described just before succumbing to his injuries. Ten to one that's what Mrs. Guerrero is going to describe, too."

Molina is translating Mrs. Guerrero's description for Ricky. He tells Mulder he has the picture of the suspect ready.

Ricky puts the finishing touches on his sketch as Mulder and Sergeant Duthie step over. Ricky turns his pad around to reveal . . . a drawing of Freddy Krueger, the killer from the *A Nightmare on Elm Street*.

"Claw monster," Mrs. Guerrero insists.

"They kill him in every movie and he just keeps coming back," Molina says with a smile.

Mulder takes the drawing. "This is strange," he admits.

Sergeant Duthie, feeling enough time has been wasted, insists, "We're looking for gangbangers."

Ricky is nervous and asks for a police escort to his car. Molina goes with him. Mulder is still puzzled by the sketch. "This is what she saw?"

"Yeah, that's the claw monster," Molina replies.

Mrs. Guerrero points to the picture of Freddy Krueger. "You catch?"

"Catch him?" Mulder asks, then nods.

A car pulls up and Scully gets out.

"How's Deputy Wetzel?" asks Mulder.

Scully says nothing but jerks her thumb back as another patrol car pulls up and Wetzel climbs out. His wrist is bandaged.

"Those weren't teeth marks, Mulder. They turned out to be insect bites."

"Hmmm."

"Individual stings or welts of some sort. Together they just look like a larger pattern . . . especially when we want them to."

Scully notices the *Cops* camera.

"Although it was an understandable conclusion that I'm sure anybody would have made." Mulder smiles at this.

"So what did Skinner say?" asks Mulder.

"He said that the FBI has nothing to hide and neither do we."

"Well, if it makes you feel any better, I'm not entirely convinced we're looking for a werewolf anymore. Something else. I'm not sure what. Some other kind of creature, though."

There is a sudden flurry of activity. Deputies are running to their cars amid the crackle of radio calls. A deputy running by acknowledges Mulder's "What's going on?"

"Six blocks from here. Could be what we're looking for."

Mulder and Scully get into their car. The *Cops* camera crew tries to climb in the backseat.

"No," says Scully. "You go with someone else."

•

Mulder and Scully race around the corner with other police officers to where a group of deputies have converged on a body lying slumped underneath an off-the-hook pay phone.

"Guys, watch out. I'm a doctor," says Scully as she pushes her way through. It's Ricky, the sketch artist.

There are five deep slashes across the front of Ricky's vest, the kind that Freddy

Krueger might inflict. As Scully presses on the vest, blood oozes out of the wounds.

"This is what I was afraid of, Scully," says Mulder.

Ricky is loaded into a waiting ambulance as Officer Wetzel talks to the *Cops* crew.

"When a fellow officer goes down in the line of duty—or even if it's not a fellow officer, if it's just someone who works part-time with a department in a support . . . um, in an artistic capacity, like Ricky—we all feel it. There's every cop's worst nightmare. But that's when you've gotta cowboy up and give 150 percent. Catch the bad guys."

Mulder and Scully go over the crime scene. Scully determines that the last call from the phone was by Ricky to the auto club, for a flat tire.

"He asked them to hurry . . . said he didn't feel safe."

Mulder pulls out the picture of Freddy Krueger.

"What's that?" asks Scully.

"Our suspect, apparently. The slash marks match up pretty well, wouldn't you say?"

She notices something laying on the ground and stoops down to take a closer look. It is a bubblegum-pink press-on nail. Scully picks up the nail and turns it over. On the underside is a bit of drying blood.

"Check out this color, Mulder. Blood red."

Mulder asks who placed the 911 call on Ricky.

•

Sergeant Duthie, with Mulder and Scully behind her, is knocking on the door of a house across the street from the crime scene.

"Steve and Edy? It's Sergeant Paula . . ."

"*The* Steve and Edie?" asks Mulder.

"They're good folks. They usually call us when there's trouble in the neighborhood."

The door opens to reveal Steve and Edy, two men in their mid-fifties. The flamboyant Edy spots the *Cops* camera and begins mugging, then goes back into the house to primp. Duthie asks if they saw what happened.

Steve says, "We heard all this screaming. Peeked out the window, and this boy with crazy hair was having a conniption fit, all rolled up by the phone."

"You didn't see his attacker?" asks Scully.

Edy comes back, with a scarf on his head, all dolled up. "I'm ready for my closeup," he coos to the camera. Steve ignores him and keeps talking.

"Now, I didn't see, whatcha say, attacker," says Steve. "No, he was all just kinda rolled up and yellin'."

Mulder pulls out the sketches of Freddy Krueger and the werewolf. "You didn't see anything that looks like this? Or this?"

Steve makes a face. "Excuse me?"

Edy hugs herself. "That's gonna give me nightmares."

Scully asks, "So, did you see anyone at all?" They shake their heads no. "Did you see a woman?"

Scully shows them the press-on nail, which they recognize.

"Mmm-hmm. Chantara," says Edy. "I know that skank-ass color."

Duthie asks, "Chantara's a streetwalker?"

Steve points to the street. "She work the corner. She on the pipe so we don't associate. You know what I'm saying?"

Mulder gets out, "We should—we'll—we should go talk to Chantara, then." They leave smiling.

The camera stays on Edy, who breaks into song for her audience.

•

Mulder, Scully, and the *Cops* crew are cruising the streets, looking for Chantara. Scully hates the camera's presence, but Mulder takes the opportunity to gab.

"So apparently we're on the lookout for someone whose hair matches her fingernails. Bubblegum pink. That'd be a good color for you, Scully."

Scully tries to ignore her partner.

"I'd have to say, at this point in the investigation, I'm usually a little more secure of what it is we're actually investigating." As he drives, Mulder addresses the camera. "But we've had so many conflicting eyewitness reports, it's hard to ascertain exactly what it is we're looking for. But the crimes we are investigating are paranormal. I can say that with absolute conviction. And the nature of

these crimes, they are always notoriously hard to quantify on any kind of rigorous scientific level, as Agent Scully will tell you."

"Oh, yeah," she replies.

"That's our job. That's why they pay us the big bucks."

"Bubblegum pink," Scully says at the sight of Chantara running down the side walk.

Mulder screeches the car around the nearest corner and catches Chantara, in a hooker outfit and a bubblegum-pink wig, in the headlights. She continues to run, but eventually stops. Her name is Chantara Gomez. Scully looks at her hand and sees four pink press-ons and one real, chewed-down fingernail. Chantara, nervous and frightened, insists she has done nothing.

Her face is blurred for the cameras.

"Earlier this evening a man was attacked. He was badly slashed," says Scully. "And you realize this places you at the crime scene."

Mulder asks, "Fisher and Belmont. That's your usual hang, isn't it, Chantara?"

"Look, I heard screaming, okay, and I went to try and help this guy! When I heard the sirens, I ran away, okay? I didn't do nothing." Chantara is clearly very scared and upset.

"Look, I believe you," says Mulder. "I think you saw something. You witnessed something. Tell me what it is."

She shakes her head. "No!"

Mulder takes a step closer to her and speaks reassuringly. "Chantara, if you're afraid that what you tell us, we're not going to believe it, don't be. Whatever it is you saw tonight . . . whatever *it is* you think you saw, however strange or terrifying or bizarre, you are not going to surprise me, okay?"

Chantara thinks for a moment. "You'll protect me from Chuco?"

"Who's Chuco?"

"*Mi novio*. He's the one who cut that guy up. Not me, I didn't do anything!"

"I'm sorry, what?" asks Mulder, confused.

"*Mi novio*—it's her boyfriend," Scully answers.

"No, I got that—"

"Look, he's been chasing me for a week, okay? He said he'd twist my neck off like a little chicken if I didn't give him more money! Chuco Munoz. The cops know who he is."

Mulder turns around, sees the camera, says, "Chuco," and walks away from Chantara.

•

Deputies are preparing to serve an arrest warrant at a house frequented by drug users. Scully and Duthie are standing by the open back door of the sergeant's car, guarding Chantara Gomez.

"I don't understand! I told you what you . . . everything you need to know! Why can't I go now? Why can't I go home?"

Duthie tells Chantara that there are still possible accessory charges pending against her until they can prove Chuco attacked Ricky. Chantara insists that Chuco will kill her and "twist my neck off like a chicken."

Scully and Duthie insist she is safe, surrounded by police officers. Wetzel is assigned to protect her.

Scully moves off and finds Mulder. They both begin getting ready for action by putting on body armor. They examine a picture of Chuco.

"He's not our guy," says Mulder.

"What do you mean?"

"I don't care how bad his rep is. He can't turn over a squad car."

"Maybe not by himself, but he's probably got friends."

At Duthie's signal, the deputies storm the house. The front door is bashed in with a battering ram. The officers flood into the house.

"Sheriff's deputies. On the floor! On the floor!"

The deputies race through the darkened house, coming upon a bunch of crackheads lounging in various rooms. They are quickly swept up and cuffed. Mulder and Scully move through the chaos, flashlight beams sweeping across faces, looking for Chuco Munoz. Sergeant Duthie approaches and leads them to a dead body. The dragon tattoo on his head identifies him as Chuco Munoz. It looks like he OD'd.

Scully studies the corpse. "Couple of days. Maybe a week. He didn't attack Ricky Koehler, that's for sure."

They hear the sound of gunfire.

"Shots fired!" screams Duthie.

Mulder and Scully race out of the house and back to the staging area along with many of the deputies. There they find a panicked Deputy Wetzel firing frantically into the darkness.

"It's here! It's getting away!"

"What the hell is going on?" yells Duthie. "What are you shooting at?"

"It came back. It was here. Oh, man, I heard her screaming. I tried to stop it. I swear, I tried—I did everything I could do. I did everything I could do."

Mulder goes to the car where Chantara is being held and aims his flashlight into the window as Scully comes up behind him.

"What is it, Mulder?"

Scully looks into the window.

The camera crew focuses in on the car window at Chantara's lifeless body. Her neck is clearly broken.

"Call it in," says Duthie.

"I wish someone would explain to me what the hell is going on here." Duthie ponders what happened.

"Keith Wetzel may be a little green, but he's a solid deputy. Nobody could have gotten past him and killed that woman."

Duthie is approached by a deputy who reports that there is no sign of whatever it was that Wetzel was shooting at. He hands his superior officer a flattened bullet that came from Wetzel's gun, found in the middle of the street. It does not look like a ricochet.

"Maybe Wetzel hit what he was aiming at," says Mulder.

Mulder walks over to Wetzel, who is standing next to his cruiser, head down.

"Hey, Deputy. Are you ready to talk to me now?"

Wetzel is silent.

"You and I both know you saw something. We're way past claiming you didn't." Scully joins Mulder with Wetzel.

"I only know what I thought I saw."

"Well, describe it for me."

With a glance at the camera, Wetzel turns to Mulder. "The Wasp Man."

Mulder considers this for a moment. "The Wasp Man?" he repeats.

"It's ridiculous. Scary stories my older brother used to tell me when I was a kid about a monster, a head like a wasp and a mouth full of stingers instead of teeth."

Wetzel stares down at his wrist and the insect bites.

"Said it would come get me in my sleep, and that it would sting me to death."

Scully listens as Mulder asks Wetzel if it was the Wasp Man that attacked him the two times.

Clearly knowing how crazy it sounds, Wetzel insists, "I'm not saying that's what it was." He references the camera crew. "They didn't see it. It's not on the videotape. This can't be real."

"I think maybe it can—just relax a moment. Excuse me." Mulder walks Scully aside. He recaps all of the eyewitness descriptions of the attackers. "Scully, what if we're dealing with one creature, one entity that, when it attacks, appears to you as your worst nightmare? Fear. Maybe that's what this thing feeds on."

Scully has no response for the moment. "Okay, well, for the sake of this argument, how would one catch something like that?"

"Probably by figuring out how it chooses its prey. It seems to spread like a contagion. One person's fear becomes the next. There's a definite chain of victims. Tonight it went from Mrs. Guerrero to Wetzel and the sketch artist to Chantara Gomez . . ."

". . . and Chantara Gomez back to Wetzel," Scully finishes. "Except you're missing someone. Steve and Edy. They were part of this chain, too. And according to your theory, they would've been attacked, right?"

•

They head back to Steve and Edy's house. Mulder chatters to the *Cops* crew as they walk to the door.

"So we're back at the home of Steve and Edy. We need to check on them as they seem to fit our victim profile." Scully asks if he was talking to her. Mulder sheepishly points at the camera.

There is a scream from inside Steve and Edy's house. Mulder and Scully draw their guns. Mulder kicks in the front door. They race into the house, where they find themselves in the middle of a lover's spat. Getting more personal information than expected, Mulder and Scully try to steer the conversation to the reason for their visit. Scully explains that they might be in danger because they witnessed the violent attack on Ricky. Edy, still hysterical from the spat with Steve, only gets more so from Mulder's and Scully's warnings. The agents tell the couple that they think it would be a good idea if they stayed awhile.

•

Hours later, the stakeout is nodding out with boredom and fatigue. Steve and Edy touchingly make up and refuse to be run out of their house by fear. "Ain't nobody gonna chase us out," Steve insists. Mulder, Scully, and the *Cops* crew leave. Outside they are confronted by Officer Wetzel and a second camera crew. "Oh God," Scully says, seeing the camera crew. "More of you?!" Wetzel questions Mulder on the evening's events.

"We're just playing catchup with this thing," says Mulder. "It doesn't do what you'd expect. We've got four or five hours until the moon sets and the attacks only occur under a full moon. We're out of luck."

Scully suggests that she go to the morgue and examine the body of Chantara Gomez for possible clues.

"Make it fast," says Mulder. "And fill that tank up with gas.

"Deputy, you're the only one who's seen this twice. So I'd like to ride with you if you don't mind."

A cameraman follows Scully into her car. She gives him a long look before getting into the car.

•

Mulder, Wetzel, and the *Cops* crew roll off into the night. The agent and the cop have a heart-to-heart about them believing him. Mulder reassures Wetzel that nobody thinks he's lying. But Wetzel is concerned about how this incident will affect his career.

"I've been on the job eighteen months. All I ever wanted to do. Right out of the gate, I get some kind of rep like I'm crazy . . . you know how cops are. How's someone supposed to live that down?"

"I don't know. I guess just do good work."

"It's a hard enough job already. I wanna help people. It's like the freakin' Wild West out here. You know people hate you? Every shift I go out thinking there's someone out there who wants to take me out. Am I going to run into him tonight? It's hard to have a fast-track career in law enforcement when everybody thinks you're nuts."

The camera pans to Mulder. "Tell me about it," he says.

•

At the autopsy bay in the L.A. County Morgue, with the assistance of a high-strung, nervous coroner's assistant, Scully is performing the autopsy on Chantara Gomez. The assistant speaks up, interrupting Scully's description of the choking injuries on Chantara.

"SCARY STORIES MY OLDER BROTHER USED TO TELL ME WHEN I WAS A KID ABOUT A MONSTER, A HEAD LIKE A WASP AND A MOUTH FULL OF STINGERS INSTEAD OF TEETH."—Wetzel

"People are saying that her pimp killed her from beyond the grave. That's the story going around. It's crazy, huh?"

"Let's just see if we can put that story to rest, shall we?" says Scully.

The assistant says that she also heard something about contagion associated with the body. Scully says that she seriously doubts that they are looking for any kind of contagious pathology. This does little to calm the assistant's nerves as she continues to babble on about how maybe they should be wearing masks.

Scully says, "Look, this is obviously a murder. This woman died of a broken neck, right? Not the hantavirus."

"Who mentioned the hantavirus?" The assistant looks even more freaked out.

"Nobody," says Scully. "It was a figure of speech."

The assistant continues to question the situation. The woman sneezes. She draws her hand from her mouth to reveal blood. The woman's eyes roll back into her head and she collapses. Scully moves to the woman. She is unconscious and trembling. Her skin is mottled and she is bleeding from her nose, mouth, and ears. Scully looks up into the *Cops* camera.

"Call 911! Get out of here, come on!"

•

Mulder and some deputies listen to Scully, in a state of confusion and shock, try to explain the death of the coroner's assistant.

"It's not the hantavirus. It looks for all the world like the hantavirus. But I can promise you that it's not. She exhibited all the symptoms, the hemorrhagic fever, the severe chills, acute shock. The thing is they all developed in a matter of seconds. And hantavirus doesn't kill that fast. No virus in the world kills that fast."

"You were talking about the hantavirus right before she died—why?" Mulder asks.

"It was like the power of suggestion. She was standing there, saying she was afraid of contagion, and then, all of the sudden, she just—"

Mulder says, "She was afraid. She was afraid, and her fear killed her. In the worst possible way that she could imagine."

Duthie asks what he means. Mulder explains it's the same pattern they've been looking at all night. Scully argues that she and the ever-present camera crew were also afraid, but nothing happened to them. Mulder mulls it over.

"You weren't afraid for your life. Neither were Steve and Edy, and it left them alone. Mortal fear. I think that's what it comes down to. This thing, whatever it is, is attracted to that. Everybody who was attacked felt that intensely."

Duthie is not convinced.

"It makes perfect sense," says Mulder. "You asked me earlier what this thing would be doing in Willow Park. Where else would it go but a high-crime neighborhood? Somewhere where people live behind barred windows and are afraid to go out at night."

Mulder asks where Officer Wetzel is. He is concerned when he discovers that Wetzel is back on patrol, alone.

"Mulder, you were walking around with him for three hours," says Scully. "You didn't see anything."

"Because I was with him. Backing him up." He leaves, hurrying.

•

Wetzel and his *Cops* crew pull up front of the crack house that was raided earlier in the evening. He decides it would be a good idea to give the place another toss. They go up to the front door. Wetzel pushes it open with his flashlight, gun drawn. He shines the light all around. Suddenly the flashlight dies and they are plunged into darkness.

Boom! Boom! Boom! The sound of heavy footsteps comes from upstairs.

"Okay," says Wetzel. "I'm calling for backup. Get out, get out now!"

Wetzel turns and pushes the camera crew toward the exit. The front door won't open.

"Oh (bleep)!" screams the cameraman.

He tries to open the door. It still won't open.

The footsteps get louder. The cameraman cries, "Oh God! No! No!"

There is a loud *thud* as something slams into the cameraman. He drops the camera, which goes out in a burst of static.

Mulder, Scully, and a swarm of officers screech to a halt in front of the crack house. Spotting Wetzel's cruiser, they race to the front door. They can't budge it. Duthie calls for a battering ram. Mulder and Scully move to the side of the house. Scully draws her pistol. Mulder eyes the piece in her hand.

"That gun's not gonna do you any good."

They find a back door and step into the darkness. A series of loud *boom*s stops them in their tracks. It is the battering ram at the front door. All of a sudden, the back door slams shut behind them.

"Wind?" says Scully.

"If you say so."

They hear a rattling sound coming from a closet. They creep up to it. Mulder grabs the doorknob as Scully raises her pistol. Mulder counts to three and whips open the door, where we find Wetzel's camera crew, who scream, cowering in fear. Scully immediately slams the closet door shut and looks at her camera crew.

"I hate you guys," she says.

Mulder raps on the closet door and asks where Deputy Wetzel is.

"We don't know," says a muffled voice from inside. "There's something out there."

"Stay where you are," Mulder calls through the door.

"(Bleep) yeah!" is the answer.

Mulder and Scully move deeper into the house. Mulder looks down and sees a trail of wet blood leading up the stairs. They follow the trail of blood to a closed bedroom door.

Mulder calls out Wetzel's name. A shriek comes from the other side of the door.

"Help me. Please, help me! It's trying to kill me!"

Mulder turns the knob but can't open the door.

He realizes that the only chance Wetzel has is not to be afraid.

"Wetzel? Don't be afraid. That's what it wants! You hear me?"

There is the sound of banging from the other side of the door.

"It can't hurt you! You're a goddamn sheriff's deputy! Don't be afraid now! And you're on national television! So cowboy up!"

There is one last bang and then silence. Mulder is finally able to force the door open. Mulder and Scully rush inside.

Wetzel is crumpled in a corner of the room. He is bleeding from his arm, semiconscious, but he is still alive. There is no sign of the monster. Sergeant Duthie arrives and demands to know what happened. Mulder moves to a boarded-up window and looks out through the slats.

"The sun just came up."

•

Wetzel, strapped to a gurney, is being rolled toward a waiting ambulance as Mulder and Scully survey the scene.

Scully turns to Mulder. "You think the deputy stopped it, whatever it was?"

Mulder considers the question. "Maybe it just went away until the next full moon. I don't know, you gotta figure there's enough fear in the world that if it doesn't show up in Willow Park, it's gonna show up someplace else."

"You didn't get the proof you wanted, Mulder," she says.

Mulder points to the camera, which is still rolling.

"Hey, it depends on how they edit it together."

"This is going to be a hard one to write up," she says as the episode ends with squawks of radio static.

BACK STORY:

We all have guilty pleasures, those lowest-common-denominator, unhip, and politically incorrect joys that fly in the face of conventional wisdom. For *X-Files* writer/co-executive producer Vince Gilligan, the vice is *Cops*.

"I've been watching *Cops* for years," chuckles Gilligan. "It's a great slice of Americana. I love it."

And for the longest time, Gilligan would regularly regale *The X-Files*'s brain trust at story meetings with his notion of an episode in which an X-File stumbled into the middle of the shooting of a *Cops* show. Frank Spotnitz recalls that Gilligan's suggestion inevitably brought a polite dismissal.

"We were afraid to do it because Vince wanted to do it on videotape, which was the way the *Cops* show was shot. And what we've discovered over the years was that a lot of the way we created effective scares was through the use of film. We also knew that to do a show *Cops*-style, which would essentially eliminate cuts and edits, would be a huge challenge."

But as they entered the seventh season, Carter had a change of heart.

"Vince had wanted to do a *Cops* show for the longest time," reflects Carter, "and at that point it was looking more and more like we had only eleven episodes left in the series and that time looked to be running out. So it looked like no time like the present."

Gilligan was soon hard at work on the script, in which Mulder and Scully are hot on the trail of a monster that appears differently to each of its victims. Gilligan and *The X-Files* staff had a good time brainstorming the horror icons Freddy Krueger, a werewolf, and an insect monster that would be seen only on the pages of a police sketch artist's pad. But it soon became evident that the key to the success of "X-Cops" was that the true identity of the monster would remain secret.

Spotnitz remembers, "What we realized was that because this was on videotape, we can't really show the monster because it would be on *Cops* and that would change the world. But we came up with the idea that videotape cannot capture everything and that some things are totally in a person's head. It became the perfect monster for a show about shooting on video."

The producers of the real *Cops* show were thrilled with the idea of having their show X-Filed and offered their total cooperation. Gilligan was invited along on an actual *Cops* shoot in the wilds of Compton, California, so that he could get a sense of the rhythms of the show. The show supplied some stock footage and readily agreed to license the rights to use their "Bad Boys" theme song. *Cops* cameramen and sound men were brought in to supervise the taping and, in a final bit of realism, *Cops* cameraman Daniel Emmett and sound man John Michael Vaughn were enlisted to play themselves in front of the camera in the episode's final act.

"X-Cops" director Michael Watkins had long had a good relationship with the Los Angeles law enforcement community and was able to call in quite a few favors, including the use of real sheriff's deputies as extras.

Casting director Rick Millikan got caught up in the reality-based approach of this episode. "This had to be played very realistically, as if it were the *Cops* show. We needed actors who could pull off the believability in just normal off-the-cuff conversation of cops out on the job. We needed actors who could play cops but who could also be believable as cops."

"X-Cops" ghetto locations were filmed in the Southern California cities of Venice and Long Beach. Director Watkins quickly picked up on the pulse and the rhythms of a typical *Cops* episode and incorporated an unorthodox approach to dealing with his actors and his video crew. When Watkins would rehearse the actors, he would deliberately keep the camera crew off the set. When it was time for the scene to unfold, he would bring the cameramen back to the set and call action. Trying to follow the actors resulted in the jerky, often unfocused quality typical of a *Cops* show.

Unlike other *X-Files* episodes, "X-Cops" was shot linearly and in real time, which was a boost for the show's budget. "Our show has gotten massively expensive since we moved to Los Angeles," explains Spotnitz. "So we thought, 'Here's a way we're going to save a lot of money.' "

Indeed, "X-Cops" moved at a lightning pace. Gillian Anderson remembers that "What was surprising to all of us was how little time it took to shoot. We basically did one or two takes of something and that was it. One night we shot three and a half pages of the script in two hours."

Shooting five to six script pages a day became the norm on the "X-Cops" set (usually three to four pages a day is the average). There were long takes and lots of dialogue, which would occasionally have the actors flubbing their lines, resulting in retakes. But that obstacle was more than balanced by the fact that no coverage shots (additional shots at different angles and closeups) were required.

The stunt side of the production was active throughout filming. In the teaser sequence, a police car was tipped upside down with the aid of a device called a Gimble. The scenes of police cars whipping in and out of frame and screeching to a stop were accomplished with the assistance of stunt drivers and real police officers. For the sequence in which a crack house is taken down, real SWAT members clashed with stunt players playing crackheads, throwing the profanity-bleeping hoods against walls and over furniture, and ultimately handcuffing them and dragging them roughly out of the house.

Despite the fact that her face is constantly obscured behind a *Cops* blur effect, quite a bit of work went into detailing streetwalker Chantara's twisted neck death. An appliance, supplied by effects house Optic Nerve, gave actress Maria Celedonio the appearance of her face on the side of her head. A wig slanted sideways on the actress's head completed the effect.

Postproduction soon commenced on the episode, with the inevitable difference of opinion, artistic versus commercial, following shortly. Paul Rabwin relates that "Vince Gilligan's original intent was not to see *The X-Files*'s logo or anything *X-Files* on the screen. He wanted it to be an episode of *Cops* that happened to involve Mulder and Scully. The network was afraid people would turn on the show and not know it was *X-Files*. A compromise of sorts was reached when we took the red-and-blue *Cops* logo and rebuilt it into *The X-Files* logo."

"X-Cops" was a crisp episode that played fast and loose with the concept of "extreme plausibility" that has long been the backbone of the show.

Staff writer Jeff Bell delighted in the irony of the "X-Cops" premise. "We had the videotape capability to finally document an X-File and the X-File turns out to be something nobody can see."

FACTS:

The average number of edits in an *X-Files* episode is 800 to 1200. The total number of edits in the first cut of "X-Cops" was 45.

A real *Cops* editor was hired to insert the trademark blur over the faces of innocent bystanders.

When a shot of a morgue was not available in the production company's stock footage file, producer Rabwin called up a friend at the Los Angeles Fox News bureau and asked if one of their roving film crews could swing by the morgue on their regular rounds and film some footage.

episode 7X13

FIRST PERSON SHOOTER

EPISODE: 7X13
FIRST AIRED: February 27, 2000
EDITOR: Heather MacDougall
WRITTEN BY: William Gibson & Tom Maddox
DIRECTED BY: Chris Carter

Mulder and Scully enter a violent video game to trade bullets and photon blasts with a deadly game vixen who does not play by the rules.

GUEST STARS:

Krista Allen (Jade Blue Afterglow/Maitreya)
Jamie Marsh (Ivan Martinez)
Constance Zimmer (Phoebe)
Billy Ray Gallion (Retro)
Tom Braidwood (Frohike)
Dean Haglund (Langly)
Bruce Harwood (Byers)
Michael Ray Bower (Lo-Fat)
Ryan Todd (Moxie)
James Geralden (Detective Lacoeur)
John Marrott (Security Guard)
Christopher Ng (Darryl Musashi)

PRINCIPAL SETTING:

Los Angeles, California

Moxie is pimple faced. Lo-Fat is chubby. Retro is lean, pierced, and tattooed. But as they eye futuristic automatic weapons in their insertion module, they all have one thing in common.

A desire to kill.

A loudspeaker booms, "T minus ten seconds to engagement."

Lo-Fat lets out a primal scream, grabs a monster gun off the wall, and racks it in Moxie's face.

"Lo-Fat's going off!" yells Moxie.

"Gonna kill! Gonna kill!" screams Lo-Fat.

Retro turns around and brandishes his own automatic weapon.

"Stay out of my way, geeks," he warns. "I'm going to the next level today. I'm a death machine."

The elevator they are in jolts to a stop.

The loudspeaker says, "Status: combat ready. Situation: guerrilla units in immediate vicinity of insertion module."

The three young men hurriedly begin putting on high-tech headsets, eyewear, and surveillance equipment, as they ready their weapons.

In a high-tech control room in another part of the building, slick retro hipster Ivan Martinez and his bright, somewhat plain assistant Phoebe are prepping for the computer conflict, watching the three boys via a monitor while other screens monitor the three's vital signs.

"Look at those heart rates!" says Martinez.

Phoebe says, "Gotta let these boys out. They're gonna kill each other."

The three teens are now fully decked out in high-tech gear and ready to do battle. The immersion module opens and the three teen commandos race out to find an urban canyon of tall buildings, garages, and hundreds of windows where snipers may be lurking. They take cover behind a barrier at the end of the "street."

Moxie asks, "Do you see them?"

"They're up there, geeks," says Retro, "looking to fry your *huevos.*"

Suddenly the street is alive with lights and the revving sounds of motorcycles surging out of side streets and melding into a flying wedge. The motorcycles race toward the commandos.

"Call it, Retro! Call it!" says Moxie.

Retro watches as the motorcycles and their faceless, helmeted, leather-clad riders close in on them, until . . .

"Now!" screams Retro.

Gunfire erupts from the commandos and the cycle raiders. Cycles hit by gunfire burst into flames and disappear. The commandos continue to fire as bullets screech against the barricade and the surrounding structures. The cycles are going down in bunches. The last surviving raider explodes into a ball of fire just a few feet from the barricade.

"Whoa—a total massacre out there," says an impressed Ivan, watching from the control room.

As the commandos peer from behind their barricade, the landscape in the canyon suddenly changes. Three kiosks appear, staggered, in the middle of the corridor.

"Phase two, geeks!" yells Retro. "Ready, knuckleheads?"

His cohorts scream, "Flank left! Flank right!"

"Go!"

The three boys leap up from the safety of the barricade.

They race down the street toward the first kiosk, firing wildly. The street suddenly lights up under a barrage of flaming muzzle flashes as gunfire rains down from the windows and doorway. All three continue to fire at the snipers as Moxie trails Retro, blasting away. Trailing is Lo-Fat, spinning, firing and screaming in all directions. The snipers start to go down one by one.

Lo-Fat's flak jacket suddenly explodes in a spreading splat of yellow paint. A jolt of voltage follows, buckling Lo-Fat to his knees.

Bullets flying all around them, Retro and Moxie pull into the kiosk. The gunfire stops. All is silence, except for the constant moans of Lo-Fat, who is being zapped by electric voltage to keep him down.

Retro and Moxie look toward a tall building and the places where snipers are awaiting their next move.

Moxie says, "Lo-Fat's down."

"Got me, Moxie?" asks Retro.

"Got ya covered."

Retro jumps up and runs as Moxie lays down a massive cover barrage and the cyborg killers fire back.

In the control room, Martinez and Phoebe are glued to their console, eyeing various screens.

"Retro's in!" screams Martinez.

Phoebe declares an adrenaline redline.

"The bloodthirst is unquenchable," says Martinez.

Retro reaches a building and goes down a flight of stairs into a very dark, warehouse-like place. Retro's weapon is poised and at the ready as he looks for something to shoot at.

He hears footsteps approaching the top of the steps he just came down. He sees an extremely curvaceous woman in a skimpy, leather fantasy warrior getup. "Who's there?" he demands. His expression falters as she walks toward him in a confident, sexy manner, Retro is struck by her beauty. The woman reaches him and puts out her hand. The hard-boiled cyberkiller dissolves into an awkward little boy. He kneels down, takes her hand, and kisses it.

"Who are you?"

"I am Maitreya. This is my game."

A gun suddenly morphs into her hand, a very old and uncyber flintlock pistol. She pulls the trigger.

The muzzle flash explodes.

•

The FPS building is a modern, spacious, impersonal place. Mulder and Scully pull open the heavy glass doors and cross to the security desk.

Showing his badge, Mulder says, "Agents Mulder and Scully, FBI. We're expected."

"I need to scan your ID," says the guard. "Retina scan, please," as he runs a light pen over Mulder's eyes.

"Cool," says Mulder.

He then repeats the process on Scully.

Mulder and Scully are put through the computer-age security check and then asked to read and sign a strict nondisclosure agreement. Scully has no idea what the initials FPS mean.

"First Person Shooter," says Mulder.

"Video games?"

"Digital entertainment."

"I can get in the Pentagon easier than this," she says.

"Dudes!" shouts Langly as he and the rest of the Lone Gunmen enter from a stairway to greet their favorite agents. "Agent Mulder. What's up, wild man? Welcome to the land where silicon meets silicone."

Frohike asks Scully, "Can I get you a latte from the bar? Or perhaps a bottle of designer H_2O?"

"How about a simple explanation as to why we're here," she says.

Langly says, "Why not take a brief moment to feel the pulse of the new American Gold Rush?"

Adds Byers, "You're standing on the launch pad of a rocket headed for the stars."

"Okay," says an unenthusiastic Scully.

The Lone Gunmen look uncomfortably at each other.

"There's been a little accident," says Frohike.

•

The Gunmen usher Mulder and Scully into the nerve center of the building.

Scully asks, "What kind of accident?"

"Like an industrial accident," Langly says.

"How did the victim die?" she asks.

Frohike says, "It's not exactly clear."

"Was there equipment involved?" asks Scully.

"Yes and no," says Langly.

Scully wants to know exactly what the Gunmen are doing at FPS. They volunteer that they are consultants. Byers admits that Langly did some programming for their new game and that they are getting stock options for their contributions to the gaming industry. "The IPO's in a week," adds Byers.

Frohike says, "Game ships on Friday. Fifty malls across the U.S. and Japan."

Scully says, "Only there's a dead body between you and untold riches."

"I don't know about you guys, but I'd be checking my shorts for cake," Mulder says.

•

"This man's been shot," says Scully, as she inspects the very dead, paint-splattered body of Retro still on the gaming floor. Standing by are Mulder, the Gunmen, and FPS technicians Martinez and Phoebe. Martinez says that death was not possible.

"No. You see, when somebody is shot there's a gun involved, and that is absolutely impossible, because there's no way anybody would ever be able to get a gun past security."

Scully holds up the monster gun lying by Retro.

"What do you call this?" asks Scully.

"Laser blaster," says Martinez. "For wasting cybertrash." Langly starts to explain, but Ivan rudely cuts him off. "The weapons feed off the FPS mainframe. The effect is intensely real, but harmless."

Scully says, "You say that this weapon is a toy, but this man clearly has gunshot wounds here. Through his . . ."

"Stun suit," says Martinez. "It's rigged with paint for wounds and kill shots. Total bleeding-edge technology."

Scully dips a finger into a bullet hole and holds up a finger coated with real red blood. Phoebe looks on.

"He's dead," says Martinez. "I got it."

Mulder asks, "Who was he playing against?"

"Against the game," says Martinez. "You waste the cyberthugs before they waste you. It's all about body count. They're computer-generated images, running on a projector. It all happens in the game space."

"It's a total digital environment," says Phoebe. "Nothing's real. It's all virtual."

Mulder asks if anyone saw the incident happen.

"I was in the control booth with Ivan," she says. "Retro was in the zone. His telemetry was solid. He looked unstoppable, like he was on his way to the next level, when suddenly he was cooked meat."

"Well, the next call is going to be to the local PD," says Scully.

Martinez flips out at the mention of police, looking angrily at Langly. "No cops! You said no cops. You said you had connections."

Scully pulls out her cell phone and begins dialing. "Well, connections or not, you've got a murder victim here."

Martinez rants as he leaves the room, "Headlines. Just what the Wall Street money dudes want to read as we're going to market."

"This is Special Agent Dana Scully with the FBI. I want to report a homicide. White male . . ."

Scully moves away as she continues the call. Mulder turns his attention to Phoebe.

"You said you were in the control booth when it happened. Can you tell me exactly what you saw?"

•

In the game control booth, Mulder and the Gunmen watch a replay of the final moments of the game.

Phoebe says, "I'm still not sure if we even saw it. I mean, one minute everything was going perfect and then we crashed. Ivan and I were sitting here. We both just looked at each other. It happened so fast. Moxie covering Retro, who's going inside after the enemy to rack up *beaucoup* points." The monitor shows Moxie firing as Retro runs off screen.

"Then *goosh!*" says Frohike. "Retro's vitals spike, like he's been shot."

"Then the system defaults," says Byers.

As Moxie is still firing on screen, the image pixilates and then goes white. Retro is lying dead on the floor when it reappears, as Moxie runs over, calling for help.

"Then they're right back in the game space," says Phoebe. "Lights up. Game over."

Mulder asks, "What happened in there?"

"We don't know," says Langly. "There's no rez images on the interior game spaces."

"What about the wireframe?" Mulder asks.

Phoebe inputs various commands, explaining they've never mapped that area since Retro was in non-combat space. The wireframe of the street scene materializes. The building that Retro entered materializes and the wire-frame figure of the gun-toting Maitreya appears above the prone body of Retro.

Phoebe reacts to this scene.

"It's a chick," says Frohike.

"It can't be," says Langly.

Mulder asks, "Can you texture wrap her?"

Phoebe types in more commands. The figure begins to fill in with color. The guys react to her exaggerated form.

"She's packing a flintlock," says Frohike.

"That ain't all she's packing," says Mulder. "Can you print that out for me?"

Phoebe nods slightly as the guys move away. She stares worriedly at the monitor as the cybercreation strides away.

"Goddess," she says, softly.

•

Retro's body is being taken out by the coroner's assistants as Scully and Detective Lacoeur go over the particulars of the case.

"Let me get this straight, Agent Scully. You've got no murder weapon, no forensic evidence, no motive, no suspect."

Mulder, printout in hand, walks over to Lacoeur.

"Have you got something?" asks the detective.

"Yeah, our killer, I believe," he says, handing him the printout of Maitreya.

Lacoeur says, "Hey, I'll put out an APB. For Frederick's of Hollywood."

Scully says, "Mulder, you're not serious. It's all in the computer. It's any voluptuous vixen out of any number of video games."

"She's not in any game, she's in this one, and no one programmed her in."

Scully says, "Yeah, but even if they had, she's not real. She's a character. She's some immature hormonal fantasy."

Their attention is diverted by the arrival of a slight Asian youth with Ivan Martinez. The Gunmen are like starstruck fans as they explain to Mulder and Scully that he is Darryl Musashi.

As Langly and Frohike trail after him, Byers explains to Scully, "Word is he slums as a game designer when he isn't contracting to the CIA. The boy wonder of virtual mayhem."

"What's he doing here?" asks Scully.

"Ivan must've called him. To go in and slay the ninja babe." Byers also takes off after the group.

Scully asks Mulder, "Mulder, why does this game have the effect of reducing grown men back into loony adolescence?"

After a beat, "That's Darryl Musashi!" says Mulder, rushing after the rest of them.

"Mulder, do you want me to autopsy the body?" asks Scully.

Mulder is on his way down the stairs. He turns, points his finger, and fires. Scully is nonplussed.

•

Darryl Musashi, dressed in body armor and sporting two handheld machine guns, is ready for action. The disembodied voice in the background announces . . .

"Immersion module in descent mode. T minus twenty seconds to engagement."

"Pay attention, worms," says Martinez from the control room, where he, Phoebe, Langly, and Frohike are watching. "Darryl Musashi's gonna show us how this game is supposed to be played."

Frohike says, "I heard he scored ninety consecutive wins in Demon Space Drifter."

"Ninety-one," says Phoebe.

A loudspeaker counts down the last ten seconds, then the metal door opens to the game space. Musashi steps out into the arena. He walks up to the barricades and stands ready.

Mulder and Byers enter the control room and Frohike urges him to watch.

Mulder asks, "Why's he just standing there?"

"Because he knows no fear," Martinez says.

The deadly motorcyclists appear and race toward Musashi, who waits until they get close to lay down a low level of fire, systematically reducing the attackers to exploding fireballs. The group in the control room is impressed. "He hasn't even broken a sweat," comments Mulder. Musashi runs into the cen-

"SHE'S A CHARACTER. SHE'S SOME IMMATURE HORMONAL FANTASY."—Scully

ter of the street and behind the barricades. He reaches the same building as Retro and steps down the stairs into the darkness, guns raised.

He turns to find Maitreya right behind him, both hands on the hilt of a massive broadsword. She slashes out and cuts off Musashi's hands with two quick moves.

Musashi screams in agony.

The others are shocked by what they've just seen.

"What just happened?" asks Martinez.

Mulder says, "She cut off his hands."

Maitreya faces Musashi, says something in Japanese, and swings her broadsword one more time, chopping off his head. The group

in the control room is understandably shocked, and Mulder especially notices Phoebe's terror.

Scully is in the Los Angeles County Morgue, examining the body of Retro. She is recording the specifics of the examination.

"Preliminary external examination of deceased, a twentyish male whose name is listed only as 'Retro,' offers no additional clues to actual cause of death." She shuts off the recorder and thinks a moment, then switches it on again. "Scratch that. Cause of death is from a large entry wound at the sternum, resulting in trauma to the internal organs and blood loss. Wound is consistent with high-velocity impact from a large projectile, which passed through a three-ply Kevlar flak jacket." She pauses again. "Scratch that. Wound is the result of high-velocity impact from an unknown object which, if it even did enter the body, left no damn trace evidence whatsoever. No powder burns, no chemical signatures of any kind of explosive propellant . . ."

Scully stops as Mulder enters.

"No luck?"

"I thought I was on to something." She holds up Retro's game suit. "You know, Mulder, this suit holds more than just exploding paint cells," says Scully. "It measures a player's vital signs, from the heart rate to the extant body chemistry, then sends that information to the computer. And then when a player's shot, a battery pack sends a twelve-volt jolt that keeps him from getting up until the game is over."

"Virtual death," says Mulder.

"Yeah, well, if only that were the case. I thought at first that maybe the suit had malfunctioned, that one of the charges had blown inward, but unfortunately that wasn't the case, either."

Mulder admires the stun suit jacket and the amazing degree of technology involved. Scully remarks that it's wasted on a stupid game. "Stupid?" demands Mulder.

"Dressing up like high-tech warriors to play a futuristic version of cowboys and Indians? What kind of moron gets his ya-yas out like that?" Mulder gives her a big smile and points to himself.

"Mulder, what purpose does this game serve except to add to a culture of violence in a country already out of control?"

Mulder says, "Who says it adds to it?"

"You think that taking up weapons and creating gratuitous virtual mayhem has any redeeming value whatsoever? That the testosterone frenzy that it creates stops when the game does?"

"That's rather sexist, isn't it?" Mulder theorizes that these games fill a void and offer an outlet for violence in today's society.

"That must be why men feel the great need to blast the crap out of stuff," answers Scully.

Mulder says, "Testosterone frenzy or no, the only suspect we have in this man's murder is a woman."

close, looks at all the men, and bites his hand. Mulder and Scully work their way to the front of the crowd.

"You get the feeling these men have something better to do," says Scully.

Lacoeur says, "We picked her up outside of a strip club in Reseda. Fits your description to a T."

"Was she read her rights?" asks Scully.

Lacoeur says with a smile, "About five hundred times."

Mulder holds up the image of Maitreya.

"Yeah, I've seen it. A computer-animated woman, Mulder," says Scully, "with a computer-animated weapon."

"A flintlock pistol, which would leave a very large entry wound."

"Pictures don't kill people, Mulder. Guns kill people."

"As do swords."

Their conversation is interrupted by a morgue technician, who wheels in a gurney with a corpse on it. Scully lifts the sheet and sees the body of Darryl Musashi, his decapitated head lying between his feet.

"The world-renowned Darryl Musashi," says Mulder, who then answers his ringing cell phone.

"Mulder . . . You're kidding. Thanks," he says, hanging up. To Scully, "L.A. sheriffs just picked up a female suspect for the murders."

At the Los Angeles Sheriff's Department, a wall of male officers is crowding the door to an interrogation room. As Detective Lacoeur exits the room, we get a glimpse of the voluptuous suspect. The detective lets the door

Mulder and Scully enter the interrogation room. Seeing the suspect, Mulder looks back at the men—and bites his hand.

"For the record, can you state your name please?" asks Scully.

A closeup view of the suspect reveals a scantily clad, voluptuous, beautiful woman who does bear a striking resemblance to Maitreya.

"For the record again, my name is Jade Blue Afterglow. I reside . . ."

Scully interrupts, "Sorry. Your real name."

Mulder is standing behind Scully. His eyes are about to pop out of his head.

"That is my real name," she says. "What were you expecting, 'Mildred'?"

"No," says Scully.

"I sure seem to be upsetting a lot of people around here."

Scully says, "You're not upsetting me, Miss . . ."

"Afterglow," says Mulder helpfully, smiling.

"I sure upset the man running the metal detector," says Afterglow.

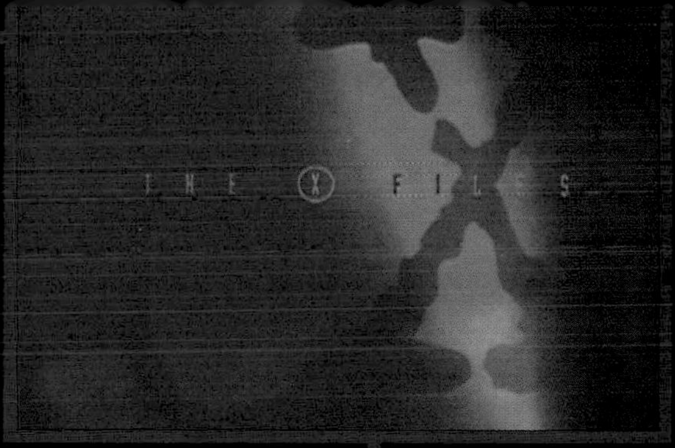

"SO WHAT DID SKINNER SAY?" —Mulder

"HE SAID THAT THE FBI HAS NOTHING TO HIDE AND NEITHER DO WE." —Scully

"YOU WANT TO MAKE YOUR THIRD WISH, CHAMP? I'D LIKE TO GET OUT OF HERE BEFORE THE BLOWFLIES HATCH."
—Jenn

"YOU KNOW, MULDER, IN THE SEVEN YEARS WE'VE BEEN WORKING TOGETHER, I HAVE SEEN SOME AMAZING THINGS. BUT THIS . . . THIS TAKES THE CAKE. IT'S GONNA CHANGE THE BOUNDARIES OF SCIENCE."
—Scully

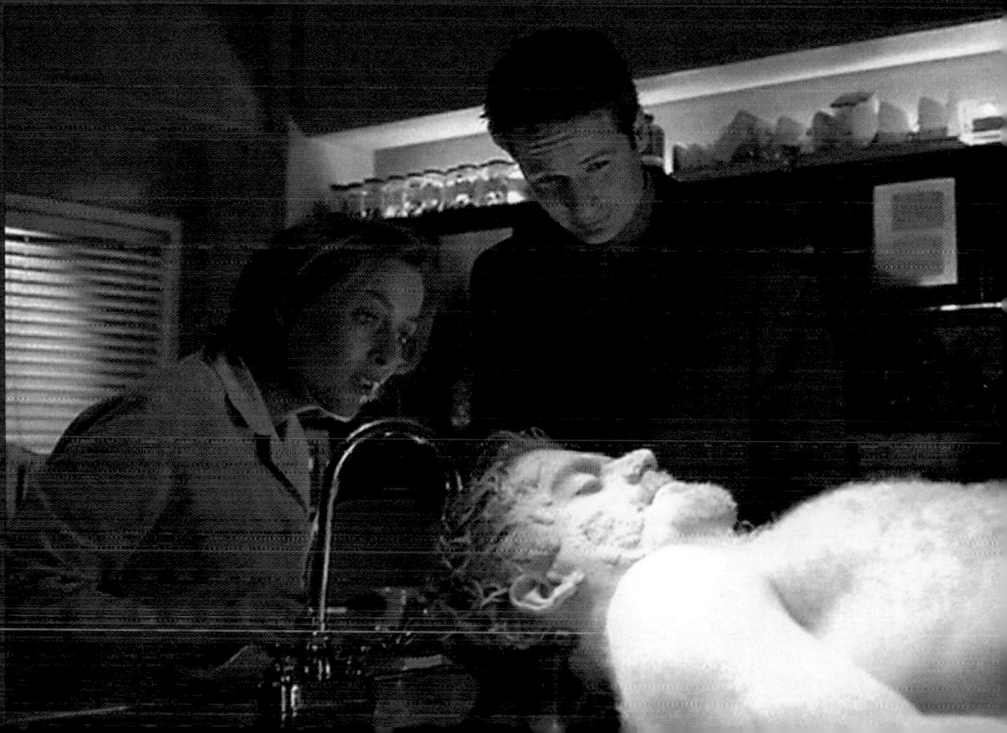

"THEY ARE NOT ROMANTICALLY INVOLVED, IF THAT'S WHAT YOU'RE THINKING." —Mulder

"NOT EVEN I WOULD BE SO FARFETCHED." —Scully

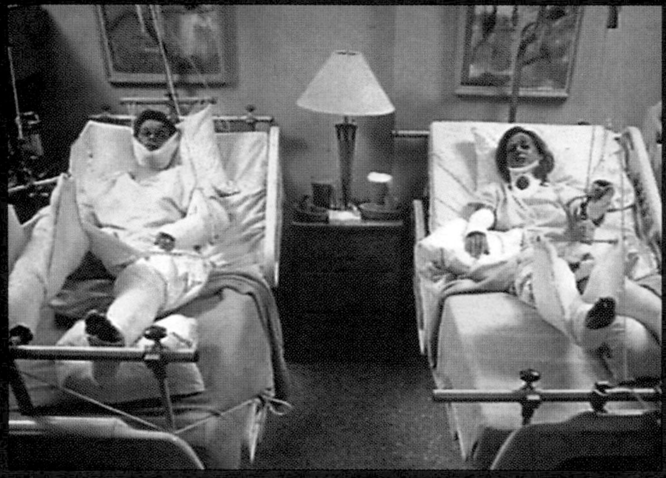

"LADIES AND GENTLEMEN! GET OUTTA YOUR SEATS AND ON YOUR FEETS FOR OUR OWN HOMETOWN BOY GONE BAD, BERT 'THE TITANIC' ZOOOPANIC!!" —Saperstein

"I DON'T KNOW ABOUT YOU GUYS, BUT I'D BE CHECKING MY SHORTS FOR CAKE."
—Mulder

"SHE'S A CHARACTER. SOME IMMATURE HORMONAL FANTASY." —Scully

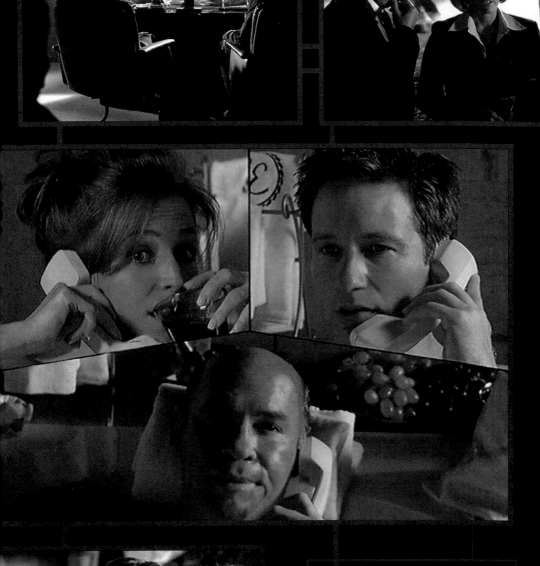

"SCULLY, SKINNER'S CALLING ME FROM A BUBBLE BATH." —Mulder

"WOW, HE'S REALLY GONE HOLLY-WOOD, HUH?" —Scully

"TOTALLY." —Mulder

Afterglow recrosses her legs. Mulder is enjoying this assignment.

Scully says, "You say that you have no knowledge of Ivan Martinez or a company known as First Person Shooter, or FPS."

"I meet a lot of men."

"Would it surprise you to know you've been placed at a crime scene in the offices of FPS?"

"Let's just say it takes a whole lot to surprise me."

Scully says, "You might want to start telling the truth."

"And what truth am I not telling you?" asks Afterglow.

Mulder says, "That you murdered two men. One with a fourteenth-century broadsword. The other with a flintlock pistol."

"Oh. You musta confused me with my sister. Xena, Warrior Princess."

Mulder unfolds the computer printout.

Mulder asks, "Are you denying this is you?"

She takes the printout. "Now I get it," she says. "The medical imaging place in Culver City. I got paid to let them do this body scan thing."

Scully asks, "They paid you to scan your body?"

Afterglow says, "You think that's the strangest thing I've been paid to do?" With a smile, Scully looks to Mulder.

"We're very sorry, Miss Afterglow," says Mulder. "We're sorry. You're free to go."

She slowly uncrosses her legs and struts out the door. Mulder strains to watch as she leaves. He turns to Scully, who is watching him, amused.

Mulder says, "I don't know about you, Scully, but I'm feeling the great need to blast the crap out of something."

•

Mulder and Scully return to the First Person Shooter control room. Scully calls out. There is no answer. From inside they hear a low moan. They see Phoebe lying on the floor.

"Phoebe?" asks Scully. "Are you okay?"

"I musta fell asleep. I was just gonna take a nap. I've been up for seventy hours straight, analyzing code. Trying to fix the game."

Scully asks, "Where is everybody? Where's Ivan?"

"He's with the money guys. They're all freaking."

"Well, we need to talk with him right away," says Scully. "About a woman named Jade Blue Afterglow. He scanned her body and created a character out of her. He put her in the game."

Mulder, looking at the monitors, sees the Lone Gunmen on the massive white floor, putting on fighting suits.

"The Lone Gunmen are on the floor," says Mulder.

Phoebe says, "Yeah, Langly and I wrote a software patch. We're going to run a rez-up test on the game."

"YOU THINK THAT'S THE STRANGEST THING I'VE BEEN PAID TO DO?"—Jade Blue Afterglow

"What for?" asks Scully.

"To bypass the problem."

As they look at the monitor, the Gunmen are surrounded by a pixilate aura, then the first level of the game appears.

"What just happened?" asks Mulder.

"I don't know," says Phoebe.

"They're in the game," says Mulder.

The Gunmen panic, yelling up to Phoebe through their headsets.

"Hey, what the hell's going on?"

"We aren't ready yet."

"Who's running the program?"

As they continue to yell, Phoebe works frantically at the keyboard, pumping in commands to no avail.

"I don't believe this. The program's running itself. This can't be happening."

The Gunmen duck for cover as bullets zigzag all around them.

"Somebody's shooting at them," says Scully.

Phoebe says, "This was supposed to be background only. There wasn't supposed to be any game play."

"They need help." Mulder leaves the room.

The loudspeaker gives off the familiar countdown refrain. Mulder stands in full battle gear, holding a big gun.

"Bring it on."

•

The door opens and Mulder runs out, joining the Gunmen at the barricade.

"You guys okay?" asks Mulder.

"Been better," Frohike answers dryly.

Langly says, "Byers is hit."

"I'm okay. It's a flesh wound," says Byers, as he's zapped by the suit.

"It's her," says Frohike. "She's out there. She nailed Byers with that flintlock."

Mulder seizes the moment. "Okay, on the count of three. I'm going to lay down some cover fire. One, two, three."

Mulder pops up and sprays the street with cyber gunfire. The Gunmen race back to the immersion module. "Mulder! Get in the module!" yells Langly. Mulder fires away as Maitreya, in a black catsuit, races across the urban landscape and down some stairs. them. The urban jungle begins to dissolve. The Gunmen are standing bewildered in the big white game space. Watching from the control room, Phoebe's concerned. They look up to the top of the stairs, where Scully enters, demanding, "Where's Mulder?"

The Gunmen look around, at a loss to explain what happened.

•

Scully races down the stairs.

"Maybe you guys didn't hear me. Come on, guys, where is he?" she asks.

Langly says, "He just took off after her."

"I saw what he did, but where did he go?"

Frohike says, "He went into the building."

Byers adds, "He was firing his weapon."

"I saw where he went, I want to know where he is!" The Gunmen have no response.

Mulder leaps out and gives chase as the Gunmen yell for him to come back.

Phoebe and Scully watch Mulder in action.

"What is he doing?" asks Phoebe.

Scully says, "Getting his ya-yas out." She leaves the control room.

"Mulder, it's suicide," says Langly.

Mulder chases Maitreya into the building and down the steps into the dark. She approaches him, twirling the sword. He sees her and orders her to put down her weapon. Maitraya disappears with swipe of her sword. He wheels around just as she swings her sword at him from behind. Mulder blocks it with his gun, firing as he's knocked down.

The Gunmen gather up their courage and race toward the sound of the gunfire. Suddenly the cyberworld begins to pixilate around

"Is there a door? An exit? Or some kind of passageway that he could have used?"

Langly says, "Just the one you came in."

"He should be right here," Frohike says.

"It's impossible," says Byers. "It's a digital environment. It's just a game."

Scully scowls at Byers, wiping his paint-splattered suit and holding up her yellow-painted finger.

"Yeah, easy for you to say."

Phoebe enters and yells, "Agent Scully, I found him."

•

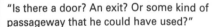

They are in the control room, looking at a monitor showing the vital statistics for each player in the game.

"This monitors everybody playing the game," says Phoebe. "There. Player four. It's his telemetry."

"What do you mean?" asks Scully.

"Player four. That's him," says Phoebe.

"On the monitor," says Byers.

"Right there," points out Frohike.

"Where?" asks Scully, looking at all the monitors.

"That's Mulder," explains Phoebe.

"He's alive," says Byers.

"Those are his vitals," adds Frohike.

"He's still in the game!" says Langly.

Scully asks, "Yes, but where's the game?"

•

Inside the cyberworld, Mulder is disoriented as he gets up and discovers Maitreya's sword buried in a wall. Maitreya is nowhere to be seen. He racks his gun, and goes out into the street. He calls out to the Gunmen but gets no answer.

Mulder spots Maitreya at the end of the street. She does a series of superfast gymnastic handsprings straight for him. Mulder opens fire, bullets whizzing past her spinning image. She leaps over him and her image vanishes.

•

Langly and Frohike are busy underneath the control console. Byers and Scully are intently working at the keyboard.

"What are you doing?" asks Phoebe.

Frohike says, "Rerouting circuitry."

"Making a kill switch," adds Langly. "So we can shut down the game."

Phoebe tells him not to, that it won't work. "There's no way to do that."

Martinez enters the control room. He looks excitedly for Scully.

"We're back in business! Baby, you are dope! We were toast! I felt the flames licking my ass! Then the bankers saw the letters on the autopsy: FBI. Cause of death? Unknown. You fixed our problems. The game's gonna ship and we're gonna be countin' Franklins." The group looks at him, astounded.

Scully says, "You're gonna be countin' teeth."

"Her partner's lost in the game," says Byers.

"Lost?"

"The game has disappeared," she says. "Jade Blue Afterglow. Does that ring a bell?"

"Jade Blue Afterglow?" he repeats.

"Oh, you'd remember her."

Phoebe bolts from the room. Scully follows her out into the hallway, where she finds the computer technician crying.

•

"I don't know how it happened."

"You knew about her?" Phoebe nods. "Then it was you. You scanned that woman's body."

"Into my computer. She was my creation. She was mine."

"But why?"

"You don't know what it's like. Day in and day out, choking in a haze of rampant testosterone."

"I wouldn't be so sure," says Scully.

"I mean, she was all I had to keep me sane. My only way to strike back as a woman. She was my goddess. Everything I can never be."

"But, Phoebe, she is still a killer. I can't explain it, but she is. And you put her in the game."

"No, I didn't. I was creating my own game. In my own computer. It was totally secret. I never told anyone. But somehow she jumped programs and she's feeding off the male aggression. It's making her stronger and stronger. I need your help. You're the only one who can understand."

"You've got to destroy her, Phoebe."

"I don't know how," she says.

"Well, there's got to be some way. There's got to be some vulnerability or a weakness somewhere."

Phoebe says, "She has no weakness anymore."

•

Mulder is running down the street. He reaches the immersion module and pounds on the door. No response. He turns and sees Maitreya sauntering down the street toward him. Mulder goes to his weapon. A light is flashing: NO AMMO. Maitreya stops right in front of Mulder and waits.

"I bet you think you're going to kick my butt up and down the block."

The first wheelhouse kick disarms him, followed by one to his head. "Okay," says Mulder. More lightning-fast wheelhouse kicks to Mulder's body send him crashing against the module door. Maitreya plants two more kicks on Mulder's body, sending him crumpling to the ground.

•

Scully returns to the control room.

"Her name is Maitreya. She's input herself into the game. We've got to download her."

"We can't even get on line," says Byers. "The system's been hijacked."

Langly says, "The program won't respond."

Scully asks what Frohike is looking at.

"Mulder's vitals are wiggy," says Frohike. "They're all over the map."

Martinez sees Phoebe and realizes she did this. He screams at her and steps menacingly toward her. Scully steps between them.

"No fair picking on a girl."

•

Mulder is getting the tar kicked out of him. Maitreya winds up for another kick. In desperation, Mulder grabs her foot in midkick and flips the fighting woman on her back. Mulder gets up on wobbly legs and runs for it. He races for the tall building where he previously fought Maitreya and pulls the sword out of the wall.

Suddenly the cyberworld begins to pixilate and the urban environment is lost. The screen reassembles and Mulder finds himself standing on the dusty street of an old Western town, holding the sword.

The Gunmen's persistence is rewarded when the game suddenly goes back on line. There is a moment of blank screens before the game completes its rez process. The Western town slowly materializes.

"That's not the game," says Scully.

"Yes, it is," says Phoebe. "It's Level Two."

Scully asks, "Where's Mulder?"

"Mulder's in Level One," says Langly.

"No, he's right here," says Martinez, as the frame changes to Mulder, alone in the Western street.

"Shut the game down," says Scully.

"No, no, no!" begs Martinez. "You can't!"

"Just turn it off!" insists Scully.

"Power down, Langly," insists Frohike.

Langly types in a series of commands.

"The computer's not responding," says Martinez.

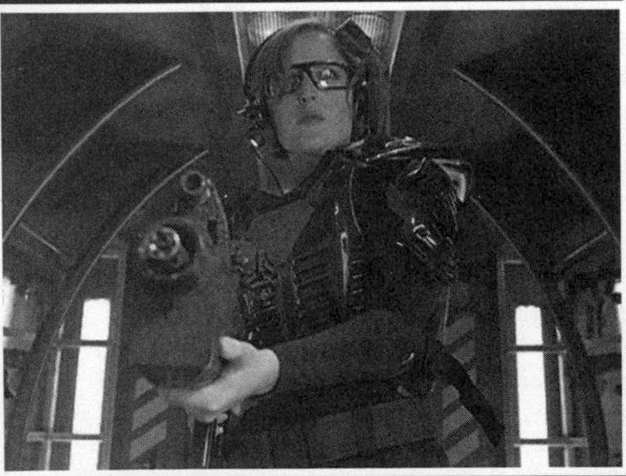

Scully says, "Look, we have to get him out of there."

"Yeah, and quick," agrees Frohike, pointing to the screen.

•

Maitreya, in a sexy cowboy outfit, appears at the far end of the street. Mulder whirls around and spots her walking confidently toward him.

"Whoa. Stop right there," he says, as he raises his broadsword.

Maitreya takes a pistol from her holster, expertly twirls it, and returns it to the holster.

"That's not really fair, is it?"

Maitreya suddenly multiplies into five identical copies of herself, all ready to fire.

"Well, that's just cheating," says Mulder. He hears the sound of the immersion module opening behind him. The door opens to reveal . . .

Scully in full gear. With a monster gun. Ready to do battle.

•

Scully steps out to the barricade and fires on the advancing Maitreyas. Mulder drops to the ground. One by one they spin and drop, like in a shooting gallery, as Scully laces them with automatic weapon fire. Back in the control room, the Gunmen are in a joyous uproar.

Frohike says, "Go girl!"

Byers says, "Scully's on fire!"

"The bloodthirst is unquenchable," Langly says.

"Are you witnessing this?" Frohike asks Martinez.

Martinez and Phoebe are not thrilled.

Langly asks, "What's wrong?"

"This is Level Two," says Phoebe. "It only gets harder."

"No one's ever beaten Level Two," says Martinez.

•

Scully leaves the barricades and joins the shaken Mulder.

"You okay?"

"Ask me if I'm humiliated."

Mulder and Scully are startled by the sound of the immersion module's door closing. They make for the door. Mulder slips the sword in just as it closes and tries unsuccessfully to pry it open. Scully sees Maitreya reforming in front of her.

"Mulder," she calls. They now face ten Maitreyas. Scully racks her gun as the firing starts.

•

"This is nuts," says Byers.

"How do you kill something that won't die?" asks Langly.

Phoebe pushes through the guys, reaching for the keyboard. "Try and stop me, Ivan." Martinez grabs for the keyboard and they wrestle for control.

"My whole life's in this game!" says Martinez.

Frohike asks Phoebe, "What are you trying to do?"

"Stay out of this!" says Phoebe.

Martinez says, "She's going to destroy it!"

Phoebe says, "It's the only way to save them."

Frohike manages to gain control of the keyboard.

Langly asks, "You can save them?"

Phoebe says, "There's a kill command."

"It kills the whole game," Martinez says.

Byers asks, "You knew about this?"

Martinez says, "She knew about it, too!"

Frohike turns on Phoebe. "You said it wouldn't work."

Martinez says, "She was trying to save her creation. Her goddess."

Phoebe says bitterly, "You don't care who dies, as long as your game survives."

Byers says, "Our friends are in there."

Langly adds, "We're not gonna let them die."

Everyone reaches for the keyboard at once.

•

Scully blasts away at the ten Maitreyas. They fall, only to be replaced by the cybervixen atop a monster tank, in sexy army gear. She fires at Scully. The tank explodes, only to be replaced by another.

•

In the control room, Frohike has regained control of the keyboard. "This is out of your hands now," he tells Phoebe.

"We have to shut down the program," Byers tells her. Phoebe and Ivan stare at each other.

"They can't keep this up," says Byers.

Langly says, "Scully's running out of ammo."

Martinez shakes his head.

Frohike demands, "What's the command?"

Martinez says, "Don't do it, Phoebe. We're so close."

Meanwhile, Scully continues to fire as the tank slowly approaches.

Langly says, "Give him the command!"

Still staring at Martinez, Phoebe tells them "Shift Alt Bloodbath."

Frohike types in the command. Images pixilate and the screens flash white. The program is being nuked. All that is left is the big, white game floor of the game space. The Gunmen and Phoebe race for the game space. Only to discover that the game floor is empty.

"Oh my God," says Byers.

"We killed the game," says Langly. "And Mulder and Scully along with it."

"Over here!" says Phoebe.

Lying on the floor is Scully's gun. They leap at the immersion module and pry open its doors, where they see Mulder and Scully lying on the floor, yellow paint marks on their chests.

"That's entertainment," says an elated Mulder, smiling.

The Gunmen and Phoebe help the agents up and, like wounded soldiers, they cross the game floor.

Mulder's voice recites a battle-weary Game Boy eulogy to the good fight.

•

Ivan Martinez sits despondent and alone in the First Person Shooter control room. The monitor screens are all dark. Suddenly the image of Maitreya rezzes up and begins its texture wrap. Martinez looks on in wonder as the wrap completes itself.

Scully's head is on Maitreya's body.

BACK STORY:

William Gibson and Tom Maddox's story idea, much like their fifth season contribution "Kill Switch," drew on the dark side of the high-tech, glamorous cyberworld, combining corporate greed and the concept of violence as entertainment into a claustrophobic, cutting-edge, visceral, visual exercise.

"William Gibson and Tom Maddox always get us into trouble," says Frank Spotnitz. "They always come up with these great ideas that are always hard to execute."

Part of that problem was translating the writers' expansive concepts, which work fine in their novels, into forty-four minutes of television airtime. Spotnitz remembers that the process of crafting the "First Person Shooter" script was a slow one. "Their idea was ultimately changed somewhat to fit the concept of an X-File. We worked with them on the first two acts and then they went away and came back to us with two more acts."

But the biggest challenge in "First Person Shooter" soon became budgetary. The sheer visual weight of the episode threatened to make it go drastically over budget. Consequently, production designer Corey Kaplan saw the cyberterrain as a personal challenge.

"Being a big William Gibson fan, I thought, 'How do I do this justice?' I'd like to brag that we created everything you see out of our own heads. But the reality is, initially, we had some video game companies send us some virtual game layouts. But we decided that we were not going to simply copy existing designs. Finally our approach was to draw some pretty pictures. We concentrated on very minute strokes and details. Everything on that episode had a price tag. It was damned expensive for a TV show."

But for all the visual flash and special effects firepower, Carter knew that "First Person Shooter" was going to live or die on the charisma and believability of the virtual game huntress Maitreya (AKA Jade Blue Afterglow). "You would think that you could toss a rock anywhere in Los Angeles and hit ten of those girls," says Carter. "But one of the toughest parts of casting that episode was the character of Jade Blue Afterglow."

Casting director Rick Millikan soon found out how tough a task it would be. "I looked at everybody: strippers, adult video entertainment ladies, erotic thriller/direct-to-video type actresses. Chris really wanted a hot-looking woman but, obviously, she had to be able to do a lot of the physical things. I had known Krista Allen for years. There was this little wholesome quality about her that initially bothered Chris. But as we went through the rest of the choices, she actually ended up being the right person."

Locations were predictably spread out. The action-packed opening sequence and much of the cybershootout sequences were shot in the more industrial part of downtown Los Angeles. The final showdown on Western streets was shot in the often-used dusty backroads of Valencia, California.

A downtown Los Angeles warehouse area, complete with a long straightaway and surrounded on either side by six-story buildings, served as the backdrop for the opening sequence in which the trio of cybergeeks meet their fate. It also put stunt coordinator Danny Weselis through the proverbial wringer. "I had fourteen stuntmen on Kawasaki 600 racing bikes riding down a corridor firing gas-powered machine guns. I was coordinating heavily with Bill Millar, who needed certain things for the visual side. We had to create fireballs so that he could coordinate with his effects to make players disappear from the game. There was lots of gunfire and hundreds of squibs. We also had doubles for Mulder and Maitreya for their martial arts fight. We had a sword master on set to teach Krista how to use a sword. And a gymnast to double Krista for the scene where Maitreya does a series of handsprings."

Gibson and Maddox are longtime fans of the Lone Gunmen and deliberately featured them in "First Person Shooter." Bruce Harwood says he was grateful for the work . . . and it was most definitely work.

"We did a lot of hard running, over and over. I know I felt terribly out of shape and ended up giving myself a charley horse. One thing I always wondered about was how the Gunmen made their money, and this was the first time we had a clue that they did this sort of game programming thing on the side."

The scope of production of "First Person Shooter" predictably manifested itself in an extremely tight production schedule. "We were still cutting the show on Saturday afternoon, the day before the show was set to air," says Spotnitz. "The show just barely made it to air."

Gillian Anderson enjoyed the episode, despite its reliance on big guns and raging testosterone. She liked the opportunity to show Scully wearing heavy metal and firing oversized weapons. "But it was kind of tricky. That episode was filmed at a time in the season when there was still a lot of stuff going on behind the scenes. It was an interesting feeling on the set with all these guys running around with big guns, just blasting away."

FACTS:

The scene involving Maitreya astride a tank was added in postproduction at the suggestion of visual effects coordinator Bill Millar. "He kept sweetening it for Chris," explains Spotnitz. "The whole scene just kept getting bigger and bigger."

ⓧ

Much of the opening action sequence was shot at the famed Rykoff food distribution company, one of the oldest buildings in downtown Los Angeles. Rykoff is the uncle of *X-Files* producer Paul Rabwin.

ⓧ

Experienced gymnast Dana Heath doubled for Krista Allen in the scene where she executes a series of handsprings.

ⓧ

Krista Allen is known for her roles as Shelley on *The Bold and the Beautiful*, Billie Reed on *Days of Our Lives*, and Jenny Avid on *Baywatch Hawaii*. She also appears in the television series *CSI: Crime Scene Investigation*.

episode 7X14

THEEF

EPISODE: 7X14
FIRST AIRED: March 12, 2000
EDITOR: Lynne Willingham
WRITTEN BY: Vince Gilligan, John Shiban, & Frank Spotnitz
DIRECTED BY: Kim Manners

A mysterious murder investigation leads Mulder and Scully to a back-woods man with voodoo powers and a vendetta.

GUEST STARS:

Billy Drago (Orell Peattie)
James Morrison (Dr. Robert Wieder)
Kate McNeil (Nan Wieder)
Cara Jedell (Lucy Wieder)
Tom Dahlgren (Dr. Irving Thalbro)
Sage Allen (Landlady)
Pamela Gordon (Proprietor)
Matthew Sutherland (Records Clerk)
Dylan Kussman (Med Student)
Michael Sidney (Security Guard)
Aaron Braxton (Radiology Tech)
Leah Sanders(Reporter #1)
Mark Thompson (Reporter #2)

PRINCIPAL SETTINGS:

Marin County, California;
Foster City, California; San Francisco, California

A Jaguar pulls through the gates and up the drive of a mansion in Marin County. Dr. Robert Wieder, his wife, Nan, and their sixteen-year-old daughter, Lucy, who carries a hefty awards trophy, enter the front door of the house, having just returned from a black-tie affair.

"Daddy, why don't you take this before my arm falls off?" asks Lucy.

The family is joined in the hallway by Nan's father, Dr. Irving Thalbro, who aims a camera at them.

"Everybody, one last shot," says Thalbro.

Thalbro fusses with the delay shutter and races to be in the picture. "Hold up that eyesore, Robert. God knows when you're gonna win another one."

Wieder says, "Irv, you want to think about staying the night? It's awful late to head back to the city."

"What? I get to stay at the home of the Bay Area Doctor of the Year? That's a deal. I'm proud of you, Robert," says Thalbro as the camera flashes, snapping the happy family.

•

A little later, Wieder climbs into bed, where he finds Nan reading the plaque on her husband's trophy.

"'Presented to Dr. Robert Wieder, M.D., for the great wisdom, skill, and compassion he exhibits in the practice of medicine.' It'll look awfully nice in your office."

Wieder takes the award from his wife. He studies it intently.

Nan asks, "What are you thinking?"

"How this is just the cherry on top. How lucky I am," says Wieder.

The happy couple snuggle together.

•

In the downstairs guest bedroom, Dr. Thalbro is getting ready for bed. He pulls back the covers.

There is dirt on the sheets, spread out in the shape of a crude stick figure. He doesn't know what to make of this. Thalbro brushes his hand through the dirt, obliterating the figure. He senses a presence. He turns to find . . .

. . . a man with a weathered face, bad teeth, and scarred eyes standing motionless behind him.

•

Wieder and his wife are aroused by the beeping and flashing of the security system.

"What is it?" asks Nan.

"The downstairs motion sensor."

"Think Dad tripped the alarm?"

"The alarm hasn't been tripped. You got me. I'll go check it out."

•

Wieder goes downstairs, where he sees a figure standing in the center of the darkened entrance hall. It is Dr. Thalbro.

"Irv?" asks Wieder.

There is no response. Puzzled, Wieder approaches his father-in-law.

"Irving? Is everything all right?"

He reaches out and touches the man's shoulder. Dr. Thalbro slowly spins around to reveal that he is hanging by an electrical cord attached to the chandelier. Blood splatters his white shirt. His throat has been cut.

Wieder backs away, slipping in the blood. He rights himself and flicks on the light switch. On a far wall, Wieder sees the word THEEF written in a massive scrawl of blood.

•

Mulder stands studying the word THEEF on the wall. Scully wanders through the hallway and joins him as he continues to stare intently at the bloody word.

"What do you think, Scully?" asks Mulder. "Is this a name, possibly? Or a code? Or an anagram?"

Scully says, "T-H-E-E-F. I assume it's supposed to be T-H-I-E-F. Thief."

"Insert your own Dan Quayle joke here. Lousy spelling aside, what do you think it refers to? Who's the thief?"

"Well, that's certainly one question. I've got many."

" 'Mulder, why are we here?' " suggests Mulder.

"To be fair, I might have used the words 'Mulder, how is this an X-File?' " says Scully.

"You see that, Scully . . . you always keep me guessing.

"This is Dr. Irving Thalbro, age sixty-six. Found hanged, his throat cut. His family, tucked away in bed not forty feet away from here. Didn't see or hear anything."

"Which would certainly shine the light of suspicion on them."

Mulder adds, "Except they're the ones who called it in. And there's no evidence whatsoever to link them to the crime."

"Which is why the police are rightly wondering if Dr. Thalbro killed himself."

Mulder points to the bloody scrawl. "Except who, then, did this? Blood pattern doesn't indicate the good doctor did it. Who, I'm assuming, could read and write above a fourth-grade level."

Scully says, "I'll admit, Mulder, this is not an open-and-shut case. But that doesn't make it an X-File."

"There's one detail that does," says Mulder.

He heads for the guest bedroom and points to the pile of black earth on the bedsheets.

"This," says Mulder, pointing to the dirt. "It's a very powerful component of hexcraft, as well as the pattern in which it was originally arranged. Check this out."

Mulder shines his flashlight on the sheets. There is still the faint outline of the stick figure. "It looks like a human form."

"Hexcraft. As in putting a curse on someone? Murdering them magically?"

"Yeah, that's what it looks like to me. I know what you're going to say, Scully."

"No. Hexcraft," says Scully, interrupting. "I mean, I'll buy that as the intent here. Certainly it jibes with the evidence. I say we talk to the family."

She heads out of the room, then stops and turns to Mulder with a wry smile.

"I'll always keep you guessing," she says.

•

Mulder and Scully talk to Dr. Wieder and his stunned and saddened family.

Scully asks, "Sir, can you think of any enemies your father-in-law might have made? Maybe inadvertently? Through his medical practice, or a business dealing, perhaps?"

"Everybody loved Irving, everyone who knew him. He was . . . No. I can't conceive of it."

Mulder asks, "Dr. Wieder, do you have any enemies? I'm sorry, I have to ask. There was a message left behind. If it doesn't refer to your father-in-law, it may refer to you."

"Theef?" Lucy says. "Are you asking if my dad's a thief? He saves people's lives! He's a good man!"

"If I have any enemies, I don't know them," says Wieder.

•

In a tumbledown boardinghouse in a rough part of Foster City, a television news reporter is giving the gory details of the Thalbro murder. Paying scant attention is the landlady, who is slowly making her way through the apartments with a carpet sweeper. She stops as a funky smell permeates the air. It appears to be coming from a particular room. The landlady moves to the door. On the other side, a scratchy, muttering man's voice is heard. The foul odor continues. Finally she raps on the door.

"Hello? Mr. Peattie? Mr. Peattie, I know you're in there. Are you cooking? You aren't supposed to be cooking."

The door opens a crack and Mr. Peattie slides his face out.

"That smell like sumthin' you wanna eat?"

"What is it, then?" she asks.

"Medicine."

The landlady says, "Oh, all right. Just so long as you're not cooking."

"Seems like you could use yourself a poultice for your back," Peattie says. "Ol' Peattie fix you right up. Be ready later."

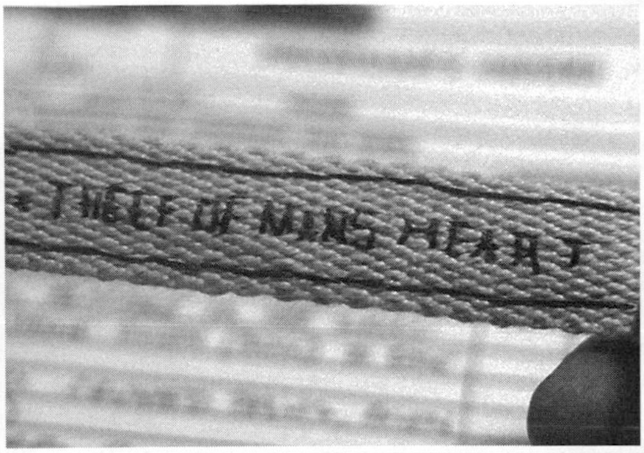

He pulls his head back and shuts the door. Peattie moves back into his tiny room, past jars containing God knows what and magic paraphernalia, to a work space where he begins sewing a crude doll. It is a female. Nearby are a male doll and a smaller female doll. Next to them, another male doll is hanging by the neck from a crude gallows.

•

Scully is looking through a microscope in an autopsy bay. The body of Dr. Thalbro, covered by a sheet, lays on a table. Mulder enters the room and holds up an evidence bag full of dirt.

"Scully, this dirt we found? Gas chromatograph shows pronounced spikes of methane and sulfur compounds: the signature of decay. It's graveyard dirt. Also known as 'conjure dust.' It's thought to be the most powerful of hexing elements, whether for good or evil. Not the kind of stuff you wanna be on the wrong end of."

"Uh-huh," says Scully, completely focused on looking through her microscope.

"Go ahead, Scully. Keep me guessing," says Mulder.

"Kuru," says Scully.

"The disease that New Guinea tribesmen get?"

Scully pulls up a microscope magnification of Thalbro's cerebellum on her computer screen. "From eating the brains of their relatives," she adds.

"I thought my grandpa slurping his soup was bad."

Scully continues, "Practically speaking, Mulder, kuru doesn't even exist anymore. Not in New Guinea, and certainly not in the U.S. But this man's cerebellum and his striatum clearly show signs of it, Mulder. I mean, these amyloid plaques? His brain is riddled with them."

"Kuru makes you crazy, right?" asks Mulder.

"Yeah, stark raving. Among other things. But in this case, stark raving mad enough to slit his own throat and hang himself. Mulder, that's what his autopsy shows, from the wound pattern to the blood spray. This man did it to himself. There's no question."

"Unless it was inflicted upon him. The graveyard dirt, the hex. He was given this disease so that he would kill himself."

•

Back home in Marin County, Nan is on her way to bed when she notices that one of the photo frames is empty. While she's examining the frame, she hears her husband's voice. Turning to meet Robert downstairs, Nan just misses seeing Peattie step into the doorway. In his hands is the missing photo.

"Who would have taken that?" Nan asks her husband as she looks at the empty picture frame.

Wieder says, "The police, probably. Could be they needed it as evidence."

Peattie is in the Wieder master bedroom, tucking an image of Nan torn from the photo into a slit in the back of a female doll. He adds a strand of Nan's hair before he closes the doll.

The bedroom door opens and Wieder and Nan enter. Peattie is gone.

Nan says, "We can't stay here, Robert. I can't live in this house anymore, Lucy can't. Not after what's happened here. And now this picture of us that's missing."

"It'll turn up," says Wieder.

"No. It doesn't make any sense. Nothing that's happened here makes any sense!"

"It does, Nan. Listen to me."

Wieder tries to console his wife. He tells her Thalbro was sick, that the FBI autopsy indicated a kind of progressive dementia. Nan moves to her dressing table as Wieder goes to the bed and pulls down the covers. He stops cold and stares down at a dirt-drawn stick figure. Wieder turns to his wife . . . just in time to see her collapse onto the floor.

"Oh my God. Nan? Honey?"

Wieder leans down to check her pulse and is shocked to see angry eruptions rising up out of her skin and covering every part of her body. She begins to convulse. Their daughter, Lucy, awakened by the commotion, appears in the doorway.

"Lucy, call 911. Call 911!" says Wieder.

Outside the house, Peattie finishes a chant and lowers the doll from his lips. He smiles up at the window.

•

Nan has been transported to the University of San Francisco Medical Center, where she lays hooked up to a heart-lung monitor in the intensive care unit. Mulder and Scully enter the ICU. Mulder signals Wieder and he steps outside the room.

Scully says, "We understand you've made a diagnosis."

"Diffuse cutaneous leishmaniasis," Wieder says. "Old World type."

"I take it that's rare," says Mulder.

"In San Francisco? It's unheard of. Maybe in Central Africa," Scully says.

Mulder says, "Maybe the rarer, the better."

"What do you mean by that?" asks Wieder.

"Someone directed this to happen to your wife. Just as someone directed what happened to your father-in-law."

Wieder says, "My enemy you were talking about. The one who thinks I'm a thief." He looks at Scully. "Agent, you're a doctor. Explain to your partner that no one can direct a person to get sick."

"The dirt you found on your bed," Mulder continues, "drawn in the shape of a body. That's indicative of folk magic. That's what I believe is being used against you."

"Folk magic," says Wieder. "You mean like Baba Yaga. Gypsies."

"I was actually thinking less Eastern and more Celtic. Maybe Scots-Irish, or Appalachian."

"I'm supposed to take this seriously?" asks Wieder.

Scully says, "Sir, regardless of the particulars, I think it's clear that there was an intruder in your home. I think it would be prudent for you to accept our protection and help us to identify this person."

"Prudent for me would be to continue treating my wife," says Wieder.

"If we don't stop who's causing this, your treatments won't matter," Mulder says.

"So. Modern medicine and all it encompasses. Artificial hearts, laser surgery, gene therapy, to name a few. All of that arrayed against a pile of magic dirt, and you tell me I'll lose? I have MRIs to look at."

Wieder heads off down the hall.

"Oh, yeah, Mulder. Win him over," says Scully.

"He will lose. Unless we can find a way to stop it."

"What do you suggest?"

"A second opinion."

•

Dr. Wieder is in a darkened room. He clicks on a lightbox and opens an envelope, sliding out MRI film. He slips the first film into place on the lightbox and the word THEEF instantly appears on the negative. He slips in another and another. All of them have the word THEEF written across them.

Wieder turns and sees a silhouette standing in the doorway. It is Peattie.

"Truth always hurts, don't it, doc?" asks Peattie.

"Who are you?"

Peattie does not answer. Dr. Wieder looks from Peattie to the MRIs.

"Is this you? You did this? What do you want from me?"

"Oh, don't you be fretting none about that. I'm getting my nickel's worth. You doin' a fine job so far."

"What the hell are you talking about? What is this all about?"

"Lynette Peattie," he says. "And don't you be saying you don't recollect her. No, no, no . . ."

"Look, if I've done anything to upset you, I . . . It's no use trying to intimidate me if I don't know how I've offended you! Tell me!

What makes me a thief?"

Peattie says, "You be a smart man. I figure you ponder it a while, it gonna come to you."

Peattie turns and walks off. "Wait!" Wieder runs after him into the hallway. But he sees no one.

•

Wieder has taken the name *Lynette Peattie* to the hospital records room, where a records clerk is tracking the name through a computer.

The clerk says, "No. No matter how I spell it, there's no Lynette Peattie."

"She's not in my patient file?"

"She's not in any doctor's patient file. No one by that name has ever been admitted to the hospital and I don't think you treated her."

"What about Jane Does?" asks Wieder as the clerk types into the computer and the screen changes.

"You've treated three in the last two years," says the clerk.

"Pull the files, please."

Wieder goes through the Jane Does. He finds nothing in the first two folders. He picks up the third folder and reads it. The report reads, "Unconscious Jane Doe, est. age eighteen, severe chest trauma, fractures of the skull and spine." Stapled to the folder is a Baggie that contains a fabric wristband embroidered with the words FLAX-HAIR LAMB, THEEF OF MANS HEART.

•

Peattie is muttering as he works on two more dolls, of Dr. Wieder and his daughter, Lucy. Suddenly he stops his work, puts down the doll, and goes to the door.

"Oh, you're there," says the flustered landlady as the door opens. "I wanted to thank you. That poultice? It worked a miracle on my back. I was about to knock and ask if I could get a little more."

She hands him a handkerchief. Peattie considers the request, retreats into his room, and scoops something out of a mason jar. He hands the handkerchief full of medicine back to her.

"Whatever that is, it sure is stinky."

"Stinky's good," says Peattie as he closes the door on her.

•

Mulder and Scully arrive at a musty, dark occult store full of voodoo and magic objects. A proprietor shelving some books looks up as they enter.

"Good afternoon. Can I help you?"

Mulder says, "Yeah. We're looking for some alternative medical advice."

"You've come to the right place. I get a lot of folks fed up with their HMOs."

"Actually, we're not here for us," says Scully.

Mulder pulls out his bag of dirt. The proprietor backs off, putting her hand up in a protective gesture. "Whoa, chief. Back in the pocket."

Scully says, "It's dirt."

The proprietor says, "It's goofer dust, is what it is! I don't know what your intentions are with that."

"Goofer dust?" asks Scully.

Mulder puts the dirt packet back in his pocket. "Conjure dust, goofer dust. How would you go about making someone sick using this? We're investigating a murder. That's why I'm asking," says Mulder, showing his badge.

The proprietor says, "Speaking strictly in the academic sense, you'd spread it on or near your victim to direct misfortune."

"So, you could give them any illness you wanted?" he asks. "One you chose specifically for them?"

"No, that's a lot trickier. It requires something special."

She pulls out a doll from behind the counter. Scully remarks that it's a voodoo doll.

The proprietor says, "They're called 'poppets.' Inside you place three thorns of a blood-red rose, a strand of hair, and a photo of your victim. Maybe other items as well, depends on the operator. Sew it up, say your spell."

Mulder takes the doll. "How would you counteract one of these?"

"Depends on who you're dealing with. But if the person you're looking for is powerful enough to bring about a murder? He's probably charmed," says the proprietor.

Scully asks, "Which would mean what?"

"It means just that. He's drawing on the energy of a charm, a source of magic power. It could be any item, provided that it's very important to him. Something that holds great meaning for him. And unless you can separate him from his charm, you're out of luck," says the proprietor.

•

Peattie is standing in a break room of the hospital, eyeing the junk food in a vending machine, particularly the "popping corn." A medical student sitting nearby instructs Peattie on how to purchase the popcorn and tells him he needs to pop it in the microwave.

"Microwave! I heard tell of such a thing. It's a true wonder," says Peattie as he follows the student's directions "Radiation, come from the heart of the atom. I think it be God's own glow."

Peattie looks out into the hallway, just as Dr. Wieder walks by and into the radiology suite with his daughter, Lucy.

Wieder says, "You're going to be very happy, I promise. The drug therapy I'm giving her is working wonders. C'mon, you'll see."

He leads his daughter into the radiology room where Nan, who is looking better, is being prepped for an MRI machine treatment.

"Mom?"

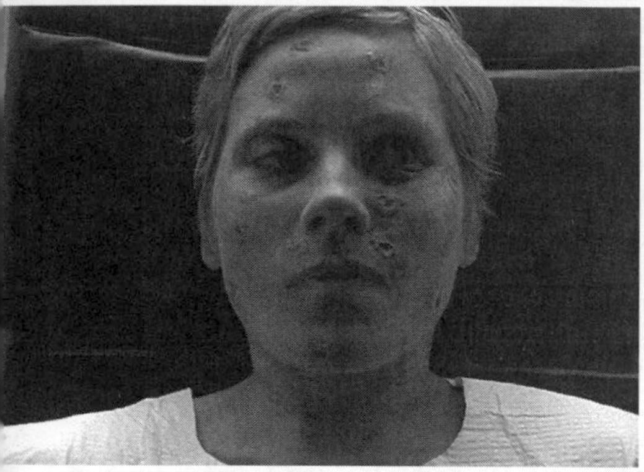

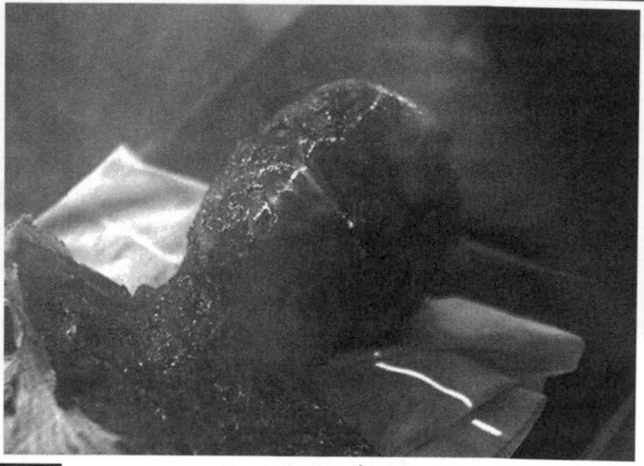

"Hi, sweetie," says Nan.

"You look good," says Lucy.

"Yeah, right. But I am definitely feeling better. So how come I have to go through this thing again?"

Wieder says, "C'mon. This thing gives off about as much radiation as a dental X ray. Nothing to worry about."

"I know," says Nan. "Still scares me. Wish me luck."

Lucy leaves the room as Nan is eased into the MRI machine. In the break room, Peattie removes the popcorn from the microwave and puts the Nan doll inside.

Wieder stands in a glass booth watching the MRI procedure. Everything seems to be going well until Nan's body begins to shake violently. She screams.

"Switch it off!" says Wieder.

He races in and grabs Nan's trembling ankles, then snatches his hands away as if burned. He grabs again and this time yanks her out of the machine, to discover Nan . . .

Nuked like a chicken breast.

Peattie pulls the Nan doll out of the microwave.

"All done," says Peattie as he exits, munching on a handful of popcorn.

•

Mulder and Scully are in Dr. Wieder's home. Wieder is in a state of shock.

"You believe that your wife was murdered?" asks Scully.

Wieder says, "It was no accident. No malfunction of the machine. Yes. I believe she was murdered."

Mulder asks, "But you still have no idea why?"

He hands Wieder a photo. It is a closeup of blackened human skin with the word THEEF burned into the flesh from the inside.

"The pathologist found this branded into your wife's chest," says Mulder.

Wieder has an odd look on his face as he looks at the photo.

Scully says, "Sir, we can't help you if you withhold information from us."

"A man came to see me yesterday," says Wieder. "My age, older maybe. Tall. He mentioned someone named Lynette Peattie. I didn't know who she was at first. It turns out she was a Jane Doe I treated last October.

She was in a bus rollover, came in amid a wave of victims. She was the worst off. I could barely put fluids in fast enough to keep up with the blood loss. We were rushing around, triaging people. Everybody knew she was dying. It was only a matter of time. And she was in agony."

Wieder takes the physician's order sheet from his desk and hands it to Scully. "This was my course of treatment."

"You gave her morphine," she says. "Lots of it."

Wieder says, "I pushed it myself. She kept screaming, her heart rate kept climbing. So I kept pushing. I took maybe the last twenty minutes of her life. It was a fair trade to make for the pain."

"Her father doesn't agree," says Mulder.

"What makes you think it's her father?" asks Scully.

"He thinks you robbed him of his family. That's why he's systematically robbing you of yours."

"What am I supposed to do? My daughter, Lucy . . ."

"You don't do anything. Let us find a way to protect you."

"How?"

"I have an idea where to start," says Mulder.

•

Mulder and Scully stand over a freshly opened grave in a potter's field, supervising the exhumation.

Scully says, "If Lynette Peattie were Carlos the Jackal, I would have had an easier time tracking her down. There's no birth certificate, no Social Security number, nothing."

"Better known to the world as Jane Doe sixty-one-forty-nine."

"Her name shows up once in the records of a VISTA inoculation program. 1981. The Allegheny Mountains of West Virginia."

Mulder says, "Deepest Appalachia."

"That's when her father, one Orell Peattie, refused to allow her to be inoculated against polio. But there's no address for him, there's no record of him whatsoever. So, Mulder, why are we exhuming this girl?"

"I'm thinking of her dear old backwoods dad and where he gets all his graveyard dirt."

"Here? His daughter's grave?"

"The occultist we spoke to said the person casting these magic spells was charmed, that he had a source of power that was very meaningful to him and he kept it close by."

Scully says, "Lynette Peattie's body?"

"That's my guess. So as long as her body remains here, resting in peace in the Bay Area, he remains powerful. But if we were to ship it off to Quantico . . ."

The workers unstrap the coffin. The lid appears to have been pried open.

Mulder pulls at the coffin lid. It pops off and he looks in dismay at the empty casket.

Lynette Peattie's body is gone.

•

The landlady is once again rapping on Peattie's door.

"Mr. Peattie? My pain is back. I was wondering if I could get a little more of that poultice. Mr. Peattie?"

There is no answer. She starts to walk away, then stops and pulls out her key. She enters Peattie's room and is immediately taken aback by a foul odor. The landlady heads for the dresser, where she knows Peattie keeps the medicine. She is startled to see somebody asleep on the bed.

"I'm sorry," she says. "I didn't know you were home."

The landlady inches closer to the bed and pulls the cover back to reveal the hideously broken skeleton of Lynette Peattie.

Screaming, the landlady turns to run and looks right into the face of Peattie.

•

Mulder and Scully are supervising new security precautions at the Wieder house. Guards man the door and windows near the entrance hall. Scully is shepherding Wieder and Lucy, who are carrying overnight bags. Mulder is finishing up a telephone conversation.

"All right. Thank you," says Mulder into his cell phone. "They'll be there before dark.

"You all set?"

"We still don't know where it is we're going," says Wieder.

Mulder says, "We've rented a cabin for you. It's important that you get out of town."

"I TOOK MAYBE THE LAST TWENTY MINUTES OF HER LIFE. IT WAS A FAIR TRADE TO MAKE FOR THE PAIN."—Dr. Wieder

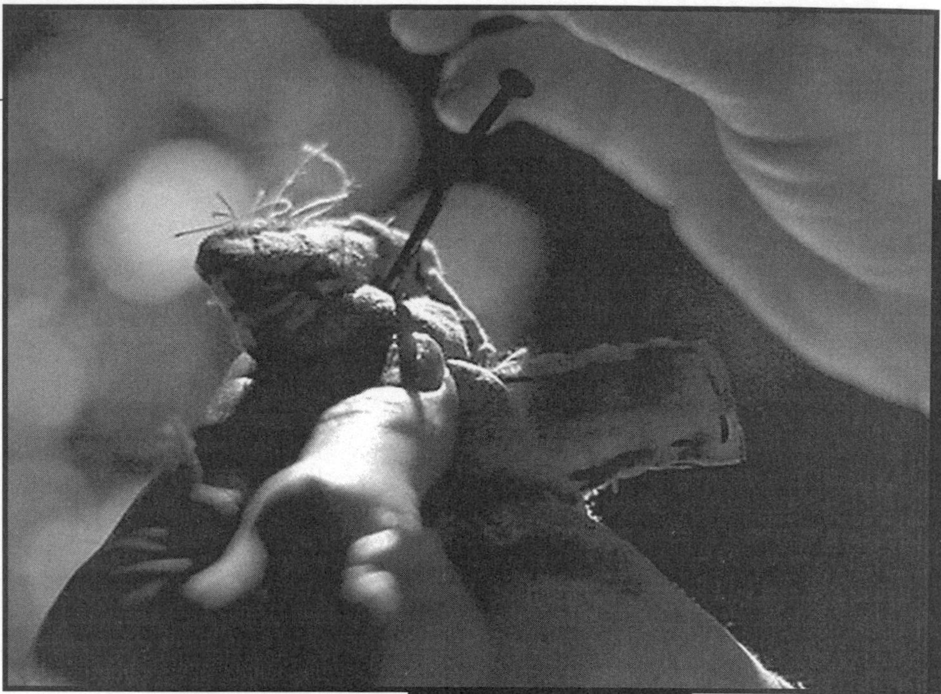

"And you believe by our leaving, we'll somehow weaken him?" asks Wieder.

Scully says, "What's important is that he believes that. At any rate, if he can't find you, he can't hurt you."

"How do you know he'll come forward?" asks Wieder.

Mulder says, "Because he hasn't gotten everything he wants."

Wieder and his daughter go to a nearby car. Scully gets in the driver's seat, speeds through the mansion's electric gates, and heads down a street.

Peattie, standing behind a tree, watches the car drive away.

That night Mulder and the security guards are in a state of high alert. Mulder is drawn to a news report on a television set a guard is watching.

The reporter says, "San Mateo County health officials admit they are at a loss to explain the sudden onset of the fifty-six-year-old woman's bizarre illness, but insist there is no cause for alarm. Although there is no official diagnosis, sources say the woman contracted the rare but deadly group A *streptococcus*, better known as the flesh-eating disease."

"Freakin' scary," the guard says to Mulder, but Mulder is already out the door.

•

The door to Peattie's boardinghouse room swings open as Mulder and a stream of uniformed cops rush in, guns drawn. Mulder's eyes go to the bed and a figure laying under a blanket. Mulder eases forward and yanks back the covers.

To reveal Lynette's skeleton . . . the head missing.

Mulder is on his cell phone to Scully who, with Wieder and Lucy, has just arrived at the cabin.

"Peattie may be on to us," says Mulder.

"What happened?" asks Scully.

"I found out where he lives, only he's cleared out. And he's taken his magic charm with him. At least as much of it as he can carry. My guess is he's looking for you."

"I didn't see anybody following us."

"Just keep an eye out, Scully. I'm on my way."

•

Peattie is watching the house. In his hands is a basketball-size cardboard box. He looks down and we see the top of Lynette Peattie's bleached skull.

"Soon. Very soon," says Peattie.

He moves up the cabin's stone driveway to Scully's car. He picks up a large rock and hurtles it through the car's window.

Inside the cabin, Scully is startled by the sound. She draws her gun.

"What was that?" asks Wieder, who, with Lucy, is hiding on the second-floor landing.

Scully says, "Stay where you are."

She clicks off the light switch and crouches low by the staircase. She sights on the door with her gun.

•

Peattie reaches in through the broken window, brushes away the glass fragments, opens the glove box, and takes out Scully's ID badge. He then looks on the driver's seat until he finds a strand of Scully's hair.

"CAN'T HURT A MAN WHO AIN'T GOT NOTHING LEFT."—Peattie

He takes the hair and the ID photo and inserts them into a female doll. He murmurs a spell. He lowers the doll and sticks two coffin nails into its eyes. At his feet, a familiar stick figure has been drawn into the earth. He sets the doll down.

•

Scully suddenly brings a hand to her face. She is in great pain.

"Oh, oh God," she says.

Wieder asks, "What is it?"

"I don't know. I can't . . . ," says Scully.

She lowers her hand to reveal her eyes are now cataracted milky-white.

"I can't see."

The front door rattles. Wieder calls down to her.

"Agent Scully?"

"Stay where you are! Stay down!"

She raises her pistol and attempts to aim by sound. The front door flies open. Scully fires. *Blam! Blam!*

Suddenly a hand flashes out of the darkness and yanks the gun out of Scully's hand. It is Peattie.

He turns and heads up the stairs toward Wieder and his daughter.

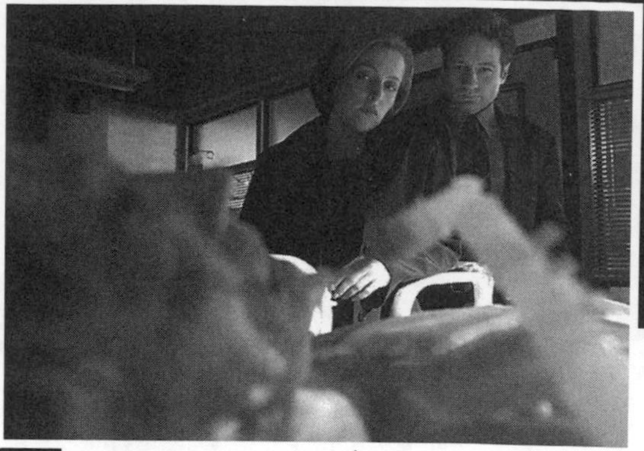

"Oh, Doctor?" he calls.

Scully says, "Leave them alone!"

On the landing, Wieder has picked up a walking stick and put himself between his daughter and Peattie.

He screams, "Get back! Get back! Don't make me hurt you!"

"Can't hurt a man who ain't got nothing left. You know who I be now? Maybe you can recollect my daughter?"

"I remember. I never forgot. I'm sorry for your loss. But I did everything humanly possible to save her."

"Arrogant little man."

The doctor says, "I did everything I could. And when I couldn't do any more, I eased her suffering."

"By killing her! If I be there, I save her!"

"You *weren't* there!" screams Wieder.

Scully listens, helpless. She feels around for her gun.

"She wanted to see the world, no name on her," says Peattie. "Far away from her people. That ain't right."

Peattie reaches into his pocket and pulls out a doll.

"Little man, I'm going to show you what be possible."

He pulls out a knife. "Show you, eye for an eye!"

"You're not going to hurt my daughter."

Peattie sticks the knife blade into the doll's chest. Wieder collapses, intense pain shooting through his chest. Peattie has induced a heart attack.

"Daddy!" screams Lucy.

"Doctor?" calls Scully. "What's happening? Doctor Wieder!"

Scully's gun is a few feet away . . .

•

Mulder arrives at the scene and strides toward the cabin. He sees the broken car window, then looks down and spots the stick figure drawn in the dirt and the doll on top of it. He bends down close to the doll and sees the coffin nails coming out of its eyes.

Wieder continues in the death throes of a heart attack as Peattie pushes the knife blade in a bit more. Scully is close to her gun. She just doesn't know it.

Blam!

A bullet tears through Peattie's shoulder. He topples backward, tumbles down the stairs, and lands at the feet of Scully, whose eyesight has returned to normal.

Mulder enters the cabin, gun drawn, and goes to Scully. Beside Peattie's body rest the Wieder doll and the knife. Upstairs on the landing, Wieder has begun to recover. Scully stands over Peattie, who lies wounded. Mulder holds up the Scully doll. The coffin nails have been removed from its eyes.

•

Scully stands alone in the University of San Francisco ICU room, watching Peattie, who is hooked up to a heart-lung monitor. Mulder enters.

Mulder says, "Lynette Peattie's body is on its way back home to Neola, West Virginia."

"She's going back to her people after all," comments Scully. "You know, Mulder, I would have made the same call. As a doctor, if I was certain that I couldn't save her life, and she was in that much pain, I would have done what Wieder did."

"It seems pretty clear cut."

"Except maybe it's not."

"You're wondering if maybe Peattie could have saved her life?" he asks.

Scully is silent. She takes one last look at Peattie and leaves the room.

"You do keep me guessing," says Mulder as he follows Scully out of the room, leaving the magic man dependent on modern medical science.

BACK STORY:

The episode "Theef" was a happy accident. The moody, low-key tale of modern medicine versus backwoods supernatural arts was not even a gleam in the production company's collective eye when Season 7 began. But things changed as the cast and crew got ready to take their Christmas hiatus.

"Originally another script was scheduled for the first episode after the Christmas break," recalls John Shiban. "But that script fell out just before we broke for the holidays."

Mentally fatigued from months of intensive work and more than ready for a few days of rest, the writers were now faced with having to create a new story concept and script literally overnight. Shiban and Frank Spotnitz wracked their brains. David Amann remembered that the original storyline that would become "Theef" was "What if you have a doctor who is prosperous but has a dark page from his past that comes back to haunt him? It was basically set up as a tale of modern versus ancient medicine."

Spotnitz remembers, "Originally the premise of the story was going to be how do you get rid of something you can't get rid of. But we just could not make it work that way. We kept at it and the story started to evolve into this *Cape Fear* type of situation which pitted this modern doctor against this man with the power of Appalachian voodoo."

Ultimately, the "Theef" script was completed by Shiban and Spotnitz over the Christmas holiday break and handed to the ever-reliable Kim Manners to direct. Even the ultra-experienced Manners found the prospect of helming "Theef" to be an unexpected test.

"It was one of those episodes that we never really had a chance to prep," explains Manners. "It was kind of a rush thing and we got the script very late. We were totally winging it while we were shooting it. We really didn't realize what the hell we were shooting while we were shooting it."

But Chris Carter, in looking back on "Theef," was able to pick out some diamonds in the rough. " 'Theef' was very well cast. We were especially lucky to get Billy Drago to play Peattie. There were also some pretty creepy moments involving patient X rays, and I felt the scene involving the MRI machine and microwave popcorn was bizarre. I also felt we came up with one of those classic *X-Files* lines in 'Stinky's good.' "

The fan and critical consensus was that "Theef's" greatest strengths were solid performances by Drago and James Morrison as Dr. Wieder. As polar opposites in this war between ancient and modern medicine, the pair was proving frighteningly believable in the roles, which went a long way toward making "Theef" a subtle character study in which the supernatural goings-on often took a back seat.

The episode was most memorable for Manners primarily for one unexpected and unpleasant reason. "It was the first time I ever got sick while directing an *X-Files* episode. We were shooting late one night and they had ordered fast food hamburgers. The burgers arrived at eleven but I was too busy to eat and so I had one reheated for later. By four the next morning I was on my knees making love to the porcelain bowl. I had a doctor to the house and couldn't get out of bed. So I called Rob Bowman up at six in the morning and he directed a day for me while I recovered."

The director recalls that "Theef" came together in the editing room. "When I looked at the footage, it was like I was looking at somebody else's film. But it cut together real nice and the result was that 'Theef' turned out to be a decent little episode."

FACTS:

John Shiban was happily surprised to discover that Leah Sanders, who was cast as Reporter #1, was a childhood friend he had not seen in twenty years.

Billy Drago has appeared in a trio of Chuck Norris movies: *Delta Force 2: Operation Stranglehold, Hero and the Terror,* and *Invasion USA.*

episode 7X15

EN AMI

EPISODE: 7X15
FIRST AIRED: March 19, 2000
EDITOR: Louise A. Innes
WRITTEN BY: William B. Davis
DIRECTED BY: Rob Bowman

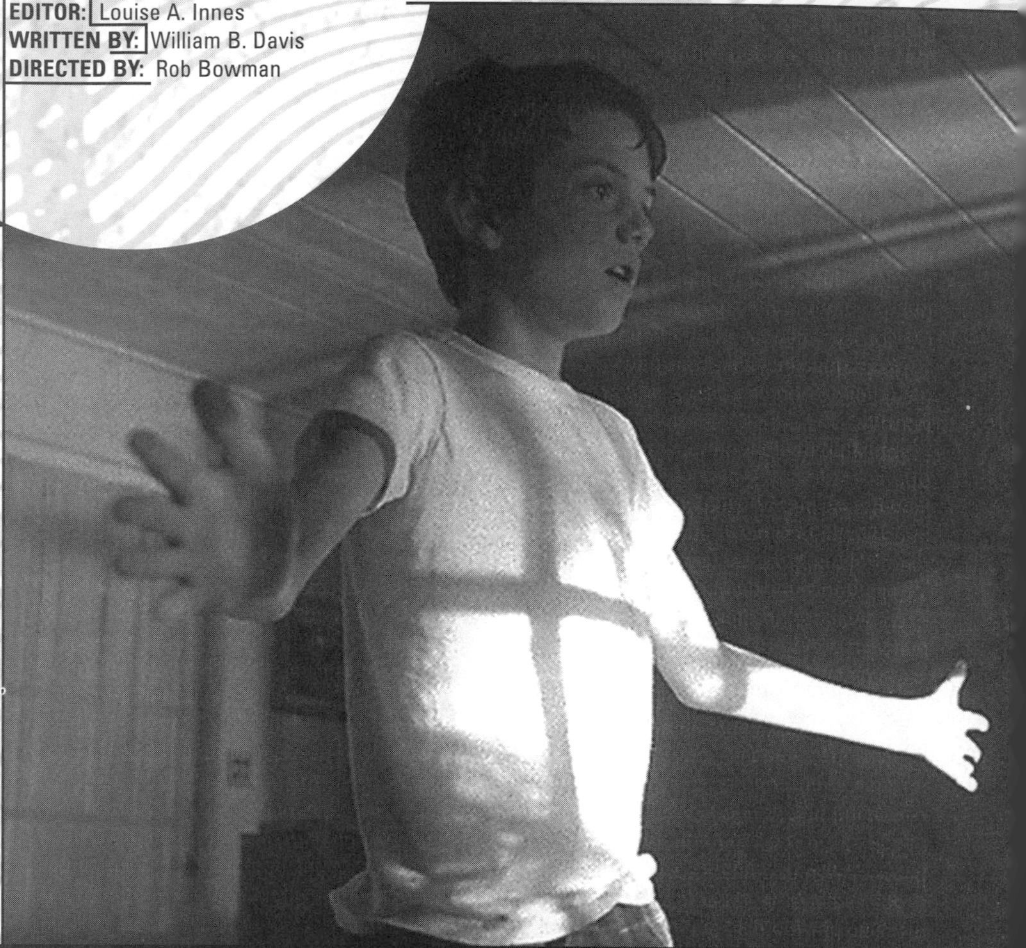

Tempted by the promise of a miracle cure for all of earth's diseases, Scully forms an unlikely liaison with the Cigarette-Smoking Man.

GUEST STARS:

Mitch Pileggi (A.D. Skinner)
William B. Davis (Cigarette-Smoking Man)
Michael Shamus Wiles (Grey-Haired Man)
Louise Latham (Marjorie Butters)
Tom Braidwood (Frohike)
Dean Haglund (Langly)
Bruce Harwood (Byers)
Michael Canavan (Cameron McPeck)
Jacqueline Schultz (Irene McPeck)
Cory Parravano (Jason McPeck)
Timothy Landfield (Cobra)
Tom Bailey (Apartment Manager)
Thomas Roe (Guard)

PRINCIPAL SETTINGS:

Goochland, Virginia; Milford, Pennsylvania

A station wagon cruises down a tree-lined street in Goochland, Virginia. Cameron McPeck glances into the rearview mirror.

"Almost home now, Jason. What do we say?" he asks.

In the back seat, his wife, Irene, sits with their son, Jason, who does not look well.

Irene joins Jason in saying, "Sticks and stones may break my bones, but words can never hurt me."

"Keep your chin up, son. We'll get through this just fine."

They pull up to their house and are set upon by reporters, cops, and a swarm of protesters who immediately surround the car, screaming . . .

"Murderers! Treat Jason! Don't let Jason die!"

McPeck gets out of the car, pushes his way through the protesters to the car door, gets his frightened wife and child out, and pushes his way through the jeering crowd.

McPeck tucks his son into a makeshift daybed in the family room. A Bible, a crucifix, and a bell sit on a nightstand. Irene enters, carrying a glass of water.

"There you go, sweetheart. If you need anything during the night, if you don't feel well, you just ring that bell. Okay?"

"Okay, Mom."

Irene kisses Jason good night and goes upstairs. McPeck lingers.

He says, "I know you're afraid. Maybe you think those people outside are right. That we should take you to the hospital and let the doctors treat you. We could do that, and they might take away your cancer. And your body might feel better. But not your soul. It's God himself who gave you this illness, Jason. For reasons that are His. If you're to be well in body and spirit, it's God who must come to deliver you."

Jason lapses into an uneasy, feverish sleep. He is awakened by a noise. He looks out the window. A blistering wind gives way to a blinding bright spotlight that shines on Jason and eventually descends to ground level.

Jason stands, his face and hands facing toward the window.

Tall, slender silhouettes appear out of the light.

•

The clock in Scully's apartment reads 8:52 as she walks through the apartment, pulling on her jacket, grabbing her bag, and going out the door. She stops at the sight of a newspaper lying at her feet, picks it up, and reads the headline:

MIRACLE ENDS CONTROVERSY

Scully tucks the paper under her arm.

She enters Mulder's office, where she finds her partner sitting behind his desk, his feet up, reading a piece of paper.

"Good morning. Here's a story to warm the cockles of your heart, Scully. An eleven-year-old boy diagnosed with lymphatic cancer. Cured with a miracle."

"Jason McPeck," she says. "Goochland, Virginia. His parents refused treatment on religious grounds. His faith forbids medical aid, so Jason's cure was delivered by angels."

Mulder nods. "Well, spontaneous remission, Mulder, isn't completely unheard of. So-called miracle recoveries attributable to no clear cause or reason."

Mulder hands Scully the piece of paper.

"It's not the miracle I'm suspicious of. It's the messenger," says Mulder, handing Scully the piece of paper he was reading. "That came as an anonymous e-mail to me from the Defense Advanced Research Projects Agency."

"DARPA?" asks Scully.

"Someone at DARPA. How'd you hear about it?"

Scully takes the newspaper from under her arm and lays it on the table in front of Mulder.

"You subscribe to the *Goochland Guardian*?" Mulder asks.

"No."

"So this just appeared miraculously on your doorstep this morning?"

"As far as I can tell, I was the only one to whom it was delivered."

Mulder says, "Someone wants us on this case."

"It's not a case, Mulder."

"Not yet. I'm going to go back over to DARPA. You see what else you can find out about that boy. I've just gotta know whether it was Roma Downey or Della Reese."

•

Scully's car pulls up in front of the McPeck house. Irene McPeck comes to the door. Scully flashes her badge and introduces herself.

"I'm here about your son."

Cameron McPeck appears behind his wife. "Are we under investigation?"

"No. I was just hoping to better understand what happened to him. May I ask, is he okay?"

Scully turns at the sound of footsteps behind her and sees Jason running up to the house.

Irene says, "Jason, you've got somebody to see you. Tell her how you're feeling."

"I feel good. Just a little out of breath."

McPeck adds, "You're looking at God's work. Jason's life owes to His grace and exalts His name in the highest. Praise the Lord." His wife and son echo his last sentence.

Scully feels awkward in the face of this outward display of faith.

"And you say that you saw angels?" asks Scully.

"Yes."

"May I ask what they looked like?"

"They looked like men. They came from the sky. In a ball of light."

Scully asks, "And what did they say?"

"They said not to be afraid. Then one of them pinched me kind of hard and then I was better right away."

"He pinched you? Where?" asks Scully.

"Right here." Jason shows Scully a small raised scar on the back of his neck.

•

Scully leaves. She is startled to see a man sitting in the passenger seat of her car, reaching for the car cigarette lighter.

It is the Cigarette-Smoking Man.

"What the hell are you doing?" she asks angrily.

"God's work. What else?"

Scully notices that CSM is looking pale and sick. But she is not sympathetic.

"Get out of my car."

"I'd hoped for more accommodation toward the man who saved that young boy's life. And yours."

"You've got your light. Now get out."

CSM gets out of the car. Scully gets in, closes the door, and sticks the key in the ignition. He leans in the passenger window.

"You're not at all curious about the chip that's been put in that boy's neck? You, a medical doctor, who has this same technology in your body, who's witnessed the wondrous miracle firsthand?

"I've taken considerable trouble to prove my intentions," says CSM. "The newspaper at your door. The e-mail to Mulder. The elaborate demonstration of curing this boy's cancer. You see, I'm dying myself. A dying man who wants to make right. To share his secrets. To bequeath this cure to millions of others just like that boy."

"So you want to give it to us."

"To you, Agent Scully. I've tired of Mulder's mule-headedness, his foolish ideas of overthrowing the system."

Scully asks, "You think I'm fooled by this?"

"I've made you my offer. Agent Mulder hears a breath of this, rest assured I'll rescind it. And take it to my grave."

CSM moves away from the car. Scully starts the engine and begins to drive away, but not before noticing a business card with no name but a single phone number on the passenger seat.

•

Back at FBI headquarters, Scully dials the number on CSM's card. She hangs up and dials again.

"Yes, I need a trace on a D.C.–area phone number. I need an address."

•

Scully enters a heavily secured government building. She approaches the security desk. A guard blocks her way and asks, "May I help you?"

"Uh . . . I'm sorry. I made a mistake," says Scully as she backs away.

The guard asks for ID. Scully is nervous. She reluctantly produces her badge.

"Third floor," says the guard.

Scully goes up to the third floor. She walks down the hall until a nameplate on a door stops her in her tracks.

The nameplate reads SPENDER C.G.B.

Scully pushes open the door and enters the office. In the hall behind her, a grey-haired man in a black overcoat watches her. She hears the voice of the Cigarette-Smoking Man calling her name. She enters an inner office to find CSM sitting behind a large desk.

"I'm glad you came."

"You obviously knew that I would."

"Well, I know you're a doctor, and a woman of compassion."

"Please."

"In the end, a man finally looks at the sum of his life, to see what he'll leave behind. Most of what I've worked to build is in ruins. And now that the darkness descends I find I have no real legacy."

"What are you dying of?"

"Cerebral inflammation. A consequence of brain surgery I had in the fall. The doctors give me just a few months."

Scully says, "So you want to use me to clear the slate, to make you a respectable person. It won't work."

"How many people in the world are dying of cancer? And here we are wasting time with the past," CSM says.

"I'm here. Where is it? This miracle cure of yours."

"We'll need to take a trip. It'll require a few days."

"I'll get back to you," says Scully as she turns to leave.

"I have access, Agent Scully. I have these miraculous chips, but the genetic research that makes them work is closely guarded. There are men in this building who would kill me if they knew what I'd offered you. They'd kill you, too, in the blink of an eye. I've destroyed a lot of things in my life, including the people most precious to me. All I want is a chance to do something in service to man before I go."

•

Mulder enters his apartment and sees the red light blinking on his answering machine. The message is from Scully.

"Mulder, it's me. I wanted to let you know that I'll be out of town for a day or two. It's a family emergency. I'll call you when I can."

Mulder returns the call and gets her answering machine. At the other end, Scully does not pick up. CSM looks on as she listens to the message.

"Hey, Scully, it's me. Pick up if you're there. Scully? You there? All right. I just got your message, and I hope everything's okay. I'll try on your cell right now."

Scully stands staring at her machine. With her back to CSM, she secretly tucks a small microphone inside her blouse before she turns around and picks up her bag. She walks out of her apartment as CSM closes the door behind them.

•

Scully is at the wheel as she and CSM drive through the night. She discreetly checks the microphone in her blouse. He reaches for the car's cigarette lighter.

"You're going to smoke?"

He opens the car window and tosses the cigarette out the window.

"It's time I quit."

"Just like that?"

He says, "No sacrifice is purely altruistic. We give expecting to receive."

"What exactly is it you expect to receive?" she asks.

"Trust. You question my sincerity. You think I'm heartless. Would it soften your opinion of me if I confessed that I've always had a particular affection for you?"

Scully flashes him a strange look.

"I assure you, my intentions are honorable. I have affection for Mulder, too. But my affection for you is special. I held your life in my hands. Your cancer was terminal. I had a cure. Can you imagine what that's like? To have the power to extinguish a life? Or to save it and let it flourish? Now to give you that power. So you can do the same."

•

Mulder is talking with the building manager at Scully's building.

"She said it was a family matter. Dropped off the key and asked me to water the plants. No biggie. Great girl," he says, taking out the keys to Scully's apartment. "Tenants like having an FBI agent in the building. Gives them a sense of security."

"Do you know how many people have died in there?"

"We don't really talk about that," says the manager.

Mulder says, "You said she was carrying a suitcase. Did you notice anything else? Anything abnormal?"

"No. Actually it wasn't her carrying the suitcase. It was her driver."

"Her driver?"

"Yeah, older guy. Tall. I've seen him here before. Smokes like a chimney."

Mulder hurries away before the manager can open the door.

•

Classical music plays softly out of the car radio as Scully and CSM drive.

"You've been at the wheel too long. Would you like me to drive?"

"I might if you let me know where we're going," says Scully.

"And knowing that, you'd feel comfortable? You'd trust me? How long did it take Mulder to win your trust?"

"I've always trusted Mulder."

"You're not being honest with yourself," he says. "Think back. There was a time when you feared for your future, for your career. When you were first partnered with this man. I told you, I've studied you for years. And if you'd permit, I'd like to make an observation. You are drawn to powerful men, but you fear their power. You keep your guard up, a wall around your heart. How else do you explain that fearless devotion to a man obsessed, yet a life alone? You would die for Mulder. But you won't allow yourself to love him."

"Wow, I'm learning a whole other side to you," says Scully sarcastically. "You're not just a cold-blooded killer, you're a pop psychologist as well."

A smile creased with sadness crosses CSM's face.

"I've been a destroyer all my life. Before I die, I would like to prove that I'm capable of something more. Turn here. On the left."

"Where are we going?"

"To show you what I'm capable of," he says.

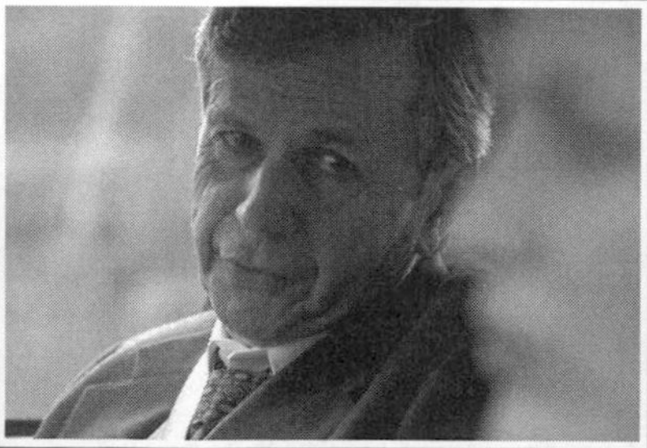

•

They pull off the highway onto a dirt road. Behind them another car coasts to a stop. Inside is the grey-haired man from outside CSM's office. His look is impassive.

Their car pulls to a stop in front of a clapboard farmhouse. An elderly woman appears from around the side of the house and begins to tend her garden. CSM says her name is Marjorie Butters.

"And what's her relationship to you?"

"Well, how should I put it? You could say that I'm her angel. Marjorie is one hundred and eighteen years old."

CSM approaches Marjorie, who is visibly happy to see him.

"I thought I'd surprise you."

"Well, I look an absolute wreck. I've tried to get in some bulbs before spring." CSM walks her to Scully, who is still standing by the car.

"Marjorie, this is Dana Scully," says CSM. "She's a very good friend of mine."

Scully greets Marjorie, who invites them into the house for some freshly baked bread. Marjorie heads inside while CSM and Scully linger behind.

CSM says, "To have this power. To visit this woman and see her joy. It must be why you became a doctor."

•

In his office at FBI headquarters, Skinner is finishing up a conversation with the FBI motor pool when Mulder enters.

"She requisitioned a fleet sedan when she left the Bureau yesterday. I don't know why and there've been no fuel charges."

"Her mother doesn't know anything about a family emergency," Mulder informs him.

Skinner says, "Look, I know you're worried about the company she's in. But from what you told me, it's not like she's sneaking out. And the truth is, she's gone to a lot of trouble to allay your fears."

"I know she can take care of herself. It's just not like her to lie to me."

Skinner's private line rings.

"Skinner. Agent Scully, where are you?"

Scully is once again driving. CSM sits beside her.

"I'm on the road. I'm sorry to call on this line."

"It's all right. We've been worried about you."

"Everything's okay. I just wanted you to express that to Mulder."

"He's standing right here. Why don't you do that yourself?"

"No, sir, that's all right. Can you tell him that I'll call him later? Just tell him that I'm fine."

Skinner hangs up the phone. Mulder heads for the door.

"She says she's fine," says Skinner.

"She's in trouble," says Mulder.

•

Scully and CSM stop at a small minimart/service station for gas.

"I'm going to the rest room," she says.

CSM moves to the gas pump as Scully enters the rest room. Inside, she moves to the sink counter and takes off her coat, speaking quietly into the recorder microphone as she unbuttons her blouse.

"Mulder, I am trusting you'll be able to make sense of what's on this tape. I have no other way of contacting you. Please try and understand. I weighed the risks. I couldn't divulge these plans without risking them, and I promise you that I weighed everything. Our current location is northbound on the Upstate Expressway. We are driving my FBI fleet sedan. I promise I will get these tapes to you as fast as I can."

Scully takes the tape out of the recorder, pops it into an envelope, and addresses it to Mulder. She exits the rest room, discreetly pops it into a mailbox, and returns to the car. CSM is behind the wheel.

"Life Saver?" he asks. "May as well get comfortable. We've got a good drive ahead."

They pull away from the station. As they drive off, the mysterious Grey-Haired Man steps out from near the mailbox. In his hand is Scully's tape to Mulder. He puts it in his pocket and walks away.

•

The car, with CSM still at the wheel, comes to a stop in front of an isolated cabin. Scully is curled up asleep in the passenger seat. CSM pulls on a pair of black leather gloves, and carefully pushes back a lock of Scully's hair.

•

Mulder, asleep in his apartment, is awakened by a knock. He goes to the door and looks through the peephole. It is the Lone Gunmen. Mulder opens the door and is surprised to find that Frohike is dressed like

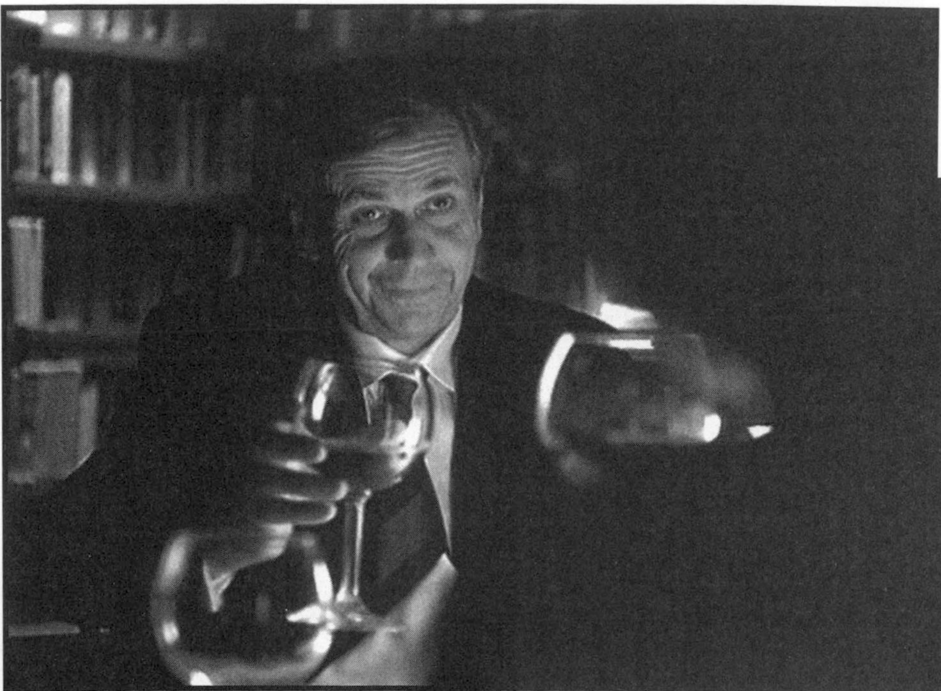

Byers, Byers is dressed like Langly, and Langly is dressed like Frohike.

"It's the masters of disguise."

"Can we laugh it up in your apartment?" asks Langly.

"We got heat on our tail," says Frohike.

"We did what you asked," says Byers, "pulled up what we could on Scully."

Langly says, "We started with her credit cards, to see if she'd purchased any airline tickets."

Adds Frohike, "And ended up hacking into some kind of Defense Department node."

Langly says, "Where they demanded we immediately identify ourselves or face prosecution for espionage and crimes against the government."

Mulder asks, "What does this have to do with finding Scully?"

Byers says, "When we went into her computer we found a series of deleted transmissions."

"E-mail that had been erased from her subdirectories, but not her hard drive," says Frohike. "A series of communications."

"From someone named Cobra," adds Langly.

Mulder says, "Who the hell's Cobra? Scully would've told me about him."

Langly says, "Well, it looks like she's gone to great lengths to keep this from you."

"I don't believe that. She knows that I'd find her no matter what."

Byers says, "Mulder, *we* can't find her. There's nowhere to start looking."

"I don't believe that either."

•

Scully wakes up the next morning in a comfortable bed. She is surprised to find herself dressed in pajamas. She gets out of bed and sees that her suitcase has been opened and unpacked, and the clothes she was wearing have been hung up. She hurriedly checks and finds the listening device still securely attached to her. She goes downstairs and faces CSM, who offers her a cup of coffee. She takes it, walks past him, and pours it out the back door.

"You drugged me."

"I did nothing of the sort."

"How the hell did I get out of my clothes and into bed?"

"I carried you. You'd been up for over thirty hours. You were delirious. I only wanted to make you comfortable."

"Where are we?"

"Milford, Pennsylvania."

Scully says, "Well, that wasn't part of the deal. I don't know what you're up to."

Scully storms out and toward the car.

"The keys are in the ignition. You're free to go, of course. The choice is still yours."

Scully hesitates a moment, then slowly moves back toward the cabin.

As the Grey-Haired Man watches.

•

Skinner is surprised to see Mulder burst into his office, followed by the Lone Gunmen. "What the hell's going on here?"

"That's my question exactly," says Mulder.

The Gunmen move to Skinner's conference table and set up a laptop computer. Frohike begins to type something on the keyboard.

"I believe you've all met," says Mulder. Langly asks if the lines are secure and gets to work. "Are you aware of a Federal fugitive code named Cobra?" asks Mulder. "For the past six months Cobra's been e-mailing Agent Scully from the Department of Defense, where he works on a shadow project for Advanced Research."

Byers says, "Shadow project is right."

Adds Langly, "Where this dude works even the shadows have shadows."

"Is that what I'm looking at here?" asks Skinner.

"No. What they're pulling up is Scully's correspondence back to Cobra."

"She has a relationship?" asks Skinner.

"No. Somebody posing as Scully. Who hacked into her computer and has been capturing all her e-mail. Passing themselves off as Scully in order to win Cobra's trust. The last five exchanges hint at a meeting, where they're going to exchange information on the project Cobra's working on."

"A meeting where?" Skinner asks.

Frohike looks up from the computer screen. "Don't know. They just ended."

Skinner demands to know who's been in her computer.

"The Smoking Man," says Mulder. "Or someone working for him. You've got to get to him. Now."

Skinner says, "You of all people should know you just don't get to him."

Mulder says, "If you don't get to him, it may be the last time we see Scully alive."

•

Scully is getting dressed, adjusting the recorder microphone, when there is a gentle knock on the door. Cigarette-Smoking Man enters, carrying a dress on a hanger.

"We'll be getting final instructions from our contact tonight. He's invited us to dinner. I took the liberty of getting you something to wear."

She takes the stunning black dress from him.

"It's beautiful."

"I'm glad you like it. I look forward to tonight," he says as he leaves Scully standing in the room holding the dress.

•

Cigarette-Smoking Man and Scully, looking ravishing in the dress, enter an upscale restaurant. They are seated at a reserved table.

"So your contact's going to join us?"

"I presume so."

Scully says, "You extol our great trust, but you still haven't told me who he is."

"He is to human genetic science as Oppenheimer and Fermi were to the advent of nuclear warfare."

"I'm still not clear what my importance is to this exchange."

"This man, call him Cobra, needs assurances. That the science he's going to hand over won't fall into the wrong hands. I've told him of you. He's expecting to meet you here."

He fills their glasses with wine and proposes a toast.

"To the future.

"I must tell you something else," he says. "Something that's so unbelievable, so incredible, that to know it is to look at the entire world anew."

"What?"

"What we are being given? It is not the cure for cancer. It is the holiest of grails, Dana. The cure for all human disease."

"How?"

"It is from that final frontier. It is largely extraterrestrial."

"Then you would be cured," comments Scully.

CSM says, "That which makes miracles can also make great evil. There are those who would use this power for their own purposes. To choose who will live and who will die. Theoretically I can be cured. Though every thing I've told you about wanting to make right . . . I'm a lonely man, Dana."

CSM excuses himself. A man watches him as he moves away. He motions to the waiter. He is Cobra.

•

CSM is outside the restaurant. He is joined by the mysterious Grey-Haired Man.

"Cobra hasn't shown."

The Grey-Haired Man asks, "What do you want to do?"

"Wait. What else can we do?"

"What trust you've won . . . Scully won't stick around forever."

Cigarette-Smoking Man is troubled.

"What's wrong?" asks the Grey-Haired Man.

"Just do your damn job," says CSM, who walks away.

Meanwhile, Scully sits alone, wondering where CSM has gone. The waiter takes her dessert plate away. Scully notices a folded piece of paper hidden under it on the table. She opens it and reads . . .

CALICO COVE. FIRST LIGHT OF DAY.

•

Scully and Cigarette-Smoking Man make their way to the nearby lake the next morning. Scully steps into a small motorboat. CSM unhooks the rope and tosses the line onto the boat as it drifts away from the dock.

"Calico Inlet is fifteen minutes out, the south end."

"What do I do when I get there?"

"I don't know. Just wait."

Scully is apprehensive as she fires up the engine and heads out.

"Be careful," he says.

Scully makes her way out onto the lake and into the shallower waters of the inlet. She arrives at the appointed spot and cuts the engine. The lake is deserted. There is nobody on the shore. She looks at her watch.

Scully hears the sound of an outboard motor. She scans the lake and spots a man in a motorboat heading out from the shore to meet her. He cuts his engine a few feet away from Scully and drifts close enough to speak.

Cobra says, "Finally we meet. You're just as you described yourself. Certainly more so last night at dinner. I only wish we could continue to correspond, but it must end after this. I hope one day we can take some time. When I'm not a marked man."

He hands Scully a CD-ROM computer disc. "This is it. The science I promised you."

Unaware that a rifle's crosshairs are trained on Scully, Cobra prepares to leave.

"Wait. Where did you get this? Where did it come from, the science?"

"Where did it come from?"

She asks, "Who developed it?"

Cobra senses he's been tricked.

"Scully?"

"Yes, I'm Scully. But I don't believe that we've spoken before, or corresponded."

A gunshot rings out, the bullet strikes Cobra and knockes him into the water. Another gunshot rings out. Scully is now the target . . .

Of the Grey Haired Man, who squeezes off shot after shot.

Scully struggles to get her boat started. The Grey-Haired Man is about to fire off another shot when another shot fires, knocking him to the ground. He is dead.

Cigarette-Smoking Man steps up to the body, then drops his gloves and a handgun to the ground. He looks out at the lake and sees that Scully has gotten the motor started and is heading for shore.

Scully pulls into the dock to find CSM waiting for her.

"They shot him. They killed him. They shot at me!"

CSM does not seem too concerned.

"Did you get it?"

"You told me that no one else knew about this!"

"I wouldn't have sent you if I thought there'd be any danger, Dana . . ."

"Yes, I got it," she says as she hands CSM the disc.

He hands it back to Scully.

"Forgive me," he says. "Here, take it. This is for you."

Scully says, "I've got to go."

CSM watches as she walks away.

•

Mulder, Scully, and the Lone Gunmen are in Mulder's apartment, watching as the CD-ROM is inserted into a portable computer. Mulder won't look at Scully because of her deception.

"There's nothing on this," says Frohike.

"It's empty," adds Langly.

"Completely," comments Byers.

Scully says, "No. It can't be! It can't be. It's got to be on there!"

•

Scully races through the corridor of the now vacant federal building, Mulder at her heels. She bursts through the office door where she had met with Cigarette-Smoking Man. The office is now empty.

"He was here! These were his offices! What the hell is this?"

"He used you," says Mulder.

She says, "Mulder, he laid it all out for me. I recorded it. I mailed you the tape. This old woman. Marjorie Butters. I met her, I saw her pictures, her birth certificate."

"You saw what you needed to see, in order to make you believe."

Scully says, "Well, then what about this boy? This boy with cancer? You can't deny that. That's undeniable proof."

Mulder says, "Even if we could convince his parents to let us march him out, how long before that chip in his neck mysteriously disappears? This was the perfectly executed con, Scully. The only thing I can't figure out is why you're still alive."

"Mulder, I looked into his eyes. I swear what he told me was true."

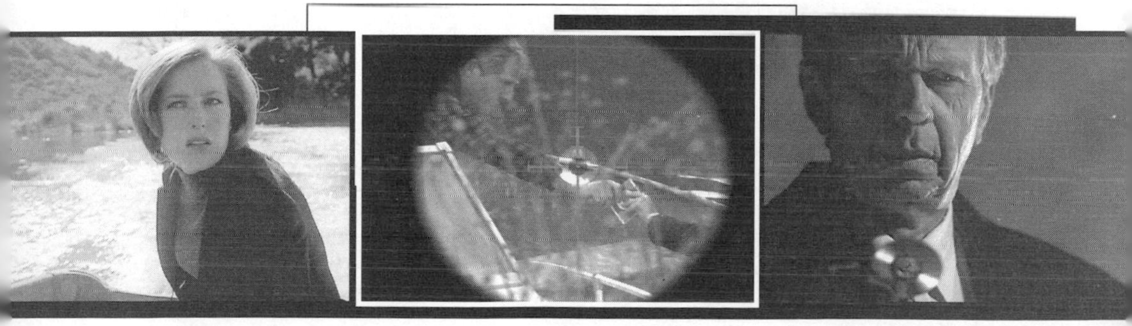

"He did it all for himself. To get the science on that disc. His sincerity was a mask, Scully. The man's motives never changed."

"You think he used me to save himself at the expense of the human race."

Mulder says, "He knows what the science is worth, how powerful it is. He'd let nothing stand in his way."

"You may be right. But for a moment I saw something else in him. A longing for something more than power. Maybe for something he could never have."

•

Cigarette-Smoking Man sits in an armchair, sipping wine and staring into a fire.

Later, he stands on the dock. He stares for a moment out at the lake, then lifts the disc out of his pocket and tosses it into the lake.

CSM reaches into his pocket, takes out a cigarette . . . and lights up.

BACK STORY:

It was a year when William B. Davis felt he finally had some time on his hands. With the whole alien mythology in transition, and the actor's infamous alter ego, the Cigarette-Smoking Man, limited to four episodes, the actor had time to sit and think. And in the process, the actor managed to come up with perhaps the most frightening storyline in *The X-Files* canon: "En Ami."

"En Ami," written by Davis, postulates the notion that CSM could make himself irresistible to Agent Dana Scully and thus, by degrees, seduce her to his agenda.

Still, Gillian Anderson notes, "It might have been a seduction in CSM's mind, but not in Scully's. She knew all along she was just playing along to get the secrets he held."

Davis, who is steeped in theater and the classics, saw much in the episode of Shakespeare's *Richard III* and, in particular, the relationship between Richard and Lady Anne. But he relates that the original inspiration for "En Ami" comes from the hand that Cigarette-Smoking Man had been dealt by past episodes of *The X-Files*.

"I've always said, if they're not going to give me a scene with Gillian, I'll just have to write one myself," chuckles Davis. "Yes, there was a lot of *Richard III* in my idea for 'En Ami,' but the main thing for me was how far Cigarette-Smoking Man would go to win Scully's affections."

Davis went to Chris Carter with the kernel of an idea. *The X-Files* creator was intrigued and urged the veteran actor, with the aid of Frank Spotnitz, to craft a first-draft script.

" 'En Ami' was another one of those scripts that went through a lot of evolution," Spotnitz remembers. "There was a lot of correspondence and a lot of long-distance telephone calls."

In early discussions of the script, Davis reports that Agent Spender and Alex Krycek were in the story and that an alliance between Cigarette-Smoking Man and Krycek was intregal to the storyline. However, those elements were eliminated early in the writing process.

Davis finished the first draft of "En Ami" in four weeks. He left his home in Canada and came down to Los Angeles, where he entered an intense four-day in-house rewriting session with Spotnitz and John Shiban.

Shiban remembers those sessions. "Sitting in the room with Bill, I really got to see his point of view. He really believed that Cigarette-Smoking Man was the romantic hero of *The X-Files*. He had an attitude about the story being a love story. Bill Davis will admit freely that he's not a writer, so it took some effort on all our parts to fashion a story."

Spotnitz remembers the Los Angeles writing session as critical to clarifying the intent of the story of this unorthodox episode. "The relationship between Scully and Cigarette-Smoking Man was one we had never explored. It's not a matter of course that you're going to say yes to one of your actors to write a script. I thought it was too great an idea not to take a chance on. [But] the last thing the audience wanted to see was Scully trusting this man she's spent seven years hating. How to make that transition believable was one of the hardest things about making this script work."

By the time the script went to Chris Carter for a final polish, Davis's initial vision of CSM as a romantic hero had been tempered by the reality of *The X-Files*'s existing mythos and past character development.

"I was basically happy with the way it turned out, despite the fact that there were many other ideas that I had that I did not get to see. My original conception of the story was that Cigarette-Smoking Man was a much better actor at winning Scully's affections and that Scully was somewhat less resistant to his attention to her. But the script got redirected."

"There were definitely some changes and some rethinking as the script went through different drafts," recalls Carter. "The big question raised by the script was what Scully's feelings really were toward CSM. She considered him to be the devil incarnate. Bill questioned whether or not that was true based on his interpretation of his character."

Originally "En Ami" was slotted to appear early in the seventh season, but Mulder's early-season emotional crisis (in the episodes "The Sixth Extinction" and "Amor Fati") made having a largely Scully episode problematic in terms of advancing characters and story tone.

Rob Bowman, whose other seventh-season contribution was "Orison," was chosen to direct "En Ami." Turning in yet another solid, understated performance in a key sequence with Mulder was Mitch Pileggi as A.D. Skinner. Pileggi was candid in assessing Skinner's character in "En Ami" and other episodes this season.

Acknowledges the actor, "It's a hard character to say that he's grown a tremendous amount. The nature of the character and what he has to do dictates not much growth. I'd have to say he's pretty stuck."

But while it was not an especially memorable episode for Pileggi, actor Bruce Harwood relates that "En Ami" was a hoot for the Lone Gunmen. "I remember that episode because we were supposed to be hiding out and we were disguised as each other. I was supposed to be Dean Haglund so they brushed my hair up so it looked like I'd stuck my finger in a light socket. Tom Braidwood had on this awful hairpiece. That show was a relief for me because usually I'm the guy in the suit and it takes me forever to get dressed and Dean is always dressed in jeans, a T-shirt, and wears his own shoes. For me, that episode was really relaxing."

Not relaxing was the fact that production on the episode ran into a time crunch, especially when shooting the restaurant scene with Scully and CSM.

Remembers Davis, "Because of the script situation, we shot Gillian's side of those scenes in the restaurant and my side of those same scenes on a different day at the studio."

The tight schedule also resulted in some last-minute construction when a small section of lake and dock were quickly built on a studio set for the sequence in which CSM finally does the noble thing.

But most of the lake scenes, including the climactic encounter between Scully and the mystery scientist code-named Cobra, were shot at California's picturesque Lake Sherwood. While it was Scully out in the lake making the exchange with Cobra, it was not Gillian Anderson driving the boat. The stunt driving was courtesy of stunt coordinator Danny Weselis.

Ultimately the most shocking element of the episode, despite her adamant rejection of him, was seeing Scully in a slinky dress on the figurative arm of Cigarette-Smoking Man. The scare was quiet and largely cerebral but ultimately very successful. Chris Carter offers that "En Ami" was something special.

"What we see is that she ultimately loathes this man beyond her ability to express it. This may have been the creepiest episode of the year."

FACTS:

A scene that did make it to an early draft of the script but was finally eliminated had Cigarette-Smoking Man teaching Scully how to water-ski.

The character of Marjorie Butters was played by veteran character actor Louise Latham, whose credits include *Adam at 6 A.M.*, *White Lightning*, and *Crazy from the Heart*.

Originally the script called for Cigarette-Smoking Man to be listening to a Brahms cello concerto on the radio when Scully gets into his car. The producers felt Mark Snow's musical backing was more appropriate and made the substitution at the last minute.

episode 7X16

CHIMERA

EPISODE: 7X16
FIRST AIRED: April 2, 2000
EDITOR: Heather MacDougall
WRITTEN BY: David Amann
DIRECTED BY: Cliff Bole

Mulder investigates the death of a housewife in a sleepy small town and discovers deep, dark secrets and a monstrous evil, while Scully gets down and dirty on a stakeout.

GUEST STARS:

Mitch Pileggi (A.D. Skinner)
Michelle Joyner (Ellen Adderly)
John Mese (Sheriff Phil Adderly)
Wendy Schaal (Martha Crittendon)
Ashley Edner (Michelle Crittendon)
Gina Mastrogiacomo (Jenny Gurgich)
Charles Hoyes (Howard Crittendon)
F. William Parker (Dr. Blankenship)

PRINCIPAL SETTINGS:

Bethany, Vermont; Washington, D.C.

Presiding over an outdoor Easter Sunday feast is Martha Crittendon, the Martha Stewart–like queen bee of Bethany, Vermont. She is joined by Ellen Adderly, a young mother, and her baby, Katy.

Ellen says, "Hey, are you sure I can't help?"

"Absolutely not," says Martha. "All set."

Ellen eyes the food and the immaculate backyard. "Oh, Martha. You make this look so easy."

Martha asks, "It's not too much, you think?"

"Are you kidding? This is just perfect. It's exactly the way I've always dreamt Easter should be."

The two women watch as Martha's daughter, Michelle, runs up to them with a half-full Easter basket. Martha applauds her daughter's Easter egg collection. The child scampers off.

Ellen says, "What you've done here is really fabulous. The kids will remember this forever."

Martha's mood suddenly changes as she turns to see Jenny, a hard-edged, inappropriately dressed bottle blonde, arriving with her son.

"I hope there are some things they won't remember. What is she doing here?" Martha asks.

Ellen says, "Her son's in Michelle's class, Martha. Be nice."

Jenny approaches with her contribution to the meal, something in a Tupperware dish. Ellen welcomes her.

"Jenny, hi, it's good to see you."

"Hey, Ellen. Martha," says Jenny.

Martha gives her a worried look, then sets her sights on the ground.

Away from this awkward exchange, Michelle continues to search for eggs. As she wanders farther from the party, Michelle is distracted by a sudden rustling in the brush. The child turns to see a raven. It stares at Michelle a moment and suddenly flies toward her. Michelle screams and covers her face as she runs away . . . right into Jenny, who stares down at her. Michelle drops her basket and dashes away.

•

Martha is on the phone, talking to her husband, Howard.

Martha says, "She's shaken up, Howard! It took me two hours to put her to bed. All I'm saying is . . . What? No, I didn't see any bird. But whatever it was, it scared her and she wants to be with her daddy. That's all I'm saying. Well, can't you come home one day early? All right. Fine. I love you, too."

Martha hangs up. Her eyes catch a curtain blowing from an open window in the living room. She walks into the living room to shut the window. She turns to see a raven perched on the mantle. The raven caws, startling Martha.

She hears another sound. Turning toward it, she briefly sees her reflection in a large mirror, just before it shatters. Martha stumbles backward in terror, right into a hideous creature, all gray skin, blackened gums, and snarling mouth. Martha screams.

The storybook house rattles with the sounds of death.

•

Working women and their customers loiter outside a dive of a strip joint whose red neon sign proclaims DIRTY DAMES ALL NUDE. They are being watched through a telescope inside a seedy motel room by Mulder. A van pulls up with JESUS SAVES emblazoned in spray paint on its front.

The stuck motel room door is forced open by Scully, who arrives with cups of coffee.

"Anything?"

"She'll come," says Mulder. "Matter of time."

Scully eyes the target of their surveillance, a photo of a blonde in a skin-tight vinyl miniskirt.

She says, "I hope you realize we have no evidence this mystery woman of yours has even committed a crime. Though her wardrobe comes close."

Mulder says, "Six prostitutes were seen with her at Dirty Dames, never to be seen again. Not only might she be a female serial killer, rare in and of itself, but twice police raided that club to arrest her."

A.D. Skinner is looking at a report in his office, when Mulder walks in.

"You wanted to see me, sir?"

"Sit down. Two weeks ago, a woman named Martha Crittendon disappeared from her home in Bethany, Vermont. Local police haven't turned up any sign of her. I'm hoping you may be able to."

"I'm already on a case," says Mulder.

Skinner says, "You're on a stakeout. I'm confident Agent Scully can continue in your absence."

"Why? What did I do?"

Skinner says, "There may be aspects to this that speak to your strengths as an investigator."

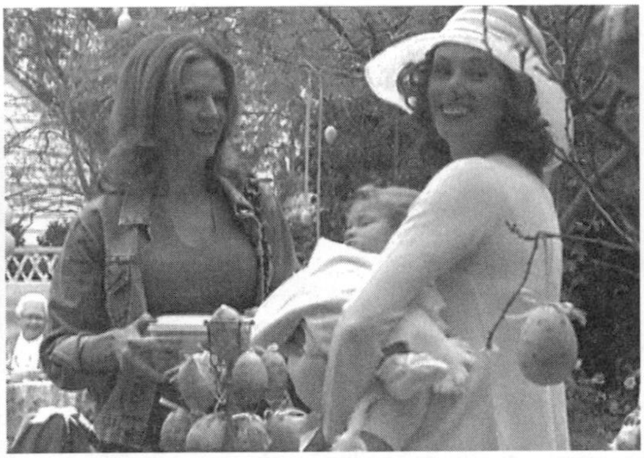

"And twice they came up empty-handed," says Scully.

"She's on the tape going in, the exits were covered, she's nowhere to be found. What happens to her? Does she disappear? Turn invisible?"

"Well, I hope we catch her so she can tell us. Before I have to spend another night here. I don't know about you, Mulder, but I find this all very depressing. This round-the-clock exposure to the seamy underbelly."

"It's the job, Scully. Vigilance in the face of privation. The sheer will that it takes to sit in this crappy room, spying on the dregs of society, until our suspect surfaces. There's something ennobling in that."

Mulder's phone rings. After a short conversation, Mulder hangs up.

"I gotta go," he says, running out, leaving behind a bewildered Scully.

•

"Specifically?" asks Mulder.

"Ravens. What do you know about them? Their mythological or paranormal significance."

Mulder explains that the raven is seen as a powerful but mostly negative symbol in Norse, Celtic, and Native American cultures. And, of course, there's the raven in Edgar Allen Poe.

Skinner says, "Martha Crittendon's seven-year-old daughter claimed she was attacked by a raven earlier the day her mother disappeared. Later, she heard one inside the house before she discovered her mother was missing."

Mulder asks, "No, really, what did I do?"

"It's the one lead that hasn't been explored. I want to know if it has any bearing on this case."

"I'm also assuming," comments Mulder, "that the fact that Martha Crittendon's father is a federal judge also has little bearing on this case."

"It's been made clear to me that locating her is my top priority. I'm making it yours, as well."

•

Mulder's car pulls to a stop in front of the Crittendon house. He is met by a local sheriff.

"Agent Mulder? Phil Adderly. Welcome to Bethany. Appreciate the help."

Mulder says, "I don't know how much help I'll be. I know you've had a lot of good investigators on this case already. Want to just take a quick look around?"

"Okay, thanks," says Sheriff Adderly as he and Mulder start walking up the driveway.

"So, tell me about Martha Crittendon."

Adderly says, "She and my wife, Ellen, are best friends. Martha's much admired here, she's devoted to her family, active in the community. And needless to say, the whole town's very concerned."

Mulder asks, "So what's your theory on what happened?"

"I'm hoping you'll tell me," says Adderly. "There's no ransom note, no prints or blood evidence."

"Her husband was out of town when she disappeared?"

"In Miami," says Adderly, "at a conference. It checks out. Howard didn't have anything to do with this."

They enter the house. Looking out the window, Mulder sees Michelle sitting silently on a swing. Her father is comforting her. Mulder watches them for a moment, then turns back to the sheriff.

"What do you know about a raven?" asks Mulder.

"Yeah, yeah. Michelle, their little girl, was saying something about that. You got me. Poor kid. You wanna talk to her?"

Mulder shakes his head as he roams the living room. He's commenting on how perfect the house is. He stops and inspects the mantel, where he sees faint scratches extending over the edge.

He asks, "How many talons would you say a raven had?"

Adderly seems surprised by the question. "Never mind," says Mulder as he moves on to an empty hook on a wall. "You know what this is? You know what was hanging here?"

"It was a mirror," says Adderly. "It was found broken."

Mulder asks, "And yet no other signs of a struggle?"

"Not a one," replied Adderly.

Howard Crittendon walks in and Adderly introduces him to Mulder.

"I appreciate you coming. I'm wondering now if this isn't just a waste of your time," Howard says. "With all the police coming and going, this place was a wreck. I was straightening up and I . . . found something."

Howard reaches into his pocket and pulls out a small plastic case. Birth control pills. "I think Martha was having an affair. After Michelle, we decided not to have more children. I had a vasectomy. They're in Martha's name. She ordered them off the Internet, because I guess small towns talk. Of course, then I started looking all around. I found this in the pocket of her favorite coat."

He holds out an old skeleton key. It's stamped #6. Mulder examines the key.

He asks, "Do you have any idea who your wife might have been seeing?"

Howard shakes his head. "But whoever he is, Martha may be with him. Which explains why we haven't found her. She doesn't want to be found."

•

Ellen Adderly is pushing a baby carriage down the street, slipping missing persons flyers with Martha's photo on them underneath car wiper blades. She hears a raven's caw and looks up at the bird in a tree.

"Cute kid," says Jenny, startling Ellen.

"Oh, Jenny. You scared me."

Jenny takes a flyer and looks at it. "I know Martha and you were good friends. You must be pretty upset."

"Of course, I'm sure we all are," Ellen says, "Hey, maybe you'd like some of these to put up on your side of town."

"My side of town. Yeah, sure."

"Look, I didn't mean that the way it might have sounded," says Ellen, apologizing.

"No. It just naturally comes out that way when you think you're better than everyone. You and Martha are two peas in a pod."

"Jenny, I don't think I'm better than anyone."

Jenny says, "You and me got more in common than you know."

Jenny takes a handful of flyers and walks away. Ellen turns away, glancing into the window of a parked car. She is startled by a reflection of a hideous creature. Ellen gasps as the car window shatters. She turns around, but the creature is gone.

•

Inside the sheriff's home, Adderly is on the phone. Sitting nearby is Mulder, who is perusing a field guide to birds of North America. Adderly hangs up.

"Whoever Martha was seeing, the two of them covered their tracks pretty good. Her phone records don't show anything. Do you think this person took her? Harmed her?"

Mulder says, "Well, I wouldn't rule it out. But I doubt it. According to your Audubon book here, a raven has four talons. That matches the scratches we found on Martha Crittendon's mantel."

"Agent Mulder, I appreciate the different tack you're taking with this investigation. But this whole bird thing . . . and keep in mind you're basing it on the word of a seven-year-old girl."

"Well, there was also the broken mirror in Martha's house. Mirrors are considered items of enchantment. A broken one means something. I'm not exactly sure what it is, but it means something."

Ellen comes into the house. Mulder is introduced.

She says, "We're so glad you're here. Look, our house is your house. We've got a spare guest room all set up. I'm sure you'll be real comfortable."

Mulder politely declines, but . . .

"Please, no arguments," says Ellen. "We are so grateful that you're here to find Martha. It's really the least we can do."

•

Mulder is sitting down to a wonderful home-cooked meal with the Adderlys.

"I should ask the Bureau to reimburse you for my room and board," he says.

"No, don't be silly," says Ellen. "It's just a typical meal around here. Phil works so much, supper is usually the only time we see each other. I like to make it special."

Mulder's cell phone rings. He excuses himself and steps away from the table. On the other end is Scully.

"Mulder, please tell me I can go home."

Oh, hey, Scully, how's the stakeout?"

"Well, the furnace broke and I can just about see my breath in here."

"Ouch. Sorry to hear it."

"That and I've witnessed a couple of hundred things I'd like to erase from my brain," says Scully, looking through the telescope at the strip joint as the same Jesus Saves van that Mulder saw earlier pulls up in front. "But as of yet, no mystery woman."

"Well, she'll come. It's just a matter of time. She'll show up. I'm sure of that."

Scully chucks a half-eaten slice of pizza. "Yeah, well, not before I die of malnutrition."

Mulder says, "Hey, Scully, tough it out. Whatever doesn't kill you makes you stronger, right?"

Mulder watches as Ellen spoons food onto his plate. "No capers, thank you."

"I'm sorry, what?" asks Scully.

"I said, what a crazy caper. I'll talk to you later, and keep warm. Bye," says Mulder as he hangs up quickly and returns to the table.

"Did I hear you say something about a stake-out?" asks Sheriff Adderly. "What's the case?"

Ellen says. "Sweetie, this is family time. Don't make our guest talk shop at the dinner table."

•

Howard and Michelle sit silently at the kitchen table, picking at a meal of macaroni and cheese.

"What's the matter, sweetheart? I thought this was your favorite."

"It tastes different when Mommy makes it."

Howard says, "Yeah, I know. How about we go get hamburgers? Would you like that instead?"

Michelle's eyes suddenly grow wide with fear.

"It's back."

Howard turns around and sees a huge raven perched outside the kitchen window. He closes the curtains and says, "Everything's all right, sweetheart. I'll be right back."

Howard makes his way across the yard toward the rosebushes, where he finds three ravens pecking at the base of the bushes.

He gets closer and spots a woman's hand sticking up out of the earth.

Martha's.

•

Police and other crime scene types swarm over the rose garden. Coroner Dr. Blankenship kneels over the body, taking particular notice of the deep gashes around Martha's face and neck. Mulder takes a look at the deep, disturbing wounds.

Mulder asks Dr. Blankenship, "What do you make of these claw marks?"

Blankenship says, "Well, one time I saw the victim of a bear attack look something like that. Only bears don't plant their kills in the rose garden. Body's been around here for a while. Probably since she went missing."

Sheriff Adderly asks, "What about your ravens? Howard said something about ravens."

Dr. Blankenship points to a spot on Martha's body where the ravens have been feasting. Adderly turns pale and walks away. Mulder goes after him.

"I'm not arresting Howard," says Adderly. "I don't care what it looks like, the body buried in his own yard. He didn't do this."

"I agree."

Adderly says, "The poor guy has suffered enough already." He sees Ellen running toward them. "What are you doing? You shouldn't be here!"

Ellen sees the body. "Oh my God! Martha! No . . ."

They turn to see Ellen standing near the body.

"Ellen, honey. I am so sorry."

Ellen says, "Oh God. It can't be. The thing that did that to her. I think I saw it today."

Ellen tells Mulder her story. "I saw its reflection. It had a face out of a nightmare. Long claws, the kind that could . . . The window shattered. I don't know how, and when I turned, it was gone. I don't know what I thought it was, I didn't think it was real. How could it be? But when I saw Martha's face . . ."

Adderly says, "Honey, you've been through a lot."

"You don't believe me."

"I do," Mulder offers. "You said the car window shattered after you saw a reflection. And there's a broken mirror in Martha's house. I don't think that's coincidence. Mirrors are considered doorways. In the Victorian era, they built mirrored rooms called psychomanteums where they thought they could summon forth spirits from the spirit world. Denizens from the spirit world were brought into this world."

Adderly questions him.

"Well, you asked about the ravens, right? The raven is a carrion bird, attracted to death and decay. What if this entity that you saw is somehow the personification of that? What if this creature was brought forth in order to attack Martha? The question then becomes, who summoned it forth? Ellen, do you know if Martha had any enemies? Can you think of anyone at all who might've wished her harm?"

"THAT AND I'VE WITNESSED A COUPLE OF HUNDRED THINGS I'D LIKE TO ERASE FROM MY BRAIN."—Scully

•

Jenny is in the middle of her workday as a waitress in a low-end greasy spoon roadhouse restaurant. It's been a long day. Sheriff Adderly and Mulder enter the restaurant with some questions about Martha's death.

"I sure as hell didn't have anything to do with it!" she says.

Adderly says, "They're just routine questions, Ms. Uphaus. Answer them and we'll be out of here."

Mulder adds, "We understand there was no love lost between you and Martha Crittendon."

"And where do you understand that from? Mrs. Sheriff, right?"

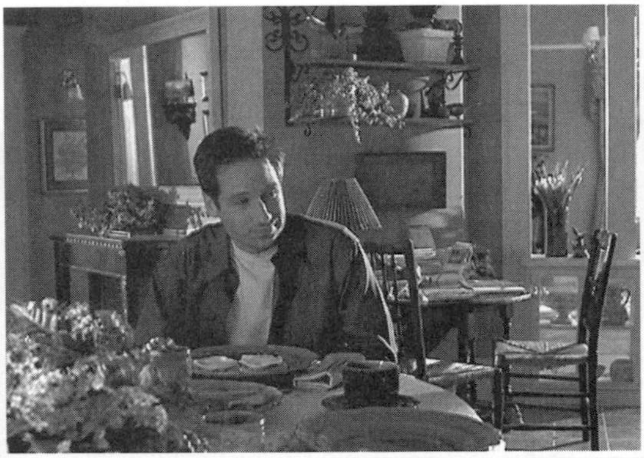

Adderly says, "It's not exactly a town secret."

Jenny says, "Right, like there's not enough of those already. Queen Martha and her perfect little Easter egg hunts. She's so above the rest of us. Except I heard she was stepping out on her husband, knocking boots with who knows who. I'm not happy she's dead and all, but you need to look into that."

Mulder reminds Jenny of her past police record. "You don't suffer people who don't give you respect. I'm thinking of the hair salon owner who you assaulted."

She says, "That was forever ago. And I paid for that. And I had nothing to do with Martha. Period."

Mulder wants to know where she was the night Martha disappeared.

"At home. All night. I gotta get back to work."

Jenny returns to her job. "I don't know about you, but I believe her," Adderly volunteers. "She didn't do it. I just don't gėt that vibe."

"Fair enough," says Mulder. "But why did she lie about her alibi? I got that vibe pretty clear."

Mulder's cell phone rings. On the other end is a very tired and dirty Scully, still on stakeout in the sleazy motel room.

"Mulder, when you find me dead, my desiccated corpse propped up, staring lifelessly through a telescope at drunken frat boys peeing and vomiting into the gutter, just know that my last thoughts were of you. And how I'd like to kill you."

Mulder says, "I'm sorry. Who is this?"

"It's a freak show, Mulder. It's a nonstop parade of every single lowlife imaginable."

"Yeah, well, the view may not be too different here. It's dressed up a little nicer, but underneath the surface, the same seamy underbelly. You know, Scully, this case has turned out to be more interesting than I thought, and I could use your help."

Scully perks up. "Are you talking about a reprieve for me?"

"Well, there's a murder victim I'd like you to autopsy for me. What do you think?"

Scully is only partially listening, her attention drawn to the telescope. "That van is back. Mulder, I'll talk to you later. Okay?"

She hangs up.

•

Ellen is in the living room, using the carpet sweeper. The sweeper hits something metallic that jams it. She flips it over and pulls out a metallic skeleton key with the number 6 on it.

She is puzzled. Her thoughts are interrupted by the loud caw of a raven coming from the direction of the nursery. Ellen walks down the hall and is horrified to see a raven perched on the crib.

She races into the room. "Get away from her!"

Ellen scoops up Katy and turns, looking at her reflection in the dresser mirror and seeing the horrible creature coming up behind her. The mirror shatters.

She runs for her life.

Ellen races into a closet and shuts the door behind her. She cowers under a pile of clothes. She sees a shadow through the closet's slats.

The door flings open.

It is Sheriff Adderly, his pistol drawn. He sees his wife and child.

"Oh God. Ellen? Ellen, what happened?"

•

Crime technicians are going over the Adderly house. Mulder checks out the nursery and the shattered mirror. A shaken Ellen is being comforted by her husband.

"What about the two broken mirrors?"

"What about them? You think broken mirrors have some deeper meaning, but you still can't tell me what it is. And in this case, I'm thinking Ellen broke them herself."

Mulder spots the skeleton key on the floor. "Number six. A match to the one Howard Crittendon found in his wife's coat pocket. What would this be doing here?"

"I don't know," says Adderly. Mulder asks Ellen if she recognizes the key. "I was sweeping the floor and it got caught up in the sweeper. I never saw it before today."

"You found it before you were attacked?" asks Mulder.

"Right before. Right before I saw the raven."

Sheriff Adderly says, "Let me see if my department can run this down, find out what lock it goes to."

Mulder gives him the key.

•

It is 12:38 A.M., and Ellen is deep in sleep. Sheriff Adderly is lying motionless in the dark, eyes wide open. He gets up, picks up his

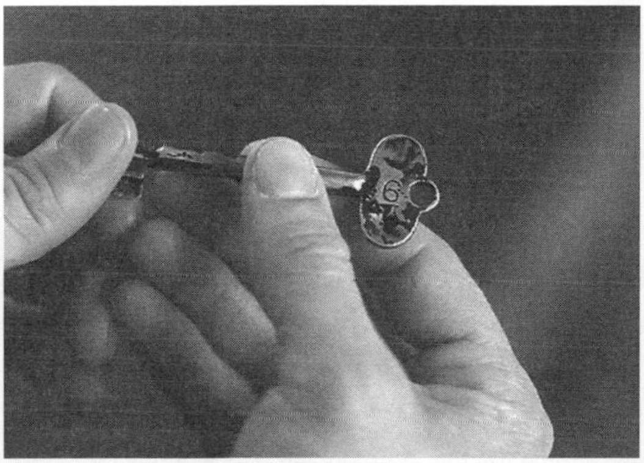

"It came back," says Ellen.

Mulder says, "It came back? The creature you saw?"

Adderly takes Mulder aside. "Please don't encourage this. This is not what she needs."

"I believe she saw something," says Mulder.

"And I believe she didn't. Her best friend just died, for God's sake. These imaginings of hers are brought on by stress. I've been through the entire house. And I didn't see any indication that anyone else was here."

clothes, leaves the bedroom, and heads for the Pineview Lodge, Room #6. He enters the darkened room. Arms reach out of the dark and grab him. He turns around.

It is Jenny.

"I can't do this anymore," says Adderly.

A light switch is flipped on.

"You can't, huh?" asks Jenny

"No. We gotta stop."

Jenny says, "Oh, that's too bad."

She kisses Adderly, hot and passionate. Adderly gives in to his desires. They fall into bed as an overhead mirror reflects their debauchery.

•

Mulder wanders into the Adderly kitchen the next morning, dressed only in his suit pants and an undershirt. Ellen is fixing up a man-sized breakfast.

"Good morning, Ellen," says Mulder. "Have you seen my shirt?"

"Oh, I'm sorry. It's over here."

His shirt and tie have been laundered and pressed.

"Oh, Ellen, you didn't have to go to this trouble."

"No, it's no trouble," she says. "Actually it helps me. Whenever my life is a mess, I just do some housework. It gives me the illusion I'm in control."

Mulder sits down to a lavish breakfast.

"It's just Phil's breakfast, times two," she says.

Mulder says, "Well, Phil is living large. Where is he this morning?"

"Probably on a call. He'll be back. But you just dig in."

Ellen is watching him eat. "I get the feeling you're not used to anyone taking care of you."

Mulder says, "Well, that has a vaguely pathetic ring to it."

"I just meant I didn't see a wedding band. Do you have a significant other?"

"Not in the widely held definition of the term," says Mulder.

"Well, the right woman will come along to change all that. Don't miss out on home and family, Mr. Mulder. With all the terrible things you must see in your work, it can be a refuge for you."

Adderly enters the kitchen. "Sorry I'm late. Paperwork. Morning, Agent Mulder."

Ellen leaves to check on Katy as Adderly sits down across from Mulder.

"Sleep well?"

Mulder pointedly says, "No, I only woke up once. When you went out."

Adderly says, "Well, I'll try to be quieter next time. I've got a deputy out and we were shorthanded. I had to take some calls."

"All night?" Mulder asks.

"Yeah. We were busy."

Mulder says, "I spoke to the coroner this morning. The autopsy shows that Martha Crittendon was four weeks pregnant when she died. Despite her birth control pills. Probably didn't even know it. Any idea who the father might be? I mean, Howard's vasectomy pretty much puts him out of the running. Any inkling who it might be?"

Adderly says, "Just say what's on your mind, Agent."

The pair is finding it difficult to stay civil in the face of Mulder's growing suspicions.

Mulder says, "You have a piece of evidence in your possession I'd like back. A skeleton key. Number Six."

Adderly gives him the key.

"You wanna tell me what this unlocks?" Adderly doesn't respond. "Once I find out, we'll talk more."

Ellen enters with Katy as Adderly leaves the room to shower.

•

Jenny is still in Room #6 of the Pineview Lodge, getting dressed while on the phone with her son, Bret, assuring him that she will be home soon. A loud caw ripples through the air, followed by another and another. Jenny moves to the window, pulls back the curtains, and sees four ravens sitting on the fence next to the window.

There is a sharp cracking sound, and the mirror atop the canopy of the bed cracks and shatters, showering Jenny with glass.

The hideous creature leaps out of the shadows and knocks Jenny to the floor. She struggles as her hand closes around a shard of glass, and she stabs it into the creature's back. It howls in pain and raises a ragged claw and strikes.

•

Mulder arrives at the Pineview Lodge. He inserts the skeleton key into a door's lock. Mulder can see the police and Dr. Blankenship going over the crime scene in the aftermath of the slaughter of Jenny Uphaus. Sheriff Adderly stands off by his patrol car, ashen-faced.

Mulder says, "Sheriff, you know that talk I said we should have?"

"I left her sleeping," he says.

"So, you were having an affair with both Jenny and Martha Crittendon?"

Adderly silently nods.

Mulder says, "I gotta hand it to you, Sheriff, you do put the service in To Protect and Serve."

"I cared about both of them," he says.

Mulder asks if the two women knew about each other. Adderly nods yes.

"But I'm assuming Ellen doesn't," says Mulder.

Adderly says, "No. But even if she did, she'd find a way to rationalize it. I'm not defending myself, but two years ago I wanted a divorce. Ellen won't hear it. She got pregnant with Katy and locked me up good."

Mulder says, "I think you've got bigger problems facing you right now."

They glance at the bagged body of Jenny, which is being wheeled out of the bungalow.

"I didn't do this," says Adderly. "I swear to you. Anyway, what about the broken mirrors and the ravens? You said it was an entity that did this, don't you still believe that?"

"I said it was an entity summoned by somebody else," says Mulder.

"Whether or not they even knew about it? Is that possible? Can I be the reason for all this, and not even know about it?"

•

The telephone rings inside the Adderly house. After several rings, the answering machine picks up. It is Sheriff Adderly.

"Ellen, this is Phil. I was really hoping you'd be home. Look, I'm in a bit of a situation here, and there's things we need to talk about. But Agent Mulder is on his way over there to explain it all to you. So if you get this message, you just wait there for him. Okay? Thanks."

The front door opens and Ellen enters the house with Katy. She takes her daughter to the nursery and lays her down in her crib. Ellen is all smiles as she bends down to cover Katy up and reveals a freshly scabbed-over cut, just below the back of her neck.

•

Ellen has filled the bathtub and is pulling her hair back. Her fingers come away from her hair with a trace of blood on them. For the first time she notices the wound on her back in the bathroom mirror. As she looks at it, she has a series of horrifying recollections of the creature attacking Jenny.

The front door opens and Mulder walks in. He calls out to Ellen but gets no answer. As he begins to look for her, his cell phone rings. On the other end, he hears a rather upbeat Scully saying . . .

"Mulder, I am free."

"You're free?" he asks.

"I'm going to go home, take a shower for, I don't know, eight or nine hours, burn the clothes that I'm wearing, sleep until late spring."

"You solved the X-File?"

"Yes. Except it's not an X-File, Mulder."

"What are you saying? You didn't catch our blonde mystery serial killer?"

Scully says, "Oh, we caught her. But she isn't a serial killer, nor is she blonde. And she isn't even a she."

Scully looks through the telescope at a man with male pattern baldness, face made up with lipstick and eye shadow, dressed in a miniskirt, talking to a group of police, one of whom is holding a blonde wig.

"What are you talking about?"

"What I'm talking about is these six missing prostitutes aren't dead, Mulder. They're all alive and well at a halfway house set up by this mysterious blonde, who happens to go by the name of Marc Scott Egbert. And Mr. Egbert wishes to acquaint lost souls with the teachings of Christ. And that's his hook, I guess. He dresses like a fellow prostitute to make the girls feel at ease. But this vanishing act is no more paranormal than a change of wardrobe, Mulder. He goes into a place like a woman and come out as a man. Right under our . . ."

"Noses," says Mulder, completing her sentence and realizing something he may have missed.

"Exactly," continues Scully.

"Well, good work, Scully. I'll call you back later."

He moves through the house to the master bedroom. He finds the door closed.

"Ellen? Ellen, it's Agent Mulder."

"Please go away," says Ellen.

"Ellen, Jenny Uphaus is dead. Your husband is in custody, suspected of murdering her. Only I don't think he did it. Do you?"

Ellen begs Mulder to leave. But he continues to reveal the truth.

"Ellen, you went out this morning after breakfast. Where'd you go?"

"It's not me. It can't be."

Mulder says, "I think it is. Ellen, I think you have a whole other side that you're afraid to face. Which would explain all the broken

mirrors. You don't want to see yourself for what you really are. Ellen, you have to come out of there."

"Then what? My marriage, my life. Everything I thought I had . . . is nothing. It's all lies."

Her eyes turn into the eyes of the creature. "I wish you'd never come here."

Mulder draws his gun as he puts his hand on the doorknob and slowly turns it. The door suddenly yanks open from the inside and the creature jumps at Mulder, knocking the gun from his hand and driving Mulder hard into a wall. The creature flails at Mulder with its taloned hands. Mulder fights back. He is tossed through the door of the master bedroom and into the bathroom. The creature follows him and moves in for the kill. It grabs him and pushes him down into the full bathtub. Mulder struggles in the water, fighting for air.

The water settles as Mulder begins to black out and the creature looks at a rippling image of itself. It retreats and Mulder breaks the surface, gasping for air. He climbs out of the tub and sees a naked, dazed, and sobbing Ellen curled up in the corner. There is no sign of the creature.

•

Ellen now resides in the Deschamps County Psychiatric Hospital. Sheriff Adderly watches as Mulder talks to his catatonic wife inside the room. Mulder leaves the room and joins Adderly.

"Do you want to see her?" asks Mulder.

"Does she want to see me?"

Adderly, now a broken man, knows the answer is no.

He tells Mulder, "The doctors say she's got some kind of dissociative disorder. A split personality. But that doesn't explain what happened, does it?"

"I think it's about as close as science can come. I think the basic idea is right. There are some multiple personality disorders where an alternate personality displays traits that the host doesn't have, like nearsightedness, high blood pressure, or even diabetes. I think in Ellen's case the changes were a lot more extreme."

Adderly asks, "Like Jekyll and Hyde?"

Mulder says, "She wanted so much from her life with you—a perfect life. And I think that at some point she found out you were cheating with Jenny and Martha. I don't know when, but at some point she did. And, like you said, I think she had to rationalize that. She just bottled up her anger, swallowed it. It had to come out some way. I think she did what she did to protect her family."

Ellen gets up, goes to the cell's outside window, and sees a raven staring at her. Ellen stares back through the bars of her new prison.

BACK STORY:

Like last season's episode "Arcadia" (6X13), "Chimera" was a compelling examination of the evil that lies beneath a prototypical white-bread suburban existence. But whereas "Arcadia" supplemented its horror with a generous dash of humor, "Chimera," with the exception of the scenes of Scully trapped on a sleazy hotel stakeout, is a straight-ahead scare, complete with a Lovecraftian monster.

Chris Carter saw "Chimera" as a chance to do something bold and new. "The concept was someone's anger taking on a form. The image of the crow has always been scary and there was definitely some potential in standing suburbia on its head. We really wanted to bust pretense and perception and expose the underbelly of a white-bread community."

These noble intentions were immediately challenged by a complex *X-Files* production schedule in which both David Duchovny and Gillian Anderson were in preproduction on their respective directed episodes ("Hollywood A.D." and "all things"). Consequently, even before the first draft of "Chimera" was written, the production team was faced with tailoring a solid story premise around limited appearances by both stars.

Greg Walker, who worked on the story with credited writer David Amann, recalls that part of their problem was solved "when David stepped up and said he had a way to do it." Amann explains that Duchovny's idea was to have Mulder carry the bulk of the story and to budget in just one day's availability by Anderson into a secondary tale "that starts out with Mulder and Scully on a stakeout looking for a serial killer before Mulder goes off to investigate a case in the 'burbs." A couple of inconspicuous telephone conversations between Mulder in suburbia and Scully on the stakeout filled out Anderson's seeming constant presence in the episode.

"Chimera" was written in a burst of twelve-hour days that saw the initial basic storyline develop a surprising number of facets. Walker describes the finished script as "a suburban parable about perfection. It ends up being about a woman who wants to control the world around her." Amann saw it as "an interesting Jekyll-and-Hyde story."

Rick Millikan's task—to fill out the cast with normal-looking suburban people—was not an easy one. "The show necessitated casting perfect people. But it's not that easy to find white bread normal-looking people. We've used so many people over the years that it's gotten harder and harder to find them."

Once filming commenced, director Cliff Bole discovered that it's tough to get crows to behave, let alone act on cue. Which is why Paul Rabwin recalls that they ultimately decided to get ravens to double for the crows in pivotal scenes. "We got two ravens. One was very good at cawing and one was good at hopping."

The opening backyard party sequence was shot in a local Los Angeles backyard. But when it came to shooting the spooky, tree-lined element, producer Harry Bring recalls that they ran into a snag. "The backyard just was not scary-looking enough. So we looked around and found some trees on the grounds of a museum in Hollywood that were perfect."

Rabwin remembers that the end of that sequence, in which the woman is attacked by the monster, also had to be reworked. "Originally we wanted to show a mirror image of the woman being attacked by the monster, but it didn't really sell. So we glued candy glass onto a piece of plywood, angled the wood, and set the camera on that angle and so we got to see the attack through the shattered fragments."

A five-hour makeup job and a full body suit turned one of stunt coordinator Danny Weselis's stuntmen into the monster alter ego of the housewife. The monster is seen in all its glory during the climactic fight scene between it and Mulder that was done in equal parts by Duchovny and a stuntman.

FACTS:

Fans of obscure genre films had a field day with this cast. Michelle Joyner's first film was the horror anthology *Grim Prairie Tales*. Gina Mastrogiacomo first came to be noticed in the movie *Alien Space Avenger*. John Mese was in the movie *Night of the Scarecrow*, and Wendy Schaal appeared in *Creature*.

Writer Steve Maeda recalls that "Chimera" originally started out as a story about a subterranean monster and was called "Subterranean Monster Blues."

episode 7X17

all things

EPISODE: 7X17
FIRST AIRED: April 9, 2000
EDITOR: Lynne Willingham
WRITTEN AND DIRECTED BY:
Gillian Anderson

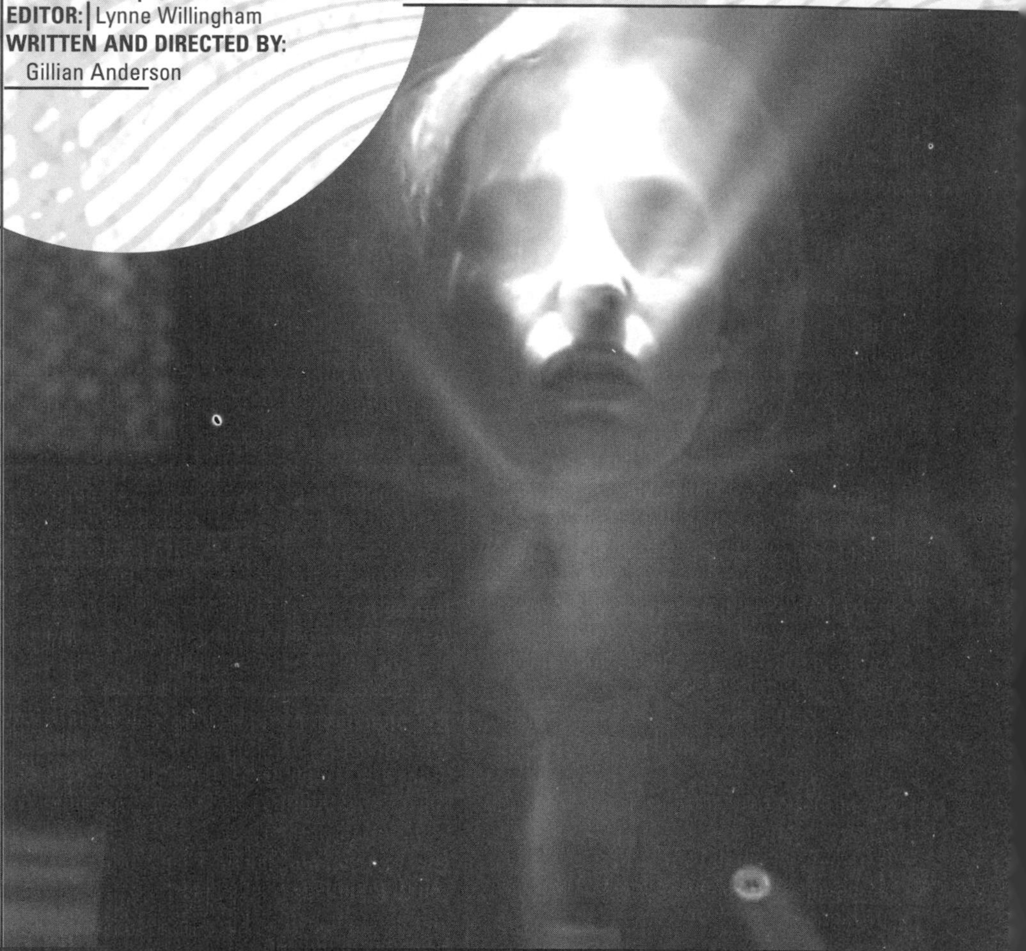

The chance encounter with a man from her past leads Scully on a voyage of personal and spiritual discovery.

GUEST STARS:

Colleen Flynn (Colleen Azar)
Stacy Haiduk (Maggie Waterston)
Stephen Hornyak (Dr. Paul Kopeikan)
Victoria Faerber (Nurse #1)
Nicolas Surovy (Dr. Daniel Waterston)
Carol Banker (Carol)
Elayn Taylor (Nurse #2)
Cheryl White (Nurse #3)
Scott Vance (Healer)

PRINCIPAL SETTING:

Washington, D.C.

Scully's face comes into view. Calm. Peaceful.

She studies her reflection in a bathroom mirror. She zips up her skirt. She is dressing in the night and thinking.

"Time passes in moments. Moments which, rushing past, define the path of a life just as surely as they lead toward its end."

Scully leaves the bathroom and enters another room, where moonlight and tree branches form a surreal pattern against her face and her thoughts.

"How rarely do we stop to examine that path. To see the reasons why all things happen. To consider whether the path we take in life is of our own making, or simply one into which we drift with eyes closed."

Scully picks up her jacket and shrugs into it. Her eyes and thoughts are fixed on something in the room.

"But what if we could stop? Pause to take stock of each precious moment before it passes? Might we then see the endless forks in the roads that have shaped a life? And, seeing those choices, choose another path?"

Scully's gaze stops on a bed. A naked leg, a bare arm. And finally on the face of a sleeping Mulder.

•

Sixty-three hours earlier.

Mulder's office is dark except for the light of a slide projector, playing out pictures of crop circles onto the screen. A small boom box pours out a Moby song. Mulder moves to the music as he watches the slides.

Scully enters the office with a brown bag.

"I got the lab to rush the results of the"—she turns off the music—"I *said* I got the lab to rush the results of the Szczesny autopsy, if you're interested," she says.

"I heard you, Scully."

"And Szczesny did indeed drown, but not as the result of the inhalation of ectoplasm, as you so vehemently suggested."

"What else could she possibly have drowned in?"

"Margarita mix. Upchucked with about forty ounces of Corcovado Gold tequila, which, as it turns out, she and her friends rapidly consumed in the woods while trying to reenact *The Blair Witch Project.*"

"I think that demands a little deeper investigation, don't you?"

"No, I don't," says Scully. She opens the paper bag.

"Well, it doesn't matter. We've got bigger fish to fry. Take a seat, Scully. Check this out. Is that beautiful or what?"

"Crop circles, Mulder?" asks Scully. She hands Mulder a sandwich.

"Computer-generated crop circles. It's a fractal image predicted by a computer program using data of every known occurrence of the phenomena over the past forty years."

Scully takes out a salad and begins to eat it, barely listening as Mulder continues talking about crop circles. ". . . then in 1997 even more complex formation occurred . . . and I'm not wearing any pants right now." Mulder stops talking. Scully looks up, her mouth full of lettuce, at Mulder's stern look.

"You're not listening."

"I am," says Scully. "I guess I just don't see the point."

"The point is a computer program has shown us that these are not just random happenstance, coincidental occurrences. And that same program has predicted that in just forty-eight hours, even more complex formations are going to be laid down in a field near Avebury."

Scully nods and chews.

"Forty-eight hours, Scully. But I wouldn't mind getting there earlier, if you don't mind."

"Getting where?"

"England. I've got two tickets on a five-thirty flight."

"Mulder. I still have to go over to the hospital and finish the final paperwork on the autopsy you had me do. And to be honest, it's Saturday, and I wouldn't mind . . . I don't know . . . taking a bath."

"What the hell does that mean?"

"What it means, Mulder, is that I'm not interested in tracking down some sneaky farmers who happened to ace geometry in high school. And besides, I mean, what could you possibly get out of this? Or learn? I mean, it's not even remotely FBI-related."

"I'll just cancel your ticket. Thanks for lunch."

There is an awkward silence between them as Mulder moves to the door.

"Mulder. Look, we're always running, we're always chasing the next big thing. Why don't you ever just stay still?"

"I wouldn't know what I'd be missing," says Mulder, leaving.

•

Scully walks through a corridor of the Washington National Hospital and up to a nurses' station.

"My name is Dana Scully. And I was told I could pick up a postmortem folder for a Ms. Szczesny here. It's for the FBI."

A nurse takes out an envelope with the name SZCZESNY on it and pushes it over to Scully. Scully signs out the envelope and moves away from the nurses' station. She opens the envelope and removes a chest X ray. Scully holds the X ray up to the light and sees the image of a human heart.

The name on the X ray is D. WATERSTON.

Scully returns to the nurses' station.

"Hi. I was given the wrong test results. This X ray marked D. Waterston was in the envelope marked Szczesny. I was expecting autopsy results."

The nurse apologizes and finds the right report. Scully asks, "Is the D. Waterston that was on the X ray, is that a Dr. Daniel Waterston?"

The nurse looks at a patient ledger. "Yes, it is. Admitted yesterday. Coronary Care Unit, Room 306."

Scully makes her way to the Coronary Care Unit and to Room 306. She peeks inside, where a doctor named Kopeikan and a short woman in her mid-thirties named Maggie are in discussion.

The doctor tells Maggie, "I'm sorry, but I don't know what else to say. Everything appears to be as it should, under the circumstances. So don't worry. If you'd like, I can show you the hospital cafeteria."

Maggie says, "Yeah . . . okay. Are there phones down there? I need to make some phone calls."

Scully backs away as they exit the room. She enters the room and pulls the curtain back from the bed.

Scully stares into the pale but strikingly intelligent and strong face of Dr. Daniel Waterston, a mid-fifties academic type who appears to be sleeping. As she stares dumbstruck at this man, a tear rolls gently down his cheek.

Dr. Kopeikan enters the room. "Excuse me. Can I help you with something?"

"I'm sorry. I'm Dr. Scully. I was just in the hospital and . . ."

"Can we step into the hallway?" asks the doctor. "I'm Dr. Waterston's cardiologist, Paul Kopeikan. Did you say your name was Scully?"

"Yes. Dana Scully."

"Dr. Waterston's mentioned you."

"I'm sorry, you must be mistaken."

"You were a student of his, right?"

Scully asks, "He has a heart condition?"

"Dr. Waterston came in yesterday with severe chest pains. And he ordered us to do an echocardiogram and a biopsy because he'd had symptoms of an upper respiratory infection the week before. Fortunately, it was the right call."

"Then it's serious."

"But treatable," says Kopeikan. "I have to wake him up soon, if you'd care to—"

"No. That's all right. But thanks for your time."

Kopeikan says, "He must have been a wonderful teacher. I've been following his work on constrictive pericarditis for years now."

"Yes, he's a remarkable man."

•

Scully returns to her apartment. She takes off her coat, tosses the autopsy report on her desk, and is about to check her answering machine for messages when the phone suddenly rings. She picks it up and answers.

"You came to see him," says the voice on the other end.

"I'm sorry," says Scully. "Who is this?"

"Margaret Waterston."

"Maggie? Is everything all right?"

"Well, that depends, doesn't it?"

"I'm sorry?"

"Whatever," says Maggie. "Dr. Kopeikan told my father you were here. Now he wants to see you."

"About what?"

"Look, he asked me to call, so I'm calling."

"I don't know, Maggie. I don't know if I've got time."

"Don't know if you have the time?"

Scully is interrupted by a beeping on her other line. She asks Maggie to hold on a second.

Maggie says, "Listen, it's your choice. But if you come, it doesn't mean I accept you being in his life."

She hangs up on Scully, who clicks onto the other line to Mulder, who is packing his bags for his solo flight to England.

"Hey, you're there," says Mulder.

"Mulder? Aren't you supposed to be on a plane?"

"I've got a five-thirty flight, remember?"

"Right. Guess I lost track of time."

"Listen, the reason I called . . . Am I catching you at a bad time?"

"No. I just walked in. Why?"

"There's this group in D.C. that is researching crop circles. And they've got a totally different set of coordinates from the one that I got already."

"Mulder, I'm not going."

"I gotta ask you a favor. One of the researchers lives out near the hospital. And they've got these sensitive photos and data and stuff that they won't fax to me. I was wondering if you would just maybe go over there, get it, and put it in a Bureau pouch?"

Scully's thoughts are elsewhere.

"Speak to me, Scully," says Mulder, bringing her back.

"I'm out for the evening, Mulder."

"Well, why didn't you just say so in the first place?"

Scully says, "Why don't you leave that address on my answering machine, and I'll try for you."

Scully hangs up.

•

Scully returns to the hospital and opens a door into a room, where she finds a group of

"AND TO BE HONEST, IT'S SATURDAY, AND I WOULDN'T MIND . . . I DON'T KNOW . . . TAKING A BATH."—Scully

strangers surrounding an elderly man in the bed. "I'm sorry," says Scully, realizing she's in Room 304, not 306.

"That's okay," says a woman standing in front of the bed.

Scully enters the correct room and sees Maggie sitting at her father's bedside. Maggie looks up at her, gets up, brushes past Scully, and leaves the room. Waterston looks at her with a mixture of sadness and joy.

"Hi," says Scully.

Waterston says, "So I have to lock eyes with the devil for you to grace me with your presence?"

"Surely not the devil. How are you feeling, Daniel?"

"It's a real drag when the body doesn't want to play anymore."

"You're extremely lucky you called that diagnosis."

"Luck has nothing to do with it, Dana. It's what doctors do every day. You may have forgotten that."

"Daniel." Scully moves to a chair next to the bed.

"So, how did you happen to be here in Washington?" she asks.

"That's a long story."

Scully is about to sit when Waterston takes her hand.

"How's the FBI?" asks Waterston after a long moment of silence.

"Is that why you wanted to see me? To remind me once again what a bad choice I made?"

Scully tries to pull her hand away but Waterston instead brings it to his cheek and shakes his head.

"Believe me. My motivations were far more selfish than that."

He brings her hand to his lips and kisses it.

"You scare me, Daniel."

"I know. I scare you because I represent that which is ingrained not only in your mind, but in your heart, that which you secretly long for."

Scully says, "You never accepted my reason for leaving."

"It wasn't a reason. It was an excuse."

"But you understood why."

Waterston changes the subject. "I can't believe the FBI is a passion. Not like medicine."

"I'm sorry I came." Waterston reaches up and caresses her face. "I just wanted to make sure you were okay."

"I know how difficult it must've been for you, just walking through that door. But you wouldn't come if you didn't want to. That says something, doesn't it?"

•

Scully leaves the hospital and goes to her car. Just as she gets in, her cell phone rings. It is Mulder, who is on a phone at the airport parking lot.

"I was just about to leave you a message. Listen, I've got that address that I wanted you to go to for me. It's a woman you're gonna be dealing with. She's affiliated with the American Taoist Healing Center."

Scully starts into the left turn lane as she speaks to Mulder.

"And she researches crop circles?" asks Scully as she rolls her eyes.

"Don't roll your eyes, Scully."

"Mulder, you want me to . . ."

A woman steps out in front of her car. Scully slams on the brakes, just as a semi truck rumbles past, rocking Scully's car. Scully realizes this woman may have just saved her life. She glances out the window as the woman, in her mid-fifties, with crystal-blue eyes, blonde hair, and a baseball cap, looks back at her with a knowing smile as she walks away.

"Scully?" asks Mulder. "Scully, are you there?"

•

Scully's car pulls to the curb in a well-manicured neighborhood in front of a quaint little house. She gets out of the car, walks up the steps, and rings the bell. The door opens.

"Hi. I'm . . ." Scully stammers. "You were . . ."

It is the woman Scully saw in Room 304 of the hospital the previous day.

"At the hospital today," the woman finishes.

"Right. That's strange. I'm Agent Scully. I'm here on behalf of my partner . . ."

"About my research."

"For the FBI. As odd as that may sound."

"Right. I'm Colleen Azar."

Colleen invites Scully inside. Scully declines, indicating she could use a little air. Colleen asks if she is all right.

"Yes, I'm . . . I'm just a little shaken. I had a near car accident, I think. But it's nothing really."

Colleen insists, "A car accident isn't nothing."

"I'm sorry?"

"In my experience, they're often the end result of us not paying attention to something."

"Look, I don't mean to be rude, but I really don't have much time."

Colleen disappears into the house and returns with some papers and black-and-white photos, which she begins to sort and hand to Scully.

"You think what we do is a little ridiculous, don't you?"

"To be honest, I don't know exactly what it is that you do."

"But you've already formed a judgment about it."

Scully says, "I really should be going."

Colleen puts the requested material inside an envelope. "There is a greater intelligence in all things. Accidents or near accidents often remind us that we need to keep our mind open to the lessons it gives."

Colleen hands Scully the envelope. "You may want to slow down."

Scully turns to walk away when the envelope opens and all the papers fall out onto Colleen's front porch. As she stoops to pick up the papers, Scully spots a paper with the symbol for the heart chakra on it. Suddenly her cell phone rings.

•

Scully returns to the hospital and is ushered by Dr. Kopeikan into Waterston's room, where she finds Maggie sitting at her father's bedside. Waterston is hooked up to all manner of tubing and machinery. He brightens as Scully enters.

"Ah, Hurricane Scully has arrived," he says.

Scully says, "I was summoned."

"Would you please tell the doc here why he should listen to me."

Kopeikan explains, "Sir, we've already agreed to doses of digoxin that are far beyond what I'd normally recommend."

Waterston says, "I guarantee you, Doctor, you're doing it right."

"But I can't be responsible for treatment that might exacerbate your illness," says Kopeikan. "There hasn't even been a double-blind analysis of prednisone's effect."

Scully says, "Prednisone. That won't complicate cardiac arrhythmia. Not if it's just a short burst."

"There," says Waterston, "an informed opinion."

Dr. Kopeikan, disapproving, exits. Maggie is angered by Scully's intrusion. "You come off so rational but maybe you know less than you think." She storms off as well.

"She's been through some difficult times, and she's very angry," says Waterston.

"How did she even find out?" asks Scully.

"There are things you don't know," says Waterston. "Things I'm not proud of."

"What things?"

"I screwed up, Dana. Things got bad at home after . . ."

Scully sighs and sits down. "Bad how?"

"I haven't been completely honest with you. It was hard for me when you walked away. I shut down from my family. Needless to say, it was very difficult for Barbara."

"You divorced."

"Only after an interminable period of discomfort for us both."

"Where did you go?" she asks.

"Here. Washington."

"When?"

"Almost ten years ago."

"Daniel, you didn't move here for me?"

"I didn't mean for it to happen this way, of course."

"Oh God, Daniel. You've come at such a strange time." Scully begins to cry.

"I know," says Waterston. "You have a life."

"I don't know what I have," she says. "Your X rays were in the wrong envelope. I never would've even known you were here if it wasn't for a mixup. It's just . . ."

"What do you want, Dana?"

"I want everything I should want at this time in my life," says Scully. "Maybe I want the life I didn't choose."

Waterston reaches out his hand and Scully puts her hand in his, tears flowing. She puts her head down on Waterston's chest and closes her eyes. Reality comes racing back in a rush of loud sounds and alarms.

Waterston is in cardiac arrest.

Scully begins to pump his chest and screams, "Nurse! We have a code in here! Nurse!"

The monitor alarm continues to sound as a nurse arrives. Over the hospital PA the words *Code Blue CCU* blare.

Scully yells, "He's in V-fib!"

Scully begins mouth-to-mouth resuscitation. Another nurse arrives with a crash cart and attaches gel pads to Daniel's chest. Scully sets the defibrillator at 200 joules and Waterston's body arcs and collapses. No luck. 300 joules. The same. Scully screams at one of the nurses for epinephrine 1 mg, IV push. Scully repositions the paddles and hits him again.

A rhythm sounds on the monitor.

"We have a pulse," says Scully, thanking the nurses.

•

Following the near tragedy at the hospital, Scully feels compelled to once again seek out Colleen Azar. Colleen's door opens to reveal another woman, Carol Banker.

"Hi. Can I help you?" she asks.

"I'm looking for Colleen."

Carol lets Scully into the house and goes off to find Colleen. She returns with Colleen and heads out the door.

"I have to go. Call me if anything interesting happens."

The women share a departing kiss. Colleen turns to Scully.

"I'm surprised to see you again."

"I'm sorry that I was rude before. I'm a medical doctor and a scientist and, you're right, I don't know what it is that you do. But there was something that you said that I wanted to ask you about."

"About slowing down."

Colleen leads Scully into the living room. Scully opens up.

"I have a friend who's ill. And I had a strange feeling today, just a short while ago actually, that he may be dying from a more serious condition than anyone realizes."

Colleen asks, "You sensed something?"

Scully nods reluctantly.

"Holistic practitioners believe, as do many Eastern religions, that living beings exist beyond the physical dimensions of time and space. That we're composed of layers of energy and consciousness. You've probably heard it referred to as an aura."

"Yes."

"Witness this energy field and truths come out that have little to do with scientific proof and much to do with faith."

"What are you saying that I saw?" Scully asks.

"Pain. And where there's pain there's a need for healing. Physically, mentally, or spiritually."

Scully says, "But he has a heart condition."

"When we hold on to shame and guilt and fear, it creates imbalance. It makes us forget who we are. This is difficult for you to accept. Would you like to have some tea?"

Over a cup of tea, Scully is stunned by the woman's intuitiveness.

"I WANT EVERYTHING I SHOULD WANT AT THIS TIME IN MY LIFE. MAYBE I WANT THE LIFE I DIDN'T CHOOSE."—Scully

"Have you ever had moments when everything gets incredibly clear? When time seems to expand?" Colleen asks.

"Yes. That's so strange."

"You may be more open to things than you think. It's just a matter of what you do with it."

Colleen is comfortable enough with Scully to be candid.

"I used to be a physicist. I was successful in my field, working eighty-odd hours a week. I thought I was happy. Truth is, I was cut off from the world and from myself. I was literally dying inside. I was in a relationship with Carol, who you met, but I was so afraid of what the world, and my family, and my fellow scientists would think, that I told no one. Then, two years ago, I was diagnosed with breast cancer."

"I'm sorry," says Scully.

"Don't be. It's the cancer that got my attention and stopped me from being on the self-destructive path I was on. It made me realize I was in a field that had little meaning for me, and it's what's allowed me to be happy for what feels like the first time in my life."

"But how?"

"I was introduced to a healer who helped me see the disease for what it was. It wasn't until I began releasing shame and telling the truth that my cancer went into remission."

Scully is impressed but still skeptical. Colleen picks up on those emotions.

"You still aren't sure. You came here looking for answers and you want something to take back with you. Everything happens for a reason."

•

Scully enters the hospital, carrying a bouquet of flowers. She heads for an elevator door. It opens to reveal Maggie exiting. She turns on Scully.

"Are you happy?"

"I'm sorry? I was just going up to see your father."

"You can't. He's in a coma."

"Since when?" asks Scully.

"Since about two minutes after you supposedly saved his life. Do you have any idea of the hell you've created in our lives?"

Scully says, "Maggie, to be honest, I left so that there wouldn't be hell in your lives."

Maggie starts to cry. "Don't try to be reasonable with me. I'm so sick of being reasonable! You moved on, but we've had to live with what you left behind!"

Maggie walks away.

Scully leaves the hospital and starts walking a downtown street, lost in thought. She walks for some time, through Chinatown, where she suddenly stops and looks skyward, at a Chinese apothecary sign swinging crazily in the wind.

Scully's gaze goes to a woman walking briskly on the other side of the street. It looks like the same woman who had previously stepped in front of Scully's car. Scully follows her. The sound of a bicycle bell draws her attention and Scully steps back just in time to avoid being hit by a bicycle rider. Scully turns to see the woman disappear behind a thick black door. Scully goes to the door, considers whether she should follow, and enters.

She finds herself at the base of a small, manicured Japanese garden. Scully looks past the garden to a small building. She walks up to the doors and peeks into a narrow room lit by candles. At one end she sees a Buddha, surrounded by cushions of worn fabric.

Scully looks for the mystery woman, but she has disappeared. Sun shines on to the

Buddha's face. Scully is overcome with sadness and confusion. She drops to her knees, closing her eyes.

A series of images flashes through her consciousness. Daniel. Mulder. Her father in military uniform. Her sister, Melissa. Cigarette-Smoking Man. Her mother.

Her thoughts smash to white and then to the image of a levitating Dr. Waterston, his body transparent, veins pumping blue blood, organs pulsating.

A black heart.

Waterston's lips are moving. Suddenly they stop. His heartbeat stops. His eyes snap open.

Scully's eyes snap open, too. She is looking into the eyes of the Buddha, trying to make sense of it all. She has a thought.

•

Inside Room 306, Colleen and a man known as The Healer, whom Scully saw earlier in Room 304, are standing over the body of Waterston. Standing nearby is Scully. The Healer solemnly speaks: "What I try to do is clear the body's energy channels, what we call chakras, which can become barriers to a doctor's ability to effectively heal the patient.

"When these channels are working improperly, whether from poor physical or emotional health, the block serves to create conditions for disease. If I can unblock the energy early on, then I can prevent the onset or escalation of an illness. Or provide a place from which . . ."

This intervention is interrupted by Dr. Kopeikan. "What is going on here? Dr. Scully, who do you think you are?"

Scully says, "We have nothing but Dr. Waterston's welfare in mind here."

"You're not his doctor," says Kopeikan.

"I understand that. What's taking place here is an alternative approach," says Scully.

Kopeikan counters, "What's taking place here is a waste of time, Dr. Scully. And I think that Dr. Waterston would be the first to agree with me. Have you considered that?"

Scully says, "I just wanted to help him. It seemed like nothing else was working."

"With all due respect, that is not for you to assess. That's for me or Dr. Waterston's family to decide."

Maggie enters the room. "Let them continue. If it isn't hurting him, we should at least be open to it."

The Healer has reached an impasse in his ministrations.

"I'm afraid there's really nothing more I can do at this time. This man, quite frankly, is ready to move on, but something seems to be holding him back. Unfinished business is binding him to the physical plane. Something he needs to release before he can let go."

Maggie and Scully look at each other.

The strains of Moby play as we see Scully in her apartment, settling in with a cup of tea. We see her back in Waterston's hospital room, staring at a bed enveloped in a halo of light. She is looking down at herself in the bed, in the same physical and emotional pain as Waterston.

She mouths the words *speak to me . . .*

. . . before she awakens from the dream in her own apartment, to the sound of her phone ringing.

"It's Maggie. I need you to come to the hospital right away."

•

She races to the hospital and Waterston's room. "Daniel?"

"You think I'd give up so easily?" Waterston says. He is looking much healthier.

Scully is amazed at his recovery. "You were slipping away. No one thought you'd come out of this. I'm still in shock."

"Imagine my shock when my doctor told me the voodoo ritual you'd arranged for me last night."

"I was afraid it didn't work," says Scully.

"Of course it didn't work. Don't be absurd. Where do you get this crap?"

Scully says, "Daniel, that crap may have just saved your life, whether you're open to it or not."

"It doesn't matter. I don't want to talk about that. Look at me. I'm going to get well and we need to talk about what happens next for us."

"I spoke at length to Maggie. It's time that you took responsibility for the hurt you caused in your family. It's no accident that you got sick, Daniel. You've been running from the truth for ten years."

"Dana, it was only to be with you. You're all I lived for."

"Maybe the reason you're alive now is to make up for that. To make it up to Maggie."

"That's Maggie talking. Not you."

"I was just looking for you."

"You're supposed to be in England."

"I'm back."

"What happened?"

"Nothing. There was no event. No crop circles. A big waste of time."

"Maybe sometimes nothing happens for a reason, Mulder."

"What is that supposed to mean?"

"Nothing. C'mon. I'll make you some tea."

Later, after a cup of tea in Mulder's apartment, they sit on Mulder's couch sharing their experiences of the past two days. The mood is warm and quiet.

"I just find it hard to believe," says Mulder.

"What part?"

"The part where I go away for two days and your whole life changes."

"I didn't say my whole life changed."

"You speaking to God in a Buddhist temple. God speaking back."

"And I didn't say that God spoke back. I said that I had some kind of a vision."

"No. I'm not the same person, Daniel. I wouldn't have known that if I hadn't seen you again."

Scully turns to walk away as Maggie enters the room.

•

Scully is sitting quietly in the hospital park when she spies the mysterious woman in the baseball cap. Scully starts after her, grabs the woman's arm, and turns her around, to find that it is actually Mulder wearing a baseball cap.

"Hey!"

"Mulder?"

"For you, that's like saying you're having David Crosby's baby."

Scully smiles. Mulder senses something is different. "What is it?"

"I once considered spending my whole life with this man. What I would've missed."

"I don't think you could know. I mean, how many different lives would we be leading if we made different choices? We don't know."

Scully says, "What if there was only one choice? And all the other ones were wrong. And there were signs along the way to pay attention to . . ."

"All the choices would then lead to this very moment. One wrong turn and we wouldn't be sitting here together," says Mulder.

"That says a lot. I mean, it's probably more than we should be getting into at this late hour."

Mulder looks at Scully, who has fallen asleep, her face pressed into the cushion. He leans toward her, brushing a lock of hair from her face, looking like he might kiss her. He reaches past her, grabs a blanket, and pulls it over her. He studies her for a moment, then gets up and walks away, leaving Scully to her dreams.

BACK STORY:

Gillian Anderson approached Chris Carter during Season 6 with the desire to write and direct an episode. It did not bother Carter that Anderson had never done either.

"We were, of course, supportive of that," says Carter. "You want to support those people who have added to the show and give them their shot to go to the next creative level."

Anderson recalls that during this period, she was also getting offers from a number of cable networks to direct.

"But suddenly it occurred to me that the best scenario would be for me to learn the ropes with what was right in front of me and what I was most familiar with. I talked about this with my manager and she asked me if I had any ideas."

Anderson did indeed have some ideas. Long an advocate of New Age/alternative lifestyles, the actress had particularly strong beliefs in Buddhism and the power of spiritual healing. What she shared with her manager was the early outline of a deeply personal X-File, one in which Scully is taken down a spiritual path when logic fails her as she attempts to deal with an interlude from her pre–*X-Files* life. The tone of her early vision for "all things" was stark, yet subtle: Scully was on a voyage of self-discovery that she would have to make on her own.

Anderson relates, "A certain concept began to form, and as soon as I got off the phone with my manager, I just wrote the entire outline for 'all things' right then and there. It all just kind of came together on the page."

The next day, Anderson went into Chris Carter's office and pitched the idea. "Gillian's idea was a real change for *The X-Files,*" says Carter. "It was very personal and quiet, but you could tell that the ideas were very close to her and that they were important."

Anderson also used the meeting to reiterate her desire to direct the episode as well. But the actress recalls that Carter's instinct was to take this very risky journey one step at a time. "Chris told me, 'Okay, let's see. Why don't you start writing. When you've written something, we'll look at it and see what we can do.' "

Weeks later, Anderson came back to Carter and executive producer Frank Spotnitz with her first draft of "all things." As befitting a maiden effort in writing, the script had problems.

"When I turned in the script, it was fifteen pages too long and it didn't have a fourth act," groaned Anderson at the memory. "It ran about eighty-eight minutes and it could have been a two-parter but there wasn't room for another two-parter on the schedule."

Spotnitz and Carter worked very closely with Anderson in the rewrite stage, walking that inevitable tightrope of wanting to keep Anderson's vision intact while having it all fit into the mandated forty-four minute time slot.

Spotnitz remembers the rewriting process. "We talked about it and changed things, all in service of her ideas about healing and Buddhism. A lot of what I did with her was the distilling of her ideas."

Carter agrees with Spotnitz. "Frank and I worked very closely with her on that script. But in the end, it was all Gillian. We were there more as backstops and she would throw things at us. Frank and I were very pleased with the courage of her convictions."

Despite her satisfaction with "all things," Anderson still regrets that the necessary script cuts were made at the expense of a clearer understanding of the relationship between Scully and Dr. Daniel Waterston. In the episode, Scully is painted as the "other woman" whose affair with Waterston broke up his family. But Anderson reveals that she originally had a different vision for the back story.

"What had actually transpired between Scully and Waterston was that there had been an attraction and that they were starting to spend some time together, things like lunch and dinner dates. She was trying to keep it platonic but there were feelings that were coming up. It started getting heavier and Waterston began talking about divorce. But they never consummated the relationship. Scully didn't want that to happen because she didn't want to be a homewrecker. At one point, another professor approached her and told her that their relationship was starting to get around and that it could hurt her career and his marriage. So Scully backed away before anything could happen physically. What Scully would later learn from Waterston's daughter, Maggie, was that her father shut down emotionally and that his wife believed he was having an affair. Eventually his wife starts to go a little nutty, is hospitalized, and eventually hangs herself."

Anderson claims that in paring down the script, many of these story details and intricacies, which were originally intended to be explained in a fourth-act conversation with Mulder, did not happen.

Anderson's next challenge was directing. It would be a relatively Mulder-lite show (as David Duchovny was busy prepping his own episode, "Hollywood A.D."), and the rhythms and beats of her character and the show were almost second nature to her after six seasons. But she cheerfully admits that she had help from everyone in the cast and crew.

"I worked with [director] Kim Manners. If I had any questions, I would go to Kim. The first thing he said was, 'Okay, you've got homework to do. I want you to spend the next two weekends doing an entire shot list of every single scene.' "

Anderson's directing debut energized *The X-Files* production. Behind-the-scenes people pushed extra hard to make sure things ran like clockwork. Production designer Corey Kaplan was one of the first to step up for her.

"There was a question in one scene about whether or not to have a Buddhist temple in one pivotal sequence," she relates. "Gillian wanted it but she felt it would be too expensive. But I said, 'I want you to have that Buddhist temple,' and so we rigged up a Buddhist temple in a cellar of one of the stages."

Casting director Rick Millikan smiles as he recalls guiding the actress-turned-director through some of the intricacies of the other side of the camera.

"I loved working with Gillian," he says. "It was fun for me to watch her go through the casting process because it was all new to her. She had never done the casting thing and she was like a little kid who you had to teach. At first she was a little embarrassed sitting there with the actors. But as she got used to the audition process, she did really well."

Anderson wielded a deft hand in her directorial debut, prodding the actors to her will, making decisions on the fly, and handling the complex special effects sequences surrounding Dr. Waterston. Kim Manners was always around the set and available for any questions or to suggest how a shot might go. And when it came to directing herself, Anderson was right on the money.

The result of this admittedly risky departure from the dark and frightening nature of *X-Files* cases was a happy surprise. Calls and letters indicated that viewers loved the vulnerability and quiet determination that Scully revealed in the unusual episode. They were equally impressed with Anderson's directorial skills. She was happy.

"When it was all over, I realized I knew more than I thought I did."

FACTS:

Previous television roles for Colleen Flynn include the role of Michelle Fazekas, who led Scully and Mulder into the dangerous Florida woods in "Detour" (5X04), and a memorable stint on *China Beach* as Dr. Colleen Flaherty Richards.

Carol Banker, script supervisor for *The X-Files*, has also performed script supervising duties on many films, including *The Prophecy, Feeling Minnesota, The Apostle,* and *Dogma*. Her role in "all things" is not her first—she played a security guard in *Mallrats*.

episode 7X19

BRAND X

EPISODE: 7X19
FIRST AIRED: April 16, 2000
EDITOR: Heather MacDougall
WRITTEN BY: Steven Maeda & Greg Walker
DIRECTED BY: Kim Manners

Mulder and Scully go up against the twin horrors of cigarettes and big business when a government witness dies a grotesque death that involves mutant tobacco beetles and a human guinea pig who has become bigger than his experiment.

[redacted]

GUEST STARS:

Mitch Pileggi (A.D. Skinner)
Dennis Boutsikaris (Dr. Peter Voss)
Richard Cox (Daniel Brimley)
Tobin Bell (Ashman/Darrel Weaver)
Mike Hungerford (Complaining Man)
Shannon O'Hurley (Ann Voss)
Arthur Rosenberg (Lead Counsel)
Ron Marasco (Doctor)
Pat Destro (Joan Scobie)
Caryn West (Dr. Libby Nance)
Rick Deats (Dr. Jim Scobie)
David Sawyer (Security Man)
Greg Poland (Second Windbreaker Man)
Matthew T. Wilson (Manager)

PRINCIPAL SETTING:

Winston-Salem, North Carolina

An upscale house is being watched by a man wearing a dark blue windbreaker. A second man in a windbreaker is patrolling the back yard.

"Radio check. Perimeter is clear," says the second man.

Inside the house Assistant Director Walter Skinner is on the other end of the walkie-talkie conversation.

"Copy that," says Skinner. "Give me a check every ten."

Skinner turns to the owners of the home, Dr. Jim Scobie and his wife, Joan.

Skinner says, "Why don't you folks make yourselves comfortable. Watch television or get some rest. Try to put your minds at ease."

Skinner moves to the windows, looks outside, and closes all the shutters.

"Just try to stay away from windows and doors, if you would."

Mrs. Scobie says, "Do we have to ask you if we can use the bathroom? I feel like I'm a prisoner in my own home."

"Ma'am, I apologize for the imposition. But my job is to protect you. As of this evening, the FBI's top priority is keeping you safe."

"For how long? A week? A month? Then what?" Mrs. Scobie turns to her husband. "Jim, don't do this, please. You don't have to testify. It's not worth it. These people have a long reach. They're powerful."

Dr. Scobie says determinedly, "I have to do this."

"I'm going to bed," says Joan, leaving the room.

Dr. Scobie lets out a ragged cough. An agent brings him a glass of water. He sips it as Skinner explains their itinerary.

"Grand jury convenes at nine. We'll leave here at seven-thirty. I'll be right outside the door if you need me."

Skinner walks away. Scobie coughs again. He takes another drink of water and puts down the glass. Scobie also goes to bed, leaving behind the glass containing a small squirming beetle, lying on an ice cube in the blood-tainted water.

Hours later, Joan Scobie awakens to find that her husband is not in bed. "Jim?" She notices a light coming from under the door of the master bathroom. She goes to the bathroom door and knocks.

"Jim? Are you feeling all right?"

She tries to open the door. It is unlocked, but something heavy is wedged against it.

"Mr. Skinner! Mr. Skinner!" she screams.

Skinner and other agents burst through the door, weapons drawn. As Joan continues to scream for her husband, Skinner calls through the door but gets no answer. He puts his shoulder to the door and it slowly opens. He enters to find Dr. Scobie slumped on the bathroom floor, blood pooling beneath his head. Skinner kneels down and turns the body over to reveal that the flesh, from the dead man's nose to his throat, has been stripped away. Joan Scobie screams in anguish.

•

Muldor and Scully arrive at the Scobie home to find Skinner on the cell phone, getting his ass chewed by his superior.

"Yes, at the time I was in another part of the house. Yes, sir, I will have answers for you."

Joan Scobie is sitting nearby in shock. She is led out of the house as Skinner hangs up.

"Rough night?" asks Mulder.

Skinner says, "It's shaping up to be a rougher morning. Follow me."

He leads them to the master bathroom. Scobie's body has been removed.

"Fingerprints everywhere," says Skinner. "But as they all belong to the deceased and his wife, they don't help us."

Scully asks, "This is where the body was found?"

"Yeah."

"What can you tell us about him?" asks Mulder.

"Dr. James Scobie, age forty-four. R&D biochemist with Morley Tobacco," explains Skinner. "If he were alive, as of twenty-six minutes ago, he'd be giving testimony against his former employer before a federal grand jury."

"Testimony concerning what?" asks Scully.

Skinner says, "Not even his wife or lawyer know the specifics, only that it concerns research he was involved in. Potentially extremely damaging to Morley. Enough so that Scobie had received death threats. Given the high-profile nature of the case, the Director charged me with ensuring Dr. Scobie's protection."

"You think that someone made good on these threats?" asks Scully.

"I do. But we have yet to determine how someone got in here. Or what killed him."

Skinner shows the agents the grisly crime scene photo.

"You can't blow the whistle with a mouth like that," says Mulder.

Scully comments, "It's almost as if his flesh has been stripped or eaten away. An assailant could have thrown acid on him."

"If it were acid in the face, he would have screamed bloody murder."

Skinner says, "We're looking at all possibilities, Agent. We need answers. We don't have a lot of time and we're going up against one of the biggest corporations in America. The Director himself personally instructed me that he wants this case closed as swiftly as possible. I trust I can count on your help."

Mulder and Scully nod their support.

Skinner turns to Scully. "I want you to perform the autopsy. The body's at the county morgue."

"I'll get right on it."

They exit through the living room. Mulder notices, "No ashtrays. Dr. Scobie and his wife don't smoke?"

Skinner says, "Not that I witnessed."

"A tobacco employee that doesn't smoke. Isn't that kind of like a GM executive who drives a Ford? If this was a hit, it seems unnecessarily high-profile. It kind of draws attention to itself, don't you think?"

"That could be the point: to intimidate potential witnesses," says Skinner. Mulder acknowledges this could be the case. "Scobie had a supervisor at Morley, a Dr. Peter Voss. I want to talk to him."

"Mind if I tag along?" asks Mulder.

After nodding his agreement, Skinner is called aside by another agent. Mulder sees Dr. Scobie's water glass and the now dead beetle floating inside. He holds the glass up to the light and looks at the beetle.

•

Mulder and Skinner enter the Morley Tobacco Company building and run into a hard-nosed security guard who insists, despite the flashing of their FBI ID, that they need an appointment to see Dr. Voss.

"Gentlemen? I can help you," says a well-dressed man entering the lobby. He introduces himself as Daniel Brimley, the head of corporate security. "You're here concerning Dr. Scobie's death, I take it. We were all extremely sorry to hear about it. Jim has a lot of friends in this building."

Mulder says, "Really? No hard feelings he was about to turn federal witness against your company?"

Brimley responds, "Nobody was happy about Jim's decision, but the timing of his death couldn't have been worse."

"So you'd have no problem with us speaking to Dr. Voss?" asks Skinner.

"A TOBACCO EMPLOYEE WHO DOESN'T SMOKE. ISN'T THAT KIND OF LIKE A GM EXECUTIVE WHO DRIVES A FORD?"—Mulder

"Absolutely not. Whatever we can do to help."

They sit down with Dr. Peter Voss, a sad-eyed professional in his late forties, in a conference room. Brimley watches Mulder and Skinner closely and a phalanx of lawyers surround Dr. Voss. Voss offers his condolences to Mrs. Scobie.

"How is she?"

"I'm sure she'll take comfort in finding out why her husband died," says Mulder.

Skinner asks, "Dr. Voss, can you enlighten us as to what Dr. Scobie intended to tell the grand jury? We know it had to do with company research."

Voss starts to nod and answer when one of the lawyers interrupts. "I'm sorry. Dr. Voss would be in violation of his employment confidentiality clause in answering that question."

Skinner stares daggers into the lawyer.

"Dr. Scobie was your friend?" asks Skinner.

"Yes. For fourteen years."

"And yet you demoted him five weeks ago," remarks Skinner. "You took him off a particular project. Can you tell us why that happened?"

Again, Voss is stopped from speaking. The lawyer says, "As before, Dr. Voss would be in violation of his confidentiality clause in answering questions regarding the nature of his work here at Morley. I'm sure you understand that our cooperation cannot extend itself to revealing corporate secrets." Voss appears frustrated by his lawyer's words.

"I'm not sensing any cooperation whatsoever," Skinner responds. "In fact, I'm one more non-answer away from getting a federal warrant and searching this entire building."

"Then this meeting is over," says the lawyer, rising and starting to leave.

Mulder pushes a small evidence bag containing the dead beetle across the table to Dr. Voss.

"Dr. Voss, can you tell me what that is?"

"It's a tobacco beetle. Why?"

"I found it at James Scobie's house."

"You find a lot of these around here. They're everywhere. There's probably a dozen in the grille of your car right now."

The lawyer asks, "Can I ask where you're going with this, Agent?"

"I'm sorry. I can't," echoes Mulder. "Answering that question would violate FBI confidentiality, due to the sensitive nature of our investigation."

•

Dr. Voss drives into the driveway of his home. He pulls into the garage and gets out of the car. He turns to see the silhouette of a man walking toward the open garage. He steps out into the light, and we see a man with sickly complexion and nicotine-stained teeth.

"Evening," says the man.

Voss asks, "What are you doing here?"

"I ran out of smokes. Me and Dr. Scobie had an arrangement, as you know. So I figured, Dr. Scobie not being around, that my arrangement with him slides on over to you."

Voss nods understandingly, opens his briefcase and pulls out two cartons of cigarettes in plain white packaging.

"That won't hold me."

Voss appears nervous. "I'll bring you more. Just don't come here anymore."

"Seems everybody's acting funny around me all of a sudden, you know? Telling me not to talk, to stay away from their houses. Too bad about Dr. Scobie. I'll bet people are wondering how he died. I've been working on my own theory, up in the old noggin. I'd be happy to share it with you someday."

"I think that you should leave now," says Voss.

"Yeah. I don't wanna wear out my welcome. We'll be seeing a lot of each other, I expect."

•

Inside the morgue, Scully is in the middle of the Scobie autopsy. She turns at the sound of Mulder and Skinner entering the room.

"Smoke 'em if you've got 'em," says Mulder.

"What have you found?" asks Skinner.

"Where are you going with this?" Skinner asks.

"That this isn't a homicide. You examined the body, Scully. Did you find any of these?" Mulder takes out the evidence bag with the dead beetle inside and shows it to Scully.

"A bug?"

"Well, it's a tobacco beetle."

Scully asks, "I didn't find anything like that, Mulder. Were you expecting me to?"

Skinner asks, "Killer bugs? This is what I'm supposed to tell the Director?"

"I don't know," Mulder says. "But judging from Dr. Voss's reaction to this, I think it's the thing we should investigate."

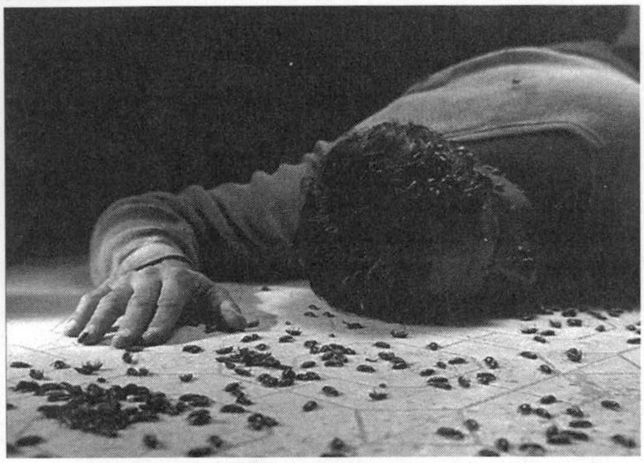

"Well, the tissue damage on Dr. Scobie's mouth extends all the way down his trachea into his lungs. His alveoli look like corned beef."

Skinner asks, "What about this being the result of some sort of corrosive agent?"

"No, that's not the case," says Scully. "There's no acids present, no caustics. This damage isn't the result of any kind of chemical reaction. His airways have more or less just been reamed out. I can tell you what killed him, though. Strictly speaking."

"What?" asks Mulder.

"Hypoxemia. The inability to transfer oxygen from the lungs to the bloodstream."

Skinner says, "He choked to death?" Scully nods. "This damage, however it was accomplished, someone did do this to him."

Mulder says, "Well, not necessarily. There weren't any signs of struggle in the room. Maybe no one was ever there."

•

The man who visited Dr. Voss earlier sits watching television and smoking in his skid-row hotel room. The man in the next room looks up at the air vent, goes to the wall, and knocks against it.

"I've been telling you all week. How many times I gotta say it? No smoking! You hear me?"

Sitting in the next room, the man yells, "America, man! *E pluribus* . . . uh . . ." and continues to blow smoke, unconcerned.

"I'll get you kicked out, you sonofabitch! You think I'm kidding? I'll do it!" The complaining man lets loose a hacking cough. "Law's on my side!"

He hacks out another long retching cough, covering his mouth with his hand. The man removes his hand from his mouth and sees that it is covered with blood. Inside his apartment, the smoking man can hear the sound of a body hitting the floor in the other room. His attention doesn't waver from the TV as he keeps smoking.

The complaining man lies dead on the floor, his head, face, and the floor around him covered with hundreds of tobacco beetles.

•

Mulder, Scully, and Skinner gather at the hotel room to check out the corpse.

Mulder says, "Guests check in, but they don't check out."

Scully adds, "Well, judging from the condition of the body, I'd say that he died in the same manner as Dr. Scobie."

"Except that this man's no corporate whistle-blower," says Skinner.

Skinner checks out the victim's wallet. "Thomas Gastall. Out-of-date Massachusetts license, food coupons, and a certificate of completion for a court-ordered anger management class."

Scully asks, "What could Morley Tobacco have against a transient from Massachusetts?"

"Probably nothing," Mulder says, kneeling down and looking at a few remaining tobacco beetles.

"What are you suggesting, Mulder?" Skinner asks.

"Jim Scobie wasn't murdered. Neither was this man."

"Well, then what killed him?"

Mulder picks up a live beetle and deposits it in an evidence bag. He holds it up to Skinner and Scully. "These."

"We didn't find these insects in Scobie's bathroom," says Skinner.

"Yeah, but there was an open window," says Mulder, "through which they could have escaped."

Scully says, "It's a long shot, Mulder, but it could be some form of contagious agent, like an insect-borne bacterium. Which would mean that there might be other victims in this building."

•

Mulder knocks at the room next door. The man from earlier appears at the door. Mulder apologizes for bothering him and is invited inside. Mulder takes in the small, dingy room.

"We're investigating the death of the man who lived right next to you. A Thomas Gastall. Did you know him?"

"Knew his voice. He yelled a lot. Said I smoked too much. Whatcha gonna do, man? It's a free country. *E pluribus*, uh . . . You mind?" he asks, holding up a pack of cigarettes.

"You don't seem surprised that he's dead."

"Guess his number come up." He lights up another cigarette and blows smoke at the ceiling. "Just glad it wasn't me."

Mulder asks his name. It is Darrel Weaver.

"Mr. Weaver, did you see or hear anything unusual last night?"

"Little Korean fellow down the hall. Dresses like Wonder Woman. But that's every night." He chuckles good-naturedly.

"Other than that?"

Weaver says, "Say, there wouldn't happen to be any reward money involved, would there? I could use an extra buck or two."

"The FBI would appreciate your voluntary cooperation, sir. That's the way it works."

"Ain't that always the way?" He takes a long drag on his cigarette and blows the smoke out slowly. "Nope. My mind's just drawing a complete blank."

Mulder hands Weaver his card and thanks him for his time. He heads back to Scully and Skinner.

Skinner is discouraged. "Two deaths in less than twenty-four hours and we've yet to come up with an answer."

Scully adds, "The only thing I have to go on medically at this point is Mulder's bug. I know an entomologist at UNC-Wilmington, Dr. Libby Nance."

"Good. Talk to her," says Mulder as he heads for the door.

Skinner asks, "Where are you going?"

"See about something else that's been bugging me."

•

Mulder goes to the home of Dr. Peter Voss. Ann Voss answers the door. Her husband appears behind her and joins Mulder on the front porch.

"I really shouldn't be talking to you without our lawyers."

"I understand your reluctance to talk, sir. You have a nice family. A lot to lose."

"What do you want, Agent Mulder?"

"There's been another victim. Thomas Gastall. He died exactly the same way Scobie did."

"I'm sorry to hear that. But what has that got to do with me?"

Mulder produces the bag containing the tobacco beetle. "We found these all over him. I believe that's what killed both men."

"The tobacco beetle. It's an herbivore. It eats tobacco, hence its name."

"I understand that. But maybe these don't," says Mulder.

"I'm not really required to talk to you, am I?"

"No." Voss starts to walk back to the house. Mulder calls after him. "But why are you hiding behind your lawyers, Doctor? How many people have to die before you do the right thing?"

Voss goes into his house and closes the door without looking at Mulder. Voss watches from inside the house as Mulder gets into his car and drives away. Suddenly his phone rings. On the other end is Daniel Brimley, who is parked across the street from Voss's home.

"What did he want?" asks Brimley.

"Are you spying on me?"

"I'm not spying on you, Peter. I'm looking out for you. What did he want?"

"There's been another death, downtown."

"How did it happen?"

"I don't know."

"This has gone on long enough. We should come forward. I should."

"Do you hear what you're saying, Peter? Now I want you to just take a moment. I want you to think about what really matters to you. Now tell me where I can find Darrel Weaver."

"Why?"

Brimley says, "This was my mistake. I'll clean it up."

"I don't know where he is."

The phone goes dead.

•

Inside the morgue, Dr. Libby Nance, the entomologist, is looking at the tobacco beetle through a high-powered microscope. Standing behind her are Skinner and Scully.

"This doesn't make sense," says Nance.

"What doesn't make sense?" asks Skinner.

"It's a *Lasioderma serricorne*. A tobacco beetle. Only I've never seen one exactly like this."

Scully asks, "What are the differences?"

"Physical differences," says the doctor. "Minor, but definitely notable. Deviations in the mandibles, the antennae, the body segmentation."

"What if such deviations arose from genetic engineering?" asks Scully.

The doctor wants to know if Scully means engineering the bugs themselves.

"No. I was actually thinking of another possibility. Transgenomics."

Skinner looks lost. Scully explains, "It's a form of DNA manipulation. Alterations made on the genetic level."

Dr. Nance says, "It is pretty widely known that the tobacco companies have been pouring money into that kind of research, changing the tobacco plant itself in order to make it heartier, give it less nicotine, more nicotine, make it naturally menthol-flavored. You name it."

Skinner says, "A form of what? Super tobacco?"

"Which possibly could have created superbugs," Scully says. "I guess the real question is, could they have become dangerous to humans?"

•

Dr. Voss has gone to the skid-row home of Darrel Weaver. He knocks on Weaver's door, calling his name.

"Sorry, doc. No vacancy," says Weaver.

Voss turns to see Weaver advancing down the hallway toward him. Voss points to Gastall's room and asks what happened.

"Well, you tell me. You're the one with the Ph.D. I'm just the big ol' guinea pig."

Weaver opens his door and enters. Voss follows.

"Listen, you have to leave town."

"And give up all this? Me, not do my part for science?"

Voss hands Weaver a fat envelope of cash. "Here. Take it. It's everything I have in the bank. Four thousand." Weaver opens the envelope and counts the cash.

"Hmm. It's not much. But it's a start."

"I'm not kidding. You've got to get out of here."

"Why? I got a good thing going here. I got cash money. I got all the coffin nails I can suck down." Weaver pulls out a cigarette and lets it dangle between his lips. "Although lately, I've been thinking this particular brand doesn't do anyone else any favors, healthwise." He abruptly flips open his lighter. Voss flinches. "You thinking that, too? Would it bother you if I lit one up?" Voss is noticeably nervous. Weaver closes the lighter without lighting the cigarette.

Weaver shows Voss the door. "Toodles."

"No, you don't understand. Morley is a multibillion-dollar global corporation. You think they're going to let you endanger that? They'll kill you first."

In his raspy voice, Weaver says, "Sounds like a Darrel Weaver problem to me."

Voss stammers for a moment, then gives up and leaves. Brimley, standing on the nearby stairs, watches Voss walk out, then turns his gaze on Darrel Weaver's door.

•

Scully is working intently over an object in the morgue. Skinner enters and looks over Scully's shoulder, flinching.

"What am I looking at?" asks Skinner.

"Thomas Gastall's left lung and bronchus."

"I guess that explains where the beetles came from."

They stare long and hard at a sliced open human lung, swarming with wriggling wormlike larvae.

Mulder enters.

"Mulder, where have you been?" asks Scully.

"Talking to lawyers over at Justice. Trying to get a look at Morley's files."

"Well, get a look at this," she says. Mulder looks, then quickly turns away at the sight. "They're the larval stage of the tobacco beetle, Mulder. And somehow they have ended up nesting in Thomas Gastall's lungs."

Skinner adds, "What doesn't make any sense is why Scobie's lungs didn't show this same condition."

Scully says, "The larvae must pupate inside the lungs. And then once they mature into beetles, exit the body en masse."

"That explains the condition of the face and throat," says Skinner. "Only, how do they get into the lungs to begin with?"

Mulder is suddenly racked by a coughing fit. Scully and Skinner look at him as he looks at his hand. Mulder looks up at them. He is shaken, unable to speak. Mulder slowly opens his hand.

His palm is flecked with blood.

•

Mulder has been rushed to the Asheford Medical Center and into surgery. Scully and a team of surgeons administer to him. A narrow vacuum wand has been inserted into Mulder's throat. The suction has filled the receptacle with mucous and larvae.

Scully slips out of surgery and into the hallway, where she finds Skinner pacing. She takes off her hospital mask.

"How is he?"

"They're using a deep-suction technique that's been designed for asthma and cystic fibrosis. So far, we're having some luck at clearing his lungs."

"But?"

"For every one of those things that are in his lung tissue, there may be a dozen eggs that have yet to be hatched."

"Eggs," says Skinner.

"His pulmonary tissue is riddled with them, and they're going to hatch. It's just . . . we're buying time."

Skinner wants to know how these things got into Mulder's lungs.

Scully says they were inhaled. Skinner appears confused at this theory. "The tobacco beetle lives out its life cycle on or around the tobacco plant. That's where it lays its eggs. If

those genetically altered beetles that we found did that, then maybe the eggs survived the processing into cigarettes."

"And been carried into Mulder's lungs as smoke?" asks Skinner.

"Right. Like spores or pollen, somehow small enough to be airborne."

Skinner reminds Scully that Mulder and Scobie were not smokers.

"Maybe they were around someone who was," says Scully.

•

Skinner and two other agents burst into the Morley Tobacco research lab, where they are met with Dr. Voss and his ever-present legal counsel. "Don't bother calling security." Skinner says as he presents the lawyer with a legal document.

"Federal search warrant," he continues. "As promised. Do it," he instructs the agents.

The agents begin to search the lab. As the lawyer scans the warrant, Skinner turns to Voss.

"You're going to talk to me, Doctor. One of my agents is dying of the same thing that killed Dr. Scobie. I believe you have information that can save him."

The lawyer says, "We stand by our contention that any and all such information is proprietary, and is therefore the sole property of Morley Tobacco."

Skinner's jaw clenches. "Listen to me, you sonofabitch. This isn't about Morley or your precious research. This is about saving lives."

Voss says, "That's exactly what we were trying to do."

"Dr. Voss, I'm advising you not to speak," the lawyer says.

"This has gone on long enough." The lawyer backs off. "We thought we were doing a good thing," Voss explains to Skinner. "We knew people were never going to stop smoking, no matter how unhealthy it was. So why not genetically engineer a safer cigarette?"

"Except you engineered the bugs as well."

"We recruited test smokers, we conducted focus groups. There were no problems. Then, after a few months in, things . . . things got bad. We had four test subjects, and, uh . . . three of them died," he finishes quickly.

"Is that what Dr. Scobie was going to testify about?" asks Skinner.

"Yeah. The company wanted us to keep it quiet. I thought, let's correct the mistakes and face the consequences. Jim didn't. He was monitoring the focus group, and that's how he got infected."

Skinner says, "You said only three died. Who was the fourth?"

•

Skinner kicks in the door of Weaver's apartment. He enters, gun drawn, followed by another agent. A smoke haze hangs over the room. Skinner discovers Brimley bound and gagged in a chair, a blood-soaked scalp evidence that he has been cold-cocked. Skinner clears the room and Voss enters, shocked at the sight of Brimley, who appears to have just come to.

"He told me he meant to get Weaver," says Voss.

"Looks like Weaver got to him first."

Skinner removes the gag, but Brimley's mouth remains wide open. "Mr. Brimley. Can you hear me?"

Brimley tries to speak. His mouth still wide open, he lets out a faint gurgle as hundreds of beetles swarm out of his mouth and quickly cover his face and chest.

•

A dark sedan pulls into a minimart/gas station parking lot. The car is Brimley's. Weaver gets out from behind the wheel. He pulls out

the last cigarette from a pack, then tosses away the package. He takes note of the NO SMOKING sign by the gas pumps, then lights up anyway. Weaver walks into the minimart and up to the clerk.

"You got Mickey's Big Mouth?"

"No smoking in here."

Weaver continues to smoke.

"Mickey's Big Mouth," he says, sliding a $20 bill into the man's breast pocket.

The clerk goes for the beer while Weaver waits. His gaze drifts to the cigarette rack as the manager brings over the beer.

"Anything else? Carton of cigarettes?"

"You don't have my brand."

As the clerk rings up the total, he hears a loud radio squawk and turns to see a sheriff's car pull up behind Weaver's car. By the time the clerk turns back, Weaver is gone.

•

Mulder is in a hospital room, in a post-surgery sleep. He wakes up to find Scully standing at his bedside, holding his hand.

"Must be bad," says Mulder in a hoarse whisper.

Scully smiles. "How do you feel?"

"Like a Dustbuster attacked me."

"We're looking for someone who may be able to help you. A Morley test subject by the name of Darrel Weaver."

Mulder, still in pain, nods at the name and says, "Mr. *E pluribus*" with a cough.

"Mr. Weaver seems to have some kind of tolerance or immunity. And we're hoping that once we find him, we'll be able to figure out how to treat you."

Suddenly Mulder is in distress. He is struggling to breathe. Monitor alarms go off. A doctor rushes in. Scully takes charge as Mulder continues to gasp for air.

"His stat's down to seventy-two! Get some O_2 on him and call a code!"

The doctor calls a code blue. He slaps a clear oxygen mask over Mulder's mouth. Scully looks at Mulder's face and swallows in horror as a lone tobacco beetle appears in the oxygen mask.

•

Scully stares grimly through the ICU room glass at an unconscious Mulder.

The doctor approaches her. "We've got him stabilized on ECMO for the moment. But we're not going to be able to maintain him on it for long. Of course you see why."

He points to an X ray which shows the infestation of tobacco beetle larvae in Mulder's lungs.

"THEY SAY THE ADDICTION IS STRONGER THAN HEROIN."—Mulder

Scully acknowledges that there are more larvae present than there were six hours earlier.

The doctor has more bad news. "They're beginning to block the flow of blood. Our best bet is to go back in there." Scully reacts with disbelief. "I think this time we have to crack the chest."

"No. He's too weak for thoracic surgery. He'd die on the table."

"I don't know what our other options are."

"I say for the time being, we just wait."

"That'll definitely kill him. Sooner or later."

The doctor leaves and Scully again turns to watch Mulder.

•

Ann Voss responds to a loud knock on the door. Skinner and several agents stand tense on the front porch. He introduces himself.

"I have to ask for your cooperation. These men are here to protect you and your family." The agents move past her into the house.

"Oh my God. Why?"

"Your husband hasn't spoken to you about this?"

"He's not here."

"He told me he was headed home," says Skinner as he turns to one of his agents. "Try Dr. Voss at work."

Ann Voss says, "I've just been trying. There's no answer."

•

Skinner races to the Morley Tobacco research lab. Pistol drawn, he makes his way through rows of tobacco. As he approaches the end of one aisle, he comes upon Dr. Voss sitting on the floor, pressing a handkerchief to his bloodied head. Voss looks up.

"Behind you."

Skinner spins around, spotting Darrel Weaver emerging from the shadows, clutching several cartons of cigarettes.

"I was just leaving. I got what I came for."

Slowly rising to his feet, Voss says, "He took the test cigarettes. I couldn't stop him."

Weaver turns to leave. Skinner yells at him to stop.

"Why? You gonna shoot me?" He takes a few steps toward Skinner.

"I'm not going to let you go and infect more people," says Skinner.

"You're gonna let me do whatever I wanna do," he says menacingly. "Dr. Voss here tells me you need me. You need me to save your boy." Weaver takes out a cigarette and puts it between his lips.

"Don't do it," says Skinner.

"They say these things kill people, you know? Any brand, sooner or later. You know, it doesn't have to be that way. I think Dr. Voss is really on to something with his research. I do."

Voss says, "It's over, Weaver. I'm through."

Weaver says, "Come on. You gotta figure, the first car killed a buncha people before they perfected it. 'Cause it's all just part of the scientific process, you know." He lights his lighter.

Skinner warns Weaver that he will shoot him. Weaver pauses for a long moment.

"No, you won't." He lights his cigarette. "I'm a regular damn scientific marvel. They're going to study me. They're gonna write scientific papers about me. I could be the cure for cancer. Me. Darrel Weaver." Weaver appears despondent. "You ain't gonna shoot me. Toodles."

Weaver walks toward the door. Suddenly Skinner fires. Weaver takes a hit in the shoulder and goes down. His burning cigarette tumbles to the floor as Skinner steps over and crushes the cigarette underfoot.

•

Paramedics bring Weaver into the hospital. Skinner is with them. Scully meets them as they race Weaver through the hallway.

"How's Mulder?" asks Skinner.

"Not good."

Scully takes a quick look at Weaver and orders bloodwork. As they prepare to move him off the gurney, Scully spots Weaver's hand.

"Wait a minute," she says, looking closely at Weaver's nicotine-stained fingertips. "Get me thirty milligrams of methyl pyrrolidine."

"Nicotine?" asks the doctor.

"Yeah. I think this could save Mulder's life."

•

Two weeks later, Scully enters Mulder's office to find him at the computer. He appears weak.

"Hey. Good to be back?" asks Scully.

"Beats the alternative." Mulder's voice is still raspy, barely above a whisper.

"Well, you'll be interested to know Morley Tobacco has subpoenaed all of our files on the case. They seem extremely interested in your recovery."

"What about Darrel Weaver?"

"He's well enough to be moved to the hospital ward at Raleigh Correctional."

"So it was nicotine itself that was keeping him alive?"

Scully says, "His fingertips were stained yellow with it. He was a four-pack-a-day smoker, far heavier than any of the focus group members who died. You know, nicotine is extremely poisonous. It's actually one of the oldest known insecticides."

Mulder says, "Good for killing tobacco beetles."

"Once we loaded your system up with enough of it, it acted as a sort of chemotherapy, except it almost stopped your breathing at the same time."

"That's not all it did," says Mulder as he crosses to his desk, opens his drawer, and holds up a pack of Morley Reds cigarettes. "I bought these on my way to work."

Scully is aghast. "You're not going to start smoking."

Mulder sniffs the pack. "They say the addiction is stronger than heroin."

Scully looks at him sternly. "Mulder." A long beat, and then Mulder tosses the cigarettes into the trash.

"Good," says Scully. "Skinner's waiting for us in his office."

"I'll be right up."

Scully leaves. Mulder looks at the cigarette package in the trash—tempted.

BACK STORY:

It has been the rare *X-File* episode that has been torn, literally, from the headlines. But "Brand X" succeeded in walking the delicate line between reality and fantasy and—at least for the space of an hour-long episode—created a nicotine-stained world in which flesh-eating tobacco beetles and corrupt and greedy corporations combined to create a very real horror.

Adding to the equation that would ultimately become the episode "Brand X" was the appreciation among the writing staff, in particular Greg Walker and Steven Maeda, for the movie *The Insider*, which took a hard look at the tobacco industry. The early stages of the brainstorming process were spearheaded by Maeda's idea for a tale about the horrifying aspects of overeating. But since the early-season episode "Hungry" had covered similar territory, the consensus was that the corporate evil that populates the cigarette industry would be a better and more timely target.

Greg Walker recalls that the grotesque vision of people smoking cigarettes and then coughing up flesh-eating tobacco beetles was a popular notion among the writers. "But we did not want to make it complete science fiction but rather something that had a foot in the real world. We wanted to use 'Brand X' to take a look at the tobacco business but not go down the standard route of corporate evil. We wanted to find the emotional core of the story, the struggling scientist and the surviving experimental test subject. Once we found those two characters, the story came together quickly."

But the episode was not without some significant logistical obstacles. David Duchovny and Gillian Anderson had both recently directed ("Hollywood A.D." and "all things," respectively) and were, at the moment, in active postproduction and so would only be available for a limited amount of time for "Brand X." In writing "Brand X," Walker and Maeda were faced with the challenge of constructing a story that would allow Mulder and Scully to be in fewer scenes together.

"Mulder getting sick in Act Two and being in a hospital bed for Acts Three and Four was the direct result of his limited amount of time," acknowledges Walker. "It was easier to shoot a bunch of stuff of him in bed than having him have to be in a lot of different locations."

The result was that A.D. Walter Skinner was able to get out from behind his desk and into the thick of "Brand X"'s action.

" 'Brand X' was probably the most activity that I've had this season," says Mitch Pileggi. "It was great to actually have Skinner getting out into the field and involved in a real X-File."

Production designer Corey Kaplan was handed a multifaceted challenge. With smoking as the overriding theme of the episode, a color scheme heavy on yellows and browns, in order to give each scene a perpetually smoky look, was required. But it was her long familiarity with the way episode director Kim Manners liked to shoot (they've worked together on nearly two seasons' worth of episodes over the last five years) that gave Kaplan the idea to enhance the cigarette company's corporate offices with long hallways and sets heavy on texture and grit.

Needless to say, "Brand X" was most conspicuous for its "gross-out" scenes of bug-induced death. The showstopper was the sequence in which the complaining man is discovered with thousands of bugs crawling all over him. The 3,000 bugs crawling over the body of actor Michael Hungerford were real. Because of the challenge of working with live bugs, this brief sequence took a full day to shoot. The bugs crawling out of the mouth of the dead Brimley and those sucked out of Mulder's throat were a combination of CGI and dummy bugs.

Producer Harry Bring recalled that the bug-infested sequences were often tedious, hours-long exercises in patience. "Bugs don't take direction very well, so you pretty much have to wait until they decide to get it right."

In both story concept and visual tone, "Brand X" was a throwback to the early seasons of *The X-Files*: moody, savvy, and a shining example of the "extreme plausibility" elements that have gone into the best *X-Files* episodes.

FACTS:

Actor Tobin Bell, who portrays Ashman, had a guest shot in an early episode of *Harsh Realm*, which was also directed by Kim Manners and created by Chris Carter.

After a long search by Paul Rabwin for the appropriate clip, a snippet from the war movie *Guadalcanal Diary* was used.

episode 7X18

HOLLYWOOD A.D.

EPISODE: 7X18
FIRST AIRED: April 30, 2000
EDITOR: Lynne Willingham
WRITTEN AND DIRECTED BY:
David Duchovny

An X-File becomes the plot of a Hollywood movie. But Mulder and Scully find their case—and themselves—distorted on the big screen.

GUEST STARS:

Mitch Pileggi (A.D. Skinner)
Garry Shandling (Garry Shandling)
Téa Leoni (Téa Leoni)
Harris Yulin (Cardinal Augustine O'Fallon)
Wayne Federman (Wayne Federman)
Paul Lieber (Micah Hoffman)
Bill Dow (Chuck Burks)
Tim Roe (Zombie)
Barry K. Thomas (Sugar Bear)
Tina M. Ameduri (Tina the Craft Service Woman)
Bill Millar (Director)

PRINCIPAL SETTINGS:

Washington, D.C.; Hollywood, California

The world is in letterbox format in a tombstone-filled graveyard. Shots are fired as a man dives behind a tombstone, a small ceramic bowl cradled under his arm. He fires back. Out of the dark and mist comes the taunting voice of . . .

. . . the Cigarette-Smoking Pontiff. "Give it up, Mulder. You've got no chance. My sniper zombies are everywhere."

A group of heavily armed, decomposing zombies deploy over the graveyard, their weapons trained on the mystery man behind the tombstone. The Cigarette-Smoking Pontiff reveals himself in the robes of a Catholic cardinal. A redheaded Scully, who looks a lot like Téa Leoni, is in his clutches.

"I'll offer you a deal. You give me the Lazarus Bowl and I'll give you Scully."

"Mulder," Leoni/Scully calls. A quick cut back to Mulder, who looks a lot like Garry Shandling.

Mulder/Shandling says, "How 'bout this deal. You give me Scully, I don't smash the Lazarus Bowl and shove the pieces where the sun of God don't shine, you cigarette-smoking mackerel snapper!" He rises from behind the tombstone and raises the bowl above his head.

The zombie snipers lower their weapons. The CSP, holding a gun to Leoni/Scully's head, and Shandling/Mulder slowly advance on each other.

"I break the Lazarus Bowl," Shandling/Mulder continues, "and all your sniper zombies go back to being good little well-behaved corpses."

"You don't fool me, Mulder. That bowl is your Holy Grail. Encoded in its ancient ceramic grooves are the words Jesus spake when he raised Lazarus from the dead, still capable of raising the dead two thousand years later. Proof positive of the paranormal. You could no sooner destroy that than let the redhead die."

The CSP cocks his gun. Shandling/Mulder readies to drop the bowl.

One of the zombies says, "C'mon, man, don't break the bowl. We don't wanna go back to being dead. There's no food, no women, no dancing. Save the bowl and we'll dump that ciggy-smoking stooge for you. And you'll be the new king of the dead."

Shandling/Mulder says, "I'd rather serve in heaven than rule in hell."

He tosses the Lazarus Bowl up in the air. The zombies race toward the bowl. Shandling/Mulder races toward the CSP. Leoni/Scully strips the CSP of his gun and trains it on him. A zombie settles under the Lazarus Bowl. Leoni/Scully turns and fires at the bowl, blasting it into a thousand pieces. Shandling/Mulder charges forward, CSP grabs Leoni/Scully, and the two agents go tumbling down a hill, into an open grave with a casket in it. The lid of the casket closes.

There is a black screen and the sound of heavy breathing.

"Is that your flashlight, Mulder, or are you just happy to be lying on top of me?"

"My flashlight," says Mulder as the camera pulls back to reveal we are looking at a movie screen at the Daryl Zanuck Theatre in Hollywood, California. The flashlight illuminates the casket. "Oh, that," says Shandling/Mulder. The audience roars with laughter. "Seven long years I've been waiting for just the right moment, Scully."

"You're a sick man, Mulder . . . go on."

"I love you, Scully. No ifs, ands, or—"

"Bees." Leoni/Scully kisses him hard.

We see the audience as we hear the sounds of Shandling/Mulder and Leoni/Scully making love. The audience includes Garry Shandling, Téa Leoni, and Minnie Driver eating popcorn out of promotional Lazarus Bowls. Everybody seems to love the film.

Everybody except the real Scully, who is staring silently at the screen, her mouth wide in disbelief. And the real Mulder, who is holding his head in his hands in abject humiliation. He turns his attention a few rows forward to A.D. Skinner, who turns around, beaming. Mulder looks back at the screen and just shakes his head.

"IS THAT YOUR FLASHLIGHT, MULDER, OR ARE YOU JUST HAPPY TO BE LYING ON TOP OF ME?"—Leoni/Scully

•

Eighteen months earlier.

Skinner is briefing Mulder and Scully on a new case.

Skinner says, "Yesterday a small pipe bomb ripped through the crypt of Christ's Church here in D.C. There were no casualties. No thefts. No note making any demand."

Sitting behind the two agents is Wayne Federman, a slick Hollywood type in his early forties.

"Who's taking credit for it?" Scully asks.

"Nobody," says Skinner.

Federman speaks into a small tape recorder. "She: Jodie Foster's foster child on a Payless budget. He's like a Jehovah's Witness meets Harrison Ford's *Witness*." Scully and Mulder turn to look at him, then back at Skinner.

"Christ's Church. Isn't that Cardinal O'Fallon's church?" asks Scully.

"Yes. O'Fallon's residence is adjacent to the crypt."

Mulder wants to know who Cardinal O'Fallon is. Federman speaks another description into his recorder. "Cardinal Oh-Fallen, perhaps." His cell phone starts to ring.

"He's one of the most powerful men in the Church today," Scully says. "His name often comes up as a possibility for the first American Pope."

Mulder says, "I don't want to be myopic here, sir, but this looks like a straight-up terrorist act for the ATF—"

"Myopic," Federman echoes into his recorder as his phone continues to ring.

"Yes, it does," prompts Skinner.

Federman's cell phone is still ringing. Mulder can't stand this intrusion.

"Are you gonna answer your phone?" he asks.

"I didn't want to be rude," he says, answering it at last.

"Sir, who the hell is this guy?"

"This is Wayne Federman. He's an old buddy of mine from college. He's a writer out in Hollywood now and he's working on an FBI-based movie. He's asked me to give him access."

"A screenwriter?" asks Scully.

"Actually, it's writer-slash-producer," says Federman.

Mulder says, "Well, that's actually just a hindrance-slash-pain in the neck."

"Yo, yo, yo . . . Agent Mulder? I don't want to eat your lunch. I'm just here for some procedural flavor, just a taste," explains Federman.

"I have no idea what you just said," Mulder says.

"The Skinman's filled me in on your particular bent. He said that you come at things a little fahkakte, a little *Star Trek*-y. Which is the exact vibe I'm looking for for this thing I'm doing, it's a *Silence of the Lambs* meets *Greatest Story Ever Told* type thing. It's beautiful and . . . I will not be in your way. I'll be strictly Heisenbergian, a hologram."

Mulder looks at Scully.

Skinner says, "Agent Mulder, Mr. Federman will accompany you today to Christ's Church, where he will act as an observer on this case. You will extend to him every courtesy and protection that you would a friend of mine and a friend of the Bureau's. Agent Scully, I require your services here for the morning." This last sentence makes Federman raise an eyebrow.

"Sir, have I pissed you off in a way that's more than normal?" Mulder asks.

•

Mulder and Federman pull up to Christ's Church just as Federman says, "I was just wondering if she's more than your partner."

"No, Wayne," says Mulder firmly as he cuts the engine. The pair meet with Cardinal Augustine O'Fallon, a powerful, vital man in his mid-sixties.

Mulder asks, "Cardinal O'Fallon, can you think of anyone who might make an attempt on your life?"

"The Church always has enemies, Agent Mulder."

"Only myself. There are half a mile of catacombs here. I like to walk here during lunch."

They enter the crypt, where they see evidence of the bomb blast. "That's where the bomb went off," says O'Fallon.

"My instinct, Cardinal, is to see this desecration of the dead less as a murder attempt and more as a terrorist act, a message—"

A cell phone rings. Mulder glares at Federman, who claims it's not his. Mulder pulls out his phone. It, too, is silent. O'Fallon pulls a cell phone out of his robes.

"Not me. I never get reception here."

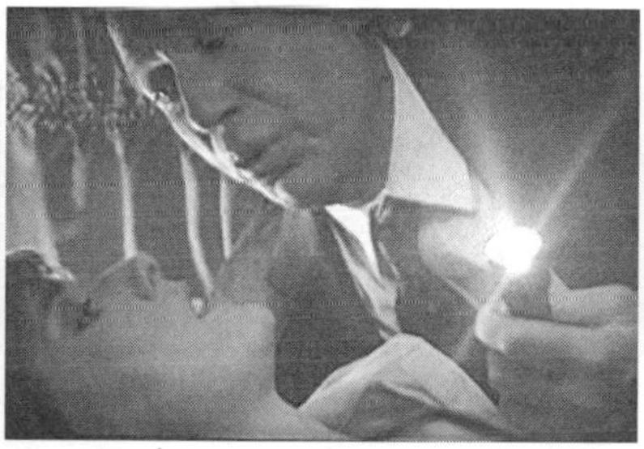

"The size of the bomb would have limited its destruction to just the crypt itself. Is there anything down there worth targeting?"

"Not really. Just some old bones, artifacts, relics, documents that we store down there in the cold. We like to think of it as God's refrigerator."

Federman says, "That's a great line."

"Thank you," O'Fallon says.

"God's refrigerator," he says into his recorder.

"Wayne, shut up," says Mulder.

O'Fallon leads Mulder and Federman down a staircase into the basement of the church.

"No treasures to the outside world. Things of negligible monetary value but great spiritual value to the Church . . . ancient devotional texts, medieval relics," O'Fallon says.

"How 'bout the Shroud of Turin?" asks Federman.

"No, afraid not. But we do have the bathrobe of St. Peter."

"You're kidding," says Federman.

O'Fallon says, "Yes, I am."

"That's a good line."

"Wayne, shut up," says Mulder.

"Who comes down to the crypt here?" asks Mulder.

Mulder bends down and pulls some stones away. The ringing gets louder. He pulls more stones away, revealing a human hand. Mulder digs feverishly and reveals the body of a man, crushed to death by the fallen rock.

"Would that be St. Jude's cell phone, Cardinal?" Federman asks.

Mulder recognizes the dead man as . . .

"No! That's Micah Hoffman," says Mulder, reaching to shut off the cell phone.

•

Mulder, Scully, and Federman are walking through the Adams Morgan district of D.C.

Mulder says, "Micah Hoffman, Willie Mays, and Frank Serpico. That's my Holy Trinity, Scully."

"Of course, I'm too young to remember, but wasn't he some kind of sixties campus radical, like a Jerry Rubin or Mario Savio?"

"Name a sixties counterculture movement and Micah Hoffman was at or near the center of it. He was one of the original Weathermen, he was the first Yippie, he was a better poet than Ginsberg, and he was also the starting shortstop for his Columbia baseball team."

"Then in the seventies didn't he go real low profile?" asks Federman.

"Yeah, right after Altamont," says Mulder. "He was never really heard from again."

Federman says, "The Stones get blamed for everything. I don't get it."

They stop at the door to a rundown house. Mulder knocks.

He asks Scully, "What did Skinner want you for this morning?"

"Just paperwork." Federman raises his eyebrows.

There is no answer. Mulder jimmies the door and they enter the home of Micah Hoffman. Mulder and Scully take in the mess, a mind-bending collection of '60s posters and artifacts.

"Mulder, we should have a warrant," says Scully.

Federman says, "Hey, it's only the constitution, no big deal . . . Ooh . . . it's feng shui."

They spot what appears to be a crude bomb-making setup.

"Mulder, sorry to denigrate a third of your trinity, but it looks like Hoffman was killed by one of his own bombs," says Scully, walking over to a table full of bomb-making equipment.

"Well, from Dharma bum to Dharma bomb," Federman says.

They notice a draftsman's table, bottles of ink, and cans of a turpentine-looking substance.

"I knew Hoffman was a master potter," Mulder says.

"It appears he was a master calligrapher as well," adds Scully. "Look, Mulder, you've got gum Arabic and sodium hydroxide here. These would be used to age the ink and the paper prematurely. It's a forger's trick."

"Well, from counterculture to counterfeiter," Federman says.

Mulder says, "All right, one more pun and I pull out my gun."

Mulder notices some old, yellowed documents.

"Scully, look at that. 'Christos.' Looks like a religious text. Can you read Greek at all?" asks Mulder.

"It's pretty rusty. But it looks like some kind of lost Gospel, a Gospel of Mary Magdalene, and an account of Christ's life on earth after the resurrection. These are heretical texts, Mulder, mythical I should say, but long rumored to be in existence."

Mulder speculates what Hoffman would be doing with the texts.

"I think the question is, what would Hoffman be doing forging them?"

Federman says, "I think the real question, Agents, is what might O'Fallon be doing with Hoffman's forgeries. You don't need a Weatherman to know which way the wind blows."

•

Mulder and Federman return to the church that night and enter the crypt.

"I like the way you guys work," says Federman. "No warrants, no permission, no research. You're like studio executives with guns. Should I call you Agent Mulder or Mr. Mulder? Do you have a nickname or something like that?"

Mulder hears a skittering sound and shushes Wayne. He shines his light at the source of the sound and sees a skeleton lying in its place.

"Like Skinman?" Federman continues. Mulder doesn't respond. "Just ignore me."

They come upon a cache of old documents, similar to those found in Hoffman's apartment.

"Looks like the same Gospel of Mary Scully ID'd over at Hoffman's place," says Mulder.

Federman wants to know if what they're looking at is a forgery or the real thing.

"There is no real Gospel of Mary, Federman. The original would be a fake."

"All right, so is this a real fake or a fake fake?"

Federman's cell phone goes off, startling both of them. He walks away, trying to get better reception.

"You're breaking up. Lemme call you back. Okay. I'm going through a crypt."

Federman hangs up. He turns to see a skull pass by on two leg bones. He lets out a gasp.

He drops the flashlight and jumps back, then looks down and sees the flashlight in the grasp of a skeleton hand, which is racing, alongside a skull, toward broken bits of pottery. It reaches the fragments, and various bones attempt to put the pieces back together.

Federman says, "Oh my God."

•

Mulder, Scully, and Federman meet at a diner the next morning to recount the previous evening's incident and to inspect the pieces of pottery.

Scully says, "Now, Wayne, I'm sure that it was dark in there. Your eyes were playing tricks on you. And you've been influenced by ghost stories and horror movies that take place in crypts and graveyards and you hallucinated this vision of these dancing bones trying to reconstruct this bowl."

"I didn't hallucinate. That was mechanical or CGI," says Federman.

Mulder says, "Federman, that wasn't a movie, that was real life."

"The difference being? Well, I have got my flavor here, so I appreciate all your help. I've got a movie to write," Federman says.

Mulder asks, "You're leaving? You don't wanna get to the bottom of this?"

"Not especially," says Federman.

"Well, you know, sometimes truth can be stranger than fiction."

"Well, fiction's quicker than truth and cheaper. You want my advice? You're both crazy."

"Why do you say that?" Mulder asks.

Federman looks at him. "You're crazy for believing what you believe."

He turns to Scully. "And you're crazy for not believing what he believes. I'll leave you with that. Thank you."

He leaves.

"I miss him already," says Mulder.

"You know, Mulder, I know that Federman's BSing you, so I'm really hesitant to mention this, but his story reminds me of the Lazarus Bowl."

"The Lazarus Bowl?"

"We had this wacky nun in Catholic school, Sister Callahan. We used to call her Sister Spooky 'cause she would tell us scary stories all the time."

"Twisted sister . . . my kinda nun, you know," says Mulder.

"She would hold up an old piece of wood with a rusty nail in it and she would say, 'This is an actual piece of the cross that Christ's wrist was nailed to,' or she'd show us a vial of red liquid and say that it was John the Baptist's blood or something."

"She'd be in prison today. You realize that."

"She would tell the story of when Jesus raised Lazarus from the dead, and she said that there was this old woman, Lazarus's aunt or something—"

"Lazarus's aunt?"

"—who was spinning a clay bowl on a wheel nearby and that Christ's words, the actual incantation to raise the dead, were recorded in the clay grooves of the pottery, just like the way music is recorded into vinyl."

"See, it's just not true that you can't get good science in Catholic school. It's a lie."

Scully says, "Well, Sister Spooky said that these words in the clay still had the power to raise the dead, just like Jesus raised Lazarus."

"That is a very cool story coming from you, Scully," says Mulder, adding, "I'll have Chuck Burks meet you over at my office to see if this clay has Christ's greatest hits on it and I'm going to go have another audience with Cardinal O'Fallon."

•

Scully meets with Chuck Burks in Mulder's office. He lectures Scully about ambient sound and tonal keys as he examines the fragments of pottery on a high-tech scanning table, as multicolored lights strobe over it.

"You see, this is my voice bouncing around in the red here," he explains to Scully, pointing to a monitor. "And all this yellow is ambient sound that we habitually tune out—the hum of my hardware, Mulder's porn tapes on pause, sounds from the street. Everything we hear but we don't know we hear I can hear with this machine.

Suddenly he whips off his headphones, the sound of a church organ rattling his senses.

"Who made this?" he asks.

Scully says, "We're not sure. Either a forger by the name of Micah Hoffman or . . . or someone else in the vicinity of Jesus Christ."

Burks laughs, then sees the seriousness in Scully's face.

"Well, whoever did it is some kind of musical genius. This clay is vibrating at all the keys at once. It's heavenly," says Burks.

•

Mulder has gone to Christ's Church. He shows Cardinal O'Fallon some of the forged pages recovered from Hoffman's apartment. O'Fallon assumes Mulder recovered them from the crypt. Mulder asks if the cardinal can translate them for him. O'Fallon begins to read.

"Did you buy these from Micah Hoffman?" asks Mulder.

"I thought they were real," says O'Fallon.

"I can understand that, sir. Hoffman was a master. My partner had these analyzed and they're virtually indistinguishable from the real thing. The paper is authentic, the ink, the hand, the diction, everything. Hoffman was also an explosives expert. Do you have any idea what he might have been doing with a bomb in the crypt? Can you think of anybody who might have wanted to kill Micah Hoffman?"

"No."

Mulder asks, "Why were you hiding the document, sir?"

"When Micah came to me with these—as I then thought—ancient texts and our experts verified them, he exploded a bomb in my heart. The Christ that lived was not the Christ in these texts."

"So you bought them in order to hide them," says Mulder.

"To keep others from feeling the despair and the anger that I felt. To protect people from what I can now see they needed no protection from."

"And then Jesus took his beloved Mary Magdalene in an embrace. An embrace not of God and woman but of man and woman. And Jesus said to Mary: 'Love the body for it is all of the soul that our senses can perceive.' "

Mulder shows O'Fallon all the documents he has found and tells him they are all forgeries. O'Fallon is surprised.

"Why didn't you just destroy the documents yourself?"

"I thought they were real. I hated them. I despised them. I would've liked to destroy them but I couldn't. Is being made a fool of a crime, Agent Mulder?"

"I'd be doing life if it were, sir."

•

Mulder is driving through the city. He punches in a number on his cell phone.

"Hey, Scully, it's me. Can you horn in on the Hoffman autopsy for me?

Scully wants to know why.

Mulder says, "I got a feeling Hoffman was dead before he died. He was blackmailing O'Fallon with those forgeries. Maybe O'Fallon retaliated."

"Mulder, this bowl. Your buddy Chuck Burks says that it has properties he's never seen before."

Mulder's other line beeps. He puts Scully on hold and is surprised to hear . . .

"Agent Mulder, it's Wayne-slash-Federman out in LA."

Federman is driving a convertible around the streets of LA.

"I can't really talk about the case."

"That's okay. Skinman's keeping me in the loop. Listen, who do you see playing you in the movie?"

"I'm in the movie?"

"It's a character loosely based on you, it's more of an amalgamation," says Federman.

Mulder puts Federman on hold and clicks Scully back on the line.

"Hey, Sister Spooky, I gotta take this."

"I'll call you after the autopsy," says Scully.

He returns to Federman, offering a suggestion of Richard Gere for the Mulder role. Federman laughs and throws back the name of Garry Shandling.

•

Scully is in the autopsy room, working on the body of Micah Hoffman. She chronicles the bodily damage and removes the heart. As she takes the heart to the hanging scale, Hoffman's body suddenly sits up.

His eyes open.

Hoffman says, "I'm gonna need that when you're done with it."

"My God." Scully jumps as Hoffman rises off the autopsy table and starts stretching in front of her.

Scully says, "Who are you?"

"I am who I am."

Scully, scalpel in hand, tries to touch Hoffman. He brushes the scalpel out of her hand and onto the floor. "*Noli me tangere*, baby," says Hoffman. Scully nervously bends to pick up the scalpel, accidentally cutting herself. Her fingertip starts to bleed. She rises and looks to where Hoffman was standing. He is gone.

Scully turns and sees Micah Hoffman's body lying on the autopsy table.

•

A little later, Mulder walks into the autopsy room, where he finds a still shaken Scully sitting next to the dissected body of Hoffman.

"What'd you find, Scully?" asks Mulder.

"In Micah Hoffman's stomach, there were traces of red wine and strychnine."

"Man, oh, Manischevitz. Communion wine, I bet. I bet O'Fallon poisoned Hoffman and

"TWISTED SISTER...MY KINDA NUN, YOU KNOW."—Mulder

"You're breaking up," says Mulder. "It sounded like you said Garry Shandling."

"Garry Shandling's signed on to play the amalgamation loosely based on you and Téa Leoni's playing the amalgamation loosely based on your partner, you stud. The movie's called *The Lazarus Bowl*."

"How do you know about the Lazarus Bowl?"

"The Skinman. Listen, Shandling and Leoni want to meet you guys, get your flavor, it's an actor-type thing. Come on out to the studio on our dime. We'll make it nice."

Mulder wants to know who's playing Skinner in the movie.

"Richard Gere."

then placed his body near the explosion to cover his tracks."

"It's possible, Mulder."

He says, "I could get a warrant for O'Fallon."

•

Mulder and Scully enter Christ's Church, where Cardinal O'Fallon is conducting Mass. They are there to arrest him. Mulder moves forward but is held back by Scully.

"Mulder, let's allow the man some dignity."

As O'Fallon finishes up the Mass, Scully's attention wanders to a three-foot-high crucifix on a nearby wall. She bows her head and genuflects, then looks back to the crucifix, where she sees a three-foot-high version of

Micah Hoffman, very much alive, nailed to the cross. The mini-Hoffman stares directly at Scully and murmurs, "*Consummatum est.*"

Scully freaks out but manages to shake off the fear. She looks back at the crucifix. The image of Hoffman is gone. Scully tells Mulder, "Let's get this over with," and they advance on the cardinal.

Mulder says, "Augustine O'Fallon, you are under arrest for the murder of Micah Hoffman."

As Mulder handcuffs O'Fallon and reads him his rights, Scully's attention is drawn to a man entering the church.

"Oh my God," says Scully at the sight of Micah Hoffman advancing on them.

"Mulder, do you see what I see?"

"Yes, I do."

"Is that Micah Hoffman?" she asks.

"Yes," answers O'Fallon, "it is."

•

Mulder and Scully are in Skinner's office, where they are being read the riot act.

"Misidentification of a corpse and subsequent unrequested autopsy," says Skinner.

Scully says, "Sir, the dead man looked very much like Micah Hoffman. He had Hoffman's ID on him."

"Agent Scully, if I'm carrying Marilyn Monroe's purse, do you assume that I slept with JFK?

"Agent Mulder," Skinner continues, "the FBI has always prided itself on the speedy expedition of its cases, but this is the first time—and I hope you're as proud of this as I am—that we've ever attempted to pursue a murder case while the victim was still alive and healthy."

Mulder says, "A bomb went off, a crime's been committed. There's a dead body nobody seems to give a damn about. O'Fallon has been less than forthcoming. And Hoffman, at the very least, is guilty of forgery and extortion."

"Agent Mulder, you will leave O'Fallon alone," Skinner instructs. "You will leave Hoffman alone. And Agent Scully, you will put your trigger-happy scalpel away. Best-case scenario, you get to keep your jobs. Worst-case, O'Fallon and the Church bring a huge, embarrassing lawsuit against the Bureau, which will feature you two as its sacrificial lambs. As of right now, I am forcing you to take a four-week leave effective immediately pending review."

•

Mulder and Scully walk into Mulder's office.

Mulder says, "I think this whole Richard Gere thing is going to Skinner's head."

"We're off this case, Mulder."

They hear a strange noise coming from the back of Mulder's office and find Chuck Burks working on the pottery.

Burks says, "*Compadres.* I teased out something very fabulous from your pottery there, layered in under the ambience. There. Guess what language that is?"

"Chuck, I've had a bad day," Mulder says.

"It's a dead language. I had a linguist in here to listen to the recording. It's Aramaic."

Scully says, "That's the language Christ spoke. Did your linguist happen to translate it?"

Burks plays a bit of sound. "Yes, he did. It's in two parts. The first part here . . . roughly translates as 'I am the Walrus. I am the Walrus. Paul is dead, coocoocachoo.' Although there is no Aramaic word for walrus, so literally it says, 'I am the bearded cowlike sea beast.' "

"What's the second part?" Mulder asks.
Burks plays a different sound. "The second part is a little freakier."
"What is it?" asks Scully.
"It appears to be one man commanding another to rise from the dead."
"Lazarus?" says Scully.

•

Mulder and Scully go to Micah Hoffman's apartment, where they confront the very much alive former revolutionary.
Hoffman says, "I am become Jesus Christ." He laughs.
"I am become skeptical," responds Mulder.
Hoffman says, "There I was totally bumming after Altamont and I thought, throw in the towel and go to law school or continue the fight and become a forger of scandalous religious documents."
"I suppose that's a choice every young gifted American male is faced with," Mulder says.
"I knew O'Fallon from college," Hoffman continues. "He was a divinity professor of mine."

"AGENT SCULLY, IF I'M CARRYING MARILYN MONROE'S PURSE, DO YOU ASSUME THAT I SLEPT WITH JFK?"—Skinner

"At Columbia?" asks Mulder.
"Yeah. And he's a decent man, but with an overweening pride and sense of responsibility borne of a fundamental lack of respect for the human animal. He believes in God, but not in man. In man's ability to choose, to live in freedom. He has Christ in his brain but not in his heart."
Scully asks, "So you created a Christ in these forgeries that was more suited to your particular worldview?"
"Yeah. But before I could write like Christ, I had to become him in much the same way I imagine an actor who plays a part becomes that part. So I immersed myself in Jesus Christ. Not just the Church and the teachings, but the man, the custom of his time, the language, the vibe, the feeling of Christ."
Scully asks why O'Fallon and the elders didn't go outside the Church to authenticate the documents.
"Because the forgeries were too damning to the Church, they couldn't risk the exposure. But then something truly weird came over me."
"Remorse?" asks Scully.
"Conversion, Agent Scully. The lightning bolt that transformed Saul into Paul on the road to Damascus. One day I was not just impersonating Jesus Christ. I had become him. That's why I blew up the crypt. These forgeries were blasphemous and needed to be destroyed."
Mulder asks, "How did your cell phone get on the dead man in the crypt?"
"God works in mysterious ways."

•

Unable to sleep, Mulder is on his couch watching the movie *Plan 9 From Outer Space*, speaking every word of dialogue along with the film. There is a knock on the door. It is Scully.
"Couldn't sleep either, huh?" asks Mulder. "*Plan 9 From Outer Space*?"
"It's the Ed Wood investigative method. This movie is so profoundly bad in such a childlike way that it hypnotizes my conscious critical mind and frees up my right brain to make associo-poetic leaps. And I started flashing on Hoffman and O'Fallon. Now there's this archetypical relationship, like Hoffman's Jesus to O'Fallon's Judas or Hoffman's Jesus to O'Fallon's Dostoevsky's Grand Inquisitor or Hoffman's Jesus to O'Fallon's St. Paul."
"How about Hoffman's Road Runner to O'Fallon's Wile E. Coyote? Mulder, do you think it's at all possible that Hoffman is really Jesus Christ?"
Mulder thinks Scully is making fun of him. She insists that she is not.
"No, I don't. But crazy people can be very persuasive."
"Well, yes, I know *that*." They share a smile. "Maybe true faith is really a form of insanity."
"Are you directing that at me?"
"No. I'm directing it at myself. And at Ed Wood."
Mulder says, "Well, you know, even a broken clock is right seven hundred and thirty times a year."

Scully is about to ask how many times Mulder has seen the movie when he responds forty-two.

"You've seen this movie forty-two times? Doesn't that make you sad? It makes me sad."

"You know, Scully, we've got four weeks probation vacation and nothing to do. And Wayne Federman's invited us out to LA to watch his movie being filmed, and God knows I could use a little sunshine, Scully."

"California, here we come," says Scully.

•

Mulder and Scully have arrived in Hollywood and walk onto the soundstage, where the movie based loosely on their exploits is being made. The agents wander past equipment, lights, cameras, and an elaborate graveyard set.

"Most of the time."

"Wardrobe!"

Shandling walks away. The now winded Scully joins up with Mulder and they watch a scene about to be shot. The assistant director yells into a megaphone, "Rollando."

"Come on now, kick it in the ass and . . . action, zombies!" says the director.

A zombie grabs Leoni and bites into her shoulder. Suddenly the zombie begins to gag.

"What is this?" says the zombie.

The director yells cut.

The assistant director yells through the megaphone, "What seems to be the problem, Mr. Zombie, sir?"

"What the hell is this? What the hell is in my mouth? What's Téa Leoni's shoulder made out of?"

"SCULLY, SKINMAN IS CALLING ME FROM A BUBBLE BATH."—Mulder
"IT'S STILL ME, MULDER."—Skinner

Federman spots Mulder and Scully and rushes up to them, kissing Mulder on the cheek, Hollywood style.

"Agents! So glad you could hang. C'mon, I want you to meet the people who are gonna play you. Garry Shandling, Téa Leoni, this is Agents Mulder and Scully."

There are handshakes and greetings all around.

"You know," says Leoni, "while I've got you here, maybe you could show me how to run in these things?" She points to her high-heeled shoes. "Right over here . . ."

Scully and Leoni walk off to another part of the studio and Scully runs back and forth to show Leoni how it's done. Shandling looks Mulder up and down for a moment.

He asks, "Seriously, could I ask you something? Do you dress to the left or to the right?"

"What do you mean?" Mulder laughs.

"Look, when I play a character, I need to find his center, his sort of rudder, so to say, and then everything comes from that," says Shandling, looking pointedly at Mulder's crotch.

Mulder looks uncomfortable. "I guess mostly to the left."

Shandling laughs, then grows serious. "Mostly?"

The assistant director yells across the set to craft services, wanting to know what Téa Leoni's shoulder is made of.

Tina, the craft services woman, steps forward. "Turkey, just like you asked for."

The zombie says, "Tofurkey! I asked for Tofurkey! I'm a vegetarian! Half the zombies are vegetarian! Oh my God!"

He runs off and yells, "The people are made out of turkey!"

•

Some weeks later, in her room at the Hotel Beverly Ernesto, Scully is luxuriating in a bubble bath. She rings up Mulder.

"Hey, Mulder, it's me. What are you doing?"

"I'm working at the computer," he says. "What are you doing?"

"I'm packing, just getting ready for our trip back to D.C. tomorrow."

"You know, Scully, I was just thinking about Lazarus, Ed Wood, and those Tofurkey-eatin' zombies. How come when people come back from the dead, they always want to hurt the living?"

We see that Mulder has been lying. He is also taking a bath.

Scully launches into a theory involving repressed cannibalistic and sexual fears and desires. Mulder says that zombie eating might be the first stage of doing all the things they missed doing when they were alive, followed by drinking, dancing, and making love.

Scully says, "Oh, I see. So it's just that we never get to stay with them long enough to see the gentler side of the undead."

"Exactly," says Mulder.

Mulder's phone beeps. "Hold on a second, that's my other line. Hello?"

"Agent Mulder, it's Assistant Director Skinner. I hope I didn't catch you at a bad time."

"No, sir. I'm just at the computer," says Mulder.

"I just wanted to apologize for coming down so hard on you during the Hoffman-slash-O'Fallon case," says Skinner.

"I appreciate that, Skinman."

"Don't call me that."

Mulder says, "Yes, sir. Where are you now?"

"I'm right underneath you," says Skinner, also in a bathtub. "I'm in LA in the same hotel as you. Right below you and Agent Scully. Federman got me an associate producer credit on the movie."

"A.*P.* Skinner, huh? So what are you up to right now, sir?"

"I'm taking a bubble bath," says Skinner.

"Hold on just one second, sir," says Mulder as he clicks back over to Scully. "Hey, Scully, Skinman is calling me from a bubble bath."

"It's still me, Mulder," Skinner replies.

"Uh . . . sorry. Hold on just one second, sir." He clicks over again. "Scully? Skinner is calling me from a bubble bath."

"Wow, he's really gone Hollywood."

"Totally."

"You know, Mulder, speaking of Hollywood, I think Téa Leoni has a little crush on you."

"Yeah, right, like Téa Leoni's ever gonna have a crush on me."

Scully says, "I think that Shandling likes you a bit, too."

"Really?"

•

Sixteen months later, Mulder and Scully are back in LA at the humiliation of the movie's premiere. On the screen, the love scene between Shandling and Leoni continues when, suddenly, Leoni breaks out of the clinch.

"Wait, Mulder, I can't."

Shandling says, "I know it feels wrong because we're friends and we treat each other as equals. But to hell with that."

Shandling moves in for more. Leoni holds him off.

"No, it's not that, it's not that," she says.

"Well, what then?"

"I'm in love with Assistant Director Walter Skinner," she says.

Mulder leaps up from his seat.

"That's it, Scully. I just can't take it anymore," he says. Scully whispers to him to sit down. Mulder heads up the aisle as Shandling asks, "What's he have that I don't have?"

"A bigger flashlight." The audience erupts into laughter. Scully looks over at Skinner, who is being kissed by his attractive date.

•

Mulder consoles himself with a Lazarus Bowl full of popcorn on the deserted graveyard set. A sudden wind kicks up. Mulder looks up and sees Scully standing by a huge fan, aiming it at him.

"I've been looking all over for you," says Scully.

"They got it so wrong, Scully."

Scully sits beside him. "I got a page from the Washington bureau. Micah Hoffman was murdered tonight, murdered in his own home by Cardinal O'Fallon, who then hanged himself, a murder-suicide."

"Jesus and Judas, Scully."

"It's all over now."

"No. It's just beginning. Hoffman and O'Fallon were these complicated, flawed, beautiful people, and now they'll just be remembered as jokes because of this movie. The character based on O'Fallon is listed in the credits as Cigarette-Smoking Pontiff. How silly is that?"

"Pretty silly," says Scully.

"Yeah, what about us?" he says. "How are we gonna be remembered now because of this movie?"

"Well, hopefully the movie'll tank."

"What about all the dead people who are forever silent and can't tell their stories anymore? They're all going to have to rely on Hollywood to show the future how we lived and it'll all become oversimplified and trivialized and cigarette-smoking pontificized and become as plastic and meaningless as this stupid, plastic Lazarus Bowl."

Scully smiles. "I think the dead are beyond caring what people think about them. Hopefully we can adopt the same attitude. You do know that there aren't real dead people out there, right? That this is a movie set?" She's laughing now.

"The dead are everywhere, Scully," says Mulder.

"Well, we're alive. And we're relatively young. And Skinner was so tickled by the movie—"

"I bet he was."

"—that he has given us a bureau credit card to use for the evening."

They both rise. "Mulder, I have something to confess."

"What is that?"

"I'm in love with Associate Producer Walter Skinner." She dumps the Lazarus Bowl on top of a statue.

"Yeah, me too," says Mulder and they both laugh as they walk off the set hand in hand. One of the branches from a plastic tree bows to touch the discarded Lazarus Bowl. Music begins to play, a hauntingly beautiful cha-cha that summons the dead from out of their graves, classy in their decomposing finery. The music kicks in and they begin to dance. Bones creak. Half skulls smile. The graveyard is alive with the dancing dead.

BACK STORY:

"The Unnatural," David Duchovny's directorial and writing debut, was an impressive addition to *The X-Files* history. The feedback was so good, in fact, that it seemed inevitable that it was only a matter of time before Duchovny decided to stretch again.

Frank Spotnitz remembers the day Duchovny once again offered up his services. "David came to me and said, 'I've got this idea and it's this and this and this.' We talked about it for a couple of minutes and then we said, 'Go ahead.' The next thing I know he's handing me a script."

"Hollywood A.D." was not the typical *X-Files* script . . . not even close. The titular X-File, a case weaving together religion and 1960s revolution, was merely the backdrop to a true Hollywood odyssey in which Mulder, Scully, and Skinner literally go up against the horrifying X-File that is the movie business. Played more for laughs than true terror and suspense, the script instantly struck a chord with Chris Carter.

"I thought David wrote a smart, intelligent, quirky, and complex idea," says Carter. "I thought it was outside the norm, even for *The X-Files,* and showed how the show could stretch in a completely new and different direction."

Once the script was accepted and Duchovny was given the directorial reins, the actor threw himself into every aspect of the episode. His conversations with production designer Corey Kaplan resulted in a bigger-than-life graveyard set as well as some impressively dark and dingy basement corridors. Each scene was intricately detailed, with each camera angle carefully plotted. When it came to casting the movie-within-a-movie concept, Duchovny came up with an appropriately surreal plan to cast the behind-the-scenes technical crew in several key sequences, including the premiere of the movie and the sequence where the movie is being made.

Appearing for the first time on camera were craft services woman Tina M. Ameduri playing Tina the craft services woman, director of photography Bill Roe as the food-phobic zombie, assistant director Barry K. Thomas as

Sugar Bear, Paul Rabwin as a producer schmoozing a chorus girl, visual effects coordinator Bill Millar as a director, and Duchovny's brother, Daniel, as the assistant director.

"David also thought it would be a clever idea to have his wife, Téa Leoni, playing the film version of Scully and his good friend Garry Shandling portraying the film version of Mulder," recalls casting director Rick Millikan. "There really wasn't a lot to cast because David knew everybody he wanted. The only thing I had to work on was getting somebody to play the reverend and we managed to get a very good actor in Harris Yulin."

By all accounts, Duchovny was good-natured but focused and intent on getting his vision during the making of "Hollywood A.D." The actor was essentially doing double duty the entire time as he appeared in virtually every scene, but the consensus on the set was that he was truly professional on all counts.

Gillian Anderson remembers, "It was a lot of fun on the set, especially with Téa and Garry around. David is always good to work with. He knew exactly what he wanted and went for it."

Mitch Pileggi was the beneficiary of many of "Hollywood A.D."'s funniest dialogue lines, which focused primarily on Skinner's going Hollywood. "David wrote some really nice stuff for me. Watching Skinner in the bathtub and at the movie premiere were so totally out of character, they were hilarious."

The stunt work on this episode was considerable; a handful of stuntmen endured five hours of makeup time to transform them into zombies for the opening graveyard action sequence. A pair of non-zombie stunt doubles were also required for the sequence where Shandling tackles Leoni and they tumble down the hill and into the open grave.

The zombie dance sequence that ends the episode required two days of actual shooting, according to producer Harry Bring. "They shot some of it during the actual day of production and then we had to schedule an additional Saturday to accommodate the bluescreen work that was required for the scene."

"Hollywood A.D." was a success on a whole range of levels. The script showcased the deep friendship underlying the Mulder-Scully relationship, which, ultimately, has been the most natural stance during the run of the show. The X-File was appropriately serious in tone and meshed beautifully with the comic goings-on without detracting from its own story. The humor was legitimate and unforced. And finally, "Hollywood A.D." proved that David Duchovny's success as a writer-director on "The Unnatural" was no fluke.

FACTS:

Chris Carter made his second on-camera appearance on *The X-Files* in this episode as a guest at the movie premiere.

(X)

Harris Yulin played the elder Watcher on *Buffy the Vampire Slayer*.

(X)

Among the stars appearing in cameos at the premiere of the movie were Minnie Driver (costar with David Duchovny of *Return to Me*) and David Alan Grier.

(X)

Paul Rabwin recalls, "David came to me before he was finished filming and asked me if I was familiar with the music from the film *The Buena Vista Social Club*. There was a track he wanted to use for the sequence where the zombies come out and dance. I had trouble licensing the music so I went to Mark Snow and he created an original piece of music for the scene."

(X)

Wayne Federman, a Los Angeles–based comedian, actor, and writer, performs regularly on *The Tonight Show*, and has appeared on such television programs as *Politically Incorrect*, *The List* on VH-1, *Baywatch*, *Living Single*, and *NewsRadio*. Fans may recognize his voice from the Cartoon Network, Nick at Night, and the Florida orange juice commercials, where he provides the voice of the talking "ham and cheese" sandwich.

episode 7X20

FIGHT CLUB

EPISODE: 7X20
FIRST AIRED: May 7, 2000
EDITOR: Heather MacDougall
WRITTEN BY: Chris Carter
DIRECTED BY: Paul Shapiro

A pair of dopplegangers on the run arrive in Kansas City, where they cause trouble for a down-on-his-luck wrestler, door-to-door missionaries, and Mulder and Scully.

[redacted]

GUEST STARS:

Kathy Griffin (Betty Templeton/Lulu Pfeiffer)
Randall "Tex" Cobb (Bert Zupanic)
Art Evans (Argyle Saperstein)
Jack McGee (Angry Bob)
Rob Van Dam (Opponent)
Gene LeBell (Bartender)
Arlene Pileggi (Woman Who Looks Like Scully)
Steve Kiziak (Man Who Looks Like Mulder)
Cory Blevins (Missionary #1)
John O'Brien (Missionary #2)
Brian Chenoweth (Koko's Manager #1)
Jim Hanna (Koko's Manager #2)

PRINCIPAL SETTING:

Kansas City, Kansas

A pair of well-dressed, bicycle-riding missionaries pull to a stop in a driveway of a small pink house in Kansas City, Kansas. A red convertible with the license plate BETTY sits in the driveway. They go to the door and knock.

The door opens to reveal a woman with red hair and a Betty Boop barrette. We only see her from behind.

The first missionary says, "Good afternoon. I hope we're not bothering you."

"Actually, I'm just—" says the woman.

"We really won't take much of your time," says the second missionary.

"I'm just waiting for a call," says the woman.

The first missionary says, "We're all waiting, ma'am. For the Good Lord to call in his flock."

The woman says, "From the cable TV people."

A moving van pulls up in front of the house.

"I'm just moving in. God bless," says the woman as she shuts the door in their faces.

The missionaries peddle down the street and stop in the driveway of a blue house. A familiar convertible, blue this time with the license plate LULU is in the driveway. After a knock on the door, the first missionary starts to go into his pitch but stops in midsentence.

"Yes?" asks the woman, who we again see only from behind.

"You're . . . weren't you? Didn't we just . . . ?"

"Didn't you just what?" asks the woman.

The second missionary says, "Speak to you."

"Excuse me?"

"We just spoke to a woman who could've been your twin."

"What are you talking about?"

"Yeah, just down the street," says the first missionary. "She's just moving in. Your spitting image."

"You're really not going to believe it when you see her," says the second missionary.

The door slams in their faces. Through the door, the woman screams, "Go away! Get out of here!"

The missionaries look at each other and then, for no reason, the first missionary pushes his partner on the shoulder. The second missionary pushes back. A shoving match quickly escalates into a full-blown street fight.

Watching through the door's peephole, the second woman is nervous and upset at the brawl she's witnessing.

A police squad car skids to a stop in front of the house. Two officers leap out and attempt to break up what has now become a crazed, bloody, no-holds-barred fight on the front lawn.

•

The next day, familiar silhouettes of a tall dark-haired man and a shorter red-haired woman stand on the doorstep of the first house. The door opens to reveal Betty. She is facing a man and woman who appear to be Mulder and Scully, although at this point we only see them from behind.

"Betty Templeton?" says the man who looks like Mulder.

"Yes?"

"We're with the FBI. We'd like to ask about an incident, a possible religious hate crime in your neighborhood."

"I just moved in yesterday. I don't know about any incident."

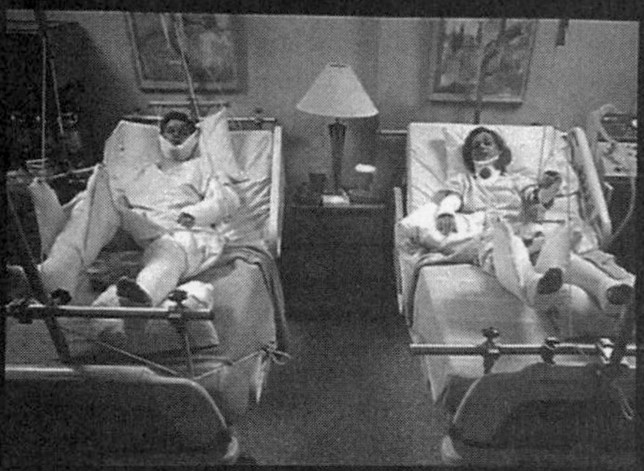

The woman who looks like Scully says, "Well, we have two young men in the car who say that you do know something."

Betty looks past them to the agents' car, where she sees the two battered and bruised missionaries.

"My God. Those are the boys who were here yesterday. What happened?"

The Mulder double says, "They were beaten to within an inch of their lives by each other. After visiting the home of a woman living a few blocks over."

"What woman?"

"A woman who by both young men's accounts fits your description," says the Scully double.

"She lives around here?" asks Betty as she pushes past the agents and looks up and down the street.

Mulder's double asks Betty if she is a practitioner of voodoo or any other black arts.

"Me? No. You know what they say, everyone has a twin out there somewhere."

We finally get a look at the agents' faces, and while they do look much like our heroes, this is not them.

"No," says the Mulder twin. "We don't know what they say."

"Well, if there's somebody else who fits my description, why isn't somebody talking to her?"

The woman who looks like Scully says, "We went to the house, but it's empty. No one lives there."

"Frankly, we're not even sure she exists," adds the Mulder double.

Betty's eyes suddenly go wide as a little blue Fiat drives by, with Lulu Pfeiffer, the spitting image of Betty, at the wheel. Their eyes lock. Lulu speeds away.

The man who looks like Mulder is sucker punched by the woman who looks like Scully. He recovers and a full-blown brawl breaks out on Betty's front lawn. Betty and the missionaries watch in horror. Finally the female agent breaks away and races to the car. She jumps inside and starts to drive away. The male agent grabs the car and is dragged off. As Betty fearfully looks on from her window, the car accordions into a tree.

•

The real Mulder and Scully study a slide of the car crash on a screen.

Mulder says, "This is an FBI fleet sedan from our Kansas City field office, requisitioned by two seasoned agents there. Driven into a tree at forty-three miles per hour by the female agent, in a novel effort to kill her male counterpart. Now, you might think I'm going to suggest psychokinesis, PK. Someone or something controlling the agents with remote, mind-bending power."

"But it's not," says Scully.

Mulder clicks to the next slide, a picture of the woman who looks like Scully banged up in a hospital bed. "Both agents sustained critical injuries. Their stories eerily similar. As if they'd temporarily lost control of their minds. Unable to alter behavior." He clicks to a slide of the two mangled agents in a hospital bed. "You might think I'm gonna say it's past lives unresolved, fate stalking the agents like an animal."

"But you're not."

"No, the interesting thing about these agents is that they had worked together for seven years previously without incident."

"Seven years?" inquires Scully.

"Yes, but they are not romantically involved, if that's what you're thinking."

"Not even I would be so far-fetched," says Scully.

Mulder clicks to a slide of the two mangled agents, side by side in their hospital beds.

"You have any ideas, Scully? Any thoughts?"

"What I'm thinking, Mulder, is how familiar this seems. Playing Watson to your Sherlock. You dangling clues out in front of me one by one; it's a game. And, as usual, you're holding something back from me. You're not telling me something about this case." Mulder pretends to think for a moment. "Okay, so these agents were investigating something. Something much like what they themselves were almost killed by. Something they came into contact with. A third party."

Mulder holds up two fingers. "Two third parties!" Scully says. She plays along and rattles off guesses. Mulder shakes his head at the notion of twins and relatives. At the mention of the term *doppelganger*, Mulder puts his finger on his nose—got it.

Scully explains, "A corporeal likeness that appears unbidden from the spirit world. The sight of which presages one's own death." Off Mulder's reaction, she continues excitedly. "Or a double conjured into the world by a technique known as bilocation. Which, in psychological terms, represents a person's secret desires and impulses, committing acts that the real person cannot commit himself." Off his silence, "Or herself."

Mulder does not agree or disagree with Scully's theory, but smiles slightly. Scully, with a smile, requests the next slide. He advances the slide to the driver's license photo of Betty Templeton. Scully lets out a victorious "Yes!"

"Don't go thinking I'm going to start doing the autopsies," says Mulder.

•

Lulu Pfeiffer, in a blue shirt and black pants, pulls up in front of Koko's Copy Center, eyeing the HELP WANTED sign in the window. She gets out of her car and walks up to the manager of the store.

"Excuse me," says Lulu. "Hi, I applied for the sales job you posted."

"Ah, yeah. I remember. How could I forget?"

"Excuse me?" asks Lulu.

"Uh, there's a problem with your application, as I recall. Miss . . ."

"Pfeiffer," says Lulu. "Are you sure?"

The manager rifles through his paperwork and finds the application. He reads off an address. Lulu indicates she has moved from that address and does not have a new address yet.

"Actually, Miss Pfeiffer, that's what's sending up the red flag. You move a lot and there's also your employment history: seventeen jobs in seventeen states in the past three years. You seem to have as many jobs here as you have addresses."

"I had a restless streak."

The manager explains he doubts her motivation.

"What I can tell is you've left a variety of jobs: Mongolian BBQ chef, high-rise window washer, wild animal trainer, palm reader."

Lulu says, "Yes, but I'm on a career path now."

There is a huge commotion in the store. All the machines begin to malfunction. Paper spews everywhere.

"I can start you immediately. There's a clean uniform in the employee washroom."

Lulu's smile fades as she spies through the window Betty, pulling up in front of the store. Betty, wearing a pink top, classifieds on the passenger seat, has been job hunting. She looks at the Koko's window just as the store manager takes down the HELP WANTED sign. Disappointed, she drives off. At a second Koko's Copy Center, Betty is speaking with another Koko's manager as he examines her application.

The manager says, "That's quite a string of positions you've had, Miss Templeton. Seventeen jobs in the last three years."

"I would've listed more but there wasn't any room left on your form. I think you'll find my former employers will only give me the highest personal references."

"It's not your references," says the manager. "It's the jobs themselves. Mongolian BBQ chef, high-rise window washer . . . wild animal trainer?"

"I'm a highly versatile employee," says Betty.

"What guarantee do I have you won't just up and quit tomorrow?"

"You have my personal word on it," insists Betty. "I'm here in Kansas City to stay."

•

Inside a room at the low-end Porcherie Hotel, Bert Zupanic, a pug-ugly fighter, is loading stacks of hundred-dollar bills into a suitcase. There is a knock on the door.

"Who is it?"

"Mr. Zupanic, it's the FBI," says Mulder from outside the door.

He freezes. "Excuse me?" asks Bert.

"It's the FBI, Mr. Zupanic. Open up."

Bert frantically slams the money into the suitcase. "Yeah, gimme a minute."

Bert opens the door to reveal Mulder and Scully standing in the hallway. "Bert Zupanic? We're hoping you can help us find the whereabouts of a woman we believe you're familiar with? Betty Templeton." Mulder takes out a photo of Betty/Lulu and shows it to Bert.

Bert denies knowing a Betty Templeton.

Scully says, "Maybe you'll want to take another look at that photograph, Mr. Zupanic. Five-foot-three. Red hair. Maybe I can jog your memory."

She pulls a yellowed newspaper clipping out of her jacket. It shows a photo of Bert in a wrestling costume in a parade car, waving to the crowd. Sitting beside him is Betty. Bert's face is flushed.

Scully asks, "Are you still pleading ignorance, Mr. Zupanic? Is that not you in last year's Fourth of July parade?"

"You know what I'm thinking?" Mulder asks.

"That Mr. Zupanic not only knows Betty Templeton, and knows where we can find her, but that he's hip to whatever she's into. And that I should take a look at that house he mentioned on Moreton Bay Street. While you go find out from Mr. Zupanic what it is exactly he's clearly hiding about Betty Templeton."

Mulder says he believes that Bert Zupanic really does not know Betty Templeton. The elevator door opens and Scully steps inside.

Scully says, "Well, I guess that's why they put the *I* in the FBI."

The elevator door shuts, leaving Mulder alone in the hallway. Down the hallway, Bert's door opens. Mulder watches from an adjoining hallway as Bert steps into an elevator with the suitcase and leaves the hotel. Mulder then heads for Bert's room.

•

Bert enters the dimly lit, downscale Froggy's Bar. He moves to a spot at the bar, rests the suitcase on the bar, and says to the bartender, "Gimme a double, Freddie."

"I thought you were in training, Bert, my man," says Freddie.

"Would you just pour?"

Bert scans the bar and notices Betty, in her Koko's uniform, nursing a drink.

"Nice outfit," says Bert as he ambles over to her end of the bar, still holding the suitcase. "Freddie, fire in the hole. Seven-and-seven for the lady, and make it stiff."

"WELL, I GUESS THAT'S WHY THEY PUT THE *I* IN THE FBI."—Scully

"Yeah," he admits unsurely.

"And who's that sitting next to you?"

"Her?"

"Try Betty Templeton," says Scully. "We can't find her, Mr. Zupanic. She seems to have left town in a hurry."

"She did? Didn't she used to live on Moreton Bay? In a pink house."

Scully says, "Alderwood, blue house."

"Alderwood?" Bert questions.

"Mr. Zupanic, do you have any reason to be lying to us?"

"No, sir. I mean ma'am."

Mulder nods at the correction.

"Thank you, Mr. Zupanic. I have no doubt we'll be in touch with you."

Mulder and Scully walk down the hallway toward the elevator.

"Ohmigod. How did you do that?"

"Do what?"

"How did *you* know my drink?" Bert looks at her, confused that she doesn't seem to know him. "I feel like you're looking right through me. Like you're reading my soul like a book."

Betty downs her new drink in a single gulp.

"Maybe you've had enough of that," he says. "You are in trouble, aren't you?"

"I don't know. I could be. What kind of trouble you looking for?"

"You don't want to go home tonight, okay?"

"It just so happens I don't got a home to go to. Anyway"—she holds out her hand, which he takes—"I'm Betty Templeton."

"Alderwood Avenue?" he asks. She yanks her hand back.

Betty freaks at Bert's intimate knowledge as he laughs. Betty looks up to see Lulu coming in the door, also dressed in her Koko's outfit. Lulu also sees Betty. Betty whispers something in Bert's ear. A big smile appears on Bert's face and he laughs some more.

Just then a pyramid of glasses begins to rattle and vibrate. Customers' drinks do the same. The drinks start to explode, followed by all the bottles and the mirrors. Glass flies everywhere. The customers duck for cover. Lulu comes up from under the bar to see as Betty and Bert slip out the door.

•

Scully arrives at Pat Devine's Kansas City Auditorium, a wrestling-boxing arena. She walks through the arena until she hears the familiar voice of Mulder calling her over to where he is sitting, comfortably chewing the fat with an elderly black man named Argyle Saperstein. Scully immediately notices that the two men are getting on famously.

"This is my partner, Dana Scully."

Saperstein says, "A pleasure and an honor."

"I take it from your posture, Mulder, you've solved this case."

"Not solved it, Scully, but I have narrowed down the search for our perpetrator with the kind help of Mr. Saperstein here."

"Narrowed it down to where?" asks Scully.

Saperstein points in the direction of the ring. "Right down there."

"Our mystery woman is indeed involved with Mr. Bert Zupanic, the man we spoke to at his hotel," says Mulder. "Who will be fighting here two days hence, with the woman almost undoubtedly in attendance."

Saperstein says, "If it's the lady I'm thinking, she's not much to look at, but he says she brings him luck."

Scully asks if Bert Zupanic is a boxer. Saperstein tells her he is, in fact, a semipro wrestler.

"So . . . what?" asks Scully. "We wait around Kansas City for a couple of days until we can talk to this woman?"

Mulder says, "Well, lots to do here. And the barbecue's second to none. Plus Mr. Saperstein's going to show me some in-your-face smackdown moves. So I can quit getting my ass kicked so often. Oh, and there's an art exhibit which traces the influence of Soviet art on American pop culture, right?" Saperstein nods. "Unless, of course, you've already found Betty Templeton."

"Well, finding Betty Templeton won't solve this case, Mulder. Not unless we find Lulu Pfeiffer."

"Who's Lulu Pfeiffer?" asks Mulder.

"Our doppelganger, who lived, until yesterday, in a pink house on Moreton Bay Street. But she's not a manifestation, Mulder. She's real and so is the path of destruction that she's left in her wake."

Mulder appears surprised at this.

She continues, "Though there seems to be no connection of any kind between the two women, Betty Templeton and Lulu Pfeiffer have traveled city to city, across seventeen U.S. states, one alternately trailing the other for the past twelve years. And wherever they have been, mayhem has followed."

"Damn," interjects Saperstein.

"It's not just car accidents and fistfights, it's house fires, explosions, and even riots."

Saperstein says, "The lady knows her stuff."

Mulder rises to leave and says good-bye to Saperstein with "Shalom Alechem."

"Yo mama," he responds offhandedly.

The agents leave. The smile on Saperstein's face fades. He gets out his cell phone and wakes Bert up from a sound sleep.

"Where's my money?" asks Saperstein.

"I got it," says Bert. "I'm bringing it."

"Yeah, that's what I heard last night! Now you got the feds on your ass! You're good luck charm don't sound so lucky anymore, boychik. Maybe I should cancel the fight."

Betty lifts her head from next to Bert and puts an arm around him.

Bert assures Saperstein that he will bring the money.

"I'm having lunch at Froggy's. No money, no fight, Titanic!"

Saperstein hangs up.

"Are you in trouble or something?" asks Betty.

"I just . . . I gotta be somewhere, okay?"

"What time is it? Oh God! I'm gonna be late for work!"

Betty gets out of bed, grabs up her Koko's uniform, and whips around the bed, stopping in front of Bert, kissing him.

"You were incredible. Why do I find myself so wildly attracted to you, Bert Zupanic?"

"I know. I'm just so wildly attracted to you, Bert Zupanic."

Despite Lulu's gushing protests, Bert ushers Lulu toward the door and out into the hallway, closing the door just as Betty comes out of the bathroom.

"Bert? Did I hear voices?"

Yelling from the room upstairs can be heard, followed by the sound of rapid-fire gunshots. Bullet holes appear in the plaster overhead as Bert and Betty hold each other in fear and surprise.

•

Saperstein is in Froggy's Bar, waiting for Bert to show up with the money. Betty walks into the bar and up to Saperstein.

"Where's the Titanic?" asks Saperstein.

"What?"

"Your boyfriend," he says. "The wrestler."

Betty says, "Wow, talk about moves! I can't believe it. We barely just met!"

"He's supposed to meet me," says Saperstein. "Here."

"PLUS MR. SAPERSTEIN'S GOING TO SHOW ME SOME IN-YOUR-FACE SMACKDOWN MOVES. SO I CAN QUIT GETTING MY ASS KICKED SO OFTEN."—Mulder

"You just can't help yourself, baby," he says with a smile.

She goes to the bathroom. There's a knock on the door. Bert opens the door to reveal Lulu Pfeiffer in her Koko's uniform.

"Where were you last night?" she asks Bert.

He's dumbfounded. "Where was I?"

Lulu pushes past him into his room. "You said meet me for a drink."

"I was there, waiting for you," he stammers out.

"Are you two-timing me, Bert?"

"How can you say that? You're my good luck charm!"

"Who is she?" she demand.

Lulu searches the room. She finds the Betty Boop barrette in the unmade bed. She breaks into a big, gushy smile. She throws her arms around Bert and kisses his neck and chest.

"You lovable lug, Bert Zupanic. I'm sorry, baby. This is mine. I just get so jealous. Forgive me?"

Bert says, "I forgive you. I'm in training. You gotta go to work. You're late."

"He's coming here?"

"He'd better be, if he wants that fight on Saturday night."

"I better go freshen up a little. I was just coming in for lunch," says Betty.

She goes to the bathroom just as Bert enters the bar with the suitcase.

"Zupanic, hey. Thought you were a no-show," says Saperstein. "Talkin' to your girlfriend."

"My girlfriend?"

Suddenly the whole room begins to vibrate. The vibrations stop just as Lulu comes through the door.

Saperstein says, "Now how'd she do that?"

"Do what?" asks Bert.

"I just saw her, I swear, I just saw her go to the can."

After thinking about that for a moment, Bert moves toward Lulu. She is happy to see the big lug.

"What are you doing here?"

"I have a business meeting. Why don't I meet you outside in the park."

Lulu says she was just going to lunch. Bert suggests they have a picnic. Bert moves Lulu toward the door and out. He hurries back to Saperstein just as Betty comes out of the bathroom. "Bert?" she calls.

The bar begins to vibrate again.

Bert says, "I have a little business to attend to here, sweetie."

Saperstein says, "You got more'n that to attend to."

As he nods, Lulu comes back through the door. The two women lock eyes. The vibrating begins again. Glass and mirrors shatter to pieces. Lulu and Betty shield themselves from the flying glass, then disappear through separate exits and the shaking stops. Saperstein rises and sees Bert has been knocked out, clutching the suitcase. He carefully takes it from Bert's hand and walks casually out the door.

•

"Mr. Zupanic?" says Scully as she and Mulder kneel over the unconscious Bert amid the wreckage of the destroyed bar, uniformed cops, and paramedics.

He slowly comes to.

"What the hell happened?"

Scully says, "There was an incident. You were struck by flying glass."

Bert notices his suitcase is missing and looks frantically for it.

"Did you lose something?" asks Mulder.

"Yeah. My good luck."

"Would that be Betty or Lulu, Mr. Zupanic?" asks Scully. "Because they're the ones who caused this and they'll do it again if we can't find them. Where are they, Mr. Zupanic?"

•

Mulder enters Koko's Copy Center. He approaches the manager.

"I'm looking for . . . that girl," says Mulder, seeing Betty right behind the manager.

"Betty, this man's from the FBI."

Betty says, "I'm just getting off work. Could we maybe talk some other time?"

Betty starts for the door. Mulder cuts in front of her.

"I think you know why I'm here."

"It's her fault!" she says.

"Lulu Pfeiffer?"

"She follows me around, trying to ruin my life! I'm not gonna let her ruin it this time. It's either me or her. I don't wanna leave Kansas!"

Betty pushes past Mulder, who follows her out of the store. He dials his cell phone. It is Scully outside the first Koko's Copy Center, watching as Lulu drives away.

"Hey, Scully. I found her at Koko's Copy Center."

"Betty Templeton?"

"Yeah, she says that Lulu Pfeiffer's trying to ruin her life. She follows her wherever she goes."

"Well, Lulu Pfeiffer works at Koko's, too. That's exactly what Lulu says about Betty. Except she says this is the end of the line; she's not leaving Kansas," says Scully.

Mulder explains that Betty told him *she's* not leaving town.

"What's going on here?"

"I don't know, Scully. You're running the show. Why don't you tell me."

Mulder watches as Betty gets into her car and rolls down the window.

Scully says, "It's more than just physical proximity, Mulder. I think these women have some kind of psychic connection."

Mulder acknowledges that that's obvious. "Hey, Scully, where's Lulu?" He turns to see a small blue car coming up the street.

"She just took off, Mulder. She just left work and drove away."

"She wouldn't be driving a little blue convertible, would she?"

"That's exactly what she's driving."

Mulder watches as Lulu stops on the opposite side of the street from Betty, who is still sitting in her red convertible—with him caught in the middle. Betty is shocked to see Lulu. "Oh crap," says Mulder, sensing what's coming. A manhole cover rattles into the sky, followed by a powerful rush of steam that knocks him down. He suddenly finds himself caught in the steam backwash, dragged along the street, and sucked into the manhole. The two women drive off in opposite directions. The manhole cover descends from the heavens and lands, a perfect fit over the hole. Mulder is gone.

•

Scully's car pulls up, right next to the steaming manhole cover. Not seeing Mulder, she heads for the Koko's Copy Center.

"I'm looking for someone," she tells the manager. "He was here, speaking to an employee. I can't seem to reach him."

"Tall guy, dark hair? He left."

"And you don't know where he went?"

"Couldn't say." Scully smiles her thanks and moves to leave. "However, I can tell you we have a two-for-one copy discount in effect!"

Scully smiles at this, then after a pause asks, "How about Internet access?" asks Scully.

"Right this way!"

•

Scully is led through the dark cellblock of the Kansas State Penitentiary. The guard tells Scully the prisoner is sleeping. "Can you wake him for me?"

"Sure you want to do that?" the guard asks.

"Will you two shut up or go away!" screams Angry Bob Damphouse as he comes out of the darkness and to the cell bars. "The sound of your voice is like a jackhammer on my eardrums!"

After a long pause Scully says, "Mr. Damphouse, I'm Special Agent Dana Scully with the FBI."

"What's special about you?" screams Angry Bob.

"It's an FBI title."

"I know it is. I'm not stupid," he yells back, beginning to pace in his cell.

"Mr. Damphouse, if you'd let me explain why I'm here, you might be able to go back to bed a little bit sooner."

"Ah, what a relief," he says.

"Mr. Damphouse, through a lot of matching up of documents that I've been able to compile on the Internet, and by comparing time and space and circumstance, and liberally applying the law of averages . . ."

Angry Bob screams, "They could electrocute me quicker!"

"I believe that you may be the father of two daughters."

At this, Angry Bob pauses and moves back to Scully, who gives a small nervous smile. "I'm no father!" he yells.

"Using documents filed by a sperm bank in Sparta, Illinois, and by mothers who may have been impregnated by your donation . . ."

"I yankee doodled into a plastic cup!"

Not making eye contact, Scully continues speaking quickly. "Be that as it may, sir, it is very likely you're the biological father. And it is very important for their safety and for the safety of others that we get as much information as possible about your mother, father, and anything about your family tree that may be able to explain the reactions being caused by these two girls."

Angry Bob says, "A big ugly dog lifted its leg on my family tree!"

•

There is a knock on the door of Bert's hotel room. He cautiously opens the door. It's Betty.

"You aren't answering your phone?"

"I'm just screening my calls."

"You sleep with me once and now you're avoiding me?"

"I got big trouble, baby. I got just one shot left at the Big Time."

Betty says, "But you got your match tonight! Your name's up on the marquee!"

"I've lost my financing," he says. "You're my good luck, baby."

Betty is confused as to what he means.

"It was my good luck to meet you," he says. "If you could help the Titanic find a way. They say I'm old and washed up. All I want's a shot. But if I don't get the money, I'm gonna lose my chance."

"Maybe I can."

Betty kisses him once and hurries out the door. A few moments later, Bert is startled by another knock on the door. He opens it to reveal a pissed-off Lulu standing in the doorway.

"You're not answering your phone?" asks Lulu.

"Lulu?"

"Someone else you were expecting? Well?"

Bert puts his arm around her and closes the door. "Baby, I got big trouble."

•

Betty has picked the lock on Koko's and is printing up sheets of $100 bills on a color copier. While, across town . . .

Lulu is in her place of employment, doing the exact same thing.

The manhole cover pushes up and slides onto the street. Mulder's hands and head pop into view. He looks around, appearing quite rumpled but none the worse for wear.

"A BIG UGLY DOG LIFTED ITS LEG ON MY FAMILY TREE!"—Angry Bob

•

Scully is sitting bleary-eyed over files and prison records in the penitentiary visiting room when her cell phone rings.

"Mulder? Where have you been?"

"Seeing a side of Kansas City few men have the privilege to see, Scully. I got sucked into a storm drain. The more pressing question is what the hell happened to Betty Templeton and Lulu Pfeiffer." Mulder is looking in through the Koko's Copy Center window.

"I don't know. But I have been able to locate the nature of their connection. Both women are nonfraternal siblings, from the same father. He's here in the state pen."

Angry Bob continues to bellow in a nearby cell.

"And he's given you insight?"

"Well, the biggest thing I can figure out right now is that he's probably the angriest man in the world, Mulder."

"Not as angry as those two women are going to be when they both realize they're in love with the one and only Bert Zupanic."

"They're both after him?" asks Scully.

"Yeah, they're both in love with him. That's why they're both staying in Kansas City and they won't leave."

Scully says, "Well, if they're the reason, it doesn't explain what's happening, what is causing this phenomena. Or how we're going to make it stop."

"Look, Scully, I don't know, you're the one who's supposed to have all the answers. Somebody's got to get to the fight and keep those two women apart. Or this time it's going to hit the fans."

As Scully hangs up, a prisoner in the cell next to Angry Bob greets her.

"Mr. Zupanic?" says Scully, incredulous, as the spitting image of Bert Zupanic smiles back at her.

•

Bert, dressed in red spandex as his wrestling alter ego Titanic, paces in the arena tunnel of Pat Devine's Kansas City Auditorium, checking out the wrestlers currently in the ring. He is approached by Argyle Saperstein.

"You said you'd have my money."

"I'll have it. I swear I will."

"I'll call off the damn fight, Titanic! I'll have these people home cursing your very name."

"I'm telling you it'll be here, I promise," says Bert.

Betty appears in the arena, carrying a big, bulging Koko's bag.

"Bert! Bert! I got it!"

Bert looks in the bag at bundles of hundred-dollar bills and bursts out laughing. Betty appears pleased at her accomplishment. Bert thrusts the bag at Saperstein, who, after peering in, declares, "Let's get ready to rumble," and walks toward the ring.

"Oh, baby, I knew you wouldn't let me down."

Betty says, "It's you and me, all the way." They hug.

Titanic's opponent, in black cape and mask, plays to the crowd. Saperstein takes the mike to address the arena's hot-blooded, standing-room-only crowd.

"Ladies and gentlemen! Get outta your seats and on your feets for our own hometown boy gone bad, Bert 'The Titanic' Zooopanic!" Bert

climbs into the ring and raises his arms to the crowd, then gives a thumbs-up to Betty.

The crowd goes wild. Betty goes wild. The bell rings.

The two wrestlers circle each other. Bert gets his opponent in a headlock. He unleashes a lethal elbow smash. Bert does a little grandstanding to the crowd before picking up his opponent and body-slamming him to the mat. The crowd continues to cheer wildly as the bout goes on. Betty is so caught up in the excitement and the action that she does not notice Mulder coming up behind her.

"Betty Templeton, Agent Fox Mulder. I'm with the FBI. Can you come with me?"

"I'm watching the fight."

"Don't make me have to remove you, ma'am."

Lulu appears behind Mulder, carrying another bulging Koko's bag. She spots Betty. She's pissed.

"I can't believe this. What are you doing here?" she asks.

Betty counters, "What are you doing here?"

"I'm Bert's good luck," Lulu insists.

"He's mine!" states Betty.

"Over my dead body!" says Betty as Mulder, looking back and forth between the two women, suddenly picks up Betty and carries her over his shoulder away from Lulu and toward the exit as Betty continues to scream at Lulu. Betty grabs on to the ring and tells Bert she loves him. Bert, busy pinning his opponent to the mat, is confused to see her like this. He is even more confused when Lulu races to the ring apron.

"Bert, I got the money!"

"Lulu?" says a distracted Bert as Saperstein appears and grabs the bag of money from Lulu.

Mulder notices the crowd has begun pushing and shoving. Punches are thrown as fights erupt. The arena turns into a riot. Mulder pulls Betty from her grip on the ring and starts walking with her as quickly as possible.

Mulder spots Scully entering the arena, accompanied by a prison guard and Bert's prison double in shackles. Betty can't believe it. Mulder sets her down. Lulu sees the double and is likewise weirded out.

The impact of all these doppelgangers brings the fight, inside and outside of the ring, to a sudden halt. Everybody is dazed and confused except Scully, who is standing amid the chaos, smiling at Mulder.

Wrestling Bert sets eyes on Prison Bert. There is a scream of rage as the doubles race at each other. The crowd resumes pummeling each other. Scully, Mulder, Betty, and Lulu look around in confusion. It's a madhouse.

•

Scully's voice is giving her expert opinion to Mulder and Saperstein, as slides of the principal characters in this strange situation flicker onto a screen.

"Fifty million anonymous donations have been made to sperm banks across the U.S."

"Most have produced healthy offspring for single mothers or fertility-challenged couples. While some of them have not."

A mugshot of Wrestling Bert, looking badly beaten, is projected.

"Bert Zupanic and his nonfraternal biological sibling, both small-time bank robbers"—a mugshot of Prison Bert, also badly beaten, appears—"and part-time pro wrestlers, both with too many idiosyncratic behaviorisms to list, stood a twenty-seven million to one chance of ever meeting. But they did."

Slides of the two Berts fighting each other appear.

"Damn, those are some odds," interjects Saperstein. Scully switches to a mugshot slide of a badly beaten Betty.

Scully says, "Betty Templeton and Lulu Pfeiffer, products of different mothers but the same father"—slide of a beaten Lulu—"an angry drifter now doing time for counterfeiting, chanced to meet twelve years ago—slides of Betty and Lulu fighting, pulling hair—"but couldn't seem to avoid each other's compulsively identical mannerisms."

Slides of pummeled Lulu and Angry Bob follow. Saperstein wants to know what it all means.

"I've been thinking hard about that, Mr. Saperstein. I would like to say it has something to do with balance in the universe, the attraction of opposites and the repulsion of equivalents. Or that over time nature produces only so many originals. That when two original copies meet that the result is unpredictable. If four should meet, the result is . . ."

Scully's face appears for the first time, covered in cuts, black-and-blue marks, and a black eye, her souvenirs of the rumble in Kansas.

"Well, suffice to say it's better just to avoid these encounters altogether and at all costs." She smiles. "I think Agent Mulder would agree with me."

Mulder nods and grimaces through a face of stitches, cuts, and bruises and a jaw wired shut.

BACK STORY:

"Fight Club" was born amid a very strange *X-Files* state of mind.

"People got really strange toward the end of the year," recalls Frank Spotnitz. "We didn't know what was going on. We were all so stressed out about whether this was the end of the series or not. It was getting toward the end of the season and everybody was kind of punchy."

Which made it the ideal time for Chris Carter to reach back into his bag of storylines and resurrect a long-lost nugget. "I had this idea for a long time to do a story about mismatched twins that had an almost nuclear reaction when they were around each other."

Carter began writing the script at the same time he was prepping the pilot for the Lone Gunmen series. Juggling two full-time jobs made this a crazy time, and his "Fight Club" script reflected the insanity. Psychic twins. Battling missionaries. Agents who looked like Mulder and Scully, and a whole lot of wrestling. Spotnitz, remembering his first look at the script, could only exclaim, "It had an odd tone. It felt like a wild show."

Casting "Fight Club" was, likewise, the equivalent of a wild ride. Rick Millikan called in former heavyweight-boxer-turned-actor Randall "Tex" Cobb as the perplexed wrestler Bert Zupanic and comedian Kathy Griffin to play the tortured twins Betty Templeton and Lulu Pfeiffer. Duchovny and Anderson stand-ins Steve Kiziak and Arlene Pileggi (wife of Mitch Pileggi) stepped to the front of the camera as the battling agents who looked like Mulder and Scully. Finally, two real professional wrestlers, "Judo" Gene Labell and Rob Van Dam, were found to play the bartender and the opponent.

First-time *X-Files* director Paul Shapiro was handed the reins of "Fight Club," which, according to stunt coordinator Danny Weselis, turned out to be a three-ring circus of action and stunts. "During the bar explosions we had a room full of stunt people showered with broken glass. And we used stunt people for much of the missionary and special agent fights."

The showstopping element of "Fight Club" turned out to be the climactic wrestling match that turns into a full-scale riot in which the crowd, overcome by the power of the psychic twins, turn on each other. The scene was filmed over a two-day period in the famed Olympic Auditorium in Los Angeles. Ads on the Internet and in selected publications recruited several hundred extras for the crowd scenes and supplemented sixteen stuntmen and 200 cardboard cutouts that were sprinkled throughout the audience. A split-screen visual image enhanced the scene by allowing viewers to focus on various angles of the action.

Harry Bring recalls that for the fight sequences "the audience members were given soft props to hit each other with. Of course a few of them got carried away and we had to tell them to settle down."

"Fight Club" was a curiosity, an enticing X-File coated in a lot of humor that took a totally unexpected departure from anything approaching reality. The hybrid worked.

FACTS:

Kathy Griffin starred in the television series *Suddenly Susan* and is a regular on the standup comedy circuit.

In postproduction, David Duchovny and Gillian Anderson looped the voices of the Agents Who Look Like Mulder and Scully.

Art Evans, who portrayed Argyle Saperstein, has also appeared in the movies *Fright Night, White of the Eye,* and *Tales from the Hood.*

"Judo" Gene LaBell is a veteran wrestler-actor-stuntman who has wrestled professionally since the early 1950s. Rob Van Dam is currently a regular on the Southern California wrestling circuit.

episode 7X21

JE SOUHAITE

EPISODE: 7X21
FIRST AIRED: May 14, 2000
EDITOR: Louise A. Innes
WRITTEN AND DIRECTED BY:
Vince Gilligan

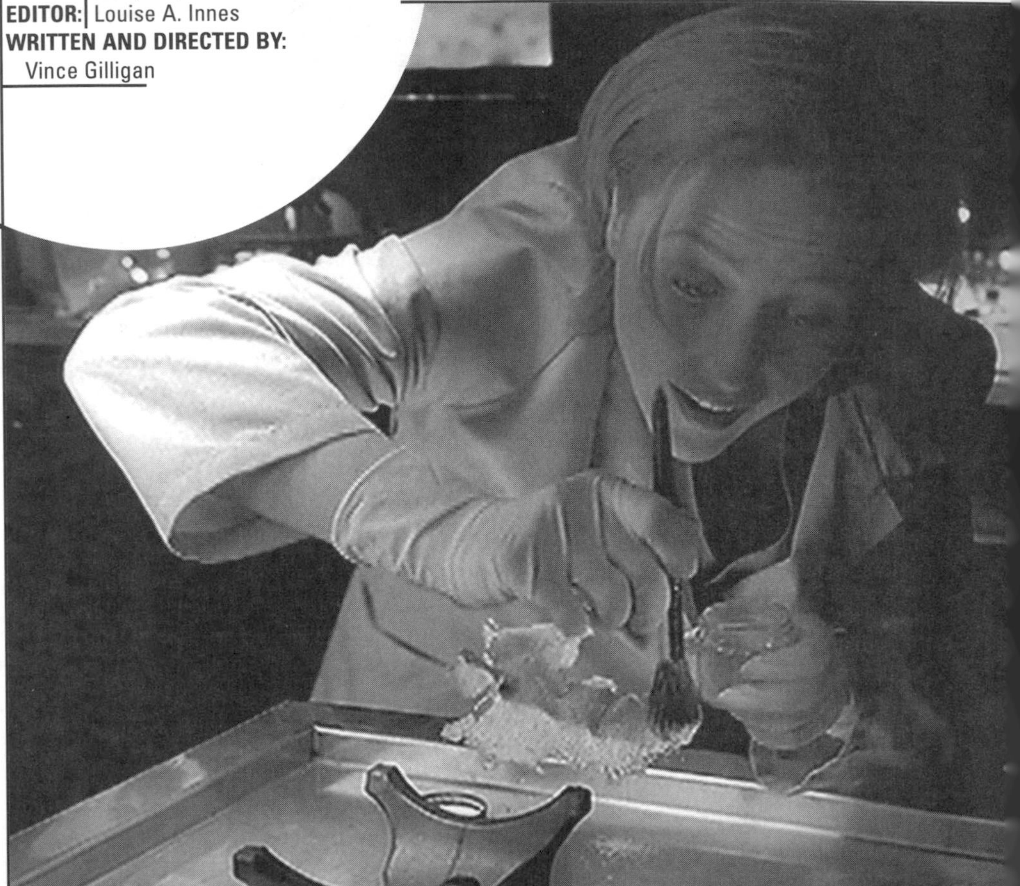

A pair of Missouri trailer park denizens discover that a genie and three wishes are not all they are cracked up to be.

GUEST STARS:

Mitch Pileggi (A.D. Skinner)
Paula Sorge (Jenn)
Will Sasso (Leslie Stokes)
Kevin Weisman (Anson Stokes)
Paul Hayes (Jay Gilmore)
Brett Bell (Morgue Attendant)

PRINCIPAL SETTINGS:

Creve Coeur, Missouri; Olivette, Missouri

A golf cart zips through the rows of buildings of a storage facility called U-Stor-It in Creve Coeur, Missouri. Behind the wheel is Jay, the fat, fortyish owner of the facility, who is talking into a walkie-talkie.

"Anson. Calling Anson. Where are you, Anson?"

There is no answer. Jay continues the search and, at one point, zips past the subject of his search, a sullen twentysomething guy reading a boating magazine inside an open storage unit. Jay screeches the golf cart to a stop and backs up to confront his AWOL employee.

"Anson, get out here.

"I've warned you about your attitude. You clean out 407? No, of course you haven't cleaned out 407. You've only had all damn morning. You think you're ever gonna own any of those boats in that magazine, the way you're going? Huh? You think you're ever gonna amount to anything? You can't even finish a simple job."

Anson says. "A monkey could do this job, right, Jay?"

"Well, you can't, so what's that say about you?"

Anson tells him to shut up under his breath. Jay stares angrily at him. "Excuse me? I didn't catch that. You clean out 407. You move out that deadbeat's stuff and you do it now. And when I come back in an hour, it better be done."

Jay zooms off.

Anson picks up a pair of bolt cutters and drags them over to Unit 407. He snips off the rusted padlock and rolls up the door. He steps inside and groans at the sight of dusty furniture and moldy cardboard boxes. He pulls out a rug. The rug gives an unexpected jerk. He drops the rug and watches as it jerks again. Anson picks up the bolt cutters and holds them like a club.

With his other hand he unrolls the rug to reveal the body of a woman, lying motionless, eyes closed. Beneath one eye is a jewel teardrop. Anson tentatively reaches out to touch her. Her eyes snap open.

Jay pulls up in front of the unit and sees that it is still a mess. The rug lies open. The mystery woman and Anson are gone.

"Anson! Oh, that's it, Anson! You hear me, Anson?"

Jay's voice strangles off and goes silent. He turns away, making swallowing sounds. He puts his hands to his jaw. Fearfully he lowers them to reveal that he has no mouth.

•

Mulder is in conference with a man in his office. He pages through the man's medical file. He offers the man some coffee. The man declines. Scully enters the office. The man does not turn to face her.

Mulder says, "Special Agent Dana Scully, this is Jay Gilmore."

Jay turns to face her. Scully nearly jumps out of her skin at the sight of his swollen and stitched distortion of a mouth. She recovers and extends her hand.

"Nice to meet you," says Scully.

"Nice to meet . . . likewise," says Jay.

"Mr. Gilmore came all the way to see us from Missouri. The 'Show Me State.' "

Jay says, "They told me you were the people to best understand my sitch . . . my situ . . ."

Jay gives up as Mulder hands Scully a couple of 8 x 10's. "This is Mr. Gilmore's situation."

Scully sees presurgery photos of Jay, which show that at one point he had no mouth.

Mulder says, "This condition came on very suddenly, about a month ago."

"Anson Stokes. He did this to me. I don't know how. I just . . . I know it was him," says Jay.

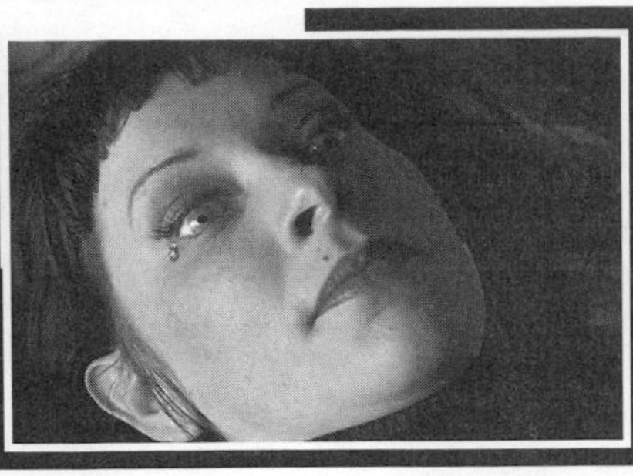

Mulder explains, "Anson Stokes is a former employee of the self-storage yard that Mr. Gilmore owns. Apparently there was some bad blood between you two."

"He told me to shut up," says Jay, pointing to his painfully reconstructed mouth.

"Then Mr. Gilmore was stricken and Anson Stokes was nowhere to be found. He resurfaced several days later. The police wanted to question him. But he refused."

"Do you know what he said? He said they had nothing on him," says Jay.

Mulder says, "To be fair, sir, they didn't, they don't."

"They had to make me a whole new mouth," says Jay. "You think Blue Cross is going to pay for this? Uh-uh. I demand justice."

•

Mulder and Scully pull to a stop in front of the Mark Twain Trailer Court in Olivette, Missouri, the last known address of Anson Stokes. They get out and walk up a street.

Scully says, "Mulder, all I'm saying is that—"

"I know. This may not be a crime and this guy Stokes may not know anything about it."

"There is a condition called microstomia, 'small mouth,' " says Scully. "It's brought on by the disease scleroderma. And it's the overproduction of collagen. It can reduce a person's mouth to a tiny little opening."

"Yeah, but that takes months to develop, right? It doesn't just happen in the blink of an eye. Gilmore's surgeons were stumped. They're writing it up in the *New England Journal of Medicine*."

"Well, there's always nasal aplasia, the complete absence of a nose," says Scully.

"That's the nose, Scully. We're talking mouth here."

"Yeah, but what we're talking, Mulder, is medical. Physiological. Not criminal, not as far as I can see."

"Well, maybe," says Mulder. "But I still want to know why Anson Stokes doesn't want to talk to the police."

They stop and look up. A huge yacht is shoehorned in between two low-rent mobile homes, nautical pennants fluttering in the breeze.

"That's a little out of place, wouldn't you say?" asks Scully.

•

Inside a trailer, Anson Stokes has spotted the two agents and is in a panic. He calls out to his brother, Leslie, a paraplegic, who wheels in on a motorized scooter.

"What? What is it?" asks Leslie.

"IRS agents," says Anson. "Gotta be. Listen, you get rid of 'em, all right?"

Mulder and Scully knock on the door.

Finally the door creaks open. There is no one there. A moment later, Leslie backs his scooter into view.

"Hi," says Scully. "We're looking for a Mr. Anson Stokes?"

"He's not here," says Leslie.

Scully says, "Would you happen to know when he's coming back?" Leslie shakes his head. "We're Agents Mulder and Scully from the FBI."

"Oh, the boat, the boat's not ours! We . . . we're holding it for someone! They pay the taxes on it! Anson's not here!"

Leslie starts to close the door. Mulder stops him. "Whoa, whoa. What's your name?"

"Leslie Stokes."

"Oh, you're Anson's brother." Leslie nods.

Mulder looks inside the trailer and sees the mystery woman. "Hi there," says Mulder, eyeing her for a moment before turning his attention back to Leslie.

"We're not here to talk about the boat, Leslie. We'd like to talk to your brother about his former employer, Mr. Gilmore."

Scully adds, "And the unfortunate condition that he's found himself in. Would you happen to know anything about that?"

"The mouth thing?" Leslie asks. "That's just like . . . chemicals."

"Chemicals?" Scully asks.

"Well, yeah, you know, people store weird chemicals," says Leslie, talking very fast. "One time my brother smelled this weird smell, you know? It was just a guy with a meth lab, you know, like in one of the storage units. That's actually probably something . . . you guys should really look into that. Okay. I gotta go."

Leslie shuts the door.

"Now I see what's going on here," says Mulder, nodding, then smiling and shaking his head.

•

Mulder and Scully arrive at the U-Stor-It and go to Unit 407. Mulder takes a particular interest in the rug.

"According to Gilmore, he was standing right where I am when it happened," says Scully.

"Well, I don't smell any weird chemical smells. And you still have both your lips."

Mulder shines his flashlight into the dark corners of the unit. He looks into a moldy box and pulls out a calendar.

Mulder says, "1978. Long time since any of this stuff has seen the light of day."

Scully paws over the furniture. "It's too bad, Mulder. Underneath all this dust, this furniture is really wonderful."

"Oh, well, you want to hit some yard sales while we're out here?"

"Mulder, this furniture is expensive. Very expensive."

"What's your point?" asks Mulder.

"My point is that there's a lot of money sitting around here. And maybe something's missing?"

"Like what?"

"I don't know. Jewelry. I mean, Anson Stokes opened up this storage unit and then he just disappeared."

"And winds up with the *Titanic* in his driveway."

"There's your crime," says Scully. "Theft."

"It still doesn't explain what happened to Gilmore."

Mulder comes upon a framed photo of a large balding man dressed in a *Saturday Night Fever* suit, smiling broadly, with a good-looking babe on each arm, standing in front of a late 1970s convertible. He notices something familiar about the woman sitting in the car.

"Scully, check this out. Does this woman look familiar to you?"

"That's the woman from the trailer."

"That's the young woman from the trailer," he says. "How many centuries now has disco been dead?"

•

Anson paces the living room of his trailer as Leslie reads a magazine and the mystery woman watches TV.

Anson says, "Two down! Two down and I got nothing to show for it!"

"We got the boat," says Leslie.

"What the hell good is that? That thing is like a big, uh . . . it's a big . . ."

"White elephant," offers the woman.

Anson asks, "What? What does that mean?"

The woman says, "It's a big, expensive item that serves no purpose and is ultimately more trouble than it's worth."

"So what the hell did you give it to me for?"

"Because you asked for it."

Anson says, "I can appreciate that! But don't you think maybe you could have found some freakin' water to put it in?"

"You didn't specify water," says the woman.

"I gotta specify you put a boat in the freakin' water? That is a given! Freakin' white elephant. I can't even pay the taxes on it."

"Why don't you just use your last wish to get rid of it?" suggests Leslie.

"You want me to put you in a home or something, maybe, right now?" Anson asks. "Because I just told you, Leslie, that I wasted two wishes. And I am *not*—now, you listen—I am *not* gonna waste the third!"

He goes to the TV and slaps it off. He turns to the mystery woman.

"Concentrate here. Now let me figure this out. Third wish. Third wish. Third wish. Final wish. Hey, I'm just spitballing here, all right? If I happen to say 'I wish' by accident, that does not count. Not until I'm absolutely ready, okay?"

The woman says, "You could always give that guy his mouth back."

"Hey, all I said was I wish that Jay would shut the hell up. If you feel bad about what you did to him, fix it on your own dime, okay?"

"It doesn't work like that."

"Whatever. Leslie, would you help me out here?"

"Money," says Leslie. "Wish for money."

The woman rolls her eyes.

Anson says, "Okay. That's not bad. That's not bad. That's not bad. But don't you think maybe we should think of something that would generate money, instead of actual money?"

The woman sarcastically offers brains, talent, and hard work as possible suggestions. Leslie says a money machine. Anson brushes the suggestion off.

"An infinite number of wishes!" says Leslie.

"Okay," says Anson.

The woman says, "Just three, boys. Settle down."

"Dammit, this is hard," says Anson.

"You know, I have a thought. Granted, it's pretty obvious."

She indicates Leslie and his obvious plight. The brothers don't get it. She indicates Leslie with more emphasis. The brothers still don't get it.

"Oh, forget it," says the woman.

Finally a lightbulb goes on over Anson's head. He snaps his fingers and grins.

"I got it. I got it," says Anson. "Are you ready? Because I am ready. Here goes. I wish that I could turn invisible at will."

"You're kidding," says the woman.

"No, no, this is perfect! I could have an advantage that nobody else on earth can have! I can, you know, spy and learn secret information. Pick up stock tips."

"Sneak into a women's locker room," says the woman.

"Not just that, okay," says Anson. "I'm talking about James Bond–type stuff, you know?"

The woman says, "Your wish is breathtaking in its unoriginality."

"Hey, you don't have to like it, all right. You just have to do it."

"Done," she says.

Anson moves to the center of the room, holds up his hand, and stares at it.

"My clothes are gonna turn invisible, too, right?"

"You didn't specify clothes," says the woman.

"Son of a . . ." Anson yells. "Screw it."

He starts to peel off his clothes.

"Oh God, turn invisible, please," says the woman, turning away.

Anson goes transparent and then vanishes. The room echoes with his laughter. The invisible Anson races to the trailer door, opens it, and rushes down the wheelchair ramp, which bounces at each invisible step. He slams into a group of trash cans, which go flying. He lets out a yell as Leslie appears at the top of the ramp.

"Anson? You all right?"

"Yeah. Yeah. Can't see my damn feet," he says, giggling with joy. "Look out, world, here I come. I'm invisible, invisible, baby!"

Anson races down the row of trailers, knocking and kicking over mailboxes, planters, and bicycles. Leslie backs inside the trailer and is surprised to see the woman has disappeared.

Anson runs through his neighborhood and comes to a crosswalk at a busy intersection. On the other side of the street he spies two attractive young women standing by their bicycles. Anson is anxious to get to them. He waits for the walk signal and then charges

"YOUR WISH IS BREATHTAKING IN ITS UNORIGINALITY."—Jenn

across the street . . . and right into the path of an oncoming truck. *Bam!*

•

A strange depression of dirt, roughly the size and shape of a body, lays on the shoulder of the road. Flies are buzzing around it. A bicyclist pedals down the road, hits the body of invisible Anson, and flies head first over the handlebars.

•

Scully is in the morgue preparing for an autopsy. The morgue doors open and two attendants carefully wheel in an empty table. The attendants are spooked and leave. Scully is left alone with what she believes is an empty table. She reaches out a gloved finger, then several fingers. She can't believe it.

She has just touched an invisible body.

She quickly searches the cabinets and returns with a container of yellow fingerprinting powder that she proceeds to brush onto Anson's face, which slowly but surely reveals itself. Much later, Scully, with Mulder standing by, is completing the job of making the deceased Anson Stokes visible.

"I think you missed a spot here," says Mulder, pointing to Anson's shoulder. "I can see straight through to his ass. This is Anson Stokes, huh?"

"It is," says Scully. "His dental records are a match. He was found a half-mile from his house. He was probably hit by a car or truck or something."

"And he's invisible," says Mulder.

"Yes, he is," says Scully. "You know, Mulder, in the seven years we've been working together, I have seen some amazing things. But this . . . this takes the cake. It's gonna change the boundaries of science."

"It is amazing," says Mulder. "But I don't think it has anything to do with science.

"Remember Mr. *Saturday Night Fever*?" Mulder holds up the photo from the storage unit. "I did a little background checking. His real name is Henry Flanken. He redefined the term *overnight success.*"

Mulder continues, "In 1977, his net worth was thirty-six thousand dollars, and in 1978, it was thirty million dollars. Then there is the interesting way Mr. Flanken died."

"How's that?"

"Chronic, morbid tumescence," says Mulder.

Scully makes a face. "You don't mean what I think you mean?"

Mulder smiles. "Schwing! On April 4, 1978, he was admitted to Gateway Memorial Hospital with an extreme priapic condition. Apparently he was quite the specimen. They had to raise the doorframe in order to wheel him into his hospital room."

"Well, what does that have to do with any of this?"

Mulder shows her a second picture, a blowup of a section of the photo found in the storage unit of the woman sitting in the convertible.

Mulder says, "I think our mystery woman is the link, about whom I can find no information whatsoever. I think she's responsible for all of this."

Scully asks how.

"I don't know. But we need to talk to her."

"I think that I should stay here with the body," says Scully. "I mean, I don't think it's a good idea to leave him unguarded. This is truly amazing."

•

Mulder is consoling-questioning Leslie. Leslie is concerned about whether his brother suffered.

"No. I don't think he suffered. The part about him being invisible. That doesn't catch you off-guard, just a little?"

Leslie shrugs.

"Leslie, there was a woman here earlier. Where is she now?"

Leslie says, "She's . . . she's gone."

"Let me tell you where I'm going with this," says Mulder. "I think that woman is a jinniyah. Are you familiar with that term? It's the feminine for jinni, as in a demon or spirit from Middle Eastern folklore."

Mulder emphasizes the point by humming a few bars of the *I Dream of Jeannie* theme song. Leslie hums along. Mulder's smile fades.

He says, "Yeah. Except, Barbara Eden never killed anybody. All right, now in Arabic mythology they speak of these beings that are composed of flame or air, but take human form. They can perform certain tasks or grant certain wishes. They live in inanimate objects like a lamp or a ring. Is this beginning to sound familiar?"

Leslie shakes his head.

"Leslie, I believe your brother found just such an object in that storage facility, didn't he? He took possession of the jinniyah. He made some pretty outrageous requests, like Jay Gilmore's mouth and that yacht out in the driveway."

Leslie asks, "Whoa. Wait. You believe all that?"

"I do. And Leslie, for your own safety, so that what happened to your brother doesn't happen to you, I think you should hand over that object to me, right now."

Leslie goes to the other side of the room and returns with a tarnished brass knickknack, a cross between an incense burner and a sugar bowl, and hands it over to Mulder.

"You're doing the right thing," says Mulder.

•

Leslie is at the U-Stor-It, struggling to open the door to Unit 407. Leslie rolls in and shines a flashlight on the rolled-up rug.

•

Scully is in the morgue, enthusiastically snapping away at the completely yellow body of Anson. Mulder comes up behind her and asks her to come outside. Scully is reluctant to leave the body for even a moment, but follows him into an adjoining room.

Scully says, "I have a group of researchers flying in from Harvard Medical. I can't wait to see their faces."

Scully notices the brass knickknack.

"What's this?" she asks.

"It's not what I hoped it would be. Judging from the odor coming from inside, I think it's where the Stokes brothers keep their weed. But that's not what I wanted to show you."

Mulder angles a computer monitor toward her and clicks the mouse. Up pops some grainy black-and-white newsreel footage of Mussolini.

"Recognize him?" asks Mulder.

"Benito Mussolini."

"What about her?" Mulder points at a figure in the reviewing stand behind the dictator. It is the woman, dressed in period clothing and in her trademark sunglasses.

"Your mystery woman," says Scully. "Or someone who looks a lot like her."

"The computer says it is her.

"I ran her through Quantico's facial recognition software and couldn't come up with a match in the known felon database. But then I took a flyer and checked with the image bank at the National Archives. Voilà."

"Well, even if it is her, Mulder, what would she be doing with Mussolini?"

Mulder clicks the mouse. "Or Richard Nixon, for that matter?"

Footage of Nixon with the woman in the background comes up.

Mulder says, "I don't know. Except they're both men who got all the power they ever wished for, then lost it."

•

Inside the Stokes trailer, the woman is glum as she kicks open the rug. Leslie rolls up and gives the rug a cursory look.

He says, "See, I told you it would look good in here. Nice rug. How do you breathe in that thing?"

"Could we just get this over with, please? Three wishes. Go."

"Okay, don't rush me, all right?" says Leslie. "I wanna do this right. I'm gonna be smarter than Anson was. Dammit, Anson."

"Then can I once again offer you a suggestion?"

"What?"

For a second time, she indicates Leslie in his wheelchair. Leslie does not get it.

"This," she says. "Your disability. There was some tragedy involved here, I assume."

"Yeah, it was pretty tragic, I guess. Me and Anson were playing mailbox baseball. God, I miss that. Anson's driving, and I was leaning pretty far out the window there . . . Wait. You mean this?" He points at his chair. "Yeah! You're right! I could wish for a solid gold wheelchair! That would be sweet."

Leslie stares at a photo of his brother Anson. "But you know what? There's something I want more than that."

•

Scully enters the morgue with the three distinguished Harvard researchers in tow.

She says, "You're not going to believe your eyes. I certainly didn't."

Scully leads them to a storage drawer. She unfastens the padlock.

"Are you ready?"

She pulls open the door and slides out the drawer. There is no yellow-coated Anson. The drawer is empty.

"Well, he is invisible, after all," says Scully.

She probes the air where the body should be. There is no body, invisible or otherwise.

"He's there."

•

The Stokes brothers are sitting at the kitchen table. Leslie is gobbling down corn flakes. A banged-up, yellow-coated Anson sits across from him, his cereal untouched, his body twitching. Leslie pushes his bowl away.

"You know what, he's creeping me out," he says. "This isn't what I asked for. He's all weird and messed up."

The woman says, "He's been hit by a truck. What did you expect?"

"I asked you to bring him back to normal!"

"You asked me to bring him back," says the woman.

"Now he's starting to smell bad. C'mon! This isn't what I wanted! He's gotta at least be able to talk! Okay, you know what? That's my next wish. Wish number two. I wish Anson could talk."

"No, you don't," says the woman.

"Yes, I do! And that's final! I wish Anson could talk!"

The woman turns to Anson, who is sitting, staring off into space. "Done." Suddenly . . .

"AAAAAAAAHHHHHHH!"

Anson is screaming in pain. Leslie cringes at this latest development. The woman shuts her eyes.

•

Back in the morgue, Mulder is attempting to console Scully.

"I should just shoot myself," she says. "I was so happy. I was so excited. What was I thinking? An invisible man?"

"You saw it. It was real."

"I don't know what I saw, Mulder. I do know that having that kind of proof in my hand . . . it was too good to be true."

"I don't think that's why the body disappeared," says Mulder.

"Why did the body disappear?" asks Scully.

"I think it was the result of a wish being granted."

"A wish. Whose wish?"

"Who would want Anson Stokes back? I mean really, really back?"

Scully says, "His brother Leslie."

•

"AAAAHHHH!"

Anson is raising the dead with his screams as Leslie and the woman hold their ears. The scream finally peters out.

"Well, this is no good," Leslie points out.

"What did you do to me?" asks Anson.

Leslie is frantic. "What? You're back from the dead, man. What kind of gratitude is that?"

Anson drones, "What did you do to me?"

"I wasted two wishes on you, that's what I did!"

"I can't feel my heart," says Anson. "I can't feel my blood. I'm yellow! I'm cold. I'm cold."

Leslie leaves the room in frustration, followed by the woman. He turns up the heat in the trailer for his undead brother. "There, I turned the heat up, are you happy now, buddy? Are you happy?" Leslie screams from the other room. "Is there anything else I can do for you, buddy? Maybe wipe your little yellow butt?" Meanwhile, Anson rises and shambles over to the stove. Opening the oven door, Anson turns the oven knob, breaking it off. The sound of hissing gas is everywhere.

"Cold," says Anson.

In the other room, Leslie turns to the woman.

"Thanks for nothing!" he says.

"You want to make your third wish, champ? I'd like to get out of here before the blowflies hatch."

Leslie says, "Yeah, well, I tell you what. My last wish is gonna be for me. You hear that, Anson? I wasted two wishes on you! You don't even give a damn about that!"

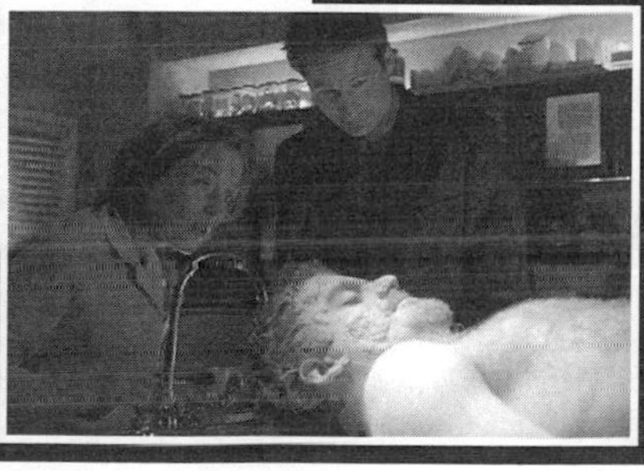

Anson fumbles open a box of matches and picks out one match in his fingers.

"All right. Third wish. I could wish for money. There's the invisibility thing. I guess that turned out pretty stupid, though, huh, Anson? To be invisible, that was real smart, huh?"

Anson reaches to strike the match against the side of the box. Mulder and Scully pull up at the front of the trailer. Anson continues to try to light the match. The woman sniffs the air and smells gas. Mulder and Scully have returned to the trailer park and are walking toward Leslie's home.

"Wait! I got it! Legs!" says Leslie.

Just as Anson's match flares.

The trailer explodes in a huge fireball. Mulder and Scully hit the dirt as the windows blow out of their car. The rolled-up rug tumbles out of the inferno and comes to rest in the street.

"Ow," says the woman's muffled voice from inside the rug.

•

Mulder has taken the woman to the manager's office, where he asks her to remove her sunglasses, exposing the teardrop near her unnaturally blue eyes.

"Do you have a name?" he asks.

"Not for a long time now," she says.

Mulder says, "How about if I call you Jenn? Short for jinniyah." The woman smiles at him.

Scully enters the office with the report that two bodies have been recovered from the fire. Mulder suggests they're Leslie and Anson Stokes.

"Looks like it," says Scully. "And Anson Stokes is visible now. Of course. But what I'd really love an explanation for is how his corpse got from my locked morgue all the way across town to the Mark Twain Trailer Park."

The woman looks at Mulder. "Ask him. He's got it all figured out."

Scully says, "I know what he'd say. He'd say you're some kind of jinni, from *The Thousand and One Nights* or something like that. And that you grant wishes."

"Well, there you have it," says Jenn.

Mulder says, "Well, one thing I haven't been able to figure out is whether you're a good jinni or an evil one. Everybody you come in contact with seems to meet a bad end."

Jenn is irritated. "That's the conclusion you are drawing, that I'm evil?"

"Well, possibly evil or possibly cursed—a curse to others."

"The only thing you people are cursed with is stupidity. All of you, everybody. Mankind. Everyone I have ever come into contact with. Without fail, always asking for the wrong thing."

"You mean, making the wrong wishes?" asks Mulder.

"Yeah. It's always 'Gimme money. Gimme big boobs. Gimme a big hoo-hoo. Make me cool like the Fonz.' Or whoever's the big name now."

"You've been out of circulation a long time," comments Mulder.

"So what? In five hundred years, people have not changed a bit."

"Five hundred years?" asks Scully.

"Granted, they smell better now, generally speaking. But human greed still reigns, shallowness, a propensity for self-destruction."

Scully is still not convinced. "You're saying that you have been a firsthand witness to five hundred years of human history?"

Jenn sighs. "I used to be human. I was born in fifteenth-century France. And then, one day, an old Moor came to my village, peddling rugs. And I unrolled one that an ifrit had taken residence in."

"An ifrit?" asks Scully.

"A very powerful class of jinni. He offered me three wishes. For the first, I asked for a stout-hearted mule. For my second, a magic sack that was always full of turnips. Did I mention this was fifteenth-century France?"

Mulder asks, "What was your third wish?"

"My third I pondered for a great while. I didn't want to waste it. So, finally, feeling very intelligent, I spoke up and I said '*Je souhaite une grande puissance et longue vie.*' I wish for great power and long life."

"And thus became a jinni yourself," says Mulder.

Jenn nods sadly as she touches the teardrop on her cheek. "Gave me the mark of the jinn, right there. It's forever. Sort of like a prison tattoo. I should have been more specific."

Jenn wants to know if she is under arrest.

"I can't think of anything we have to hold you on," says Scully. "Not surprisingly, we don't have any evidence of any of this. So, I think she's free to go."

Jenn says, "No, I'm not. He unrolled me."

Mulder gets it. "I get three wishes."

•

Mulder enters his apartment, followed by Jenn.

"So your partner left the airport rather quickly," says Jenn. "I don't think she likes me very much."

"I don't think she knows what to make of you. I don't think I do, either, really."

"Well, you can always give up your three wishes. I'll disappear, no hard feelings."

Mulder is silent.

"I didn't think so. So what's your first wish?"

Mulder asks Jenn what her wish would be.

Jenn says, "I'd wish that I'd never heard the word *wish* before. I'd wish that I could live my life moment by moment, enjoying it for what it is instead of worrying about what it isn't. I'd sit down somewhere with a great cup of coffee and I'd watch the world go by. But then again, I'm not you. So I doubt that's your wish."

"You know, I think I'm beginning to see the problem here. You say that most people make the wrong wishes, right?"

"Without fail. It's like giving a chimpanzee a revolver."

"This is because they make their wishes solely for personal gain. So the trick would be to make a wish that's totally altruistic, that's for everyone. So I wish for peace on earth."

"Peace on earth. That's it?"

Mulder says, "What the hell's wrong with that? You can't do it?"

"No. I can. It's done."

Mulder stares at Jenn, not understanding what's going on. He does notice that it is very quiet. He looks out his window and on to the street. There is no sign of life. Mulder leaves his apartment and wanders the deserted street.

"I guess I should have seen this coming," he says.

He goes in search of Scully at his office, inside the FBI building, and in Skinner's office. He is frustrated at the result of his wish.

"Jinni? Whatever the hell your name is," says Mulder.

She appears behind him. Mulder is relieved and pissed.

"What the hell is this?" asks Mulder.

"It's what you asked for, peace on earth. Listen."

"You know damn well that's not what I meant," says Mulder.

"You didn't specify."

"This has nothing to do with specificity. You don't have to wipe out the entire population of the whole planet just to effect a little 'peace on earth, and good will toward men.' "

"You didn't say 'good will toward men.' So, you expect me to change the hearts of six billion people? No religion in history has been able to pull that off, not Allah or Buddha or Christ. But you'd like me to do that in your name so what? You can feel real good about yourself?"

"Did I say that?" says Mulder. "I didn't say that."

"How grotesquely egotistical of you. I bet you wish you hadn't made your first wish."

Mulder says, "Yes, I do. Since you butchered the intent of that wish so completely."

Jenn nods as Mulder continues his rant, unaware that A.D. Skinner and a table full of agents are behind him.

"And another thing. I think you've got a really horrible attitude. I guess that comes from being rolled up in a rug for the last five hundred years. But we're not all that stupid, we're not all chimpanzees with revolvers. I think there's another possibility here, and that's just that you're a bitch."

Jenn motions Mulder toward the agents staring at him.

"Agent Mulder?" asks Skinner.

Jenn has disappeared, leaving Mulder in an embarrassing situation.

"Sir."

"How did you get in here?" asks Skinner.

Mulder forces a weak smile.

•

Jenn reappears in Mulder's office, where the agent is busy at his computer, drafting something that has a lot of legalese in it. Jenn reads over his shoulder.

"What are you, a lawyer?"

"I have to be with you," he says. "To get this last wish perfect I'm not gonna leave you any loopholes, not gonna let you interpret this as an edict to bring back the Third Reich, or to make everyone's eyes grow on stalks."

"Geez, and I was so looking forward to that."

Scully enters.

"Skinner called me, Mulder. Is everything all right?"

"You don't remember disappearing off the face of the earth for about an hour this morning?"

Scully gives him a strange look. "No."

"Then I guess everything's okay."

Scully turns to Jenn. "Could you give us a minute, please?"

Jenn says sure but doesn't move.

"Like today," says Scully.

Jenn is instantly gone.

Scully says, "Where the hell did she go? It's gotta be hypnotism, or mesmerism, or something."

"Scully, it is what it is. You examined an invisible body, remember?"

"I thought I did," says Scully. "Mulder, all right, say you're right. Say this is what it is. Then what you're doing is extraordinarily dangerous. I mean, you even said that yourself."

"The trick is be specific, to make the wish perfect. That way everyone is going to benefit. It's gonna be a safer world, a happier world. There's gonna be food for everyone. Freedom for everyone. The end of tyranny of the powerful over the weak. Am I leaving anything out?"

"It sounds wonderful," says Scully.

"Then what's the problem?" asks Mulder.

"Maybe it's the whole point of our lives here, Mulder, to achieve that. Maybe it's a process that one man shouldn't try and circumvent with a single wish."

Scully studies Mulder for a moment and then quietly leaves. Mulder starts typing again. Jenn reappears.

"You ready?" she asks.

Mulder shuts off his computer. He turns back to Jenn.

"Yeah. I'm ready," he says.

•

Mulder and Scully are sitting on the sofa in Mulder's apartment. "Can't believe you don't want butter on your popcorn. It's un-American," says Mulder.

He is putting a video in his VCR. Scully studies the video box.

"*Caddyshack*, Mulder?" she says.

"It's a classic American movie."

"That's what every guy says," says Scully. "It's a guy movie."

"Hey, when you invite me over to your place, we can watch *Steel Magnolias*."

Mulder and Scully uncap a couple of beers.

"So what's the occasion?" she asks.

"Just felt like the thing to do.

"Cheers," says Mulder as he and Scully clink bottles. "I don't know if you noticed, but I never made the world a happier place."

"Well, I'm fairly happy. That's something. So, what was your final wish anyway?"

He smiles as the movie starts.

•

Jenn is sitting at the lunch counter of an urban diner. She takes off her sunglasses. The teardrop has disappeared. A waitress approaches and sets a cup of coffee on the table. Jenn sips her coffee as she glances out the diner window at the passing parade. Jenn smiles.

After five hundred years, she has finally gotten her wish.

BACK STORY:

Vince Gilligan signed on to *The X-Files* four and a half years ago with a definite agenda.

"From the beginning I always had the intention of directing an episode," recalls Gilligan. "But I kept putting it off because I figured I didn't know enough."

But as the seasons came and went, Gilligan slowly became accustomed to the techniques of directing an *X-Files* episode, picking the brains of established *X-Files* directors like Kim Manners and Rob Bowman and, on one occasion, directing a couple of hours of insert shots. However, as Season 7 approached and the rumors persisted that this would be the final season, Gilligan knew it was time to fish or cut bait. He approached Carter and was given a slot to write and direct his first episode.

David Amann remembers Gilligan's odyssey. "Initially Vince was planning on writing a real stark and scary show. But as he got closer to the date he was scheduled to direct, he decided to go with a lighter show."

Gilligan was beginning to feel the heat. "For months and months I knew the deadline was looming and I had to write a story that I would direct. It was very scary."

And it was with fear and uncertainty as his guide that Gilligan created "Je Souhaite," a tongue-in-cheek bit of lunacy in which Mulder and Scully encounter a centuries-old genie and Mulder is granted three wishes. Chris Carter remembers being impressed with Gilligan's storyline.

"Vince had been playing around with somebody finding something in a storage locker. He played around with several different ideas and one day he came in with this idea of a genie and three wishes. The one thing I noticed right away was that the relationship between Mulder and the genie was very sweet."

As he was writing "Je Souhaite," Gilligan remembered that he started to be concerned that he might be painting himself into a corner. "I did not intend to make it a hard episode to direct. I thought I was writing a very simple story. But before I realized it, I was blowing up a trailer, having a truck hit an invisible man, and all sorts of strange genie effects."

Gilligan stepped onto *The X-Files* soundstage for the first day of "Je Souhaite" in a state of panic. "I looked at all the people on the set, standing around and looking at me, and I thought, 'Oh man, I'm going to be exposed as an impostor.' Fortunately everybody decided to take pity on me."

Gilligan eventually overcame his first-day jitters and settled into a natural, easygoing style of directing, managing the inevitable surprises and unexpected turns calmly. In particular, the actors found that the working environment under Gilligan was impressively stress-free.

Gillian Anderson remembers, "Vince was a very calm and even influence on the set. He had a very casual and knowledgeable approach to things."

Paul Rabwin recalls that Gilligan's calmness stood him in especially good stead during the sequence when the dead invisible man is painted with gold powder by Scully. "The actor who played Anson was being covered with yellow powder when he suddenly announced that he was having an allergic reaction to the powder and started scratching himself. They ended up playing around with the powder mixture and finally came up with something the actor could tolerate."

Rabwin also spent many hours going through newsreel footage to find historical footage of Mussolini and Nixon in which they could computer-insert the image of the genie.

Easily the most logistically challenging sequence in the show centered on Mulder's wish for world peace and his resulting walk down deserted city streets. Producer Harry Bring recalls that the only way they could effectively shut down eight blocks of downtown Los Angeles was to shoot the scene early on a Sunday morning.

"We shot four takes and wouldn't you know it but on the one perfect take, a derelict had somehow eluded all our security people and walked right through the shot. We printed it anyway." (The man was removed digitally at the editing stage.)

"Je Souhaite" turned out to be a lighthearted episode with a thoughtful subtext. Scully was decidedly out of character in her dealings with the dead invisible man, but Mulder's obsessive nature in casting the ultimate three-wish list was perfectly in character.

"It was real tough," said Gilligan. "But now that it's over, I'm glad that I didn't simply write a talking heads show."

FACTS:

Janeane Garofalo was originally approached to play the role of the genie but was not available.

Paula Sorge has appeared on *Malcolm & Eddie* and *Rude Awakening,* and played Tracy in the cult fave *Bar Girls*.

episode 7X22

REQUIEM

EPISODE: 7X22
FIRST AIRED: May 21, 2000
EDITOR: Heather MacDougall
WRITTEN BY: Chris Carter
DIRECTED BY: Kim Manners

Mulder and Scully return to the place where it all began to investigate the collision between an American plane and a UFO. Their quest leads to the sudden disappearance of Mulder and Scully's discovery that the inexplicable truth may lie inside her.

GUEST STARS:

Mitch Pileggi (A.D. Skinner)
Leon Russom (Detective Miles)
Andy Umberger (Special Agent Chesty Short)
Peter MacDissi (Prison Guard)
Laurie Holden (Marita Covarrubias)
Nicholas Lea (Alex Krycek)
Eddie Kaye Thomas (Gary)
Judd Trichter (Richie)
Zachary Ansley (Billy Miles)
Gretchen Becker (Greta)
William B. Davis (The Cigarette-Smoking Man)
Sarah Koskoff (Teresa Hoese)
Darin Cooper (Ray Hoese)
Tom Braidwood (Frohike)
Dean Haglund (Langly)
Bruce Braidwood (Byers)
Brian Thompson (The Bounty Hunter)
Grace and Kelly Demontesquiou (Baby)

PRINCIPAL SETTINGS:

Bellefleur, Oregon; Washington, D.C.;
Borj Sidi Toui, Tunisia

A sheriff's cruiser races down a dark, rural highway in Bellefleur, Oregon, its light bar strobing into the night. Over the radio is heard . . .

"Unit four. I got a fire out on the horizon! Something burning out here at the twenty-mile marker!"

A dispatcher's voice crackles back. "Unit four, confirmation of downed aircraft burning."

The dispatcher's voice alerts all units to a 10-13.

"Unit four, this is Detective Miles. I'm coming right at you, Ray. Now you wait for backup before you head out, alright? Unit four. Come back, deputy."

Miles waits for a response. All he gets is static.

Suddenly the cruiser's clock begins to race backward. The car's engine seizes up and dies. He spots another sheriff's cruiser stopped up ahead in the road. Miles's cruiser fishtails and skids to a crashing stop against the other cruiser.

Miles, a cut over one eye, is dazed as he works his way out of the car. In the distance a fire is burning. Miles notices that his watch is also racing in reverse. He approaches the other car.

"Deputy Hoese? Ray?"

He sees Deputy Ray Hoese slumped against the wheel, unconscious, his face battered, blistered, and burned, but apparently alive. Detective Miles begins to panic. He looks down to see a green bubbling substance eating at the asphalt and the bottom of his shoes. As he looks up from this, Miles notices a figure standing behind him. It is an exact duplicate of Ray Hoese. He is unscathed, except for the green substance oozing out of the three bullet holes in his chest.

•

Deputy chief auditor Special Agent Chesty Short is talking to Mulder.

"Lariat car rental. The totals." He whistles. "Would you like to see the figure?" asks Short.

Short holds out the stack of receipts and paperwork to Mulder.

Mulder asks, "Is that a lot?"

"A lot?" asks Short. "Gas, expenses, the motel rooms alone. By FBI standards, these numbers are out of control."

Mulder says, "We could start sharing rooms."

Short does not have much of a sense of humor. "You're under evaluation. There has to be a point when we say no."

"You can't really compare what we do to other departments in the Bureau."

"Right," says Short. "This business with aliens."

"Well, there's more to it than that."

"But at the end of the day, you'd say aliens are your real focus."

"That's the reason I got started, yeah," says Mulder.

"Investigating your sister's abduction and the government conspiracy around it. Both of which've been resolved. Correct?"

"Nothing has been resolved, exactly," says Mulder.

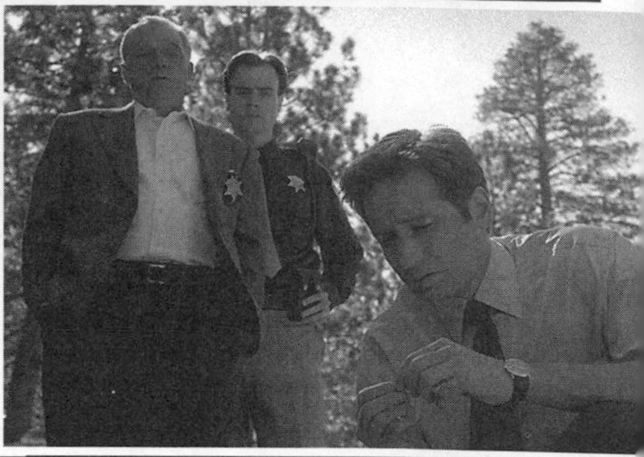

Short says, "In this case report here it's concluded your sister is dead. As well as the men who took her. This is your handwriting here on the report, Agent Mulder?"

"Yeah," Mulder admits.

"So what exactly's left to investigate?"

•

A din rises up at the far end of the overcrowded cell block in a dark prison in Tunisia. The prisoners go berserk at the sight of an attractive blonde woman being escorted into the cellblock by a burly Tunisian guard.

It is Marita Covarrubias.

She walks to a particular cell and stares coldly at the mass of humanity inside.

"Your release has been arranged," says Covarrubias.

A prisoner appears at the bars.

It is Alex Krycek.

Krycek says, "Marita Covarrubias. Last time I saw you I left you for dead."

Covarrubias says with a small smile, "Alex, if it was strictly up to me, I'd leave you here to rot, too."

•

Back in the FBI office, it is Scully's turn to talk with Short.

"I see the money bleed out, but it just doesn't seem to make the results of your work any better. So many of the cases you investigate are left unexplained. It makes it hard to justify the expense," says Short.

Scully says, "So much of the work that we do cannot be measured in standard terms."

"How would you measure it?" asks Short.

"We open doors with the X-Files which lead to other doors."

"Doors leading to a conspiracy of men," he quotes from a report, "who cooperated with alien beings to create human/alien hybrids. So we could all become slaves of an alien invasion."

"I believe that there was once a conspiracy," says Scully. "I believe I was taken by men who subjected me to medical tests which gave me cancer and left me barren."

"But you don't believe in aliens?"

"I've seen things that I cannot deny."

•

Covarrubias watches at Krycek as he showers.

"Who sent you?" asks Krycek.

"The Smoking Man," says Covarrubias. "He's dying."

This gets Krycek's attention.

•

Mulder pays another visit to auditor Short.

"You said you were finished," says Mulder.

Short says, "I turned in my report and was asked to go over a few things. As you know, the times we live in, the world is changing fast."

"I'm missing your point," says Mulder.

"As I said, this is an evaluation, Agent Mulder. To understand what you do, so if you go forward, you can do so more responsibly."

"That sounds more like a threat."

"Cost-benefit analysis. But if you want the truth, I really don't care one way or the other. You mostly record bizarre facts on bizarre cases. In other words, information-gathering. Something, it seems to me, you can easily do on the Internet."

Mulder explains that he can't do his job sitting in an office.

Short says, "If you spend so much time and money looking for aliens, responsibly you should narrow your search."

"To where?" asks Mulder.

"Wherever they are," says Short. "It's not unreasonable. It's just a matter of reducing your vision."

•

In Oregon, a car pulls to a stop at the sight of the wreck of the two sheriff's cruisers and two young men get out. They spot Detective Miles coming out of the woods toward them.

"What's the problem?" asks Miles, who, despite a cut, is seemingly none the worse for the previous night's experience.

"Isn't that your car, Mr. Miles?" asks the first young man.

Miles says, "Yeah. There was a small accident. Everything's all right. What are you boys doing out here?"

"Well, we heard there was a plane crash," says the second young man. "Military jet fighter collided midair with a UFO."

Miles says, "Navy found their plane about three miles away. We've seen no evidence of any other crash."

The second boy says, "But we heard a sheriff say he saw a fire burning off the highway at the twenty-mile marker."

"There's nothing out here," says Miles. "No fire. No sign of a fire. You boys go on home." He starts to leave. "There's nothing to see here."

•

Mulder walks into his office to find Scully staring at his "I Want To Believe" poster.

"I think I'm in big trouble," says Mulder.

Scully says, "C'mon, Mulder. How many times have they tried to shut us down?"

"Yeah, but I've never actually assaulted an auditor before."

"Did you hurt him?" she asks, smiling.

"I reduced his vision a little bit," he says.

The phone rings. Mulder picks up and puts the call on the speaker.

"Agent Fox Mulder?"

"Speaking."

"My name is Billy Miles. I don't know if you remember me."

Mulder and Scully trade looks. How could they forget?

"Oregon, seven years ago," says Mulder. "You had multiple abduction experiences. I'm here with Agent Scully."

Scully asks, "Billy, are you all right?"

"Yeah. This may seem weird, me calling like this, but I don't know where else to turn."

"Is it happening again, Billy?" asks Mulder.

A door in Billy's house opens. Billy lowers his voice.

"Yeah. But not to me this time," he says as his father, Detective Miles, approaches. Billy quietly puts the phone back on the cradle.

Mulder turns to Scully as the phone clicks off.

"More alien abductions, Scully," he says.

"I don't know how we could possibly justify the expense."

"We'd probably turn up nothing."

"Let's go waste some money."

•

Krycek and Covarrubias climb a flight of stairs in the darkened, spare Watergate apartment building in Washington, D.C. They approach a door and knock. A woman named Greta opens the door.

"Hi," she says. "He's anxious to see you."

She walks Covarrubias and Krycek into the apartment and up to the Cigarette-Smoking Man. He sits in a wheelchair, his face pale, his hair thin and white. He is breathing through a shunt that has been put into his neck. His dead eyes light up at the sight of Krycek, who is shocked at his appearance.

"I was worried about you, Alex," says CSM.

Krycek says, "Cut the crap, old man."

"I heard about your incarceration."

"You had me thrown into that hellhole."

CSM says, "For trying to sell something that was mine, was it not? I hope we can all move forward and put the past behind us. We have a singular opportunity now."

"A singular opportunity?" asks Krycek.

"There's been a crash in Oregon," says CSM in a labored voice. "An alien ship has collided with a military aircraft. Recovery is all-important. It's Roswell and Corona all over again, fifty years later. It's our chance to rebuild the project."

Greta hands a lit cigarette to Cigarette-Smoking Man. CSM takes a deep puff on the cigarette through the shunt as Covarrubias and Krycek stare in stunned silence.

"How do you know someone hasn't already recovered it?" asks Covarrubias.

"It's never quite so easy," says CSM.

•

The two young kids, Gary and Richie, are again prowling the woods with a flashlight and a Geiger counter. There is an increase in the static being picked up.

Suddenly Gary is captured by a force field. He is shaken and begins vibrating at warp speed. Richie, far ahead, is unaware of what is happening to Gary, concentrating on the Geiger counter readings. His flashlight suddenly strikes something ahead. The beam seems to refract at odd angles.

Richie turns back excitedly to Gary, only to find that his friend has disappeared.

Richie calls out to his friend. Suddenly his flashlight begins to glow red-hot. He drops it like a hot potato. The Geiger counter begins to go crazy. Richie takes off as the flashlight bursts into flame.

Mulder says, "You find the UFO and he won't be able to deny the truth."

Another sheriff's cruiser, this one banged up, pulls up in front of the house. It is Billy's father, Detective Miles.

"Talking to some people you might remember, Dad," says Billy. "From the FBI."

Scully introduces herself and Mulder.

"What brings you folks out here? You're not thinking this incident is some kind of UFO?"

Mulder says, "Crash of an unidentified craft."

"Well, I've been on with the FAA. You might want to follow up. Looks an awful lot like there was no crash at all."

•

Mulder, Scully, and the two sheriffs pull to a stop on a stretch of highway where Miles says the collision occurred. As they step out of the car, Mulder's foot comes down on a weathered and worn X spray-painted on the asphalt.

"RECOVERY IS ALL-IMPORTANT. IT'S ROSWELL AND CORONA ALL OVER AGAIN, FIFTY YEARS LATER. IT'S OUR CHANCE TO REBUILD THE PROJECT."—The Cigarette-Smoking Man

Mulder and Scully pull up in front of Billy Miles's house. Deputy Billy Miles comes down the steps of the house to greet them.

"Agent Mulder and Agent Scully."

"You're wearing a badge," says Mulder.

Billy says, "Never thought of myself as a cop, but it's been three years now. My dad got them to fudge the psych qualifications."

Their conversation reveals that Billy is divorced and living with his father. Mulder and Scully notice the sadness surrounding him.

Mulder asks, "Have you ever been able to get over the abductions?"

Billy says, "Well, I have, but people haven't. No one really believes it. My dad still denies it ever happened. That any one of us was taken."

Mulder says, "Does he deny that it's happening now?"

"There was a crash. A Navy pilot hit an unidentified aircraft outside of town. The military found their jet, but the other craft hasn't been recovered."

Scully asks why not.

"It's our county," says Billy, "and we're in charge of coordinating efforts. But my dad has really been no help. Even though we have a deputy missing."

Mulder says, "Déjà vu all over again."

"That was there already, in case you're wondering at all about it," Miles says.

Scully says, "I watched Agent Mulder paint that there seven years ago."

"What for?"

"To mark an anomalous electrical disturbance," Mulder explains. "The kind where time gets bent or goes missing, or where your car loses power and dies in the middle of the road."

They continue to scour the roadway for clues. Scully hangs back. Miles points out skid marks that he says are his. Mulder kneels down, looking at a spot on the pavement that looks acid-eaten.

Scully calls them over to the other side of the road, where she has picked up a shell casing. Other shells lay on the roadside shoulder.

"Did the deputy carry a thirty-eight?" she asks.

"Thirty-eight Super," says Billy. "Why?"

"Three shots were discharged," says Scully. "I imagine they could've rolled from up there."

"What was he shooting at?" asks Miles.

Mulder says, "Probably nothing."

"Nothing?" questions Miles.

"Nothing's all you seem to find out here, Detective."

Mulder heads back to the car as Billy opens an evidence bag for Scully to deposit the shells.

"Was the missing deputy a good cop?" asks Scully.

"Yeah, sure. I guess," says Billy.

"Married? Single?"

"Married. New baby." Billy's father calls him over.

Mulder and Scully drive off, leaving Miles and Billy alone in the road. Billy hands the evidence bag to his father.

"You know, they only want to solve this," says Billy.

Billy gets in the car while Miles moves to the trunk, opens it, and places the evidence bag inside next to the face of a blistered and burned Detective Miles.

•

Mulder and Scully are on a quiet residential street, knocking on the door of a modest wood-frame house. A pretty young woman comes to the door.

Scully says, "I'm sorry to bother you, Mrs. Hoese. We're with the FBI."

The woman asks, "Is this about my husband?"

Mulder asks, "You're Teresa? Teresa Nemman?"

"Yes," says Teresa.

"Seven years ago. You came to Agent Scully and I for help. You were afraid of being abducted."

"Oh my God." A baby begins to cry inside the house. Teresa invites the agents in as she goes for her baby.

The agents sit with Teresa, who holds her baby, in the living room.

"I'm sorry," says Teresa. "I sort of lost it when I realized who you were."

Scully says, "We came to see if there was anything that you could tell us that might help to find your husband."

"We had no idea you were his wife," Mulder says.

"I don't know if it's important. Maybe I just hope it's not, but Ray and I have a connection that's even deeper for us."

Mulder understands. "He's an abductee, too."

"He kept it a secret from almost everyone," says Teresa. "It doesn't make you real popular around here. His experiences were a lot more terrifying than mine. He was taken many times. And tested. I have extensive medical records on him. And photos of his scars. I'll get you the files."

Teresa hands Scully the baby as she goes for them. Scully is soon cooing to the baby as if it were her own. Mulder watches her.

•

Mulder is laying in his motel room bed, studying the records and photos of Ray Hoese's encounters with aliens. He is deep in thought when suddenly there is a knock on the door.

"Who is it?" he asks.

"It's me," says Scully.

Scully enters. She is pale, perspiring.

"What's wrong, Scully?" asks Mulder. "You look sick."

Scully says, "I don't know what's wrong."

Mulder brings her inside and gets her to the bed, where she sits down.

"I was starting to get ready for bed and I started to feel really dizzy. Vertigo or something. I started to get chills."

"Do you want me to call a doctor?"

"No. I just want to get warm."

Mulder helps her into bed and under the covers. He lies down next to her on top of the covers and holds her.

"Thank you," she says.

"It's not worth it, Scully," Mulder says softly, his mouth at her face.

"What?"

"I want you to go home," he says.

"Mulder, I'm going to be fine."

"No, I've been thinking about it. Looking at you today, holding that baby, knowing everything that's been taken away from you. The chance for motherhood and your health. And it made me think that maybe they're right."

"Who's right?"

"The FBI. Maybe what they say is true, if for all the wrong reasons. It's the personal costs that are too high. There's so much more you need to do in your life. So much more than this."

Mulder caresses her face.

"There has to be an end, Scully." He gently kisses her cheek.

•

Outside the motel, Krycek sits in a car, keeping tabs on Mulder and Scully. He is on a cell phone to the Cigarette-Smoking Man's apartment, where Covarrubias watches as Greta gives CSM an injection.

Krycek says, "In spite of a great deal of effort, no one seems to be able to find this UFO of yours."

"Of course they can't," says the Cigarette-Smoking Man.

"You know why? 'Cause it's not here," says Krycek.

"It's there, Alex. I'm certain of it. Hidden in plain sight."

"You listen to me. If you're going to play games, the two of them, Mulder and Scully, they're going to beat me to it."

"Are you saying that Mulder and Scully are there looking for the UFO?" asks CSM.

"They're looking for a missing deputy," says Krycek.

"Well, they're looking for the right thing, but in the wrong place."

Krycek says, "You said we were looking for a ship."

"Find the deputy, find the ship," CSM says, then hangs up.

•

A knock on the door startles Teresa out of her sleep. She slips on a bathrobe and cautiously goes to the door.

"Who is it?" she asks.

She sees a silhouette of a man on her front porch. It looks like a cop.

"Ray?" she says as she opens the door to reveal her husband, Ray Hoese. "Oh my God, oh my god. I was worried. I was so sure."

Teresa clutches her husband to her. "What did they do to you this time?

"Ray, talk to me." Teresa notices her husband's blank expression and backs away. "You're not my husband."

She races back into the house and up the stairs, followed by zombie Ray. Teresa grabs a pair of scissors and leaps at the man, driving the scissors into his chest. There is no effect, other than the holes in his chest beginning to bubble green. Teresa doubles over, trying to shield her face.

Her eyes begin to burn and blister.

Teresa, now unable to see, frantically flails and crawls back toward the baby's room. She reaches the baby's crib just as Ray comes around a corner and reaches down for her, carrying her away as the baby cries.

•

Billy Miles walks out of the Hoese house to meet Mulder and Scully, who have just pulled up to the scene of a full-scale police investigation.

"What happened, Billy?" asks Mulder.

"Teresa's gone. She's been taken. They took her."

"How do you know?" asks Scully as they head back toward the house.

"The door was open," says Billy.

Mulder heads for the nursery. He stops and looks down.

"Scully. The floor. What do you see?"

She sees a spot on the floor that has been eaten away as if by acid.

"Same thing as out on the road," says Mulder. "You've seen it before."

"Yeah. I have. We both have." Mulder leaves the nursery.

Billy does not know what they're talking about.

Scully says, "It's a biological toxin, emitted as a gas through the bloodstream."

"From who?" asks Billy.

"From what is arguably an alien," Scully says.

Scully experiences another wave of vertigo. Billy moves to steady her.

"Are you okay?" he asks.

"Yeah. I'm fine. Thanks."

•

The Cigarette-Smoking Man takes another hit off his cigarette through his throat shunt with the aid of nurse Greta and thanks her as she walks away. He turns his attention to Covarrubias.

She asks, "Why the trouble to bring Krycek here and then toy with him?"

"Do you trust Alex, Marita?"

"Then why bring him here at all?" she asks.

CSM says, "You misunderstand. I have great faith that Alex will find the ship. But if I told him how, he'd be tempted to sell the information."

"And you're certain it's there?"

"Yes. But it won't be there forever. It's rebuilding itself."

Covarrubias wants to know what will happen if he finds the ship.

"To possess it is to possess the answer to all things. Every possible imaginable question."

"To God?" she asks.

CSM smiles at this question coming from the normally cold and clinical Covarrubias.

"There is no God, Marita. What we call God is only alien, an intelligence much greater than us."

"They're coming here, aren't they?"

"They're only coming back," he says.

•

Scully comes out of the house, looking for Mulder. She sees him in the car. Mulder's eyes lock onto Richie, who is standing across the street, watching what's going on with the other neighborhood looky-loos. Mulder jumps out of the car. Richie sees Mulder coming at him and begins to walk the other way.

"Hey, what are you doing?" asks Mulder. He grabs Richie and turns him around.

"I was just standing there. Is that against the law?"

They are joined by Scully and Billy.

"Do you know this guy?" Mulder asks Billy.

Billy asks, "What are you doing, Richie?"

"They took him," says Richie. "They took Gary. He was just gone!"

"Relax," says Mulder. "Slow down."

"They're out there! I don't care what your dad says, Billy!"

"My dad?" asks Billy.

Richie says, "He was out there, too! He knows!"

Billy takes off.

•

Mulder and Scully have persuaded Richie to take them to the spot on the isolated stretch of highway where Gary disappeared. They get off the highway and tramp over rocks into the woods.

"I was shining my flashlight into the dark," Richie says, "looking for the UFO, and the beam hit this spot in space and it, like, bent the light."

"And then what happened?"

"I yelled 'Gary!' and I looked, but he wasn't there, you know, he wasn't anywhere, man. Then the flashlight got really hot and I dropped it. Right around here somewhere."

Mulder stomps through the brush as Richie continues to scour the ground. Scully moves off in a slightly different direction. After a few steps, her body is suddenly taken control of by some invisible force. She begins to vibrate, shake, and levitate within the force field.

Richie comes upon the flashlight, just as Mulder turns around and notices that Scully has disappeared. He calls after her but gets no answer. Mulder begins a frantic search and finds her semiconscious on the ground. She is afraid and confused. He urges her to stay still. Mulder sends Richie for some water and props Scully up and holds her.

"I just hit the ground," she says breathlessly.

"Lie still," urges Mulder.

"Why is this happening to me?"

"It's okay."

"What the hell is going on, Mulder?"

Mulder says, "I don't know. But these aren't just random abductions, Scully. And we'd better warn Billy Miles of that."

"Warn him of what?"

"These abductees aren't just systematically being taken. They're not coming back."

•

Billy enters his house and calls for his dad but gets no answer. He starts at the sound of the floor creaking, draws his gun, and turns to see his father stepping out of the shadows.

"Billy, what are you doing?" Miles asks.

"You stay where you are," says Billy, his gun aimed at his father.

Detective Miles steps forward. "Billy, it's me."

"I said stay where you are!"

"Dammit, Billy. Listen to me."

"No. I don't know who you are, but you are not gonna take me."

"I'm your father. Are you going to shoot your father?"

"If you're my father, then why won't you believe me?"

"I believe you, Billy. I just want it all to go away. Give me the gun, son."

Billy's hand begins to shake as his father reaches out and touches the gun. He breaks down as his father takes the gun from his hand, collapsing into a chair.

Detective Miles instantly morphs into the Bounty Hunter, just as Mulder and Scully's car pulls up outside.

Mulder and Scully call for Billy as they open the front door. They get no answer and draw their guns as they enter the house to find it empty.

•

Two days later, Mulder is leaning back in the chair in his office, idly tossing a basketball, in the aftermath of their adventures in Oregon. A.D. Skinner suddenly appears in the doorway.

"Agent Mulder."

Mulder turns to him. "What's our punishment this time? Thumbscrews or forty lashes?"

Skinner is impassive.

"C'mon in, Walter. Sit a spell. This could be the last time you take a trip down to these offices."

"You went to Oregon," says Skinner.

"Guilty as charged. If they're coming down on you for that, I'm sorry, I truly am."

"Fortunately, they think that I make a contribution to the Bureau," Skinner says.

"Oh, well, yeah. Stick to a budget and they say you're making a contribution. But push

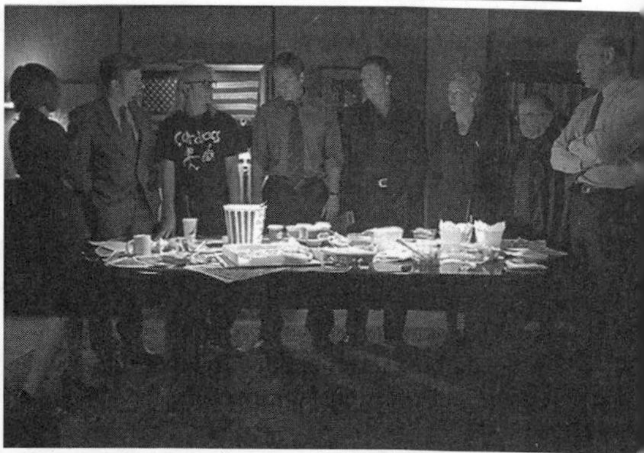

the limits of your profession and they say you're out of control."

"You could bring home a flying saucer and have an alien shake hands with the president. What it comes down to, Agent Mulder, is they don't like you."

Mulder knows what Skinner is saying is true.

"Well, we didn't bring home a flying saucer. Or an alien."

"Yeah. So I've been told."

Krycek and Covarrubias step up behind Skinner. Mulder immediately rushes for Krycek as Skinner moves to stop him from taking his enemy's head off.

"Mulder! I think you should listen to him," says Skinner.

Krycek says. "You've got every reason to want to see me dead. But you've got to listen to me now. You have a singular opportunity."

"Here? Or you wanna step outside?" Mulder asks.

Covarrubias says, "Agent Mulder, Cancer Man is dying. His last wish is to rebuild his project. To have us revive the conspiracy. It all begins in Oregon."

looking at maps, computer printouts, and all manner of relevant data.

Frohike says, "What's amazing is that even the military satellites don't see this."

Langly says, "But JPL's Topex Poseidon shows it only as waveform data."

Byers says, "And here it appears simply as a micro burst of transmission error on the European Space Agency's ERS Two."

"In other words?" asks Skinner.

"In other words, you'd never know it's a UFO!" says Frohike.

Byers says, "If you didn't know what you were looking at. Or looking for."

"No wonder we couldn't see them!" says Langly.

Krycek says, "Listen, it's not gonna be there forever."

"As we all stand here talking, it's rebuilding itself," adds Covarrubias.

Scully leaves the room. Mulder catches up with her in the hallway.

"Mulder, if any of this is true . . ."

"If it is or if it isn't, I want you to forget about it, Scully."

"SCULLY, YOU HAVE TO UNDERSTAND! THEY'RE TAKING ABDUCTEES. AND YOU'RE AN ABDUCTEE. I'M NOT GOING TO RISK LOSING YOU."—Mulder

"The ship that that collided with that Navy plane . . . It's in those woods," says Krycek.

"There's no ship in those woods," says Mulder.

Krycek says, "It's there, cloaked in an energy field. While he mops up the evidence."

"Who?" asks Mulder.

Krycek says, "The Alien Bounty Hunter. Billy Miles, Teresa Hoese, her husband. He's eliminating proof of all the tests. We're asking ourselves, 'Where are they?' They're right there. They're right under our noses.

"I'm giving you the chance to change that," says Krycek. "To hold the proof."

Mulder asks, "Why me? And why now?"

"I want to damn the soul of that cigarette-smoking sonofabitch."

"Mulder?" Scully enters the office, shocked at who she sees.

•

The Lone Gunmen have joined the others around a table in Skinner's office. They are

"Forget about it?"

"You're not going back out there. I'm not going to let you go back out there."

Scully asks, "What are you talking about?"

"It has to end sometime. And that time is now."

"Mulder—"

"Scully, you have to understand! They're taking abductees. And you're an abductee. I'm not going to risk losing you."

They embrace.

"I won't let you go alone," says Scully.

•

At dusk, a car stops on a familiar stretch of Oregon highway, and Skinner and Mulder get out. Mulder moves to the trunk and reaches into a small pack. Skinner stares off into the woods.

"This is starting to feel like the snipe hunt I was afraid of," says Skinner.

"No such thing as a snipe, sir," says Mulder.

"You know my ass is on the line here, too, Agent Mulder."

"I know that."

They enter the woods.

Back at Skinner's office, Scully and the Lone Gunmen are continuing to go over the stacks of file folders and records. Scully is going over a particular file.

"This just can't be," she says.

The Gunmen gather around.

"What are you looking at?" asks Frohike.

Scully says, "Medical records. Billy Miles and other known abductees in Bellefleur, Oregon. They all experienced anomalous brain activity."

Scully passes the information around the table.

"Electroencephalitic trauma," Byers adds.

Scully says, "Which is exactly what Mulder experienced earlier this year."

"I don't understand," says Langly.

"There was something out there in that field. It knocked me back. Because it didn't want me. Mulder thinks that it's me that's in danger of being taken."

"When it's Mulder who's in danger," says Frohike.

Scully's eyes suddenly lose focus. Her balance goes and she falls as the Gunmen rush to her aid.

•

As Mulder and Skinner move through the woods, Mulder's laser pointers shoot out into the darkness. Mulder takes out other laser pointers and places them in a row, their beams shooting out into the darkness.

"How's this supposed to work?" asks Skinner.

"Not exactly sure, sir. But budgetarily, I'd say we're looking pretty good."

Mulder follows the red beams as they bend and converge in space. Suddenly the laser lines begin to stop in space, defining the rough shape of a dome behind an energy field.

Mulder reaches the field. He reaches out to touch it. His hand enters the field and begins to vibrate at top speed.

Skinner lays out another laser pointer and looks up.

Mulder is nowhere among the beams. Skinner begins looking for him and calls after him, but he has vanished.

Inside the field of energy, Mulder appears with an expression full of disbelief. A bright circle of light illuminates figures standing inside the cone: Billy, Teresa, Deputy Hoese, and others. There are blank, resigned expressions on their faces. On the outside, Skinner is still looking for Mulder, unaware that Mulder is right near him, but has disappeared behind the field.

Mulder approaches the circle of light, pauses, then enters as the others appear to welcome him.

He looks up and sees a massive spacecraft hovering overhead, so big that it appears to go on forever. Stunned, Mulder looks back at the group of people around him.

Approaching is the Bounty Hunter. Mulder's look of awe turns to fear. The bright lights of the craft overtake the group.

Outside the force field, Skinner is in a panic, still unable to see Mulder. Blinding bright lights suddenly shine in his face. Skinner watches as the craft rises above the tree tops, the light beam disappearing. "Mulder," Skinner says, watching the ship disappear, leaving Skinner alone in the darkness . . . and Mulder nowhere to be seen.

•

The Cigarette-Smoking Man's breathing is dry and raspy as he deals with Krycek and Covarrubias. "We've failed then. Perhaps you never meant to succeed. Anyway, the hour is at hand, I presume."

Krycek moves to CSM's wheelchair and spins it.

His assistant, Greta, asks, "What are you doing?!"

"Sending the devil back to hell," says Krycek.

As Covarrubias holds off Greta, Krycek pushes through the door and to the stairs outside CSM's apartment. For the first time, there is genuine fear on CSM's face. But, as always, his final words are chilling.

"As you do to Mulder, and to me, you do to all of mankind, Alex."

Krycek hesitates only a moment, then sends the wheelchair careening down the stairs; CSM falls from it and tumbles to the bottom. Krycek and Covarrubias descend the stairs and step over his motionless body.

•

Skinner has arrived at the hospital and is shown to a room where Scully sits in bed, looking thoughtfully out the window. She is looking much better.

"Agent Scully," he says as he enters the room.

"Hi," she says.

"How are you feeling?"

"I'm feeling fine. They're just running some tests on me."

Scully notices that Skinner is very emotional, unable to meet her eyes. She senses that he could cry at any moment.

"I already heard," she says, near tears herself.

Skinner breaks down.

"I lost him. I don't know what else I can say. I lost him. I'll be asked . . . what I saw. And what I saw I can't deny. I won't.

"We will find him. I have to." Scully is on the verge of tears.

Skinner turns to leave, then stops at the voice of Scully, who seems unsure of what she's about to say.

"Sir, there is something else I need to tell you. Something that I need for you to keep to yourself. I'm having a hard time explaining it or believing it. But . . . I'm pregnant."

BACK STORY:

The rumor had begun toward the end of Season 6. Season 7 would be the last season for *The X-Files*. Or would it?

"We always anticipated that, most likely, we were going into the final season," recalls producer Paul Rabwin. "We knew David's contract was up and we felt that, maybe, the show had run its course."

And so Season 7 started out in a decided state of flux. Many crew members felt they had to protect themselves and their families by investigating potential jobs for the year following the current season, while others insisted that they would wait for a final answer. Needless to say, Chris Carter was on the horns of a dilemma, one that he was agonizing over.

"I just remember that I felt bad because I had no clear and firm answers to give everyone about whether we were coming back," he admits. "It was all about David. I kept saying that I would not do it without David. Fox was asking me to commit to doing another season with or without him."

But Paul Rabwin remembers that things began to change as Season 7 got under way. "As the season progressed, we found ourselves starting to get energized again. Word started getting around that maybe this would not be the end. The network certainly wanted us back and Gillian was still under contract for another year. As we got toward the end of the season, everyone was kind of hopeful."

But hope did not translate into a final decision as the days counted down to the point where the final script of the season had to be written. There were several options. The episode could end the series, it could be a cliffhanger for an eighth season, or it could be the cliffhanger for the long-talked-about series of *X-Files* feature films. Early on there was talk about the season finale being a two-hour or ninety-minute show, but those ideas were quickly discarded. Staff meetings between producers and writers took on an extra sense of urgency.

John Shiban recalls what was going through everybody's mind during those meetings. "If this were the end, what would we want the end to be? Where should Mulder and Scully end up emotionally? Where should the conspiracy and the aliens end up? We didn't know what the status of the show was and so we decided that whatever we did would have to apply as either a conclusion of the series or a cliffhanger."

"The first thought we had was, what the hell are we going to do?" recalls Spotnitz, reflecting on the frustration of that time. "We were tossing all kinds of ideas back and forth and finally the suggestion was made to go back to the pilot. Our idea was that if this was going to be the end, let's go back to the beginning. At that point, we only had one idea that was definite. Since the beginning of the season, we had known that Scully's pregnancy would be a great idea as a whole, a wonderful way to end things if this was going to be the end. So we had to devise a story that would allow for all possibilities."

It went without question that Chris Carter would write the script. And, in an attempt to keep the element of surprise, the particulars of that episode were made known to only a select few. Consequently the rumors began to fly thick and fast, along the Internet superhighway as well as around the Fox Studios lot. There were hints that since Duchovny would, most likely, not return to the show, a recurring cast member would step into the Mulder role. Mentioned quite often as a possible replacement was A.D. Skinner.

"Me?" Mitch Pileggi laughed during a break from filming "Requiem." "That's probably the most ridiculous rumor I've heard so far. I've heard millions of them and that's all they are."

Now, an *X-Files* script being completed at the last possible moment was not uncommon. But as the days wound down and the time when the production company would have to begin prepping the episode drew closer, everybody connected to the show mentally geared up for yet another wild ride.

Paul Rabwin remembers the day the first draft of the script came out. "The first clue as to the kind of script it might be was its title, 'Requiem.' It was a significant title: a Mass said for the dead. The first thing I read on the script was *Bellefleur, Oregon*. I immediately recognized the site of the pilot episode. It sounded like a full circle situation. I didn't know what to make of it."

Slowly but surely, literally one act at a time, the script came out. Cast and crew were finally getting an idea of what "Requiem" would be. Rabwin relates, "By the time we started shooting, we knew Mulder was in the woods, there was a spaceship that took off, and Mulder was nowhere to be found. But, like anything else in *The X-Files*, that really didn't answer any questions."

Some clues came to light in the casting process. Since "Requiem" returned to the scene of the very first *X-Files* episode, casting director Rick Millikan brought back the slightly older Leon Russom (Detective Miles), Zachary Ansley (Billy Miles), and Sarah Koskoff (Teresa Hoese). Also returning to the fold were Laurie Holden as Marita Covarrubias and Nicholas Lea as mercenary Alex Krycek.

"I wasn't surprised that they called me back," insists Lea. "I would have been shocked if they hadn't. They're opening up the closet and bringing everybody back, so why not Krycek? It's always been that way. Nobody knows where I'm at or even if I'm alive and then I just sort of pop up."

Filming began on "Requiem" on April 20, 2000, on Soundstage 5 at the Twentieth Century Fox lot. There was the usual joking and good-natured banter during the first few days of filming. But there was also the underlying tension of not knowing, even as the last episode began filming, whether *The X-Files* would be back.

Chris Carter remembers his unease: "I honestly did not know, even through the filming, if we would be back."

Adding fuel to the uncertainty and rumors on the set was the fact that the now-completed script was missing the final two pages.

Pileggi acknowledges, "I don't know what I was feeling at the time. I was kind of numb."

For Anderson the missing script pages were not the major source of concern. "It had more to do with not knowing if we were coming back for another season or not and if a new season was going to be involving David."

But the mystery surrounding *The X-Files*'s future did not get in the way of finding moments to remember. William Davis offers wryly that wearing the prosthetic neck appliance that allowed him to smoke through a blow hole in his neck "was not too much fun."

Nicholas Lea adds, "I got a kick out of the scene where I toss CSM down the stairs. I think the script clarifies the fact that Krycek has his own agenda. Once he gets out of jail, his one mission is to see that CSM doesn't take another breath."

In contrast, Bruce Harwood saw "Requiem" as the prototypical Lone Gunmen episode: "That was actually the most typical appearance we had that year. Basically we just showed up and used our supertechnological information to move the plot along."

There was nothing typical about A.D. Skinner's role in "Requiem." Mitch Pileggi was enthusiastic about the fact that after a season of being largely office-bound, he was now in the thick of the action. "He goes out into the field and is there when what happens to Mulder happens. He's definitely involved."

The X-Files production wrapped up shooting at the studio at the end of Day 4 and relocated to the mountain resort of Big Bear, California. The picturesque mountains, glassy lakes, and long stark stretches of forest made Big Bear the ideal backdrop for the final days of the "Requiem" shoot. The Big Bear stay coincided with a number of the episode's most demanding visual effects and stunts. Stunt coordinator Danny Weselis recalls a particularly nasty car wreck on a lonely stretch of mountain road and the day that Gillian Anderson was hoisted into the air on a harness to simulate her encounter with the alien force field. But Bill Millar created much of the visual FX sequences involving the alien craft and its encounters with humans in a building in Big Bear.

Back in Los Angeles, Chris Carter was sitting in front of his computer. The final day of shooting "Requiem" was a day away. It was time to write the final two pages.

Carter remembers, "I did not write the final two pages until the day before they were to be filmed. We had been talking about those two pages for a long time, but I held back on writing them until the last minute because I didn't want to create something that would let the cat out of the bag and give anybody the opportunity to spoil our fun. Then I called line producer Michelle MacLaren and asked her to make sure she scheduled the final hospital sequence between Skinner and Scully as the last shot."

Frank Spotnitz was well aware of the attempts to keep the ending secret. "Clearly the idea of the pregnancy was built into the structure of the show but we didn't want anybody to know until they had to know. We wanted the element of surprise. We knew Mulder's abduction would get out, but we wanted the pregnancy to be a surprise. Chris finally wrote the ending, showed it to me, printed up one copy with the exception of the last paragraph, and had somebody drive it up to Big Bear at ten o'clock on the morning of the last day of filming. Chris left at four that afternoon with the final paragraph and drove up to Big Bear."

Carter arrived at the Big Bear Hospital shortly before the scene was to be shot. He approached Kim Manners, Gillian Anderson, and Mitch Pileggi and calmly handed them the final paragraph. Carter remembers their reaction. "Gillian said she knew it. She thought it was a great idea and it just blew everyone else away."

"Requiem" wrapped filming on May 5, 2000. The consensus was that the season finale was a stark, bleak, and ultimately satisfying episode. But there still were no answers.

"Nobody knew when we started that episode that we were coming back," concludes Spotnitz. "Nobody knew it at the wrap party. It was a very odd wrap party. We were all saying. 'This can't be the end because it doesn't feel right.' It just didn't feel like we had closure."

Shortly before "Requiem" aired, Fox announced that *The X-Files* would be back for an eighth season. David Duchovny had agreed to come back but would only appear in a total of eleven episodes.

AWARDS AND HONORS

1999–2000

PRIME-TIME EMMY AWARDS

—**Winner**, Outstanding Makeup for a Series—Cheri Montesanto-Medcalf, Kevin Westmore, LaVerne Basham, Gregory Funk, and Cindy Williams for "Theef"

—**Winner**, Outstanding Sound Mixing for a Dramatic Series—Steve Cantamessa, David J. West, Harry Andronis, and Ray O'Reilly for "First Person Shooter"

—**Winner**, Outstanding Special Visual Effects for a Dramatic Series—Bill Millar, Deena Burkett, Monique Klauer, Don Greenberg, Jeff Zaman, Steve Scott, Steve Strassburger, and Cory Strassburger for "First Person Shooter"

—**Nominee**, Outstanding Music Composition for a Series (Dramatic Underscore)—Mark Snow for "Theef"

—**Nominee**, Outstanding Sound Editing for a Dramatic Series—Thierry J. Couturier, Cecilia Perna, Debby Ruby-Winsberg, Donna Beltz, Jay Levine, Ken Gladden, Mike Kimball, Stuart Calderon, Susan Welsh, Jeff Charbonneau, Mike Salvetta, and Sharon Michaels for "First Person Shooter"

—**Nominee**, Outstanding Special Visual Effects for a Dramatic Series—Bill Millar, Deena Burkett, Monique Klauer, and Don Greenberg for "Rush"

SCREEN ACTORS GUILD AWARD

—**Nominee**, Outstanding Performance by a Male Actor in a Drama Series—David Duchovny

—**Nominee**, Outstanding Performance by a Female Actor in a Drama Series—Gillian Anderson

AMERICAN SOCIETY OF CINEMATOGRAPHERS AWARDS

—**Winner**, Director of Photography—Bill Roe for "Agua Mala"

INTERNATIONAL MONITOR AWARDS

—**Nominee**, Best Achievement in Visual Effects—"Rush"

TEEN.COM ENTERTAINMENT AWARDS

—**Winner**, Best Drama Series

—**Winner**, Best Actress in a Series—Gillian Anderson

ENVIRONMENTAL MEDIA AWARDS

—**Nominee**, "Brand X"

WORLDWIDE BROADCAST OUTLETS:

During the 1999–2000 season *The X-Files* was licensed for broadcast in the following countries:*

Afghanistan
Algeria
Argentina
Armenia
Aruba
Australia
Bahrain
Bangladesh
Barbados
Belarus
Belgium
Belize
Bhutan
Bolivia
Bosnia/Herzegovina
Brazil
Brunei
Bulgaria
Cambodia
Canada (English)
Canada (French)
Chile
China
Colombia
Costa Rica
Croatia
Cyprus
Czech Republic
Denmark
Dominican Republic
Dubai
Ecuador
Egypt
El Salvador
Estonia
Fiji
Finland
France
Germany
Ghana
Greece
Guadeloupe
Guatemala
Guyana
Honduras
Hong Kong
Hungary
Iceland
India
Indonesia
Iran
Iraq
Ireland (Eire)
Israel
Italy
Jamaica
Japan
Jordan
Kazakhstan
Kenya
Kuwait
Kyrgyzstan
Laos
Latvia
Lebanon
Lithuania
Luxembourg
Macao
Malaysia
Malta
Mauritius
Mexico
Mongolia
Morocco
Myanmar (Burma)
Namibia
Nepal
Netherlands
New Zealand
Nicaragua
Norway
Oman
Pakistan
Panama
Paraguay
Peru
Philippines
Poland
Portugal
Puerto Rico
Qatar
Romania
Russia
Singapore
Slovak Republic
Slovenia
South Africa
South Korea
Spain
Sri Lanka
Sweden
Switzerland
Syria
Taiwan
Tajikistan
Tanzania
Thailand
Trinidad & Tobago
Turkey
Turkmenistan
Ukraine
United Arab Emirates
United Kingdom
United States
Uruguay
Uzbekistan
Venezuela
Vietnam
West Samoa
Yemen

*Broadcast license windows last up to two years; the series may or may not be on the air at any given time.

RATINGS: SEASON 7

AIR DATE:	EPISODE:	RATING/SHARE:	VIEWERS: (in millions)
11/7/99	THE SIXTH EXTINCTION	10.6/15	17.82
11/14/99	THE SIXTH EXTINCTION II: AMOR FATI	10.1/14	16.15
11/21/99	HUNGRY	9.6/14	16.17
11/28/99	MILLENNIUM	9.1/13	15.09
12/5/99	RUSH	7.9/11	12.71
12/12/99	THE GOLDBERG VARIATION	8.8/13	14.49
1/9/00	ORISON	9.4/14	15.63
1/16/00	THE AMAZING MALEENI	9.4/14	16.18
1/23/00	SIGNS & WONDERS	8.5/12	13.86
2/6/00	SEIN UND ZEIT	8.4/12	13.95
2/13/00	CLOSURE	9.1/13	15.35
2/20/00	X-COPS	9.7/14	16.56
2/27/00	FIRST PERSON SHOOTER	9.3/13	15.31
3/12/00	THEEF	7.4/11	11.91
3/19/00	EN AMI	7.5/11	11.99
4/2/00	CHIMERA	7.5/11	12.89
4/9/00	ALL THINGS	7.5/11	12.18
4/16/00	BRAND X	6.8/10	10.81
4/30/00	HOLLYWOOD A.D.	7.7/12	12.88
5/7/00	FIGHT CLUB	6.9/11	11.70
5/14/00	JE SOUHAITE	8.2/13	12.79
5/21/00	REQUIEM	8.9/14	15.26

Each rating point equals 980,000 homes, or 1 percent of all households in the United States. Share is based upon the percentage of TV sets in use within the time period. Total viewers for each episode is measured by Nielsen's people-meter service, which draws its figures from a small sample designed to represent all television viewers in the United States.

Source: Nielson Media Research

SEASON ONE

PILOT 1X79
FBI Agent Dana Scully is paired with maverick agent Fox Mulder, who has made it his life's work to explore unexplained phenomena. The two are dispatched to investigate the mysterious deaths of a number of high school classmates.

DEEP THROAT 1X0
Acting on a tip from an inside source (Deep Throat), Mulder and Scully travel to Idaho to investigate unusual disappearances of army test pilots.

SQUEEZE 1X02
Mulder and Scully try to stop a mutant killer, Eugene Tooms, who can gain access through even the smallest spaces and awakens from hibernation every 30 years to commit murder.

CONDUIT 1X03
A teenage girl is abducted by aliens, compelling Mulder to confront his feelings about his own sister's disappearance.

THE JERSEY DEVIL 1X04
Scully and Mulder investigate murders thought to be the work of the legendary man-beast living in the New Jersey woods.

SHADOWS 1X05
Mulder and Scully investigate unusual murders committed by an unseen force protecting a young woman.

GHOST IN THE MACHINE 1X06
A computer with artificial intelligence begins killing in order to preserve its existence.

ICE 1X07
Mulder, Scully, and a small party in the Arctic are trapped after the unexplained deaths of a research team on assignment there.

SPACE 1X08
A mysterious force is sabotaging the United States space shuttle program and Scully and Mulder must stop it before the next launch.

FALLEN ANGEL 1X09
Scully and Mulder investigate a possible UFO crash site, which Mulder believes the government is covering up.

EVE 1X10
Two bizarre, identical murders occur simultaneously on different coasts, each involving a strange young girl.

FIRE 1X11
Mulder and Scully encounter an assassin who can start fires with the touch of his hand.

BEYOND THE SEA 1X12
Scully and Mulder seek the aid of a death row inmate, Luther Lee Boggs, who claims to have psychic abilities, to help them stop a killer who is on the loose.

GENDERBENDER 1X13
Scully and Mulder seek answers to a bizarre series of murders committed by one person who kills as both a male and a female.

LAZARUS 1X14
When an FBI agent and a bank robber are both shot during a bank heist, the robber is killed but the agent begins to take on the criminal's persona.

YOUNG AT HEART 1X15
Mulder finds that a criminal he put away who was supposed to have died in prison has returned, taunting him as he commits a new spree of crimes.

E.B.E. 1X16
Scully and Mulder discover evidence of a government cover-up when they learn that a UFO shot down in Iraq has been secretly transported to the United States.

MIRACLE MAN 1X17
The agents investigate a young faith healer who seems to use his powers for both good and evil.

SHAPES 1X18
Mulder and Scully travel to an Indian reservation to examine deaths caused by a beastlike creature.

DARKNESS FALLS 1X19
Mulder and Scully are called in when loggers in a remote Pacific Northwest forest mysteriously disappear.

TOOMS 1X20
Mulder becomes personally involved when Eugene Tooms, the serial killer who extracts and eats human livers, is released from prison.

BORN AGAIN 1X21
A series of murders is linked to a little girl who may be the reincarnated spirit of a murdered policeman.

ROLAND 1X22
Mulder and Scully investigate the murders of two rocket scientists apparently linked to a retarded janitor.

THE ERLENMEYER FLASK 1X23
Working on a tip from Deep Throat, Mulder and Scully discover that the government has been testing alien DNA on humans with disastrous results.

SEASON TWO

LITTLE GREEN MEN 2X01
With the X-Files shut down, Mulder secretly journeys to a possible alien contact site in Puerto Rico while Scully tries to help him escape detection.

THE HOST 2X02
Mulder stumbles upon a genetic mutation, the Flukeman, while investigating a murder in the New Jersey sewer system.

BLOOD 2X03
Several residents of a small suburban farming community suddenly turn violent and dangerous, prompted by digital readouts in appliances telling them to kill.

SLEEPLESS 2X04
Mulder is assigned a new partner, Alex Krycek, and they investigate a secret Vietnam-era experiment on sleep deprivation that is having deadly effects on surviving participants.

DUANE BARRY (PART 1 OF 2) 2X05
Mulder negotiates a hostage situation involving a man, Duane Barry, who claims to be a victim of alien experimentation.

ASCENSION (PART 2 OF 2) 2X06
Mulder pursues Duane Barry in a desperate search for Scully.

3 2X07
Mulder investigates a series of vampiresque murders in Hollywood and finds himself falling for a mysterious woman who is a prime suspect.

ONE BREATH 2X08
Scully is found alive but in a coma, and Mulder must fight to save her life.

FIREWALKER 2X09
Mulder and Scully stumble upon a deadly lifeform while investigating the death of a scientist studying an active volcano.

RED MUSEUM 2X10
Mulder and Scully investigate a possible connection between a rural religious cult and the disappearance of several teenagers.

EXCELSIUS DEI 2X11
Mulder and Scully uncover strange goings-on in a nursing home after a nurse is attacked by an unseen force.

AUBREY 2X12
Mulder and Scully investigate the possibility of genetic transferrence of personality from one generation to another in connection with a serial killer.

IRRESISTIBLE 2X13
A psycho who collects hair and fingernails from the dead steps up his obsession to killing his soon-to-be collectibles himself.

DIE HAND DIE VERLETZT 2X14
Mulder and Scully journey to a small town to investigate a boy's murder and are caught between the town's secret occult religion and a woman with strange powers.

FRESH BONES 2X15
Mulder and Scully journey to a Haitian refugee camp after a series of deaths, finding themselves caught in a secret war between the camp commander and a voodoo priest.

COLONY (PART 1 OF 2) 2X16
Mulder and Scully track an Alien Bounty Hunter, who is killing medical doctors who have something strange in common.

END GAME (PART 2 OF 2) 2X17
Mulder pursues an Alien Bounty Hunter who has taken Scully prisoner while discovering that his sister may not be who she seems.

FEARFUL SYMMETRY 2X18
Mulder and Scully investigate animal abductions from a zoo near a known UFO hot spot.

DOD KALM 2X19
Mulder and Scully fall victim to a mysterious force aboard a Navy destroyer that causes rapid aging.

HUMBUG 2X20
Mulder and Scully investigate the bizarre death of a retired escape artist in a town populated by former circus and sideshow acts.

THE CALUSARI 2X21
A young boy's unusual death leads Mulder and Scully to a superstitious old woman and her grandson, who may be possessed by evil.

F. EMASCULATA 2X22
When a plaguelike illness kills ten men inside a prison facility, Scully is called to the quarantine area while Mulder tracks two escapees.

SOFT LIGHT 2X23
An experiment in dark matter turns a scientist's shadow into a form of instant death.

OUR TOWN 2X24
Mulder and Scully investigate a murder in a small Southern town and its strange secrets surrounding a chicken processing plant.

ANASAZI 2X25
Mulder and Scully's lives are jeopardized when an amateur computer hacker gains access to secret government files providing evidence of UFOs.

SEASON THREE

THE BLESSING WAY 3X01
With the Cigarette-Smoking Man pursuing the secret files that prove the existence of alien visitation and experimentation, and Mulder still missing, Scully finds her own life and career in jeopardy.

PAPER CLIP 3X02
Mulder and Scully seek evidence of alien experimentation by Nazi war criminals while Skinner tries to bargain with the Cigarette-Smoking Man for their lives.

D.P.O. 3X03
Mulder and Scully investigate a series of deaths related to a teenage boy who can control lightning.

CLYDE BRUCKMAN'S FINAL REPOSE 3X04
Mulder and Scully enlist the help of a man who can see when people will die while searching for a serial killer who preys upon fortune tellers.

THE LIST 3X05
A death row inmate makes good on his promise to return from the dead and kill five people who wronged him.

2SHY 3X06
Mulder and Scully track a serial killer who preys on lonely, overweight women via the Internet.

THE WALK 3X07
A suicide attempt and subsequent murders at a military hospital bring Mulder and Scully into contact with a quadruple amputee veteran who may have the power of astral projection.

OUBLIETTE 3X08
The abduction of a young girl prompts Mulder to seek the help of a woman who was kidnapped by the same man years earlier and who has the ability to feel what the victim feels.

NISEI 3X09
Video of an alien autopsy puts Mulder and Scully on the trail of a conspiracy involving Japanese scientists that may shed light on Scully's abduction.

731 3X10
Mulder is caught on board a speeding train with what might be alien cargo and a government killer, while Scully seeks her own solution to the conspiracy.

REVELATIONS 3X11
Mulder and Scully seek to protect a young boy who displays wounds of religious significance from a killer, causing Scully to question her own faith while being cast in the role of the boy's protector.

WAR OF THE COPROPHAGES 3X12
A number of deaths seemingly linked to cockroaches cause widespread panic in a small town.

SYZYGY 3X13
Two high school girls born on the same day are involved in a series of deaths thanks to an odd alignment of planets that causes strange behavior in all the townspeople, as well as Mulder and Scully.

GROTESQUE 3X14
A serial killer maintains that an evil spirit was responsible for his actions, as Mulder's own sanity comes into question when the murders persist.

PIPER MARU 3X15
A French salvage ship finds mysterious wreckage from World War II that unleashes a strange force causing radiation sickness and leading Mulder into a web of intrigue.

APOCRYPHA 3X16
Mulder pursues Krycek and the mystery of the sunken World War II wreckage, while the shooting of Skinner brings Scully new clues to her sister's murder.

PUSHER 3X17
Mulder and Scully investigate a man possessing the power to bend people to his will who engages Mulder in a scary battle of wits.

TESO DOS BICHOS 3X18
The unearthing of an ancient Ecuadorian artifact results in a series of deaths potentially linked to a shaman spirit.

HELL MONEY 3X19
The deaths of several Chinese immigrants missing internal organs leads Mulder and Scully to a mysterious game with potentially fatal consequences.

JOSE CHUNG'S *FROM OUTER SPACE* 3X20
A novelist interviews Scully about a rumored UFO abduction of two teenagers that seems open to a number of different interpretations.

AVATAR 3X21
In the midst of a marital breakup, Skinner becomes a murder suspect, while a clue to the case may lie in the form of a strange woman who appears to him in dreams.

QUAGMIRE 3X22
Mulder and Scully investigate a series of deaths that may be linked to a lake monster known to the locals as Big Blue.

WETWIRED 3X23
Mulder and Scully discover a conspiracy involving mind control through television signals that's responsible for a series of murders in a small town and begins causing Scully herself to behave strangely.

TALITHA CUMI 3X24
Mulder and Scully search for a mysterious man with the power to heal, whose existence risks exposing a conspiracy involving the presence of aliens on Earth, while various forces seek a strange weapon that comes into Mulder's possession.

SEASON FOUR

HERRENVOLK 4X01
As Mulder's mother lies dying, he and Scully are given tantalizing glimpses of a plan to secretly catalog—and clone—human beings. Only by putting the pieces together can they hope to save Mrs. Mulder's life.

UNRUHE 4X02
Someone is abducting, mutilating, and murdering the inhabitants of a small town. The primary evidence is a series of photographs depicting the killer's psychotic fantasies.

HOME 4X03
While investigating the death of an infant in a close-knit rural community, Mulder and Scully uncover an even darker family secret.

TELIKO 4X04
African-American men are disappearing. Their bodies, when found, are dead white—drained of pigment. Were they killed by a virulent new disease? Were they murdered? Or does the answer lie elsewhere?

THE FIELD WHERE I DIED 4X05
In an effort to prevent a mass suicide at a fanatical religious cult, Mulder and Scully interrogate one of the wives of the polygamous cult leader. Under hypnosis, her accounts of her past lives—and deaths—are inexplicably tied to the agents' own.

SANGUINARIUM 4X06
At a busy—and lucrative—cosmetic surgery clinic, doctors are murdering patients with the tools of their trade. Several clues point toward demonic possession.

MUSINGS OF A CIGARETTE-SMOKING MAN 4X07
The secret biography of a sinister, all-powerful conspirator. Some old mysteries are cleared up—and some new ones are created.

PAPER HEARTS 4X08
Prompted by a series of prophetic dreams, Mulder reopens the case of a convicted child killer. The murderer claims to know the circumstances of Samantha Mulder's abduction.

TUNGUSKA 4X09
Diplomatic couriers are bringing a lethal alien life form into the United States. Mulder and Scully's investigation points to a high-level international conspiracy beyond even their comprehension.

TERMA 4X10
Stranded in the gulag, Mulder discovers the effects of the alien toxin—firsthand. In Washington, Scully battles a corrupt U.S. senator to keep their investigation alive.

EL MUNDO GIRA 4X11
Fear, jealousy, superstition, and prejudice converge when a young female migrant worker is killed by a mysterious yellow rain.

KADDISH 4X12
Someone—or something—is killing the members of an anti-Semitic gang. To find the truth, Mulder and Scully delve into the ancient canons of Jewish mysticism.

NEVER AGAIN 4X13
On a solo assignment out of town, a lonely Scully meets Mr. Wrong—a single guy who thinks his new tattoo is talking to him.

LEONARD BETTS 4X14
A headless corpse escapes from a hospital morgue. Mulder and Scully investigate; what they find leads them to the jagged dividing line between life and death.

MEMENTO MORI 4X15
Scully learns she has inoperable cancer—of the same type that killed nearly a dozen female UFO abductees. While she undergoes radical treatment, Mulder works desperately to unravel the conspiracy behind her disease.

UNREQUITED 4X16
A Marine Corps prisoner of war, abandoned in Vietnam by his superiors, returns to the United States with a vengeance—and a special talent for hiding in plain sight.

TEMPUS FUGIT 4X17
A former UFO abductee is killed in a catastrophic plane crash. Mulder suspects a conspiracy—and a cover-up.

MAX 4X18
Mulder and Scully get close to proving alien involvement in the crash of Flight 549. As they do so, they trigger a massive military disinformation campaign—and the deaths of several friends and colleagues.

SYNCHRONY 4X19
For centuries, scientists have debated whether time travel is possible—and if it ever will be. For Mulder and Scully, this age-old conundrum is the key to solving several baffling murders.

SMALL POTATOES 4X20
Mulder and Scully investigate several not-so-blessed events in a small Southern town.

ZERO SUM 4X21
Walter Skinner makes a deal with the devil—AKA the Cigarette-Smoking Man—in an effort to prevent Scully from dying of cancer.

ELEGY 4X22
Several young women have been murdered on Mulder and Scully's home turf. Their prime suspect is a mentally disabled man, Harold Spüller, who has been beset by a series of frightening apparitions.

DEMONS 4X23
After experiencing a series of blackouts and seizures—and what might be the recovery of repressed memories—Mulder gains new insights into his younger sister's abduction. However, while taking his inner journey, he may also have murdered two people.

GETHSEMANE 4X24
When a controversial scientist claims to have discovered evidence of extraterrestrial life, Mulder and Scully find their lives—and belief systems—in grave peril.

SEASON FIVE

UNUSUAL SUSPECTS 5X01
In an important chunk of X-Files pre-history, up-and-coming FBI agent Mulder crosses paths with an unlikely trio of eccentrics, pursues a beautiful alleged terrorist, and gets a searing glimpse into his own future.

REDUX 5X02
After faking his own suicide to shake off Syndicate and FBI surveillance, Mulder secretly searches for the cause of—and cure for—Scully's terminal cancer.

REDUX II 5X03
While Scully, dying from cancer, undergoes the desperate treatment her partner has stolen for her, Mulder penetrates the inner circle of the Syndicate-FBI conspiracy. He finds many of the truths that have long eluded him—as well as disillusionment, despair, and danger.

DETOUR 5X04
A primeval forest is threatened by encroaching civilization. Its secret inhabitants—fierce predators with glowing red eyes—fight back.

CHRISTMAS CAROL 5X05
While spending the Christmas holiday with her family, Scully receives a mysterious phone call. She is summoned to help a desperately ill child, whose tragic history is inexplicably linked to her own.

THE POST-MODERN PROMETHEUS 5X06
Deep in the American heartland, Mulder and Scully encounter—then attempt to unravel—the twisted schemes of a modern-day Victor Frankenstein.

EMILY 5X07
Scully's biological daughter is dying. Mulder uncovers the little girl's role in the alien conspiracy—while Scully fights to save her only child.

KITSUNEGARI 5X08
The serial killer known as "The Pusher"—a man with the inexplicable ability to impose his own will on others—escapes from a maximum security prison. He immediately pursues the man who captured him: Mulder.

SCHIZOGENY 5X09
In a blight-stricken farm town, a series of murders is attributed to child abuse. The real cause, however, lies deeper.

CHINGA 5X10
With the help of an eerie playmate, an autistic child is able to express her innermost feelings—and terrorize an entire New England village.

KILL SWITCH 5X11
A dying computer genius creates a murderous cybernetic life-form. Mulder and Scully—aided only by the dead man's disciple—must somehow purge this predator from the Internet.

BAD BLOOD 5X12
Mulder sticks his neck out—and then some—to capture a small-town serial killer.

PATIENT X 5X13
As a disillusioned Mulder denies all evidence of extraterrestrial visitors, Scully—along with thousands of other abductees—is drawn toward a final confrontation.

THE RED AND THE BLACK 5X14
The world turned upside down: Recovering from a near-death experience, Scully is convinced that her memories of alien encounters are true. For his part, Mulder clings to skepticism and science and uncovers new, even more dangerous, conspiracies.

TRAVELERS 5X15
One year before reopening the X-Files, young Agent Mulder investigates a bizarre murder. The answers he seeks lie in the not-so-distant past: during the Red Scare of the 1950s.

MIND'S EYE 5X16
A sadistic murderer is on the loose. The only witness to his crimes: a totally blind young woman who somehow "sees" through the killer's eyes.

ALL SOULS 5X17
After a handicapped young woman is killed in the act of prayer, Scully is pulled into the case and forced to search her own soul for answers.

THE PINE BLUFF VARIANT 5X18
Playing a dangerous double game, Mulder infiltrates a gang of domestic terrorists.

FOLIE À DEUX 5X19
A giant buglike creature is sucking the life out of humans. Or so says one gun-toting, apparently mentally ill man, who holds a group of his coworkers, plus Mulder, hostage.

THE END 5X20
A child chess prodigy has the ability to read minds. If Mulder and Scully can protect him, he could be the answer to the mysteries they've long been exploring. If the rulers of the Syndicate capture him, he could be the key to world hegemony and the final destruction of the X-Files.

SEASON SIX

THE BEGINNING 6X01
A vicious creature—possibly of extraterrestrial origin—is cutting a murderous swath through the American Southwest. With Syndicate infiltrators in control of the X-Files, Mulder and Scully must find it—and determine its place in the alien conspiracy.

DRIVE 6X02
A carjacking and subsequent highway chase have an inexplicably deadly ending: an innocent victim's head explodes. Disobeying FBI orders, Mulder investigates—and becomes a high-speed chase hostage himself.

TRIANGLE 6X03
Hauled onto a World War II–era ocean liner trapped in the Bermuda Triangle, Mulder must get his bearings, fight off Nazi raiders—and ensure that democracy survives in the twentieth century.

DREAMLAND 6X04
After a close encounter near Area 51, Mulder becomes trapped in the body of another

man—who, unbeknownst to Scully, assumes her partner's identity.

DREAMLAND II 6X05
While Mulder learns how he's switched bodies with Morris Fletcher, Scully discovers the true identity of her "partner." But this knowledge leads only to an unsolvable—and tragic—dilemma.

TERMS OF ENDEARMENT 6X06
In a "normal" middle-class community, a mother is accused of murdering her late-term fetus. Mulder, however, suspects an even more shocking crime.

THE RAIN KING 6X07
In rural Kansas, thousands of drought-stricken citizens are being forced to enrich the town drunk—who seems able, through mystical means, to control the weather.

HOW THE GHOSTS STOLE CHRISTMAS 6X08
On Christmas Eve, Mulder and Scully are trapped in a house haunted by its murder-filled history. They encounter the mansion's original owners—and struggle to stay alive until midnight.

TITHONUS 6X09
Separated from Mulder and teamed with another FBI agent, Scully pursues a crime photographer with an uncanny ability to predict death—or, perhaps, to cause it.

S.R. 819 6X10
An unknown, deadly microorganism—connected to a shady U.S. government trade deal—is found replicating in Walter Skinner's bloodstream. In just a few precious hours Mulder and Scully must identify the bioagent, discover its human propagators, and save their friend and former supervisor.

TWO FATHERS 6X11
As a prelude to the colonization of Earth, Syndicate scientists successfully create a human-alien hybrid. The slave-race prototype is abductee Cassandra Spender, who returns, reveals many secret conspiracies and connections—and plunges Mulder and Scully into a climactic battle for global domination.

ONE SON 6X12
Cassandra Spender outlines the real connections between the Syndicate, the warring alien factions, a half century of sinister experiments, and the abductions of Scully and Samantha Mulder. Using her information, the agents reach the end of their long quest—and confront a worldwide apocalypse.

ARCADIA 6X13
Residents of an upscale, uptight suburb are disappearing without a trace. Mulder and Scully go undercover—as a "typical" married couple—to investigate.

AGUA MALA 6X14
A deadly creature is slithering through the water system of a seaside town. Mulder and Scully are called down to investigate—and arrive in the midst of a killer hurricane.

MONDAY 6X15
Trapped in an endless time loop, Mulder and Scully are fated to live the same day—the day that they die—over and over again.

ALPHA 6X16
A wolflike creature from China—long thought extinct—is cutting a murderous swath through California. Aided by an animal behavior expert with suspicious motives, Mulder and Scully must somehow track it down.

TREVOR 6X17
A violent prisoner gains the ability to walk through walls—unleashing a series of horrifying murders.

MILAGRO 6X18
A struggling young writer, obsessed with Scully, seemingly has the power to make his grisliest fantasies come true.

THREE OF A KIND 6X19
On a fishing trip to the desert, the Lone Gunmen find murderers, shadow-government conspirators—and true love.

THE UNNATURAL 6X20
A rabid baseball fan—Fox Mulder— makes a startling discovery: Something alien has infiltrated his beloved national pastime.

FIELD TRIP 6X21
After being exposed to a hallucinogenic, Mulder and Scully are trapped inside a subterranean cave—and the dark recesses of their own minds.

BIOGENESIS 6X22
An extraterrestrial artifact may hold the key to the origins of life on Earth. Fox Mulder must decipher its mysteries before it destroys him.